A Handbook of Practicing Anthropology

A Handbook of Practicing Anthropology

Edited by Riall W. Nolan

WILEY-BLACKWELL

A John Wiley & Sons, Ltd., Publication

This edition first published 2013
© 2013 John Wiley & Sons, Inc.

Wiley-Blackwell is an imprint of John Wiley & Sons, formed by the merger of Wiley's global Scientific, Technical and Medical business with Blackwell Publishing.

Registered Office
John Wiley & Sons Ltd, The Atrium, Southern Gate, Chichester, West Sussex, PO19 8SQ, UK

Editorial Offices
350 Main Street, Malden, MA 02148-5020, USA
9600 Garsington Road, Oxford, OX4 2DQ, UK
The Atrium, Southern Gate, Chichester, West Sussex, PO19 8SQ, UK

For details of our global editorial offices, for customer services, and for information about how to apply for permission to reuse the copyright material in this book please see our website at www.wiley.com/wiley-blackwell.

The right of Riall W. Nolan to be identified as the author of the editorial material in this work has been asserted in accordance with the UK Copyright, Designs, and Patents Act 1988.

Wiley also publishes its books in a variety of electronic formats. Some content that appears in print may not be available in electronic books.

Designations used by companies to distinguish their products are often claimed as trademarks. All brand names and product names used in this book are trade names, service marks, trademarks or registered trademarks of their respective owners. The publisher is not associated with any product or vendor mentioned in this book. This publication is designed to provide accurate and authoritative information in regard to the subject matter covered. It is sold on the understanding that the publisher is not engaged in rendering professional services. If professional advice or other expert assistance is required, the services of a competent professional should be sought.

Library of Congress Cataloging-in-Publication Data

A handbook of practicing anthropology / edited by Riall W. Nolan.
    p. cm.
    Includes bibliographical references and index.
    ISBN 978-0-470-67460-4 (cloth) – ISBN 978-0-470-67459-8 (pbk.)   1. Anthropology–Methodology–Handbooks, manuals, etc.   I. Nolan, Riall W.
    GN33.H25 2013
    301.01–dc23
                                        2012039876

A catalog record for this book is available from the British Library.

Cover image: Top: Ante-natal clinic, Lesotho, South Africa, photo © Gideon Mendel / Corbis for UNICEF; Left: Close-up of tube with liquid in clinician gloved hand by the microscope © Pressmaster/Shutterstock; Right: Archeologists at work © thumb/Shutterstock; Bottom: Man at the phone with collapsed building in background © Claudia Dewald/iStockphoto.
Cover design by Richard Boxall Design Associates.

Set in 10.5/13 pt Minion by Toppan Best-set Premedia Limited

1   2013

Contents

Notes on Contributors

Linda A. Bennett is a medical sociocultural anthropologist who has worked in academic anthropology positions (Wright State University, 1966–9; University of Memphis, 1986 to date) and in a research faculty position in a medical school environment (George Washington University Medical Center Department of Psychiatry and Behavioral Sciences, Center for Family Research 1974–86). She has served as president of the National Association for the Practice of Anthropology and the Society for Applied Anthropology.

Lenora Bohren is director of the National Center for Vehicle Emissions Control and Safety and Director of Research for the Institute of the Built Environment at Colorado State University. For over 20 years, she has worked on environmental issues with organizations such as the US Environmental Protection Agency (EPA) and the US Department of Agriculture (USDA). She has also conducted air quality studies throughout the United States and Mexico and helped organize national and international clean air conferences.

Elizabeth K. Briody is a cultural anthropologist and founder of Cultural Keys LLC, which specializes in improving organizational effectiveness and understanding and reaching customers. Her recent publications include *The Cultural Dimension of Global Business* (with Gary Ferraro, 2012) and *Transforming Culture* (with Robert T. Trotter, II and Tracy L. Meerwarth, 2010).

Gordon Bronitsky is the founder and president of Bronitsky and Associates, an organization which works with indigenous artists and performers around the world, both traditional and contemporary. They also work with indigenous communities in festival development. Bronitsky and Associates has an e-newsletter, *From All Directions*, which goes out every other month to nearly 7,000 people around the world.

Mary Odell Butler has worked for 35 years in research design, management, and supervision of evaluations for public health projects. She has been employed by Battelle and Westat and holds adjunct appointments at the University of Maryland and the University of North Texas. She has delivered numerous courses and workshops in evaluation for anthropologists and public health professionals. She is co-editor of *Evaluation Anthropology: Creating an Emerging Sub-field* (2005) and of *Practicing Anthropology in the Global Village* (2011).

Paula Chambers founded the first ever online community for humanities PhD students interested in non-academic careers while she was earning her PhD at Ohio State University. After graduating in 2000, she continued to manage the community while pursuing her own successful non-academic career as a grant writer. In 2010 she founded The Versatile PhD, an online service that helps universities provide graduate students with non-academic career information.

Mari H. Clarke is a senior gender consultant for the World Bank. Over the past 40 years, she has also played various roles in the Asian Development Bank (ADB), the United States Agency for International Development (USAID), the Millennium Challenge Corporation (MCC), Gesellschaft für Technische Zusammenarbeit (GTZ), NGOs, and consulting firms, addressing gender issues in a wide range of sectors and countries. Her PhD in anthropology is from the University of North Carolina at Chapel Hill.

Cathleen Crain, one of the two founding partners in LTG Associates, designs and manages project work and leads development for the firm. As a professional social scientist, Crain has worked for 35 years with ethnic, vulnerable, and hard-to-reach populations domestically and internationally, focusing on the development of evaluation and research methods that reach communities and engage them in expressing their concerns and their agency to focus and refine programs serving them.

Timothy de Waal Malefyt is visiting associate professor at Fordham Business School, Center for Positive Marketing, in New York City. Previously he was vice president, director of cultural discoveries for BBDO advertising in New York City, and D'Arcy, Masius, Benton & Bowles advertising in Detroit. Malefyt holds a PhD in anthropology from Brown, is co-editor of *Advertising Cultures* (2003) and co-author of *Advertising and Anthropology* (2012).

Paul E. Farmer, a medical anthropologist and physician, is a founding director of Partners in Health, an international nonprofit organization that provides direct healthcare services and has undertaken research and advocacy activities on behalf of those who are sick and living in poverty. He holds appointments at Harvard Medical School and Brigham Women's Hospital, and is UN deputy special envoy for Haiti. He has written extensively on health, human rights, and the consequences of social inequality.

Shirley J. Fiske is an environmental and policy anthropologist with over 20 years' experience working for the National Oceanic and Atmospheric Administration as a research manager and program director; and subsequently in the Senate on energy, natural resources, public lands, climate change, and ocean and fisheries policy. She is currently a research professor with the Department of Anthropology, University of Maryland, College Park. She has been president of NAPA and WAPA, and on the AAA executive board.

Kerry B. Fosher is the director of the Translational Research Group at the Marine Corps' culture training and education center, which integrates social science perspectives across a broad range of Marine Corps initiatives. She was a member of AAA's commission on engagement with military and intelligence organizations from 2006 through 2010.

Martha Hare is a program director at the National Institutes of Health (NIH)/National Cancer Institute (NCI). At NIH she has administered research studies concerned with health disparities, HIV/AIDS, and palliation. After receiving her PhD in anthropology (New School for Social Research), Hare conducted public health evaluation research. She earned a BA in anthropology from Binghamton University and a BS in nursing from the Cornell University–New York Hospital School of Nursing.

Suzanne Heurtin-Roberts is a health scientist at the National Institutes of Health (NIH)/National Cancer Institute (NCI). She has worked for several federal offices and agencies in research and program management on issues including health equity, culture and service delivery, policy, and behavioral and community health. She has a PhD in medical anthropology, and an MSW, and has published in the areas of culture and chronic illness, adherence, health equity, and mental health services.

Susanna M. Hoffman is a disaster anthropologist, author, co-author, and editor of ten books, including *Catastrophe and Culture* (2002) and *The Angry Earth* (1999), both with Anthony Oliver-Smith. She has written numerous articles, and has made two ethnographic films. She was the first recipient of the Fulbright Foundation's Aegean Initiative, shared between Greece and Turkey after their earthquakes, and helped write the United Nations Statement on "Women and Natural Disaster." She is frequently a national and international speaker on disaster issues.

Adam Koons has worked in development and relief for 31 years, including 17 years overseas. He has worked for the Peace Corps, USAID, international NGOs, the UN, and consulting companies. Koons specializes in food security, economic development and income generation, and disaster relief. He has served as training coordinator, evaluation director, food aid adviser, program manager, relief director, department director, and country director. He holds a PhD in economic and applied anthropology.

Grant McCracken is the author of a number of widely read books; his latest is *Culturematic* (2012), from Harvard Business Review Press. He has been the director of the Institute of Contemporary Culture at the Royal Ontario Museum, a senior lecturer at the Harvard Business School, and a visiting scholar at the University of Cambridge. He is now a research affiliate at C3 at Massachusetts Institute of Technology. He consults widely, and serves on numerous marketing boards.

Crysta Metcalf is the manager of experiences research within Motorola Mobility's Applied Research Center, and leads a cross-disciplinary team of social scientists, computer scientists, and designers. She has worked in applied research in Motorola since 2000, on a variety of projects utilizing team-based, transdisciplinary methods for technology innovation. Her work has been primarily focused on emerging interactive media applications, and consumers in both the home and mobile spaces.

Riall W. Nolan is professor of anthropology at Purdue University, where he was associate provost and dean of international programs until 2009. He worked overseas for nearly 20 years as a practicing anthropologist, in Africa, Asia, and the Middle East, mainly in international development. In addition to teaching, he writes and consults frequently on issues of international development, international education, cross-cultural adaptation, and applied anthropology.

William L. Partridge recently retired from Vanderbilt University where he was professor of anthropology and professor of human and organizational development. From 1986 to 2001 he worked for the World Bank in Washington, DC and Buenos Aires, Argentina. He is a specialist in social analysis and resettlement, and is the author of numerous publications on these and other aspects of international development. He is the joint editor (with Elizabeth Eddy) of *Applied Anthropology in America* (1987).

Tracy Meerwarth Pester is a corporate officer at Consolidated Bearings Co. in Cedar Knolls, New Jersey. She worked at General Motors Research and Development from 2001 through 2008, prior to which she received an MA in applied anthropology from Northern Arizona University. She is interested in cultural modeling, cognitive anthropology, and symbolic anthropology. She is a published author, a competitive golfer, and a yogi.

Amy S. Porter is a candidate in the MD/PhD program in clinical medicine and social and medical anthropology at Harvard University. She has been working with communities affected by HIV/AIDS and tuberculosis in South Africa since 2005. Her prior work focused on postpartum illness in the United States and Fiji.

Terry Redding is senior editor and research associate with LTG Associates in Takoma Park, Maryland, currently working on projects for the Robert Wood Johnson Foundation and the Duke Endowment. He also coordinated the 2009 CoPAPIA MA career survey. Redding holds an MA in applied anthropology from the University of South Florida (1998) and BA dual majors in journalism and sociology.

Susan Squires, from the Anthropology Department of the University of North Texas, is an anthropologist working with businesses to find innovative solutions to their challenges. She is a recognized expert on customer insights research and her edited book, *Creating Breakthrough Ideas* (2002), chronicles the application of her research theory and methodology as used by anthropologists in business and design.

Nathaniel Tashima is one of the two founding partners in LTG Associates, Inc. He has overall administrative responsibility for the firm, and oversees contract management, project design and implementation. He maintains a strong interest in the ethics of social and health research and the role of affected people and communities in the policy discussion. Throughout his career, Tashima has focused on developing opportunities for consumers to participate in policy discussions through program evaluation and community organizing.

Frank J. Tortorello, Jr. is a sociocultural anthropologist employed by Professional Solutions, LLC as a researcher for the USMC Center for Advanced Operational Culture Learning. He studies issues arising from the Corps' need to be capable of accomplishing missions ranging from humanitarian relief to combat in any culture around the world.

Judy Tso currently works for a large strategy and technology consulting firm. She is a certified coach and certified master facilitator and applies her anthropological skills to help organizations navigate change. She has a bachelor's degree from the Wharton School and a master's in applied anthropology from the University of Maryland.

Linda Whiteford is a professor of anthropology and was vice provost for academic program development and review, associate vice president for global strategies, associate vice president for strategic initiatives and chair of the Department of Anthropology at the University of South Florida. Her most recent book, *Global Health in Times of Violence* (2009), is co-edited with Paul Farmer and Barbara Rylko-Bauer.

Dennis Wiedman holds a PhD (1979) from the University of Oklahoma. From 1990 to 2000 he was assistant to the provost at Florida International University. He has served as treasurer for the Society for Applied Anthropology; executive board member, practicing/professional seat for the American Anthropological Association; and president of the National Association for the Practice of Anthropology. Currently, he is associate professor of anthropology in the Department of Global and Sociocultural Studies at Florida International University.

Robert Winthrop is a cultural anthropologist and leads the socioeconomics program at the US Department of the Interior Bureau of Land Management in Washington, DC. His publications include "Defining a Right to Culture, and Some Alternatives," *Cultural Dynamics* (2002) and *Dictionary of Concepts in Cultural Anthropology* (1991).

Preface and Acknowledgments

There has never been a better time to be a practicing anthropologist, as across the globe, people work together to confront and address our societal and environmental challenges at a variety of levels and in a variety of ways. Anthropology has much to contribute to these efforts, but until a few decades ago, I think it's fair to say that our discipline sometimes took a somewhat off-hand and haphazard approach to issues of application.

Fortunately, this is no longer the case. Anthropology outside the university is now the fastest-growing – and arguably most exciting – facet of our discipline, bringing theory and practice together in new and exciting ways. More and more of our graduates now choose practice, and more and more of our academic programs are gearing up to help develop these practitioners. Essential to this undertaking is the inclusion of practitioner voices in our disciplinary conversations about what anthropology is and what it is becoming. This book is a modest contribution to that effort.

My intention here was not to provide a survey of the literature and theory relating to practice, but instead to bring together insider accounts from experienced professionals, accounts of what it's like to be them. I wanted them to tell us, from their perspective, what they do and how they do it; what they see as major issues and opportunities in their work, and how they address these. Consider this, if you like, an attempt to provide an emic perspective on practice, and one which connects our discipline and its concerns to wider structures, interests, and issues.

No book of this size and scope can be created without the efforts of many different people. My thanks and appreciation go out to my original small group of "sages," with whom I consulted at the outset and who helped me with ideas, encouragement, warnings, and advice. Later, I received helpful suggestions from many other practitioners as the project proceeded, regarding possible authors, topics, and approaches. And throughout, I was encouraged and supported by the editors at Wiley-Blackwell, in particular Rosalie Robertson, Julia Kirk, and Jennifer Bray.

But most of all, my thanks go to our authors, most of whom are engaged in full-time practice, and who gave generously of their precious time and energy to make this book possible. They did not write their chapters for the purposes of promotion or tenure. Nor did they do it for the money. They did it, as I learned, because they are passionate about their work, because they understand how integral anthropology is to what they do, and because they want to tell that story to others.

I am proud to claim them as friends and colleagues. I am impressed with the skill and dedication with which they approach their work, and I am equally impressed with their accomplishments. I think you will be too.

Riall Nolan
Lafayette, IN
September 2012

Chapter 1

Introduction

Riall W. Nolan

What is "practicing" anthropology, and how does it differ from academically based anthropology? What is the nature of the relationship between these two sides of the discipline? What has been their history together? These are the main questions addressed in this chapter by Riall Nolan, as a way of introducing the rest of this book, its rationale, and structure.

The Development of Practice in Anthropology

This is a book about what anthropologist practitioners do and how they do it. "Practice," as we use the term here, has a very specific meaning: it is anthropology done largely outside the university, by non-academic anthropologists.

"Applied," "action," or "engaged" anthropology – terms often used synonymously – can refer to virtually any extramural work done by university-based anthropologists. The "practitioner" distinction, however, is important because their work isn't an optional or part-time activity; they work as insiders, full-time. And the contexts in which they work, varied as they are, are all significantly different from university environments, particularly with respect to issues of security, support, and role definition.

Engagement and application have always been an integral part of anthropology, of course, and have had a large hand in shaping what the discipline has become (Rylko-Bauer et al. 2006: 179). The history of practice, moreover, is by now well known (see, e.g., Chambers 1985, 1987; van Willigen 1986, 2002; Gwynne 2002;

A Handbook of Practicing Anthropology. First Edition. Edited by Riall W. Nolan.
© 2013 John Wiley & Sons, Inc. Published 2013 by John Wiley & Sons, Inc.

Nolan 2003; Ervin 2004; Kedia and van Willigen 2005). Up through World War II, much anthropology was both "engaged" and "applied." Following World War II, for a variety of reasons, academically based anthropologists rose to dominance, effectively redefining the limits and possibilities of the discipline. The application of anthropology became, for many, somewhat suspect.

At the same time, however, increasing numbers of anthropology graduates began to choose non-academic careers, and by the 1980s, this trend was clearly established. At that time, John van Willigen remarked:

> It appears unlikely that the large numbers of anthropologists entering the job market as practicing anthropologists now will take academic jobs in the future. They will not return because there will not be jobs for them, their salary expectations can not be met, and they just do not want to. (1986: 34)

As the trend continued, concern began to surface about the relationship between the growing body of independent practitioners and the academy.

Today, although we lack precise figures, there are probably more anthropologists working outside the academy than within it. The demand for the kinds of skills anthropologists possess is strong, and growing, and "practice" – as we have come to call it – is no longer a secondary or alternative career choice. Anthropology's constituency now includes a majority of people with little or no academic experience, and few ties to academia. Many of these people, furthermore, now consider the MA rather than the PhD to be their professional qualification.

Practitioners work across a wide variety of sectors, doing an enormous number of different things. They are planners, managers, policy-makers, project and program directors, advocates, and designers. To an increasing extent, they are also influential decision-makers within their organizations. Their work – and how they do their work – differ significantly from that of their university-based colleagues.

Why Is Practice Different?

Some in the traditional anthropological mainstream have had difficulty grasping the nature and extent of these differences. Some academicians, who work or consult regularly outside the university, see their applied work as little different from that done by practitioners. Overall, there has been a tendency to minimize – or even deny – differences in this respect. Others insist that all anthropology is really applied in one sense or another. Mullins, for example, says that "virtually all anthropology can claim some measure of practicing engagement somewhere along a continuum of political possibilities." Practice, for Mullins, "is research that consciously positions itself within public dialogue" (2011: 236, 235).

New names for the use of anthropology have appeared. And so we now have "public" anthropology, "engaged" anthropology, and even "activist" anthropology, together with exhortations for more collaboration, interdisciplinarity, and connection. One result of this has been to downplay or minimize practice. Naming, as several writers have pointed out, is a way of creating distance (Rylko-Bauer et al. 2006: 182). "New approaches," say these authors, "tend to be presented in opposition to existing ones." Merrill Singer, among others, has lamented this tendency on the part of the academy to invent new labels for what are essentially long-established practitioner activities, in the process "usurp[ing] the role of public work long played by an existing sector of our discipline" (2000: 7).

Other debates center on ethical concerns. Ethics in anthropology is a broad field, but ethical concerns with respect to practice have focused on issues such as informed consent, the ownership and use of information, and the appropriateness of work for large and powerful institutions (see Baba 1998: B5). Within the academy, discussion of the ethics of practice tends to be hampered by the relative lack of understanding of and experience with what practitioners actually do on a daily basis. Given that many if not most of the jobs done by practitioners don't actually have the word "anthropology" in the title, academics are prone to ask, "But it this really anthropology?" John van Willigen provides a clear and straightforward answer when he reminds us that there are really no such things as *anthropological* problems. There are client problems, and our job is to figure out how to use anthropology to address these (van Willigen 2002: xi–xii, 233).

Discussion within the disciplinary mainstream been preoccupied with such stuff in recent years, while one of the most fundamental aspects of anthropological application – its relation to a client base – has largely been neglected. And here, I think, we need to acknowledge a set of essential differences between anthropologists working within the academy and those working outside it. These differences are significant, both constraining and enabling how anthropology is done, how it is used, and to what effect.

We can begin with a fairly basic difference: where problems come from and how they're dealt with. Problems, for academic anthropologists, tend to be self-selected, generated and defined from within the discipline itself. In anthropological practice, however, problems usually come from the needs of external clients. These clients not only define problems, but they may also specify the criteria that solutions must satisfy.

Academic anthropologists often see themselves as providing "critical perspective" on issues or problems, whereas practitioners are expected to provide solutions. And the solutions often have the effect of changing lives, as well as minds. As one practitioner said, "we don't just stand outside and critique, but work inside to change, guide, and innovate" (Kitner 2011: 35). For practitioners, action and outcomes are assumed to be the top priority. What they work on is defined and prioritized within the overall social and political context, and not simply in terms of what the academy might think important. And whereas anthropologists – academics and practitioners alike – are very good at providing "thick description" of specific contexts and situations, practitioners must often simplify and prioritize these descriptions to turn them into policy.

Other differences between academia and practice are also important. These include aspects of structure, patterns of reward and constraint, and work style.

Structures

An anthropologist will have either a base in the university or a base in the world of practice, and where that base is located will determine important things about how they are seen, what they do, and how their work is judged. University-based anthropologists, however "exotic" they might appear to their academic colleagues, generally have little if any difficulty in defining and presenting themselves to others in the university. Practitioners, whose job title rarely includes the word "anthropologist," must make repeated decisions about how to represent themselves and what they do.

Structurally, academia is remarkably homogeneous. Although each of our many institutions of higher education can be said to be a distinctive culture unto itself, they are organized in very similar ways. There are a relatively small number of rungs on the academic ladder, and a fairly well-established set of rules and procedures for climbing up them. And there is fairly clear agreement across institutions as to what rights, roles, and responsibilities accompany these different ranks.

Outside the university, organizations are considerably more diverse in structure, mission, and mandate. Anthropologist practitioners occupy a very wide range of roles here, at a variety of different levels, and with a bewildering array of titles. Moreover, these organizations are themselves often changing, sometimes fairly quickly, in response to outside forces.

Rewards and constraints

In like manner, the pattern of rewards and constraints which shape jobs and careers, while relatively uniform within the academy, is again highly diverse and variable outside it. Academics, by and large, are rewarded (i.e., hired, tenured, and promoted) for a very limited number of things, principally teaching, research, publication, and service, and while each of these activities is highly complex and requires a great deal of skill, the path to success is clear. Judgments about how well or badly these things are done, moreover, are typically made by one's academic peers.

In contrast, practitioners generally work on a succession of projects or assignments, each requiring a somewhat different set of skills, approaches, and activities. Only some of these activities involve research. These assignments, moreover, are not usually chosen or created by practitioners themselves, but by the needs and requirements of the wider organization and its clients. And as a result, outcomes are judged by those clients, and not by peers. The consequences of these judgments are, of course, significant for future practitioner assignments and opportunities.

Work styles

Work styles also differ significantly between academics and practitioners. Academic anthropologists tend to do their work as individuals, beginning in graduate school, and extending through fieldwork, tenure, and beyond. Work assignments and deadlines are usually self-imposed, limited mainly by the academic calendar, funding deadlines for grants, and tenure and promotion reviews.

Practitioners, on the other hand, often work in multidisciplinary teams. Their work tends to be collaborative and highly result-oriented. Often, these results may not be individually attributed. Although their work is not devoid of theory, practitioners tend to be judged on the basis of what they can do, not simply on what they know. Time pressures, of course, can sometimes be intense.

A History of Missed Opportunities

Years ago, in a gloomy moment, one of my academic mentors remarked to me that "the history of higher education in the US is, to a large extent, a history of missed opportunities." This is nowhere more true for anthropology than in the history of the relationship between practitioners and their academic cousins. The details of this troubled and inconstant relationship are by now well known. What is striking about it is how unnecessary, for the most part, it has been.

This has been a tremendous missed opportunity. Today's practitioners are skilled, influential, and well networked. In their work, they test anthropology's theories, concepts, methods, and perspectives against the demands of society. They work collaboratively with other disciplines to do this, and they do much more than research: they are decision-makers and implementers. Slowly but surely, they are bringing anthropology into the workplace, and securing its position there.

To a large extent, most of this has been studiously ignored by the academy. Practitioner work is all but invisible to the discipline, its products lying for the most part outside the mainstream of academic literature. We do not even know with any degree of precision how many practitioners there are or what they do, for the simple reason that no one is counting. And as we all know, what gets counted *counts*.

As a result, the discipline is largely cut off from any nuanced understanding of how, why, and with what effect anthropology is actually being used outside the classroom. What's been lost includes an enormous amount of information and understanding about how significant issues and problems are constructed by different groups in society at large; and how and why solutions to these problems succeed or fail. Additionally, we have lost opportunities to both test and build theory by looking closely at instances of practice. And finally, of course, we have missed significant opportunities to build awareness about anthropology among the general public and, with awareness, influence.

There are clear signs that some of this, at least, is changing. In some respects, there isn't a moment to lose. Outside the academy, awareness is growing of the magnitude and importance of what are termed "grand challenges," and within the academy, disciplines like engineering and agriculture are beginning to reorganize themselves – often to the extent of major curriculum reform – to respond to these.

But in this global effort to bring creative thought and action to bear on some of our most pressing problems, anthropology as a discipline seems curiously absent.

Individual anthropologists, of course are not at all absent, and some – like Merrill Singer and Paul Farmer – have had a substantial impact on public thinking and awareness. But there is little programmatic discussion within the discipline regarding how we might direct our efforts more intentionally. We have what amounts to a knowledge management problem here, as well as a problem with getting what we are learning into the curriculum for our students.

Until quite recently, the discipline appears to have suffered from a form of "naive realism": the belief that the way one's own culture sees the world is the way the world really is. From this perspective, practitioners can appear as failed academics, ethically challenged rogues who peddle "anthropology lite."

Expecting practitioners to behave like academics seems oddly ethnocentric. One of the most frequently repeated criticisms of practice, for example, is that it is atheoretical. The evidence for this claim is generally taken to be the relative dearth of writing by practitioners in refereed journals. But expecting practitioners to generate peer-reviewed research as a way to legitimate what they do is to ignore the essential realities of their work. It calls to mind the classic Doonesbury strip where Jane Fonda urges her cleaning lady to do more exercise. If I can fit exercise into my busy schedule, Jane reasons, then surely the cleaning lady can. To which the woman replies, "Ms Fonda, you're as busy as you wanna be. I'm as busy as I gotta be."

Students today are more interested in practice careers than at any other time in my own 40-year experience within the discipline. But most of our institutions are still preparing them only for university careers. If anthropology is so useful in the world at large – as practitioners demonstrate on a daily basis – then why are most of us still not training our students to actually do this?

Fortunately, there are clear signs today that all of this is changing. We have seen, for example, the first comprehensive surveys of who practitioners are and what they do (Fiske et al. 2010). We now have a growing number of excellent applied Master's programs in the country, as well as several full PhD programs. More are undoubtedly on the way. The *American Anthropologist* has begun regular features involving practitioners and practice-based themes. And discussion has been ongoing for some time regarding the reform of tenure and promotion guidelines at universities, to support practice activities.

How This Book Is Structured

Any attempts to improve graduate training in anthropology and to prepare people for careers in practice must perforce include a better understanding of what practitioners actually do and how their professional lives are constructed (see Rylko-Bauer et al. 2006: 187). One of the most difficult things to do, however, is to bring practice – and practitioners – directly into the classroom. Structural incompatibilities alone make it difficult to involve practitioners in more than marginal ways in academic programs. But it is possible to bring the experience of practice to students through the stories of practitioners themselves.

Hence this book, which is an attempt to describe – to some extent at least – the world in which practitioners live. Not all of the contributions here are from practitioners, of course, but the majority of them are. Several chapters are collaborations between a practitioner and an academically based anthropologist. My request to potential contributors was very simple: tell us what your professional situation looks like from your personal perspective, and through your own eyes.

Some contributors provided what are essentially autobiographical accounts; others attempted a more comprehensive description of their job or sector, often drawing on other literature and other professionals. Others gave us a case study. In each case, however, contributors were at pains to provide personal perspectives, as practitioners, of a particular aspect of practice.

The principal readership for this volume includes three groups of people. One of these, of course, is anthropology students interested in practice. The second group includes those faculty members teaching applied and practice-oriented courses, some of whom may also be interested in the possibility of becoming a practitioner at some stage. The third group comprises, of course, practitioners themselves, particularly those relatively new in their career.

The book is divided into four parts. The first, "The Practitioner Career Arc," includes chapters on practitioner training, what it's like to move out of academia, job-hunting and job success, career management, and coping with stress and failure. Part II, "Practitioner Bases," provides a series of accounts from practitioners about what it is like to work in various sectors. Included are four chapters from independent practitioners, as well as chapters on work in small and medium enterprises, NGOs, multilateral organizations, the corporate sector, the federal government, and the university sector. Part III, "Domains of Practice," looks at a series of important areas of practice. There are chapters on methods and approaches, health, international development, the military, marketing and advertising, design, the environment, and disaster and humanitarian work. Part IV, "Issues," takes up a number of key concerns for practitioners. Included here are chapters dealing with relations with the academy, professional communication, networking, and working with others. Also included are three detailed case studies, one dealing with ethics, one on the integration of medical and social data, and one on practitioner training.

In 1997 James Peacock wrote a provocative essay on the future of anthropology. The discipline, he said, would either flourish, stagnate, or disappear, depending on the choices that we made from now on. To avoid either stagnation or extinction, Peacock recommended that anthropology do three things: initiate projects which reach beyond the concerns of the academy; do more than merely provide critical analysis; and think and communicate beyond both the discipline and the academy (1997: 14).

Ironically – but very fortunately – practitioners have been doing these things for years. This book describes how some of them are doing that.

References

Baba, Marietta (1998) "Anthropologists in Corporate America: Knowledge Management and Ethical Angst." *Chronicle of Higher Education* (May 8), B4–5.
Chambers, Erve (1985) *Applied Anthropology: A Practical Guide*. Prospect Heights, IL: Waveland Press.
Chambers, Erve (1987) "Applied Anthropology in the Post-Vietnam Era: Anticipations and Ironies." *Annual Review of Anthropology* 16: 309–337.
Ervin, Alexander (2004) *Applied Anthropology: Tools and Perspectives for Contemporary Practice*, 2nd edn. Boston: Allyn & Bacon.
Fiske, Shirley J., Linda A. Bennett, Patricia Ensworth, et al. (2010) *The Changing Face of Anthropology: Anthropology Masters Reflect on Education, Careers, and Professional Organizations. The AAA/CoPAPIA 2009 Anthropology MA Career Survey*. Arlington, VA: American Anthropological Association.
Gwynne, Margaret (2002) *Applied Anthropology: A Career-Oriented Approach*. Boston: Allyn & Bacon.
Kedia, Satish and John van Willigen (2005) *Applied Anthropology: Domains of Application*. Westport, CT: Praeger.
Kitner, Kathi (2011) "Letter from the Field: Practicing Anthropology at Intel Corporation." *Anthropology News* 52(3): 35.
Mullins, Paul R. (2011) "Practicing Anthropology and the Politics of Engagement: 2010 Year in Review." *American Anthropologist* 113: 235–245.
Nolan, Riall (2003) *Anthropology in Practice*. Boulder, CO: Lynne Rienner.
Peacock, James (1997) "The Future of Anthropology." *American Anthropologist* 99(1): 9–29.
Rylko-Bauer, Barbara, Merrill Singer, and John van Willigen (2006) "Reclaiming Applied Anthropology: Its Past, Present and Future." *American Anthropologist* 108(1): 178–190.
Singer, Merrill (2000) "Why I am Not a Public Anthropologist." *Anthropology News* 41(6): 6–7.
van Willigen, John (1986) *Applied Anthropology: An Introduction*. South Hadley, MA: Bergin & Garvey.
van Willigen, John (2002) *Applied Anthropology: An Introduction*, 3rd edn. Westport, CT: Praeger.

Part I
The Practitioner Career Arc

Chapter 2

Professional Training and Preparation

Terry Redding

Drawing on several recent surveys of practitioners and their activities, Terry Redding provides us with a comprehensive look at the main questions and concerns with regard to how practitioners prepare themselves for careers. Included here are discussions of key job skills, the range and scope of practitioner employment, and whether to choose a master's or a PhD. Redding also looks at the role of advisers, of internships and practicums, and offers some insights on preparing yourself for the marketplace.

Introduction

This chapter is designed for those who are newly arrived or arriving on the practitioner scene, in particular graduate students and recent graduates. It will introduce some relevant issues, examine making the most out of graduate school and the transition into practice, and explore building a career by applying anthropology.

This chapter and some others in this volume have a distinct advantage over previous books; we are able to cite actual data from a relevant survey of your peers. In the summer of 2009 the AAA Committee on Practicing, Applied, and Public Interest Anthropology (CoPAPIA) conducted an online survey focused on the education and careers of anthropology master's degree holders. Of the 758 respondents, all had completed master's degrees in anthropology, and a third had gone on to undertake or complete doctorate degrees (although not always in anthropology).

These real life data will be invaluable in helping to understand the perspectives of those who have already been through the process of graduate education and

A Handbook of Practicing Anthropology. First Edition. Edited by Riall W. Nolan.
© 2013 John Wiley & Sons, Inc. Published 2013 by John Wiley & Sons, Inc.

employment. We will refer to this survey (the CoPAPIA survey) often in this chapter because it is the largest and most comprehensive survey of its kind to be done, and (at the time of this volume) the most recent. However, it should be noted that respondents were overwhelmingly female and white. How this represents anthropology as a whole is uncertain because no one keeps track, but it is not wholly dissimilar to many cohorts of current graduate students. The survey was also conducted using a snowball sampling method, so the results should be considered illustrative and comparative without being exactingly scientific.

Foundational Issues

Anthropologists fall out all across the career intent spectrum. That is, some went into graduate school knowing exactly what career path they wished to pursue, while others (such as the present author) had more vague ambitions and were more motivated by the subject matter itself. Career paths in anthropology can sometimes be based more on serendipity than rigid pursuit: a chance encounter at a professional meeting with a leader in a sub-specialty, or a shot-in-the-dark job application that yielded both what the applicant wanted and needed. That is simply the nature of this profession.

Nonetheless, wherever you fall, you can assist yourself at some point by clarifying the big picture in terms of the life you envision for yourself. Do you need a job or a career? Will you bounce around every couple of years, or do you need stability in your life? Unlike, say, Masters of Public Health (MPHs), Masters of Business Administration (MBAs), doctors of law (JDs), or physicians (MDs), many if not most applied anthropologists do not have a practitioner certification that is widely recognized and immediately understood by the general public. (I should note that there are graduate anthropologists who also hold the aforementioned certifications.) Archaeologists do enjoy some recognized practices, such as salvage archaeology or cultural resources management (CRM), and you may occasionally see job announcements calling for those skills. There are also firms that will post job positions for various archaeological specializations.

You probably discovered long ago that a majority of people do not know precisely what anthropologists do. Indiana Jones has been a mixed blessing for the public recognition of archaeology. And at the time of this writing, the star of a popular television program is a forensic anthropologist, a fact she mentions in several episodes. The series is based loosely on the show's producer, who in real life is a novelist and forensic anthropologist.

Still, for practicing cultural anthropologists, we have not had a recognized "star" in the public spotlight since Margaret Mead. So, if you are an accountant, you are an accountant, and everyone knows what that means. If you are an anthropologist, many employers may ask you why they should hire someone who studies bugs (or, if you are lucky, they will think you collect dinosaur bones). In a way, this is good; you can create whatever role for yourself in the job market you wish to pursue and see how it goes. On the other hand, you may have to reinvent yourself each time you look for a job.

In part, specific geographic or sector preferences may limit your flexibility. If you are looking for the stability and certainty of a state or local government job, then you can go just about anywhere. Alternatively, if you want to work in any kind of university, lab, or museum setting in general, you may also have plenty of options to pursue. If you want to work for the federal government, a big NGO, or association, however, the odds are high that you will have to move to Washington, DC or some other major city.

If you wish to work in the private sector or be an entrepreneur, you should have more flexibility in your job search, although your choices may be limited geographically if you are looking at a particular industry or sector (e.g., agri-business, communications technology, and nuclear energy activities do not happen everywhere).

For reasons laid out below, and more clearly in the next section, much of the discussion in this chapter will be more relevant for those in the cultural and social anthropology fields (and possibly for physical and linguistic anthropologists) than for archaeologists. Still, the discussion will be broad enough to be relevant for all fields of anthropology, whether you attended a program with an applied or an academic focus.

You might be thinking, "What is it that anthropologists actually do in the workplace?" Let us turn to the data. An exploration of non-academic job titles in the 2009 CoPAPIA survey showed that archaeologists tended to work in recognizable positions, according to their job titles: archaeologist, museum curator, cultural resources manager, and historic preservation. The majority of non-archaeologists, however, held a dizzying array of job titles: in addition to the expected researcher, ethnographer, curator, and evaluator job titles were director, manager, program associate, program assistant, educator, writer, and information specialist, along with legal and policy-related titles. Some of the more interesting, specific job titles were archivist, artist, business owner, community organizer, environmental analyst, executive planner, grants manager, health analyst, immigration consultant, intelligence analyst, librarian, nurse practitioner, real estate agent, restaurant worker, sales representative, senior speechwriter, staff development coordinator, strategy manager, training consultant, and urban sustainability consultant. Therein lies the complexity in trying to relate what it is that anthropologists actually do. The answer is: they do everything.

That revelation is probably not of great assistance to you in knowing what specific skills you will need to bring to or to gain in the workforce, so perhaps your peers can help. The CoPAPIA survey respondents were asked to name the top two or three skills they would need in the next few years to do their jobs. As this was an open-ended question, responses were refined into several broad categories, shown in Table 2.1 in order of frequency.

What about your degree level? If you have not gone to graduate school, a bachelor's degree will almost always need to be combined with another degree to get on a career-building track. Still, it is a great co-major to possess; it may give you an edge

Table 2.1   Job skills needed in the near future

Skill or skill area needed
Methods (general)
Writing skills (all areas)
Management (all types)
Grant writing/funding
Teaching
Research (not specified)
Statistics
GIS/GPS
Communications (general)
Computers or software (general)
Verbal skills
Technical skills (general)
Laws and regulations
Evaluation
Fieldwork (all kinds)
Language (additional)
Project or program design and/or development
Budgeting/finance
Analysis (all types)
Community engagement/ organizing/development

in the workplace to be a valuable analyst and problem-solver when working in a non-social-science setting. But if you wish to work more closely in the profession, you likely will need to go to back to graduate school.

Will a master's degree get you where you want to go in the long run? A number of comments in the CoPAPIA survey indicated that some respondents found they had to go back to pursue a PhD to achieve their career goals. If you hold a master's but think you will go back someday to complete a PhD, keep in mind various family and geographic constraints that may change over time (e.g., you have quadruplets, or your husband gets the world's best job and it is located 1,200 miles away from your graduate school of choice). And if you wish to be a principal investigator (PI) on your own projects, you are almost certainly going to need a doctorate for applied work outside of archaeology.

There will also be differences in potential employment for master's and doctorate holders. While doctorate holders may find some jobs off limits because they are considered overqualified, they will typically have more options in the long run, and more flexibility if they change their mind about careers and directions. Many upper-level government jobs, for example, require a PhD, and you will usually need PhD status to be the PI on a grant application or proposal. You can more easily dabble in academia, and publishers of all stripes may prefer seeing a PhD after an author's name. Nonetheless, your ongoing work experience will be the most significant determinant of your access to future jobs and career paths.

Here are some reworked quotes from the CoPAPIA survey to put this in perspective (or simply cloud the issue):

- "The master's program was the highlight of my academic career, including another master's and, subsequently, a PhD."
- "I found I could do what I wanted with a combined MA/MPH, so I did not pursue a PhD."
- "Having a master's has been quite successful for me. I would like to pursue a PhD but am unsure if I will."
- "I am pursuing a PhD outside of anthropology, and my anthropology MA has been a good basis for this. Anthropology is my passion, but public health will get me a well-paid job."
- "I got a PhD because I realized a master's would not take me where I wanted to go professionally."

Related issues on going into the workforce include knowing exactly what is required of the types of jobs you wish to apply for, and what salaries you can expect vis-à-vis the job role and your individual skills (more on this in later chapters). This is information you need before you start looking for a job, and understanding your limits will help in your ongoing life choices (e.g., do you take a higher-paying job you do not really want in order to pay off your student loans more quickly?).

You may also be curious about where anthropologists work. The CoPAPIA survey found again that anthropologists are broadly employed across many types of organizations and institutions. The top 10 employers from the pool of 758 respondents are listed in Table 2.2.

Other employers include nongovernmental or community-based organizations, international organizations, independent consultancies, and K-12 education.

Table 2.2 Top 10 employer types of anthropologists

Type of organization	Frequency
Academic (college, community college, and/or university)	305
Nonprofit organization	98
Consulting firm	95
Government (federal)	87
Government (state or local)	79
Research institution/organization	67
Museum/exhibition/curatorial	64
Larger corporation (100 or more employees)	53
Small or medium business/LLC (under 100 employees)	46
Self-employed or with own business	46

Table 2.3　Domain or type of primary employment

Domains of employment	Frequency
Education/outreach	259
Administration/management	221
Archaeology	220
Ethnography/cultural anthropology	153
Cultural resource management (CRM)	137
Evaluation/assessment	133
Historic preservation	123
Museum/curation/project design	97
Health (international/public health)	97
Environment and natural resources	78
Community development	64
Business	58
Advocacy (human rights/social justice)	57
Tourism/heritage	53
Human/social services	51
Healthcare management/services/delivery	46
Computers/software development/information technology	43
Management consulting, organizational development/training	40
Design (products and/or services)	37
Social impact assessment	35
International development/affairs	30
Market research	30
Forensics	26
Law/criminal justice/law enforcement	25
Mass communication	19
Humanitarian efforts	13
Other	138

And what domains of work are undertaken by anthropologists? Table 2.3 shows the primary types of employment held by respondents to the CoPAPIA survey. (Respondents were able to select more than one category, so the totals exceed the *n* of 758.) It is important to point out that these domains may have more to do with the nature of the survey and respondents than the exact nature of the kinds of work anthropologists do, but the results provide a good baseline for your consideration.

Along with considering where you can work, and who you will work for, you may ultimately find your choices come down to finding the balance between your personal and professional goals. For better or worse, you can be assured that your career will rarely be boring.

By the way, the CoPAPIA survey showed that, in general, those holding doctorates earn somewhat more than those with master's degrees, with both being at or slightly below national income averages for their respective degree levels. At the doctorate level, there is rough income parity between females and males, although males earn slightly more at the master's level. The good news is that the income gap is smaller than national averages.

Concluding Your Graduate School Experience

If you are still finishing your graduate education, it can be difficult to know if you are receiving all the information needed to pursue your career dream; you might not discover this until you are fully engaged in the workplace. But there are some general basics to review to ensure you are on the right course.

Key questions you should be asking yourself are: Can I get hired in my chosen area of focus? Are the skills and knowledge I am absorbing currently relevant in the real world? Get a sense of the answers by searching through postings for the jobs you want; see how the required skills align with your experiences. Query your faculty regarding where previous graduates have been employed; contact these alumni and ask how they made a successful transition.

You may also wish to ask yourself a life question of whether you are looking for a specific course of training, or more of a broad education in graduate school. Not that they are mutually exclusive, but you will probably have to work harder at getting a job if your graduate school provides you with conceptual and theoretical classes (reading and writing term papers) more than hands-on and practical training-oriented classes (conducting interviews, learning computer-assisted qualitative data analysis). If you want the latter but cannot get them in your program, look to other departments or other campus resources, volunteer opportunities, part-time work, or alumni.

The ideal program will provide you with both experience and knowledge to put you on the right trajectory. Along with accumulating knowledge about anthropology and anthropological applications through coursework, you will gain both technical and functional skills and knowledge. Technical skills include specialized computer software (e.g., ATLAS.ti, GIS), languages (Spanish, French, and Arabic are most in demand but any extra language helps), and methodological applications (e.g., running a focus group, designing and implementing surveys). Functional skills include organizing information and writing reports, presenting information coherently to a group within a specified time, and planning and preparing a project.[1] It is up to you to put all the elements together to address your larger career goals.

In addition, the ideal program will offer not just a solid grounding in workplace-relevant methods and skills, and instructors who care and are responsive, but also:

- an adviser or committee chair who looks out for you, meets deadlines, and knows department and university rules and requirements;
- a stable curriculum, with flexibility in course offerings and scheduling;

- collaborations with other departments and faculty;
- opportunities to get involved in local projects conducted by faculty or others;
- a good match for your professional interests;
- good mentoring;
- networking potential.

The first item above relates to your adviser or committee chair. This may be the key relationship in your graduate school experience. Ideally, this is someone with whom you are professionally compatible and who can offer honest and constructive critiques of your work, insights into managing the academic program, and wisdom in helping your see your way forward in the direction you wish to go. If your current adviser is not working out, other students may be helpful in helping you find out which advisers offer appropriate and timely feedback, have reliable meeting hours, and give proper credit to students. You may also wish to explore where former students of different advisers are in their lives now, and who has a good record of helping students transition appropriately and successfully into the workplace.

Another key item noted above is the opportunity for involvement in projects outside of the department. When reviewing your résumé, potential employers are going to focus more on what you did rather than what you learned. Field experience is thus a key aspect of your education, and if your program offers only limited possibilities, you will have to find them on your own. Take heart; there are plenty of opportunities to volunteer in your community, attend a field school or two, and set up some kind of internship or practicum. Not only should these experiences give you practical, real life experiences from which to learn and grow, but they will also be things employers will want to know about. All graduates have had coursework. Your fieldwork experiences may be what highlight your abilities the best, especially if you have participated in some unique or compelling work on a specific project, and if you can cite a specific role you played in making it happen.

Job opportunities are going to be different for anthropological subfields, so let's turn back to the data for a while. One of the more interesting CoPAPIA survey results was a divergence between how archaeologists and non-archaeologists approached their educations (as there were only a few self-identified physical and linguistic anthropologists in the survey, they were lumped with cultural and applied respondents). Two-thirds of archaeologists had a specific career goal in mind when they entered graduate school, while only one-third of the non-archaeologists had a specific career in mind. Archaeologists were also much more likely to be satisfied with their educations than non-archaeologists. Indeed, as touched upon previously, an analysis of job titles listed by respondents showed that archaeologists were likely to have job titles that reflected their specialization. However, only 11 percent of non-archaeologists held job titles that would indicate they were anthropologists (take this with a grain of salt, though; about half said that anthropology was indeed part of their general position description). Most of the survey comments in this chapter, then, focus more on those with cultural, linguistic, or physical anthropology backgrounds than on archaeologists.

A significant survey finding was that, for all respondents, more than half said they had planned to combine anthropology with some other education or training in pursuit of a specific job or career. Rather more surprising was that 87 percent of all respondents, both archaeologists and non-archaeologists, indicated that skills learned outside the discipline were significant to their career positions. Various responses suggest that these skills and training would include specialized areas of research; communication skills such as writing and speaking; community-based research methods; project design, development, and management, including grant-based work; and the work domains of health, business, environment, history, education, development, and public administration. It is no surprise, then, that practicing anthropologists often find themselves as the lone representative of their discipline on a multidisciplinary team, doing work far outside of what they have trained for in graduate school.

Despite this, it is important to note that 63 percent of respondents said that holding a graduate degree in anthropology was important in their job offer. In any case, it was clear that anthropologists were working in an amazing array of sectors, most of which would indicate that multiple skills and a holistic, multidisciplinary approach would be vital. If you do not hold a diverse skill set outside of anthropology, do not despair. As alluded to before, two-thirds of respondents said the job skills they currently used were learned on the job.

The following points synthesize key lessons (not quite actual quotes) from respondents to the CoPAPIA survey.

- "I got a job through an internship/practicum."
- "An off-campus research project helped gain needed skills, experience, and contacts."
- "Having volunteer opportunities was very helpful for experience and networking."
- "The most important learning experiences came from on-the-job training. My best 'advisers' were other students, employers, and informal conversations with faculty."
- "The course work outside my department led to important networking."
- "My second degree offered the most practical training and the best job opportunities."
- "Working on research projects was the most helpful part of my graduate school experience."

Finally, if you are closing out your student days, consider the following points:

- use networking, leverage an internship, and find job search collaborators;
- do not assume your committee chair will come through for you in the clutch without you pushing to meet deadlines;
- take full advantage of your student discounts by joining relevant associations before you graduate;

- if you have not already done so, try to present at a professional meeting, and make contacts with movers and shakers in your chosen specialty;
- find a mentor to help you transition out of school life and into the workplace.

Choose your first job with a strategic sensibility. It could set a tone or put you on a course you will follow for the rest of your career. Or not. In the CoPAPIA survey, in fact, there was a huge dip in job tenure at the 10-year mark for most respondents. One of the interesting things about anthropology is that it allows you to re-create yourself from time to time, to blend and merge your skills into new career paths that you may not have anticipated in graduate school.

Making the Transition to the Workplace

Chapter 4 will review strategies on getting a job, but we will lay a bit of groundwork before getting there. Addressing these issues should assist in making a smooth transition out of graduate school.

After completing school, graduates will divide into two camps, based on life priorities: those who will follow their bliss and take whatever means of making a living best matches their life situation, and those who will follow a more structured approach to job and career pursuits. Still, it is something of a false dichotomy to think of this as pursuing either happiness or professional satisfaction. Hopefully both will fall into place, or at least a middle ground will develop. In any case, since it is presumptuous to tell others how to follow their bliss, this section really addresses graduates or career changers who want to be more directive and systematic in a career pursuit.

Those who are best placed to move from the classroom to the workplace will have already made presentations at an annual meeting or two, been in contact with various movers and shakers in their preferred specialty, thought about preferred living locales, and put out several employment feelers. They also will have considered how to leverage the thesis/dissertation, internship/fieldwork, and any outside skills and specializations in the search for a dream job.

On a very practical note, a large student debt seems to be a growing barrier to flexibility for many graduates. If you have not yet racked up a mortgage-sized debt, do everything you can to keep it that way. It took me six years of part-time work and attendance to complete my three-year master's program, but those extra three years were worth leaving school with virtually no debt.

Start your career quest with networking. A members' survey conducted by the Washington Association of Professional Anthropologists (WAPA) in 1987 showed that some 98 percent of members found their jobs via networking, and the other 2 percent found theirs through job postings.[2]

It could be that this reflects the nature of Washington, DC or WAPA. However, the CoPAPIA survey shows a similar trend, although the numbers are quite different. When respondents were asked how they obtained their current positions, by far the most frequent response (38 percent of respondents) was that a colleague or friend had referred them to the position or organization. Only half as many (18.5%) indicated that they had been promoted within their organization, the second most frequent response. Others found jobs through websites or non-web job postings. Perhaps surprisingly, only 4 percent said they had been hired through an internship or practicum.

The lesson is important for practicing anthropologists. Here are some thoughts on proactive networking:

- From your literature reviews, you may already know the players in your field of interest. Ask faculty for suggestions and tips, even personal anecdotes.
- Write to potential contacts with a few insightful questions, and let a dialogue develop.
- Introduce yourself after annual meeting sessions or in the halls, and have a business card to hand out.
- Former faculty and alumni from your program should not be overlooked; they may even be your best advocates.
- Follow up. Sadly, a majority of individuals I respond to never send a follow-up message or acknowledgment after their initial queries are answered.

Happily, in the CoPAPIA survey, most respondents said they had found some type of job within six months of graduation. As noted above, 63 percent said that holding an anthropology degree was important in their job offer. And some three-quarters said their degree played a significant role in their overall career satisfaction.

A crucial component of moving from graduate school into the workforce may be selling your skill set to an employer who does not know what an applied or practicing anthropologist does. You may have already had a taste of this via an internship. Brainstorm with peers; discuss ideas and strategies for getting interviews and job offers. The good news is that, according to CoPAPIA survey respondents, two-thirds agreed that their supervisors understood the positive contributions an anthropologist brings to their positions once they are on the job. If we include the archaeologists, the number goes even higher.

As we have seen, many practitioners have or plan to pursue skills outside of anthropology. The key focus now is how to package and present an anthropological skill set and possibly other skills and experiences as a relevant whole to potential employers. Get used to the process, because the chances are that you will be doing it more than once. Colleagues of mine have combined past social service experience, Peace Corps service, entrepreneurship, language abilities, and technical prowess as part of their overall skills and experience package.

Not that this is a bad thing for a discipline that embraces a multidisciplinary approach. It may, however, affect the way you present yourself. Many practicing anthropologists will refer to themselves as social scientists or social researchers to those not familiar with what applied anthropologists do. You might find practicing anthropologists filling roles at various health and human services-type organizations and agencies, both public and nonprofit: child welfare, juvenile justice, aging services, adult literacy, and community health are just a few. Your potential colleagues and team members may represent other social and biological sciences, law enforcement and legal services, medical and clinical services, and education.

Some of the main things you may be called upon to do (competencies) in typical modes of anthropological practice are well detailed in workshops presented by Riall Nolan at yearly Society for Applied Anthropology (SfAA) meetings, and discussed in detail in his book on practice (Nolan 2003). These competencies boil down to the following:

- finding out things (asking the right questions and understanding the answers), for example, performing literature reviews, survey designs, interviews, and rapid assessment;
- analyzing and learning things (figuring out what the facts mean), for example, conducting data analysis;
- communicating things (telling others what you have learned), for example, giving presentations, writing reports and briefings;
- planning and designing things (how to get things done), for example, designing projects and programs that function and address the need;
- managing things (organizing, managing, and sustaining actions), for example, working with others, assigning roles and duties, monitoring progress, and problem-solving;
- judging things (measuring progress and accomplishments and assessing the results), for example, assessment and evaluation, identifying success and failures and knowing why they succeeded or failed.

To make all this happen, Nolan points out you will need some of the following abilities, more or less in order: research design, interview techniques, database search techniques, statistics, content analysis, writing and editing of all kinds, speaking, audiovisual presentation and graphic design, project and program design and management, budgeting, policy analysis and formulation, negotiation and conflict resolution, facilitation, supervision, and delegation, time management, evaluation and monitoring, and troubleshooting and modification.

Much of the above may be familiar to you, and may even be things of which you have some experience. However, many if not most of these competencies will be learned on the job. Still, while an employer will not expect you to have expertise in these competencies early in your career, any relevant experiences you do have should be highlighted in résumés and interviews.

The CoPAPIA survey highlights the need to be adaptable. In particular, since you will likely not be hired as a "practicing anthropologist," you will learn by doing a variety of assignments, many of which may not relate to your job title or training. Your adaptability in learning new skills will determine whether you take on greater responsibilities. Flexibility will be critical as you and your employer sort through your strengths and weaknesses. This may be more true for master's degree holders than doctorates; PhD roles may often be clearly defined in job postings or position descriptions, with roles for those with master's degrees more vague and varied. Perhaps the benefit is that the latter can more easily tweak their resumes or CVs to suit a particular job opening.

Building a Career Path to Suit Your Interests

The fundamental issue at hand is how to realistically build a career that suits your interests and needs, one that ideally pays the bills while making you and those around you happy. However, just as there are dozens of possible career courses in professional anthropology, there are numerous strategies for reaching particular career goals. Many of these career courses will be explored in the subsequent chapters of this book.

You will already know the basics of managing a professional career:

- build and maintain a network of relevant co-workers and colleagues;
- present and publish when possible;
- attend meetings and events, in particular annual association meetings;
- become involved in committees with relevant organizations and associations;
- keep track of developments in the field;
- undertake professional development, training, courses, and activities as needed;
- keep vigilant for trends and developments.

Focus on your particular career long-term goals, but remain flexible. Things change. Imagine a poor inventor who perhaps developed a revolutionary way to store vinyl LPs just as CDs came to prominence, or an innovator after that who perfected CDs just as electronic file sharing became the next big thing. Things are dynamic in this realm, too, so remain aware of them: the profession of anthropology continues to evolve. You will change too, and what thrills you now may be a bore in 10 years.

Throughout an anthropologically based career, you may be called on more than once to make the fundamental life choice of following the market or your bliss. Fortunately, anthropology has the flexibility to allow you to do either, or both. And you control your fate: no one will come looking for you unless you have an extremely well-defined niche or very good connections. And if you hope to get rich, anthropology is, in financial terms, a rather dubious mechanism for achieving that aim. In personal development, however, it can indeed provide a wealth of experiences and memories.

Consider one more long-term career development strategy: find a successful person to emulate. There is probably someone whom you would like to imitate, whose career comes the closest to your ideal for yourself. Find out how that person, or perhaps persons, got there: their training, their experiences, the steps they took, their trajectory. Learn as much as you can about them. Get them to communicate with you, maybe even to mentor you. If they have already created the wheel you want, try to determine how they did it.

Provided this is not a library book, be sure to read this volume with a highlighter or two nearby, and mark passages and tips that resonate with you as you go through it. If all goes well, when you are finished, the book will be a dog-eared, multicolored, coffee-stained wreck, but you will have a much more solid idea of where anthropology can take you.

Notes

1   See Nolan (2003) for a more detailed discussion of these issues.
2   Charity Goodman, WAPA President (2006), personal communication.

References

Fiske, Shirley J., Linda A. Bennett, Patricia Ensworth, et al. (2010) *The Changing Face of Anthropology: Anthropology Masters Reflect on Education, Careers, and Professional Organizations. The AAA/CoPAPIA 2009 Anthropology MA Career Survey*. Arlington, VA: American Anthropological Association.
Nolan, Riall (2003) *Anthropology in Practice*. Boulder, CO: Lynne Rienner.

Chapter 3

Making the Transition from the Academy to Practice

Mary Odell Butler

Mary Odell Butler draws on both her own experience and that of other colleagues as she describes how and why she decided to become a practitioner, and what the transition was like. She offers valuable and thoughtful insights into how practitioner identities are constructed and maintained, the core role played by the discipline in this, and role of on-the-job learning in expanding both capacities and possibilities. She concludes this chapter with some very specific suggestions for people just beginning a career in practice.

I am a practicing anthropologist. For the past 25 years, I have loved my job. There have been tough moments, of course. But by and large, I have gone to work in the morning bemused that someone was paying me to do this and paying me pretty well. I have done ethnography in all of the states except North Dakota (and I almost made it there) and in five foreign countries. I have grown professionally as an anthropologist, as a scientist, and as a human being in ways that I would not have dreamed of at the beginning.

Each year many practicing anthropologists move from academic to non-academic settings for many different reasons. Some of us began practice right out of graduate school because we had trained to do this or because a graduate internship or field-work had sold us on this kind of work. Some of us chose to practice anthropology because this was where we saw ourselves being the best professionals we could be

A Handbook of Practicing Anthropology. First Edition. Edited by Riall W. Nolan.
© 2013 John Wiley & Sons, Inc. Published 2013 by John Wiley & Sons, Inc.

or because practice was a good complement to the rest of our lives. Some of our careers evolved in the direction of practice. Some of us entered practice because the anticipated academic job failed to appear. Some of us were thrust out of academia to practice new forms of anthropology that we knew very little about. All of us learned a lot from the transition. But for many of us, things would have been so much easier had we known then what we know now.

The precise circumstances in which we made our transitions into practice varied across time. I made my own transition in the1980s when I was denied tenure after 14 years in the academy as a graduate student, an instructor, and an assistant professor of anthropology. Things were different then. First of all, practice wasn't talked about much in polite circles – like American Anthropological Association (AAA) meetings. Practitioner networks were small and few people knew about them. Like many of my peers, I was convinced that practice was a distant second choice for those who somehow didn't make it in academia. When I was denied tenure, I thought I would have to forget about anthropology and get myself a "real" job.

I am pleased to report that it didn't turn out that way. After a few missteps, I found my feet as an anthropologist in the private sector when I began to do program evaluations in public health. I tell people that my career worked out much better than anything I could have planned in the beginning. I was completely ignorant of the possibilities and I could not see beyond the academic setting.

At this point I have hired a dozen anthropologists into the private sector. I have mentored many more. Things are changing now. As anthropologists have moved out into the government, nonprofit, and private sectors, people have begun to see what we can do and have come to value it. I still don't see ads for "cultural anthropologist" in the *Washington Post*, but nowadays at least some clients come to us because they know that they need an anthropologist to do what they want done. Still this anthropology occurs in a field that must – like all field sites – be researched and understood before we can navigate it successfully. All of us, whether at the beginning of our careers or later, experienced the same push to adapt to new environments, often with little help from our graduate schools. This is true even for many of those students – now found everywhere – who make practice a career goal and pursue it from early in their studies.

I wanted the story in this chapter to be broader than my own experience. Therefore, in preparing it, I talked to 12 anthropologists with experience in practice, anthropologists who were considered successful practitioners by their colleagues. In telephone interviews, I asked these people to recount their career trajectories, their expectations when they came into anthropology, and the learning experiences that were most important to them in retrospect.[1]

It is important to remember that the people represented here were chosen because they are successful practitioners; that is, they have or have had employment in the practice of anthropology for a non-negligible period of time, they make their living primarily from practice rather than teaching, and they are respected by colleagues in and out of the academy. Their stories have much in common, but there is no way to tell whether these career paths are typical of successful practitioners or if these people are successful practitioners because of the specific career decisions they made.

My Experience

I am the senior citizen of this cohort. I received my PhD in 1978. The anthropology that I was trained to enter was changing quickly, but few of us were aware of that in the 1970s. Mostly we became absorbed in our graduate studies and put off the whole issue of what we would do if and when we got our degrees. I had finished fieldwork in western Guatemala and was beginning to think about writing a dissertation when, due to a series of coincidences, I got a tenure-track academic job a year and a half before I received my PhD. In my small, joint sociology–anthropology department, I was a utility cultural anthropologist. I taught three sections of introduction to cultural anthropology each year. Beyond this, like each of the four anthropologists in my department, I "owned" one of the four fields. Because I had a bachelor's degree in pre-med and because of my interests, I was given biological anthropology. I taught human evolution, physical anthropology, cultural evolution, medical anthropology, the emergent field of biocultural anthropology, Latin American ethnography, the North American Indian. In fact, I was allowed to teach just about anything I was willing to pull together. In my eight years in this job, I taught 15 different courses. I used to joke that this was my eight-year bachelor's degree in anthropology. It was a wonderful job and I loved it.

Everything changed in 1984 when I was denied tenure. There were a lot of reasons for this which no longer matter. Suffice it to say that I found myself on the streets, an unemployed assistant professor of anthropology. And that was *all* I was. In my 15 years in anthropology till then, I had never given a single thought to the possibility of this kind of situation – anxiety yes, but not much thought. Nor had any of my colleagues in the department. When word came that I had ultimately been denied tenure, my friends avoided me as if afraid of some kind of ritual pollution. It was awful. Choked by my own sense of failure, I believed that I was no longer an anthropologist. I did what anyone would do in the situation: I got depressed and refused to do anything for eight months. I moved to Washington with my husband and sat in the house for a long time. Once in a while I called one of the three or four friends I had in Washington and talked to them about how to find a job, but I wasn't really very interested. I was too demoralized to do anything.

In the end one of these calls produced a job for me as an economic analyst in a two-person firm, one of whom was me. You may ask, what did I know about economics? Not much. But I knew how to learn. I read up like crazy and basically I faked it until I got smart enough to do the job, just like I had when I was learning enough economics to support my dissertation research. During my economics job, I learned to program in the Statistical Analysis System (SAS). The next job I got was as an SAS programmer on a clinical study that my new employer was doing for the National Cancer Institute (NCI). After a few months of that, I became project director on the NCI project. Looking back, I realize that at this point I had made the transition.

My transition took a while and it was difficult. Eventually I got back to where I had been professionally when I left academia. I had work that excited me, opportunities to develop intellectually, a vibrant working environment, stimulating colleagues. Things were good again. I was productive. I was also in my own mind no longer an anthropologist. I kept my membership of the AAA but didn't go to any meetings for nine years. I read the *American Anthropologist* about as thoroughly as I do today. I finally came back to the professional associations on the practice side of things. When I began talking to other practitioners and to anthropology students, I saw how common my experience was in its essential elements. I was not uniquely afflicted, nor a poor anthropologist, nor a failure. I was just living an experience that many of us had in building careers and that many more were to face in the future.

One of the respondents said: "I'm always an anthropologist. It's just who I am." This was my experience as well. No matter what doubts I had about a successful career in anthropology, I always knew that I was an anthropologist in some essential way. For many other anthropologists in practice, this isn't so. I have often worked with a client or even a colleague for months only to discover in a casual conversation over lunch that they have a graduate degree in anthropology. They self-identified as a program manager or a social researcher or an epidemiologist. I don't have the numbers, but I suspect there are a lot of anthropologists like that out there. It you ask them straight out what they studied in graduate school, they will admit to anthropology. If you never ask directly, you will never know. They're just smart professionals of some sort. This tendency to de-identify from anthropology comes at a cost to the profession, especially to practitioners. No one ever knows that the good work these people do is part of anthropology.

Becoming a Practitioner

In this section, I would like to present some themes that emerged in my interviews with my non-random sample of successful practitioners of anthropology. I will begin by outlining the basic career trajectory that we took from graduate school to where we are today and summarize common ideas that emerged from these discussions. I would like to describe what the transition from academic settings looks like from the other side, that is after you've left academia, discuss the role of anthropology in this wider world, talk about how to sell anthropology (yes, sell!) in terms that can be understood by non-anthropologists, and share some lessons learned.

Most of us came into anthropology because we found it fascinating, empowering, exciting. We wanted what it had to offer. We went through graduate departments that – by and large – prepared us for academic jobs that were decreasing in availability even as we were learning to do them. We heard sometimes that there weren't many academic jobs, but many of us thought – if we thought about it at all – that we would get one of the few available. Our professors, our colleagues, our mentors were usually unaware of alternatives to academic jobs, even threatened by them. If we were not archaeologists, we were unlikely to be taught the methods that we would need in research jobs. Even those of us fortunate enough to study in programs stressing applications of anthropology had few mentors with hands-on experience in non-academic practice. While conditions vary somewhat, this is where many of us stood at the moment of our transition.

Nine of my respondents are cultural anthropologists of some kind, and three are archaeologists. Some are full-time practitioners in corporate, nonprofit, and academic settings. Some combine anthropological practice with academic or other kinds of careers. One of them, after many years of successful practice, moved into an academic job in a department that focuses on practice. Some hold master's degrees and some hold PhDs. Some were trained in programs designed for applied or practicing anthropology. Others came from traditional anthropology programs. Some – like me – were trained as four field anthropologists. Insofar as possible, I tried to choose anthropologists at several stages of their careers. My respondents all received their degrees between 1978 and 2003.

The current work of these people was or has been the application of anthropological method and theory to concrete problems that a client of some kind needed to resolve. Many of them have grown into executive jobs in their companies and become involved in management, business development, and marketing. Two people had completed MBAs to support these activities. People work for corporations, private businesses, nonprofit organizations, governments. Three of them are entrepreneurs with their own businesses.

Ethnography is widely used to explore a wide range of topics and problem areas in practice. Practicing anthropologists work on projects such as understanding organizations and solving organizational problems, building communities around health and the environment, and describing markets for a wide variety of programs and products. You probably already know how to use ethnography in your own area. Training in the approach itself is very valuable. You have learned to suspend judgment, listen more than you speak, respect diversity and difference, and resist conclusions until the data are all in.

For archaeologists, cultural resource management (CRM) is important. CRM jobs are available to graduate students seeking support as well as to graduates. One of my interviewees commented that getting CRM jobs in the area of his practice is "no big deal." There is a massive shift toward private organizations in CRM work, one that is likely to make these jobs the wave of the future. Interestingly, archaeologists in CRM and heritage archaeology do substantial ethnography with modern people in coming to understand the value, meaning, and context for their work.

A fairly common career path was a combination of academic and non-academic work either simultaneously or sequentially. Usually their academic work was not the standard tenure track pattern of starting as an assistant professor, obtaining tenure, and moving up the ranks. Often they were in cross-disciplinary academic programs with, for example, business schools and schools of public health. The majority of people I talked to had or had had academic experience of some kind as part-time or adjunct faculty. Many of them have served on graduate committees, arranged for student internships, and otherwise mentored individual students.

The successful practitioners in this group had attended fairly traditional depart-ments of anthropology. About half of them had planned academic careers and discovered alternatives when they began seeking employment. People who got their degrees before about 1985 expected to be professors when they were in graduate school. People who got their degrees in the 1990s or later were more diverse in their reported career expectations. Many had known all along that they would practice. Two people had planned academic careers and chose non-academic jobs because they were impressed by their experience in interviews with potential corporate employers.

Most of the people I talked to had worked as practicing anthropologists before receiving their degrees, either as part of internships and fieldwork or to support themselves in graduate school. It was common across this group for people to drop out of graduate programs for a time to work, to try out things, to learn on the job prior to graduation. This was very helpful in shaping their later careers. Those with practice jobs in graduate school had some experience and understanding of what was available for them and what kinds of things they like to do. Sometimes practi-tioners were so successful in graduate school jobs that they required a long period of time to complete their graduate degrees.

About half the people I spoke to had left the AAA, but belonged to some other professional association such as the Society for Applied Anthropology (SfAA) or the Society for American Archaeology (SAA). Some participate in the Ethnographic Praxis in Industry Conference (EPIC). Whether or not they were members of AAA, they all identified themselves as anthropologists.

Transitions

Career transition is a lifelong experience. As practitioners we have to divorce our-selves from the idea that careers incorporate lifelong security doing basically the same job from initial employment to retirement. Only in the academy does this occupational model persist. It has long since faded from the private sector because organizations needed the flexibility to adapt to rapid technological and societal change in the latter half of the twentieth century. Now this impetus is beginning to affect academic institutions and the traditional tenured jobs are becoming rare, so rare that only a small percentage of anthropologists will ever become tenured professors.

Most of us change both the kinds of jobs we do and the settings in which we do them several times in our careers. For practitioners the focus must center on building a corpus of knowledge and skills that will carry us across transitions. We need to think of ourselves as what we can do, how we can bring this to the market, and what our role is in moving the world ahead. This is not always easy even to conceptualize.

The biggest surprise that I encountered in my own transition was learning – very gradually –that anthropologists can do a lot of things, but they may not see the value of what they do. We have skills that are more and more in demand because people need to know the questions as often as they need answers. This is pretty fundamental to the ethnographic method, where our task is not to measure observation as much as it is to define what is important, what issues confront the people we work with. We do this by listening carefully until we begin to see the big picture, probing as appropriate. No matter where I am or what I am doing, I'm usually doing ethnography. This skill is a big asset not only in doing ethnography to research something, but also in marketing, meetings, boardrooms, negotiations in a business environment. My personal rule in any kind of business setting is "The person who talks most learns least."

I had to learn a different work rhythm. In my academic career I used to say, "I can work my 60 hours a week whenever I want." The open schedule of the academy and – certainly – long breaks in the summer and around holidays feel like a big benefit. However, I was responsible for two children, so the summer break meant seasonal unemployment for me. I had to find a "summer job" while doing the prep for the fall; I took a two-week vacation just like everybody else. I thought at the beginning that working 40 hours a week 48 weeks a year would be difficult. But it didn't turn out that way. First of all, there was a lot of flexibility in the corporate environment. Some weeks you worked 60 hours; other weeks you worked 30 or so depending on crunches in project work or proposals. I found that I tended to work to the job and not to the clock and that this was fine with my employer. I just had to get the job done. However, I was also shocked to discover that I had to account for 40 hours of work a week. This was a challenge but once I learned it, it wasn't hard. Now it's instinctive.

A finding repeated over and over was the importance – and the value – of teamwork in the practice of anthropology. This is a significant break from the "lone wolf" orientation common in tenure track or tenured academic jobs. The reward systems in academia and outside are set up differently. Universities sometimes discourage teamwork with tenure policies like giving less than full "credit" to co-authored articles or requiring the publication of books for tenure. Outside of the academy, the criterion for success is effective project work that pleases clients and passes scientific muster. In scientific work, an organization's reputation is the product that it sells and it must be protected at all times. The likelihood of projects being successful is improved by building interdisciplinary teams that bring multiple and complementary theories and skills to the job. So this is what's rewarded in salaries and promotion. It is also intellectually stimulating to build something that incorporates the strengths of multiple disciplines and lots of different people. Some of my younger interviewees reported that they got into practice because they discovered that they preferred working on teams to working alone. Normally they learned this by serving in practice-related jobs or internships in graduate school.

I had to learn to sell myself and I had to learn to sell anthropology. It was an expectation of my job that I work to raise funds to support myself and my colleagues through face-to-face discussion with potential clients and by organizing and writing successful proposals. They called it marketing and it sounded very daunting to me. Making sure that work continues is a requirement of almost any job, academic or not. One of my respondents told me that it is an illusion that anyone ever gets a job based on "hard money," that is, money guaranteed to be there. We all have to work to generate the revenue that supports us. Once I got used to the idea, marketing was not difficult in the least. It consists of talking to potential clients, eliciting their problems, understanding their points of view, devising ways to meet their needs. This should sound familiar. It's ethnography and most anthropologists do it pretty well.

Lessons Learned

Here are some suggestions that I have developed over my own fairly successful career as a practitioner. First of all, learn to sell anthropology. Don't worry. You'll get used to the idea. The central thing here is very simple. Every time you can teach someone – especially someone who hires people – that anthropology can do something that they, or someone they know, can use, you serve not only your own cause but the cause of anthropology generally. As I said before, a lot of people need an anthropologist but don't know that it's an anthropologist they need. It's incumbent on us to teach them who we are.

In job interviews, don't lead with "I'm an anthropologist." Anthropology has a questionable reputation out there. You've probably experienced it in social settings. "What do you do?" "I'm an anthropologist." "Oh . . . [long pause] That must be interesting." Can you imagine the images that might be running through the mind of someone who may never before have met an anthropologist? Savages with bones in their noses, who dig up mammoths, live in Bora Bora? You can bet it has little to do with what we actually do for a living, especially if we're in practice. I hasten to add that not everyone is like that. This is one of the many things that are getting better. People do have a more sophisticated idea of who we are. But none of that matters if you are interviewing a person who is one of the other kind.

Also the interviewer has your résumé. They already know you're an anthropologist. In fact, they may be interviewing you *in spite of* that fact. So do ethnography in job interviews. Get the interviewer's idea of what the job is, what it needs. I have written up enough job ads to know that employers often don't know what they need and are not really sure what kind of person will fill the bill. So they write pretty generic job descriptions, disperse them widely, and see who shows up. Before you start to present who you are, get some idea of what they need, so that you can respond appropriately with the training, skills, and so on that you have to approach that job.

Remember, job interviews are two-way. You are also interviewing them and you probably are more comfortable doing this than they are. Compile a list of questions before you arrive. Figure out what you need to know about the job. Do adequate homework before the interview. Once you are in the interview, your task is to decide for yourself if you can fit in here. Let them decide if they want to hire you.

Conversely, we have a responsibility to promote our talent as anthropologists in work environments. In any situation where you work with people – whether they are colleagues, clients, bosses, or competitors – make sure that everyone realizes you are an anthropologist. For our own good and for the good of anthropology in the future, we should do everything we can to make sure that everyone we work with knows that the good work we produce comes from anthropology. We are almost invisible in many of the contexts in which we practice. There are probably a number of reasons for this. But one I have experienced over and over is that, a couple of years into practice, anthropologists cease to identify themselves as such. I have often gone to lunch with someone I have worked with for months and discovered in casual conversation that they have a master's or even a doctorate in anthropology. They have lost track of or interest in the larger anthropological endeavor. As a result, when they do a good piece of ethnography no one knows that anthropology had anything to do with it. So sound the horn for anthropology wherever you are. You are the only one who can do this.

Some Concrete Tips

In my own experiences and in my conversation with colleagues for this chapter, some simple, concrete ideas for how to approach the transition to practice came up. Many of these we learned along the way; some of them are things we wish we had thought about at earlier points in our careers. We learned these things from each other and from friends and students who have sought our advice.

- Plan ahead for what you will do if you find yourself on the job market. Until I was denied tenure, jobs had always fallen into my lap without a great deal of effort on my part. I refused to believe that I would ever need to present myself to the world as a job candidate. As a result, when I had no job, I stumbled around for months trying to get my legs under me. When I finally looked for a job, it didn't take too long. It would have been so much easier if I had made myself plan in advance.
- Do your ethnography. This has been a recurring theme in this chapter. We have very good tools for entering the job market, for moving about in it, for succeeding. We are trained in the skills needed to penetrate a social situation, to find out how the people who are there experience it, and to use this knowledge to generate strategies for understanding and acting in new situations. Yet often anthropologists forget to use these skills to their own advantage in researching jobs. I sometimes go on job interviews just for the experience. Since I already have work and my life isn't riding on the outcome, I sometimes focus on interviewing the interviewer. I've always gotten a job offer when I've done this, every single time. Interesting, huh?
- Inventory your skills. What can you contribute to the workplace? Be able to articulate this to a potential employer. Your understanding of this is more important

than your résumé in landing a job. Your résumé just gets you the interview; *you* get the job!

- In your graduate work and on your jobs, focus in on methodology. It's not that theory isn't important: you will use it every day. It's just that methods are what employers usually need and what you will sell. This is especially important for us since we are not always trained to prioritize methods.
- Build networks. Start today. Everyone you meet, whether or not an anthropologist, is a potential contact and/or employer. You never know who will help. My first two jobs came from friends of mine that I met in other contexts and had never mentally connected to my job search. They knew of places and opportunities that I wouldn't have thought of. When I say build networks, I mean more than schmoozing at conferences. Networks should be concrete, written down somewhere with contact information, where you met the person, possible connections – whatever you need to remember. If you're visual like me, add photos if you can find them. Write this down as soon as possible. You will forget. If I don't do this, I come home from meetings with a whole bunch of business cards that I don't know what to do with.
- Solicit other people's stories. Practicing anthropologists tend to be eager to tell their stories. They have usually worked hard to define their jobs, even while doing them. And, like all humans, I guess, we really love to talk about it. What happened to them? How did they get in this line of work? What is good about their job? What would they change?
- Develop an elevator speech on what anthropologists are and what they do. People will ask you this question constantly when you are looking for a job, after you get one, and in your work itself. Be prepared to deliver it over and over, sometimes in real elevators on the way to lunch.
- Try really hard to clean the anthropological (or any other) jargon out of your working vocabulary. When I first entered the workplace, I used the emic/etic distinction like they were real words in the English language. People gave me this really strange look. Eventually I learned to say, "From the perspective of [whoever] . . ."
- Be careful about strong ideological orientations. I once interviewed an anthropologist who had great qualifications for the job but classified himself as a "Marxist anthropologist." This was fine with me – I was a Marxist anthropologist myself for a few months in 1973 – but it was all he would talk about. We weren't looking for a Marxist anthropologist. Needless to say, he didn't get the job.
- Stay in anthropology. Your colleagues are the underpinnings of your career. They will make you feel better while you're unemployed and eventually they will connect you to a job if you are there to be connected. Had I been thinking clearly, I would have joined my local practitioners' organization (LPO) long before I did. But I was mad at anthropology for the tenure denial and I found it necessary to sulk for 10 years before I discovered that colleagues are power.
- Reach back. When you get your career going and are happy with it, help other anthropologists get there too. It's hard to find mentors in practice. They tend not

to come built in to your graduate program. Mentoring can only come from us. Professional organizations, universities, and colleagues can connect you with people who are seeking a mentor. Most LPOs and the National Association for the Practice of Anthropology run mentoring programs. Mentoring is the lifeblood of practice. Get it, give it, and encourage those you mentor to pass it forward.

Note

1 I identified the 12 persons I interviewed by making up a short list of practitioners whom I knew from previous discussions. I then networked out using recommendations from these individuals. In addition, I published a note on the NAPA discussion page requesting volunteers to talk to me about this issue and received three responses. I endeavored to obtain a distribution by age (actually year of the most advanced degree received in anthropology) and by area of expertise. I made a special effort to reach out to archaeologists because this is an important area of practice whose needs are not always considered. My respondent group included only sociocultural anthropologists and archaeologists.

Chapter 4

Job Hunting in the Twenty-First Century

Judy Tso

In this chapter, Judy Tso outlines a clear and straightforward strategy for finding a job as a practitioner, whether it is a first professional job, or the next. She focuses in particular on understanding your skills and your potential contribution as an anthropologist, and making this an integral part of your search. Anthropologists, she maintains, are particularly well qualified, by virtue of their training and perspective, to compete effectively in today's job market, but they need to understand how to present themselves and their abilities in the most persuasive way. Included in this chapter are suggestions for how to narrow down your job search, how to write an effective résumé, the value of networking, and finally, zeroing in on specific job opportunities and interviewing successfully for them.

Introduction

This chapter will address what the job search process looks like in the twenty-first century. As I write this chapter, there is a temporal dimension to the discussion; we are still in a recession. Unemployment is hovering between 8 and 9 percent, and many people have given up looking. In some areas, unemployment is even higher.

It's currently a tough environment. While these conditions may ease over time, the approach I lay out will work at all times. In a down economy when jobs are scarce, you really need to stand out; your résumé cannot read like a million others. And standing out will always be relevant.

You can think about the job search in five big steps:

A Handbook of Practicing Anthropology. First Edition. Edited by Riall W. Nolan.

1. Determine what job you want: research, reflect on, and determine what positions you are looking for and are well suited for.
2. Write your résumé: create a résumé and cover letter for each position.
3. Apply for jobs: choose which organizations interest you and apply for jobs.
4. Network and build your connections to support the job search.
5. Interview, interview, and land the job.

Step 1: Determine the Job You Want and How You Are Qualified for It

The first step requires a great deal of reflection on your part. You need to have a sense of your interests, your values, what you are passionate about, and where your skills are to formulate a list of positions that might suit you.

Be flexible and develop a list of three or four possible positions. One of the books I always recommend to people is *What Color is Your Parachute*, by Richard Bolles. This book is a classic and has endured because it includes a number of really useful exercises to help you get clear on your skill set. If you complete these exercises you will have some good data to inform your decisions. You can also browse the website O*NET online at www.onetonline.org/.

In addition to getting clear on what you bring to the table, you also need to articulate what is so valuable about your anthropological background. In the next section, I have summarized what is valuable about the perspective that anthropologists bring. Some of the questions you can consider as you reflect include:

- What jobs or tasks have you enjoyed in the past?
  - Think about all the jobs you have had or all the activities you have accomplished. What were peak experiences for you? Jot down a description of each peak experience and then look for themes. Are there similarities across these situations?
  - What situations are your pet peeves? Make a list of your pet peeves. Your pet peeves may also direct you to careers, focus areas, issues.
- What are your top values and how might they shape your search?
- What topics or issues interest you?
- What type of organization do you want to work in (corporate, nonprofit, government, etc.)?
- What size of organization do you prefer – large, medium, or small?
- What geographic area(s) are you targeting?

You need to be adept at translating the skills you have gained from an education in anthropology to any possible position you are interested in. Below you will see some of the perspectives and skills that are often gained from this background.

Communicating the value of anthropology

There is no better time to market and position your skills as an anthropologist than in the twenty-first century, despite the recession and high unemployment, given that the US economy is now predominantly a knowledge production economy and not a manufacturing economy. The best-paying jobs are ones that require a global and systems perspective, a thinking mind, and a laptop. Anthropologists have good skills for these jobs.

So let's start with a rundown of some of the skills that the contemporary economy requires and how those skills overlap with the anthropologist's toolkit. Required skills include:

- cultural competency – understanding global and international markets and cross-cultural systems;
- understanding complex systems;
- strategic and analytic ability;
- ability to work across disciplines;
- ability to work inductively and from a customer perspective;
- training in ethnographic research methods.

Cultural competency Anthropologists are grounded in culture and understanding difference and the interdependent world economy is a reality that sorely requires more people with the anthropologist's mindset and training. We understand the importance of looking at human diversity and cultural diversity and making sure that different mindsets, customs, practices and beliefs of the world are honored, taken into account, addressed. In the US especially, we are still slow to get out of the dominant cultural mindset and make sure the approach considers different cultures.

Understanding complex systems We live in a time when helping organizations understand complex systems is essential for making the cultural transformations that are needed in the world. As anthropologists, we naturally hold a systems view. We bring that lens to all we do. Holism is a concept we talk about frequently in anthropology and this holistic viewpoint is a strategic advantage.

Strategic and analytic ability Similarly, anthropologists are big-picture thinkers. We need and want to know the context, to understand the environment, and we naturally think in strategic terms. Rather than focus on the minute details, we back up and seek to see the landscape. Most people are focused on the details and not on the strategic picture. Needless to say, anthropologists utilize various analytical methods to make meaning and to understand the world. Making sense of the world is a particularly important skill set.

Ability to work across disciplines Practitioners rarely work by themselves. Anthropologists, by training, are good at entering unfamiliar cultures and gaining understanding of them. Other professions and disciplines, in this sense, are indeed other cultures, and we need the ability to work with others who think differently from us, but no less well. It is far better, when you come into a meeting, to ask people to explain their reality and to let an understanding emerge than to tell people what you think. Rather than come in as experts about an organization, we should come in with curiosity and let the data emerge.

Ability to work inductively and from a customer perspective Our focus on ethnography, on speaking to the people involved in order to understand the situation, is participatory in nature and the world is in desperate need of more participatory processes. All the top-down, authoritarian approaches yield very poor answers and fail to meet most people's needs. The anthropologist's training and bent for talking to everyone involved, no matter their rank, means that we can uncover many key pieces of information that others do not bother to collect.

Similarly, because we are participatory, that often naturally lends itself to being customer-focused, patient-focused, client-focused. We want to understand the experience of the people, whoever they are and often we seek to understand the people no one cares to ask. In the hospital or school, we want to talk to the janitor. In the immigration debate, we want to talk to the illegal alien. In the study of AIDS, we want to talk to the homeless, the drug addicts, and the men who self-identify as both straight and gay. We don't exclude, we aren't prejudicial. We seek to talk to everyone in the field and on the ground, those being impacted, affected, and so on.

Ethnographic training As anthropologists, we have some basic training in ethnographic techniques and qualitative research. The ability to use these ethnographic approaches to observe, study, and understand people, groups, and cultures is a distinct asset.

Positioning yourself

Your ability to portray your anthropological background as a unique asset will increase your chance of making a distinct impression. Therefore, I ran a number of National Association for the Practice of Anthropology (NAPA) workshops back in 2002 and 2003 at American Anthropological Association meetings to help students to articulate the benefits of having this background. The workshops were usually entitled: "Promoting Your Anthropology Background in 30 Seconds . . . *in Plain English*."

From these workshops I compiled this list of what anthropologists are particularly good at doing. Anthropologists have the ability to:

- appreciate the perspective of others and capture their stories;
- see the big picture in strategic terms;
- take a systemic view, i.e., see systems as a whole;
- take a holistic view;
- be customer-focused;

- be participatory and empowering in their dealings with people;
- conduct qualitative research;
- gain the trust of people;
- understand the cultural implications of plans, proposals, and changes;
- understand what is going on between people, that is, group or organizational dynamics;
- get at what people can't say through their skill of observation.

Given these skills and attributes, the following are some of the topics that anthropologists are well positioned to study or address:

- the shrinking earth;
- demographic changes;
- the global workforce and globalization;
- issues of race and power;
- non-verbal behavior;
- issues of space.

Using the language of the target audience

When you have determined which types of organizations interest you, you need to choose language that is common and well understood in the organizational culture you are targeting. It is important to get a handle on the trends and developments in your targeted industry or sector. What are the buzz-words in use in that sector? For example, within the health field, culturally competent care has been an important concept, as has patient-centered health. In corporate environments, people have talked for years about the voice of the customer or, lately, consumer insights. Ethnographic research also became more popular in market research and product development circles. You will want to include critical phrases and buzz-words in your résumé and in the cover letter. The ability to the speak the target organization's language will demonstrate your understanding of what the sector considers important as well as your ability to "translate" your anthropological skills into language your target audience understands.

   In the academic environment no one likes the words "synergy" or "leverage" but in corporate environments they are the rage: how can you *leverage* your skills and take advantage of *synergies* with your teammates to get the task done? In the environmental field people speak about sustainability and leaving a legacy. This is exactly what anthropologists do when they study people. They learn to use the language our subjects use in order to build rapport, fit in, be trusted. Use the same set of skills when you seek a job, to find out what the current buzz-words and trends are. You know how to do interviews, so set up a bunch of informational interviews and note what words they are using.

Job titles suitable for anthropologists

These are some of the job titles that require the skills anthropologists have to offer (look for titles that have the words "analyst" and "social science"):

- program or management analyst (federal jobs)
- policy analyst
- strategy consultant
- research associate (think-tank)
- research analyst
- research scientist
- anthropologist
- ethnographer
- qualitative researcher
- research consultant
- market researcher
- marketing analyst
- product development analyst
- social scientist
- program evaluator
- program manager
- health policy researcher
- manager, customer relations
- associate insights manager
- media research analyst
- management consultant
- product specialist.

Some other key terms that may indicate you have what the hiring officials may be willing to consider:

- user-centered design
- voice of the customer
- product development.

Step 2: Write Your Résumé

Today, the majority of résumés are being processed, screened, and reviewed by electronic means. They are inputted electronically through a website and a machine looks at them first; rarely are they reviewed first by a person. Should they make it through to a person, it is most likely that a lower-level administrative person or human resources person, often a person who is not an expert in your field, will review it first. Therefore the words you use in your résumé are crucial. The person reading is looking for key words. If you paraphrase, this layperson may not understand that your skills match the qualifications. That is why it is imperative to tailor or customize each and every résumé to the particular job you are applying for and to use the language you find in the job description.

In addition, there are four other important things you should do as you craft your résumé:

- Tailor your résumé to the job you are applying for.
- Make it short.
- Summarize your experience and qualifications at the beginning.
- Finally, describe your accomplishments as quantitatively as you can.

Tailor your résumé to the job

This may seem like a pain, but it is absolutely essential to revise and customize your résumé to address the specific requirements for a job opening. It may take you two hours but it is absolutely essential to make sure that your résumé rises to the top of the heap.

A lot of résumés are now reviewed by automated systems. A human being may not review your résumé in the first round, so if the key word search fails to yield as many matches as is desirable, your résumé will never be seen by a pair of human eyes. Even if it reaches a person, he or she may not be well versed in your area of expertise and likely isn't an anthropologist, so if they are looking for key words and you have used synonyms, they may not recognize them. It is best to aim to use the wording that the hiring official is most likely to recognize and that is the wording in the job description. A job application is not a research paper and creativity and originality are not rewarded. This is especially important for government jobs where a non-expert will look at your résumé and will not recognize terms that were not found in the job listing. Again, don't try to be creative.

Make it short

A résumé, the predominant document that the non-academic world relies on as a summary of your professional experience, is short. If you have less than five years of work experience, your résumé should be no longer than two pages. If you have 10 or more years of experience, you could go to three pages but keep it focused on the last 10 years of experience. There is no need to go all the way back to the first job. There aren't too many résumés that are much longer than three pages. A résumé is not a curriculum vitae.

The non-academic world is in a rush and no one has the time to read a long document.

Summarize your experience or qualifications at the beginning

At the top of your resume, use a summary paragraph that highlights your best qualifications and experience. This is your abstract if you will or your condensed bio. It should differentiate you from the pack. If it sounds generic rewrite it until it reflects your unique set of skills. This paragraph is your opportunity to explain "why hire me." This paragraph should already be making the pitch to the potential employer.

Describe results quantitatively

Today, the name of the game is results and impact. Do not simply describe what you have done. Most people make a list of all the things they have done but neglect to describe the results of the work. What happened next as a result of your work and your contribution? It is essential to cite these results in quantitative terms whenever possible. For example, if you conducted research, how many surveys were collected and how did you use the data? What impact did the data have on subsequent decisions? Did the survey lead to program improvements or other positive impacts?

To describe only what you did (the mechanics) is a poor approach, e.g. "I designed and implemented a survey that was sent to 500 employees." It would be better to say: "I designed and implemented a survey achieving a response rate of 50 percent, and findings were used to shape the communication plan for the project. As a result of the communications sent out, employees have provided feedback that they understand and are committed to the new initiative." Even better would be to say: "As the research lead for the Jasper volunteer project, I designed, tested, and conducted a survey with 300 volunteers. Findings from the 150 responses indicated that the project needed additional resources and a clearer set of benefits. The program manager used the findings to secure additional funding and clarify the benefits, which resulted in a 20 percent increase in volunteer participation."

There may be 20 people who can design a survey, but who was most effective in making an impact through the survey? The market is extremely competitive, and you are more likely to be hired if you can demonstrate results you have achieved, using statements such as:

- By using the findings from the employee engagement survey, several new employee initiatives were created and the percentage of employees that responded favorably increased from 25 to 40 percent between 2010 and 2011.
- I developed a new customer service training course and, as a result, the first call resolution rate (number of calls resolved on the first call) increased from 80 to 85 percent.
- I wrote 20 grants during a one-year period and had a success rate of 70 percent, bringing in a total of $550,000.

Once you have a good draft, circulate your résumé to people who can critique it. Send it to someone who might be a potential employer.

Step 3: Apply for Jobs

These days the application process for most organizations take place on line. You will often need to register and provide a username and password to create an account in the talent management software, after which you can usually upload résumés and cover letters. Sometimes you can also attach other background documents. If you have copies of articles you have written or other writing samples, copies of any certifications you possess, or award certificates, you can attach these as proof of your skills and credentials.

It is important to prepare a customized cover letter with each résumé. Your cover letter is your chief opportunity to present yourself when applying. You will want to make the strongest arguments in this letter and attract the attention of the human resources staff. Make sure to customize your cover letter to the job description and desired qualifications.

Step 4: Network and Build Your Connections

In seeking a job today, it is your ability to utilize the connections in your network that can help to push your résumé to the top of the pile. Some organizations really pay attention to employee referrals. So if your connection can refer you for a particular job, that is a great way to proceed. If you don't feel your network is very big, create a plan that will enable you to add people to your network. Even acquaintances may help you out.

A networking plan is a simple tool you can use to list the people you know. Make a list of people you need to get to know and then think of some next steps to develop those relationships. If you are an introvert and hate to mingle, I am sorry to say, you will have to move out of your comfort zone. People trust those they have met in person. Personal contact enables someone to get a sense of who you are. So work on getting yourself involved in events. Table 4.1 shows a simple way of keeping track of your many networking contacts. As the number of people in your network grows, you will find a system like this helpful for remembering them.

Social media

Much recruiting activity takes place online these days. The top professional networking site is LinkedIn, and it is important to have a presence there. My recommendation is that you link only to people you would feel comfortable referring. If you don't know them that well, don't link to them. If you link to them and they ask you for

Table 4.1 A networking contact chart

Name/type of contact	Organization	Degree of familiarity (hot, warm, cold)	Next steps
Joseph Daniels	Red Cross	Cold	Send email requesting informational interview
Connection to City Year	City Year	Cold	Need to look at LinkedIn to see if I know anyone at City Year

a recommendation, which you don't feel you can give them, you probably don't know them well enough to benefit from the linkage.

Recruiters trawl through accounts in LinkedIn and may approach you with job openings. Also, once you apply for a job, it is not uncommon for a recruiter to check out your profile and look at your recommendations. Recruiters may also to seek to connect to you. I recommend you accept connections from recruiters, as once they have a sense of your skills they may become a useful connection in the long term. You can also use LinkedIn to see if you are connected to someone who can refer you to an organization or provide the name of a contact for informational interviews.

While I don't do much with Facebook and Twitter, some of their activity is related to job search as well. You can follow recruiters on Twitter and tweet a link to your résumé. If you enjoy tweeting, you can use Twitter to advertise your thinking and expertise in a way that can demonstrate your qualifications.

Step 5: Interview and Land the Job

These days it is common for recruiters to conduct a telephone interview to screen you. If you have the skills for the job, the recruiter will schedule a time to speak with you by phone and confirm your background. This is a phone interview. If you do well in it, it is likely you will get a face-to-face interview.

Prepare for every interview as seriously as you would prepare for the doing the job itself. Make sure you have scripted answers to the most popular questions interviewers ask, for example:

- Tell me about yourself.
- Why should we hire you or what makes you the best candidate for the job?
- Why do you want to work here?
- Why did you leave your last position?
- Tell me about your work experiences.
- What are your strengths and weaknesses?

Many organizations also use behavioral interviewing questions. These questions are designed to understand how you would approach different situations or have addressed past situations, for example:

- How do you handle a challenge? Give an example.
- Have you ever made a mistake? How did you handle it?
- Give an example of a goal you reached and tell me how you achieved it.
- Describe a decision you made that wasn't popular and how you handled the implementation of it.
- Give an example of how you set goals and achieve them.
- Give an example of how you worked in a team.
- What do you do if you disagree with someone at work?

Once you have scripted your answers, ask a person to conduct a mock interview so you can practice giving these answers aloud. Afterwards, ask the "interviewer" what they thought of your answers and how you could improve them. Practice your answers many times before the interview. The more confident you are in providing the answers, the better your performance in the interview.

Job hunting can be difficult and time-consuming, but people with anthropological training are very well suited for the challenges. Unlike many others in the job market, they will be able to quickly assess opportunities, understand local organizational cultures, and find ways of demonstrating the usefulness of their skills, experiences, and abilities. As with all aspects of practice, the job hunt is only partly about you: it's really about you in relation to others.

Chapter 5

Job Success 101
A Quick Graduate Course

Cathleen Crain and Nathaniel Tashima

Cathleen Crain and Niel Tashima pick up where the previous chapter left off, with an extended discussion of how to excel at one's job. Getting a job is only the first step, they remind us: keeping that job, and excelling in it, is the next challenge. Practitioners are urged, as in previous chapters, to recognize the value and power of their anthropological skills in understanding and dealing with the organizations within which they work. The chapter covers formal and informal aspects of organizational culture, appropriate and inappropriate behavior in the workplace, and the importance of working in teams. It provides suggestions for advancing in the job, working with mentors, and knowing when (and how) to leave an organization.

Introduction

Congratulations on entering the world of professional work, whether for the first time or since becoming an anthropologist! In this chapter, we are going to focus on some of the things that you will need to know and skills you will need to acquire and practice to be successful in the professional world. As you go through this chapter, you may find that some of the items are already on your radar while others may not be yet. We are going to provide you with the perspectives of both an employer and a co-worker as we explore issues that will affect your short- and long-term success as a professional.

Perhaps the most important thought is to use your anthropological training to understand the culture of any organization you join. Your anthropological training

A Handbook of Practicing Anthropology. First Edition. Edited by Riall W. Nolan.
© 2013 John Wiley & Sons, Inc. Published 2013 by John Wiley & Sons, Inc.

has prepared you as no other discipline prepares its graduates to understand not only the specifics of a culture at work but also the cosmology. Exploring history, initiation rites, rites of passage, social networks, social hierarchies, special language, values, roles, and responsibilities are all important in understanding how to become successful in an organization.

The Formal and the Informal

As all good anthropologists know, there are formal and informal ways to learn about a new culture, and in your case a new organization. A first and most essential lesson in job success is to be a good anthropologist! In this section we will discuss some of the ways to collect information about an organization both formally and informally.

The informal

Listen and learn from the people around you. Ask the natives about the cosmology of the organization, the cultural norms, and the cultural prescriptions and proscriptions. Ask them how things are intended to work, how they see things working or not, and the important rules (both written and unwritten). Ask them about who's who and how people relate to one another.

And, as in any good fieldwork, be sure to ask a variety of people about these issues and then triangulate what you think you are learning. As the new person to any culture, you should proceed to learn the culture thoughtfully, respectfully, and gradually. Don't interrogate the natives if you want them to be welcoming. Also, be prepared to offer and keep the confidence of the people who provide you with information. The more sensitive the information, the more likely people are to need to rely on your discretion; if you betray their trust, the likelihood of receiving useful information in the future will be reduced.

Understanding where and how you fit into the organization will help you to understand the information that you receive from the people with whom you inter-act. If you are the new person and you are being groomed to conduct interesting research, for example, you may find that there are people with whom you are to work who will be concerned or even feel threatened by your presence. Or, if you are a new person and the most junior of staff, you could find that people are happy to help you learn and grow. You will need to try to determine, as you learn about the organization, how others see you and if their view of you affects the information that you receive.

Learn how people are expected to fit into the culture. For example, do teams eat lunch together? Is there an expectation of socializing after work or on the weekends? Do people work beyond the 8 to 5 day? What are the unwritten rules of the organization that can either be beneficial to you or a potential hazard? Once you learn how the organization functions, you will know how to make informed decisions about how you should function.

In the university you should have been challenged to be an independent thinker, to question ideas, and to state your views clearly. In the workplace, these are still valued skills. However, it is critical to your success to understand how your new organization hears those ideas, how the people you work with value what you say and how you say it, and how they express that value to you. Part of your job is to understand how to function in the organization and become a valued member who constructively contributes to the success of the unit, section, or business.

The formal: personnel manual

Be sure to read the personnel manual from cover to cover and annotate as appropriate. This is the place where the organization tells you formally what the policies are about such things as:

- the relationship between you and the organization;
- rules and regulations regarding hiring, including the kinds of checks carried out on you before you are cleared for employment;
- the categories of employees and what they mean;
- hours of work, timekeeping procedures, and scheduling expectations;
- when you will be paid and how you will receive your pay;
- how the organization treats its employees, and who you can go to with concerns and questions;
- how the organization addresses issues of workplace harassment or violence;
- the organization's policies on alcohol, drugs, and tobacco;
- how employee performance will be judged and how and when you will receive reviews;
- the company and the employee's rights in relation to information about the employee;
- policies on data and inventions ownership and use;
- rules regarding communication with the media;
- how the company expects employees to dress and why;
- policies regarding the use of vehicles;
- travel policies and reimbursements;
- policies regarding the use and misuse of equipment;
- policies and practices regarding technology, the Internet, and social media for the organization;
- policies and allowable holidays, vacation, and, sick and other leave time;
- availability of 401(k), health insurance, and other benefit plans;
- organizational support for employee access to training programs;
- organizational support of memberships and subscriptions; and
- how the organization terminates employment.

While this is not a negotiable document, it will provide you with a great deal of information about how the organization approaches sensitive topics, the rules about how it treats employees, and what kinds of benefits may be available to you. As you read the manual, you should be clear about zero tolerance policies, that is, behavior or activity for which there will be immediate consequences, up to and including termination of employment. Many organizations, for example, have zero tolerance for sexual harassment; the definitions will be provided in the manual, as will the consequences. These are policies that should be taken especially seriously as the organization will have to follow them in order to treat all employees equitably.

The topic of benefits is particularly important for you and you should pay special attention to what the organization offers and how they can be accessed. In the above list there are several places where the organization will give you information about access to the pension or 401(k) plan, and access to training, memberships, and subscriptions. Other benefits, such as public transportation subsidies, are not unusual.

401(k) and other employer contribution plans If your new employer offers a 401(k) plan, in many cases they are saying that if you contribute to the plan the company will provide a stated amount of matching funds. The matching funds are free money to you. You will have the opportunity to decide whether or not to participate in the plan early in your employment. Some employers want you to "opt in," which means that you fill out paperwork saying that you want to join. Some will have an "opt out" policy, which means that you will have to specifically decline to join the plan. Generally speaking, if you have an opportunity to enroll in these programs they are a truly good investment.

Access to training, memberships, and subscriptions For you to continue to develop your skills is a good thing for you and for the organization. Many organizations will provide some percentage of support and, potentially, time off if you want to take courses that directly benefit the organization. So, for example, if your organization is involved in evaluation and you, as a social scientist, want to take some advanced evaluation courses with the American Evaluation Association, this would be a good opportunity for organizational support. Some organizations will pay for your membership in a professional organization; this too is seen as of benefit to both you and them. Many organizations will also pay for subscriptions to professional journals that will allow you to continue to keep up with the latest developments in your discipline.

All of these benefits are valuable to you and you should look to take maximum advantage of their availability and to share the benefit with the organization. Some organizations will expect, for example, that if you go for training you will return to provide a briefing on the content. This both provides benefit to those who attend your briefing and extends the benefit for you as you have an opportunity to be seen by people in the organization.

Minding Your Ps and Qs

In the workplace, which is for most a fairly intimate environment, being mindful of (or learning and exercising) good manners is important. It is easy to assume that you can be casual in the workplace only to suddenly find that you have offended your supervisor or co-workers. Maintaining comfortable, collegial working relationships with as many people as possible should be your aim; this doesn't mean that you will develop friendships with all of these people, but rather that you will be on good terms with those around you. In this section, we will provide a few guidelines about office manners. While these are basic, there are times when new professionals in particular may not recognize their importance.

Show up on time

Starting times at most organizations are not really suggestions; they are a part of the working culture and are required of all staff. If everyone begins their work at 9 a.m., it is not likely to be acceptable for you to come in consistently at 9.30. This is a simple thing to learn and a silly thing to end up being called to your supervisor's office to discuss. This is also the kind of issue that can cause co-worker unhappiness if not addressed.

Dress like a native

If you have been in school for the past 20 years, you may not be familiar with how people are expected to dress for work. Be a good observer and harmonize what you wear with the rest of the organization's staff. You do not need to become a corporate clone, but wearing shorts and flip-flops are not likely to help you fit into your new professional environment. Also, depending on your work environment, there may be guidelines that have been set for work dress that you will need to learn. This may include guidance on such things as showing cleavage (for women), wearing shorts to the office, or walking around barefoot. Most workplaces provide guidance that is in keeping with their organizational culture, the regularity with which clients or customers visit the office, and workplace safety. It is your responsibility to learn both the rules and the culture and to adhere within reason to both. Again, no one expects you to be a cipher, but making a statement about your unique character through dramatic or proscribed dress may be counterproductive to your goals.

Help out, clean up, put it away

Again, becoming a member of what is likely a relatively small group of people, even if you are at a large corporation, is analogous to moving into a small community.

In every office there are the people about whom co-workers grumble. Very often it is about someone acting as if they are privileged or better than others, as shown by their lack of willingness to pitch in and help as needed. Learn what the office norms are about helping out, whether it is cleaning up in the break room after lunch, or helping the administrative assistant to prepare materials for a meeting you are attending. While it is not a good use of your time to do anyone else's job, helping out as opportunities present themselves is an important part of becoming part of the new community that you have entered. If you use something, clean up after yourself. If you take the last of some office supplies, make sure that the appropriate person knows so that it is time to reorder.

Mind your language

There are many ways to alienate yourself from others with your use of language. You can alienate people by using language that is clearly outside their zone of experience; if you hear the words "discourse" or "hegemony" slipping from your lips, rethink your language. You can alienate people by speaking in the code of a particular age group, from the latest popular trends, or from a place, or by using expletives and swear words as a part of your everyday pattern of speech. The ability to understand another through a shared language is an important part of our interest in and ability to communicate clearly. If you make it difficult for people, then they will move away.

In most instances you may be the only anthropologist in the unit or on the staff. You may find it difficult to be the only anthropologist. In graduate school you are constantly with anthropological peers and work in a world of terms and concepts that have shared meanings. Once you step outside this protected world, you must be able to communicate as part of a general community. Your specialized language and knowledge may not be understood or appreciated by those around you. Even though they have brought you into their working world, they most likely will have assumptions about what an anthropologist is and how you will contribute to the work of the group. Figuring out how to help them to understand and value what you bring is a central issue for you in creating your own success.

Think about what you are saying

Most work environments are delicately balanced ecosystems. There are generally lots of different groups that are distinct for one reason or another but which have learned to live in (relative) harmony. You can rapidly undermine that balance in a variety of ways. You can alienate people by being outspoken about your political or other beliefs and insisting that they must agree with your views. You can insist that you be allowed to do something that others are not allowed to do. You can hear and share gossip that creates divisions within your co-workers. You can show your superiority through distaining those without advanced degrees similar to yours. You can show your independence by denigrating the organization, your co-workers, or your managers in public. This last indiscretion is one for which your employment can be terminated. This is also critical for electronic communication. Once you have pushed the "send" button, that piece of communication cannot be recalled, deleted, or forgotten. Reread what you have written; be sure it is not written in the heat of the moment and that it accurately makes the point you are trying to convey. If the message is overly emotional, think about how it might sound to an uninvolved party before you send it. Electronic communication in the workplace is formal and serious. Do not confuse it with your private email or Facebook account.

Teams and Tasks

Few workplaces in which you are likely to find yourself will support the independent work of a social scientist. Most workplaces are based on the use of project, topic, and/or organizational teams. If your training has not already prepared you to work as a part of a team, and to not necessarily owning the product of your efforts on an individual basis, then workplaces based on a team concept will be a shock to your system.

What is a team and how does it work?

Most people think they know what a team is and how one works. In reality, teams are highly complex forms of organization and functioning and rarely work as well as they could. Here are some thoughts on being a good team member and producing good outcomes. First, a good team has a clear purpose that everyone understands (whether they agree to it is a different issue). Here is an example of a team purpose statement:

> We will work together to develop a plan for the implementation of the Wallace project. Marilyn will be the team leader and will make and monitor assignments. She will be responsible for assigning individual team members to work groups and for appointing leaders. We will meet together once a week to update one another on progress, to plan next steps, and to update the time line. We will also use this time to ask other members of the team for their input to ensure the appropriateness and quality of the outcomes.

A good team is not internally competitive, but may be competitive with another team. Individuals do the work that is assigned and submit it to the team leader or others in the agreed time frame. Senior members of the team provide guidance and support to more junior members and do not dump work on junior members. In most teams, communication is critical. Learn how your organization communicates and be prompt. Be proactive when appropriate. Being passive and waiting may not be the best strategy. Again, learn how your organization values communication and understand how to behave appropriately.

Part of effectiveness is understanding how to communicate and what to communicate. Judging what your team or supervisor/manager needs to see of your work or needs to understand is important to your success. Too much material and they might become overwhelmed; too little and they will not know how to make a decision. Ask your supervisor/manager for guidance on what, how much, in what format, and on what time line information will be useful. This will help to ensure that what you provide meets their needs.

In some organizations telephone or mobile phone contact is encouraged; in others it is seen as a social activity. Too many voice mails can waste a team or manager's time; too little and they may not have a complete picture. Deciding how much conversation to have in the hallway, lunch room, or across cubicles is also important to consider. Some level of this type of conversation goes on in all organizations. Important information can be exchanged quickly and may assist in making the team feel cohesive. At the same time, too much of this type of conversation and you may be seen as a gossip, wasting your time and the time of members of your team.

If you find yourself working on a team that has clear deficiencies, the challenge is to help to strengthen the team without undercutting leadership. One of the good ways to help others to see a deficiency is to place yourself in a learning mode and ask careful questions about how the team is functioning. An example is: "Can you please let me know what our time frame is for the completion of the whole task/ our particular subtask?" This allows leadership to address the issue without calling particular attention to the oversight. Your acting as the naive learner allows them to move the whole team process forward.

Time lines, products, or deliverables are critical to a team's success. Often your work or your team's work will be nested within a larger product or outcome. To be successful, it is critical that you deliver the product, report, or briefing on time. Being an hour or a day late will have negative consequences for your team, your managers, and your success in the organization. Unlike your university experience, there is no "incomplete" with an opportunity to complete the work tomorrow.

If you find yourself on a team that is imploding owing to internal strife, poor management, or for other reasons, you have a delicate problem. You should not sit by and let the task or the team self-destruct. You should also not jeopardize your own position by gossiping about the problems to others. If you have a good manager in whom you can confide, ask her or him for a private meeting to share your concerns in confidence. With clear, non-judgmental information, a good manager will determine avenues of intervention that can help the team get back on track. This is also your opportunity to show yourself as supportive of the mission of the organization and to distance yourself from any impending train wrecks. It is critical, however, that you get agreement from the manager that the information shared will not come back to you and that the actions taken will be supportive of better team functioning.

Computers and Other Electronics

In any modern organization there are myriad, often expensive, electronics to which you will have access as a member of the staff. As a new professional, become a good student of the electronics that are entrusted to you.

Computers

Software Learn the software so that you are competent to do your job effectively and efficiently. If you are really good with a piece of software, you might offer to share some of your knowledge with others. Do not install any software on your computer without permission from your supervisor or the organization's electronics supervisor. You may think it harmless to download an application onto your computer, but if the application is infected with malware or a virus, you could be the source of network-wide problems for the organization. Not the speedway to popularity with your co-workers or managers!

Traveling on the Internet When you are in an organization, what you do on your computer belongs to the organization. Be thoughtful about where you go and what you do, as the organization has the right to monitor the sites you visit. And if you visit inappropriate sites or spend excessive time on Facebook or other social sites, your organization may limit your access to the Internet. If that happens, it also calls into question your work ethic and your judgment.

Other equipment

Many good copiers cost approximately the same as a new car and require training to use appropriately. LCD projectors can be delicate and finicky to use. Shredders will not cross-cut telephone books. Laminators are not intended to be used on your family photos. Binding machines can bind fingers almost as readily as they bind reports. All of the equipment in your organization cost time and money to acquire and is intended to be used for the purposes of the organization. Most organizations designate a key operator who is responsible for the use, care, and maintenance of its equipment. If you want to use a particular piece of equipment, be sure that you seek training so that you don't misuse it or end up damaging it and depriving others of its use. If something goes wrong with equipment that you are using, let the key operator know immediately; trying to fix such equipment could do more harm and negate warranties.

How to Advance in Your Career in the Organization

Be mentored and mentor others

As a new professional, it is important for you to create relationships with successful people that will allow you to be mentored both within the framework of the organization and in your development as a professional.

Identifying mentors Identifying such individuals should be a matter of careful study when you join a new organization. Choosing mentors who are successful in the organization and in their careers is essential. Be thoughtful about people who are potential mentors. Their role in the organization can facilitate your career or side-track it. Before you engage with someone as a mentor, consider how they are seen by others and how their information is received. Also, remember that even if you are not specifically identifying someone as a mentor they can be helpful to you in moving toward a successful career.

Use your mentors wisely Determine the use of each of your mentors carefully. You may have one on whom you rely for internal knowledge of the organization and perhaps another who will help you to think about your career-building steps. A mentor should be someone to whom you can speak in confidence about issues of concern, who will give you their best advice and potentially use their networks to your benefit. You, in turn, need to be thoughtful about the use of their time and social capital and continuously gauge the appropriateness of your requests.

If you have created a relationship with a mentor, listen to them carefully. If you decide not to accept or heed their advice, be open and clear with them about the choices that you are making. If they are a good mentor, they should respect your decisions even if they disagree.

Professional development

It is also important to understand the expectations your organization has about continuing professional development. If the personnel manual offers opportunities to support you in classes or to attend professional meetings, there is an opportunity to enhance not only your knowledge, but also how your managers see you. Taking advantage of these opportunities signals that you are willing to take responsibility to make yourself a greater asset to the organization.

If you subscribe to journals, you have the opportunity to share information from those publications with others, either informally, or formally during the development of projects, for example. Being an information resource, bringing new methods to the organization, and being knowledgeable and available with information will all be valued by supervisors. And you will be seen as someone who continues to develop themselves professionally; this is often an important asset when personnel reviews are conducted.

In addition, think about volunteer work in the community or with service organizations. At times organizations appreciate staff making an investment of their time and expertise in the community and may be willing to give you release time to participate in community work.

How to Leave the Organization Like a Professional

There comes a time for many professionals when they need to change jobs. Change may come because you need new challenges, the organization doesn't appreciate your skills as you think they should, or you are moving to a new place. Whatever your reason for determining that you need to leave, leave like a professional. You may not think that it matters how you leave an organization; however, there are several reasons why it does. First, many fields are small, and how you leave may be communicated to others, affecting how they view you. Second, the goodwill of your soon-to-be-former employer will affect the potential for a good reference. Third, your current employer can make your final days more or less comfortable and decide the time of your leaving rather than allowing you to decide; an alienated employer may opt to make you leave now. In this section, we provide some guidance on how to leave professionally so that the bridge behind you remains intact.

Deciding that it is time to go

If are leaving because you have taken full advantage of the opportunities in your organization, then you are in a good position to create a favorable end to your association with your current employer. However, you may first want to test the assumption that you have no place to go in the organization. You should have been saying in your annual review discussions the direction in which you want to go. Don't expect your supervisor to guess correctly what you are interested in, tell her or him.

If your reviews have been consistently good and you are getting positive feedback from your supervisors, you may want to consider approaching your supervisor with a clearly thought through discussion about how you would like to continue to develop your career. For example, you may want to move into more of a management role and to gain new skills. You can say this to your supervisor and explain that you enjoy your work and working in the organization (and with her), but that you don't see new opportunities for development in that direction. This is not yet the moment to say that you are definitely leaving; this is the moment to explore with your supervisor what she and the organization see as options. This gives her the opportunity to respond in likely one of two ways. She can say that it is good that you are interested in moving in that direction, and that she will discuss it with her supervisor to see if there may be ways of moving you in that direction. Or she can say that she values you and your skills but that there are not going to be such opportunities in the near future. This is an interesting place to be, where you may be able to negotiate for more money and benefits, or if those are not of interest or are not a possibility with the organization, for support in finding your next position.

If you have decided that it is time to go and are not interested in the possibility of staying under better conditions, then be clear and professional in informing your employer. Be as flexible as possible in the timing of your leaving in order to reduce disruption of work for your team and your employer. Avoid telling your team and others that you are leaving for a better job in a much better organization even if you think that is the case. You want to leave behind you a team that continues to value you as a professional colleague and an employer who will be a part of a past to which you can refer with confidence.

Someone else decides it is time for you to go

There are many reasons an organization might shed staff. Generally people are terminated for cause (e.g., they have done something wrong) or because the organization does not need or cannot afford to support them and their particular skills (as a result of reduction in workforce, reorganization, etc.). These are clearly very different conditions, but in both cases handling yourself with dignity and professionalism will go a long way to make the termination as drama- and trauma-free as possible.

Terminated for cause

If you are told that your employment will be terminated for cause, that is, you have not performed adequately or you have done something wrong, you will need to consider your options carefully. If you have a history of being told that your work is not judged as adequate, you may have seen the termination coming and be prepared to leave the organization as gracefully as possible.

If your employment is being terminated because you have been accused of activities or actions that are prohibited or not tolerated by the organization, you will certainly want to see and understand the charges against you and how they have resulted in the most serious personnel action being taken. It is unusual for someone not to be aware of a pattern of concern from management about their activities and behavior. For example, if you have had a series of verbal altercations with other staff, you should have received warnings from management that you appear to be the aggressor and that you must change your behavior. Management should be sharing concerns with you about your activities and behavior. If you don't believe the charges are true or if you have never heard them before, you may want to consult an employment attorney.

In either case, you must carefully consider your goals in how you proceed. You may decide to be loud and public about your unhappiness and potentially reveal details to others about your employment history that will not serve you in the future. You may decide to leave quietly, but if the charges are unjustified you may live with that burden and your subsequent inability to point to that job and refer to your successes with the support of the organization. This is also a place to engage with your mentors and get the best advice you can about how to leave or fight in the best possible way.

Reduction in force (RIF) or reorganization

If your employer is letting you go because the organization does not need your skills or cannot afford to keep you, you are in a good position to negotiate the terms and timing of your leaving. Here are some of the items that you may be able to negotiate:

- a sum of money as part of a severance package;
- money in lieu of notice;
- continuing your health insurance for a period of time before you need to be on another employer's insurance, or in the United States, to exercise your COBRA option;
- continuing other benefits for a similar period of time;
- a letter of recommendation (depending on the organizations' policies);
- names of other organizations where your skills may be needed;
- introductions to other employers through your supervisors' networks; and
- a time line of reducing work that will allow you to be active in the job market while still being employed.

It is unlikely that your employer wants you to leave unhappy. Therefore, you may be able to request and receive such benefits or others that are important to you. It is very important that you allow yourself time to think when you are told that you are going to lose your job. Some organizational personnel policies mandate that a terminated individual be told, allowed to pack, and escorted out the door. If you can avoid that kind of circumstance, you have a far better opportunity to negotiate a more comfortable transition. In any case, leaving with dignity is important for you as a professional.

Creating and Nurturing Professional Networks

For anthropologists and others, developing and nurturing professional networks is an important part of a maturing career. There are several reasons that professional networks will be important to you over the course of your career.

- It is through professional networks that most people identify job opportunities. It is also through these networks that you may be moved to the head of the job line as your colleagues talk about your skills and attributes.
- It is through professional networks that you will be invited to join with others in the development of professional publications and presentations.
- Professional networks provide you with a reference group for problem-solving and methods development.
- Professional networks are particularly important for anthropologists who are very often the only anthropologist in their employment area; being able to consult with others regarding career growth challenges, skills development, recognition, and other topics is essential.

For many young and aspiring professionals, your networks will begin with those with whom you studied: both other young anthropologists and faculty. As you move out into your professional life, there are new opportunities to develop networks. The first is with your work colleagues; many of you will move on to other jobs over the course of your career but if you remain in contact, you may continue to benefit one other. A second is by becoming active in professional organizations and networks. The National Association for the Practice of Anthropology (NAPA), a section of the American Anthropological Association, provides a ready-made network of new and young professional anthropologists. The Society for Applied Anthropology (SfAA) also provides opportunities for creating or expanding networks. In addition, local practitioners' organizations (LPOs), which exist in metropolitan areas around the United States, provide relatively local networks of professional anthropologists.

Final Thoughts

A career is something that you build, and it is greater than the sum of the jobs you have held. It is likely that over the course of your career you will have many jobs, each (if managed well) helping you to build your career. Managing each job well, learning from those with whom you work, teaching as you go, growing in your skills and vision, and finding and honing your voice as a professional will result in a satisfying career.

Chapter 6

Careers in Practice

Susan Squires

Susan Squires draws on her own experience and that of others to discuss the sometimes circuitous path followed by practitioners as they build careers and develop their professional identities. The chapter begins with a look back at how the practice option developed within anthropology, and how Squires herself made the decision to go into practice. Using examples from her own career, she discusses the importance of continuing to learn on the job, and how practitioner career arcs involve progressive increases in roles and responsibilities, while also noting some of the salient differences between practice and the academy. The chapter concludes by offering some lessons learned, as well as a reminder that the field of practice is still evolving.

Introduction

In this chapter I begin by looking back at practice, and how current practitioners created a career path for themselves starting as ethnographers. As their careers progressed, many moved away from fieldwork and into management where they now shape projects, mentor staff, and participate in decision-making. The trajectories that their careers have taken provide lessons for those wanting to become practitioners themselves. But the path that these now senior practitioners took is, for most, unavailable today. What does this mean for new practitioners and what are the lessons we can glean from those now in senior roles? To answer this question I will try and create a frame for understanding how and why practice has come to be as

A Handbook of Practicing Anthropology. First Edition. Edited by Riall W. Nolan.
© 2013 John Wiley & Sons, Inc. Published 2013 by John Wiley & Sons, Inc.

it is, and to outline how future careers and career trajectories in practice will not be the same.

For this chapter I draw on a number of sources for my information. First of all I use understandings from my own career. Second, I call on the stories of the growing number of highly talented anthropologists working in both public and private sectors in the United States and around the world, including interviews with business practitioners conducted by Mack and Squires (2011). If it had not been for these pioneering anthropologists, none of us would have had such an exciting career opportunity.

A sample of senior practitioners is included. To learn about them and others in more detail, their individual stories can be found in NAPA Bulletins on *Careers in Anthropology: Profiles of Practitioner Anthropologists* (Sabloff 2000) and *Careers in Applied Anthropology in the 21st Century: Perspectives from Academics and Practitioners* (Guerrón-Montero 2008). Further readings that I would recommend reflect specific practice areas, such as design and new product development (Reese 2002), emergency and disaster (Williams 2001), working as a federal contractor (Reed 1997), consulting on organizational culture (Jordan 1994), working in business (Jordan 2003), facilitating workplace performance (Briody and Trotter 2008), and applying anthropology in "the global village" (Wasson et al. 2011). The volume edited by Wasson and colleagues (2011) focuses on the work of practice in a variety of field settings.

All have their own individual stories and unique career time lines, yet we all share some fundamental things in common. For example, practitioners, more often than not, work in their home country rather than in an "exotic" or "foreign" field site. As Barbara Pillsbury noted in the mid-1990s, we have all "come home" (1995: 74). Another commonality among practitioners is our foundation in anthropology, which Mari Womack noted, "contains both a methodology and a value system" (1995: 51).

To some degree we all shared stories about our initial identity crisis and where we belonged. During my career I was called many things: social scientist, researcher, evaluator, and ethnographer. With each new job I took on a new name and a new identity. Even today, being known as an anthropologist can invoke mystified looks and puzzling questions.

Using a title such as "social scientist," "ethnographer," or "evaluator" was not a deception. That was who I was within the organizations in which I worked. However, I struggled to reconcile my title with my identity as an anthropologist. When I adopted the title that my colleagues had in their vocabulary, was I shortchanging my profession and myself? Was I missing key learning moments to explain the value of anthropology? Over time I realized that these titles presented opportunities for building bridges from what was known and understood to what I could teach others about anthropology.

While practitioners still have to navigate identity, recently anthropology has become more and more recognized and understood as a legitimate profession outside the academy but the challenge still exists.

Some History

Anthropologists have been applying their knowledge to problems in our society for a very long time. For example, the Society for Applied Anthropology was founded in 1941

> to promote the integration of anthropological perspectives and methods in solving human problems throughout the world; to advocate for fair and just public policy based upon sound research; to promote public recognition of anthropology as a profession; and to support the continuing professionalization of the field. (http://www.sfaa.net/sfaagoal.html, accessed Aug. 24, 2012)

However, breaking entirely from the academy to follow a career in practice is relatively new. Beginning in the 1980s, full-time ethnographic jobs began to appear sporadically within a variety of private, governmental, and not-for-profit organizations. This trend began to take on momentum in the 1990s when positions for social scientists and ethnographic researchers came into demand peaking during the period between 1997 and 2001 (Mack and Squires 2011: 20). Anthropology seemed to be coming into its own as many organizations discovered ethnographic methods and our methods took on a certain "spin" in business, health, and international development, to name a few areas. It was becoming increasingly clear to many that the theory and methods of anthropology had the ability to provide a holistic picture of a people or a problem in ways that traditional research-gathering techniques of focus groups and survey questionnaires could not. Anthropology has a tradition of systematically collecting cultural knowledge and then providing that information in the "native" language and within the "native" context. Critical concepts such as culture provide explanatory models that can go beyond behavior to explain cultural knowledge systems. The value of this approach is what this knowledge can tell us about a cultural system in a way that is unmatched by any other method. It is within this context that practice and the roles of practitioners were established.

This is also the context in which my own career in practice began. It was not anthropology per se which drew me into practice; it was ethnography. By the time I had finished my coursework and was preparing to conduct my dissertation research, I realized that I did not want a career in teaching, but there appeared to be few alternatives with the possible exception of working in international development, as my major adviser had done. Despite her work experience, she could offer little advice on how to find such a position beyond telling me to go to Washington and bang on doors.

So, after I got my PhD in 1990, I began teaching anthropology at the University of New Hampshire. Like many of those who found their way into practice, I still did not want to teach and continued to look for non-academic employment, hoping that the teaching was a temporary thing. And, as with many of my peers, my career path reflects the intersection of professional opportunities and chance.

While driving home from the University of New Hampshire, I had noticed an employment office on my route. It was nearing the end of the semester, and I was looking at yet another year of teaching ahead of me. I was not expecting to find any job listings for anthropologists, but I was wrong. What I did not know at the time was that education had discovered the value of ethnography in understanding the context of teaching and learning and had started to recruit anthropologists to conduct educational research. The Network, an educational consulting group, was looking for anthropologists to conduct "classroom ethnography." I got the job and the real learning began for me.

Practice Isn't Like the Academy

Most of us were unprepared for a career in practice and learned our craft in the workplace settings in which we found ourselves and through workplace communities of practice. For example, I was trained in a traditional academic department at Boston University where I was required to take courses in the four subfields: linguistics, archaeology, and biological and social-cultural anthropology. I did my dissertation fieldwork on fishing crew recruitment in Newfoundland, Canada.

At Boston University, I had lots of courses on theory but very little on method. When I received my PhD in 1990, I expected to find employment in international development as my adviser had done, consulting with, for example, the World Bank or USAID. I never considered becoming a practicing business professional, nor had I thought about how anthropology might be used in a private or not-for-profit organizational setting.

If you are planning a career in practice you need to understand the differences between working inside and outside the academy, and plan accordingly. In the early days we did not always have the foresight to prepare ourselves. More often than not, we were learning while in the process of doing. And we made it up as we went along. Early practitioners have referred to this career path as a "random walk" (Butler 2006: 20) or "spiral path" (Wali 2006: 209). This was true for me.

In my first "real" job in an educational consulting firm, I discovered that while my theoretical knowledge was sound, my methodology skills were woefully weak. The traditional departments from which I graduated provided me with a crucially important theoretical foundation, and throughout my career I have drawn from anthropological theory to construct valid explanatory models that can be used in applied settings. But when I got my first job outside of the academy, it became embarrassing clear that I was not prepared for my role as staff ethnographic researcher – I lacked a strong grounding in methods.

However I was offered an opportunity to improve my methodological knowledge when the consulting firm decided to send me to a workshop offered as part of the annual meeting of the American Evaluation Association (AEA). Through the workshop and following conference, I was introduced to an extensive repertoire of qualitative and quantitative tools. My story is not so different from other practitioners. Graduate school and teaching did not prepare me for practice. I did not have good method skills. I was ill prepared to collaborate with others: a crucial skill to have. I had no understandings about how private, governmental or not-for-profit organizations were structured, what they expected of their employees and how they might reward them.

One early practitioner writes about how unprepared he was when confronted with introducing ethnographic fieldwork to engineers at Fujitsu, because we ethnographers have learned "through a mostly unstructured and, to be honest, self-directed process" that was enhanced by informal discussions with peers and faculty. Therefore, he not only had to introduce methodology to professionals from another field, they had to dig into differences of mind-set and value (Ikeya et al. 2007). Not only did the engineers understand little to nothing about anthropology and ethnography, but they had a real bias against working with "social scientists" such as anthropologists and using "soft or fluffy" methods such as ethnography. In my experience I have found that most "hard scientists" and engineers have been educated to believe that qualitative methods are not rigorous and are therefore less reliable. They don't value such methods. And because they believe qualitative methods are "fluffy" and unstructured they also believe anyone can use them successfully. This belief and value system can be a major hurdle for the practitioner.

If you are planning a career in practice, the key insight from these examples is to get a good grounding in both theory and methods, and be well prepared to defend them. You can do this in one of several ways. Consider a department of anthropology which has an applied program. Alternatively if you are in a more traditional program where method courses are few or absent, seek out methods courses from other departments. Become familiar with both qualitative and quantitative methods. Knowing about both will help you better prepare for difficult questions concerning your methodical approach.

And remember that quantitative methods are an important part of your anthropology toolkit. You may be asked to create and conduct a survey one day. At the very least you will likely work within a team in which there are members who do use such methods.

Learning on the Job

These early workplace experiences had an impact on the evolving careers of individual practitioners, like me, and their career trajectories. For one thing these practitioners not only had to learn on the job but they had to learn in a business, government, or not-for-profit organization along the way.

At my first job I was also surprised by the differences between academic expectations and routines and those expected by organizations. Most practitioners with whom I have talked have also mentioned this. Writing about his experiences, one practitioner noted that ethnographers' "work was rooted in our professional (anthropological) traditions, passed on through various kinds of apprenticeship, and was essentially under our direct control" (Lombardi 2009: 42). Now we were finding ourselves in a different context, where we were part of a team or in research group with its own work rules, dress code, and expectations for success.

Public and private organizations have a culture that needs to be understood if you are to be successful. Learning about the organization is not so different from any other culture that anthropologists have investigated where its members share a system of values, beliefs, and historical traditions. Within the work setting there is a class system, as well as status issues and power relationships. As with my peers, my first job experience taught me that practitioners need to understand the organization or area of expertise in which you work or want to work. To those who are new practitioners or want to become practitioners, I recommend that they conduct informational interviews with members of those organizations and consider an internship.

The Career Arc of a Practitioner

Like many of my fellow practitioners, I did not stay long in my first job but was soon recruited by a large corporation. They were looking for a qualitative evaluator who had a background in education and could design and conduct assessments of the company's education and training programs. Apparently the director of evaluation unit believed in the value of anthropology and liked having an anthropologist on staff. I got an interview and the job.

My experience moving from job to job is not unique, I have learned. A career in practice is much more like other careers in the "real world" than academic careers. Skills development, work settings, and job changes are normal. In my own career I have worked as a program manager in a governmental agency. My first ethnography job was in an educational consulting group which was investigating teaching and learning in the classroom. I was a classroom ethnographer. My next job built on my educational experience. I became an evaluator for a business training center, surveying students to determine their knowledge gained from business classes. Because I had also developed my ethnographic skills, I was next recruited to conduct consumer research for a design consultancy. The goal was to develop new products and services based on consumer needs. Understanding consumers led me to Yahoo! where I became involved in researching the online experience of consumers. My combined experiences in ethnography and computer–human interactions then brought me to Sun Microsystems where I studied "consumers" using supercomputers. In this case the consumers were computational scientists who were modeling problems associated with long-range weather forecasting and protein folding, an important exercise for certain medical research. More recently I led a team of medical researchers to learn about aging in Ireland and what technical interventions might keep the elderly healthier and happier and enable them to remain in their homes.

As you can see, I have moved around a bit. Each change has built on the skills and knowledge from the previous job and each change has provided exciting challenges, allowing me to learn and grow. In contrast to the academy, where there is a relatively simple, visible, and uniform career arc, practice has a different pattern. In the interviews I conducted with practitioners, including those I did with Alexandra Mack, I have found that, while each individual followed their own unique career trajectory, there are clear commonalities and themes. Many of those I have interviewed or whose biographies I have read, told a similar story. Many had not wanted to teach but saw no other alternative. Others, like me, had a teaching position but did not feel that teaching suited them. When each discovered that there were job opportunities as practicing anthropologists, they all actively pursued this career. As one practitioner explained, "Because I already had an inclination in that direction, I think, that is why I sought out something different [from academia]." Another noted that "It wasn't until later that my natural inclination and my passionate interest came together" (Mack and Squires 2011: 21).

All also described the new skills and knowledge they had to acquire to pursue a career in practice. In one interview Mack and I conducted we were told, "No one can just be a field-worker." Another summed up what everyone told us, "What I do is a combination of ethnographic practitioner but also other kinds of practitioner fields: leadership, management, consulting" (Mack and Squires 2011: 22). Teamwork, the ability to integrate viewpoints and approaches and to be responsive to another, is a big part of almost any practice job. Learning to collaborate in multidisciplinary teams, which might include engineers, medical professionals, environmental scientists, and other social scientists, is an important skill to actively cultivate.

In addition to learning new skills on the job, practitioners have had, and will continue to have, career arcs similar to the rest of the US workforce, changing jobs several times as they advance. With each promotion they will take on more responsibilities and even leadership roles. Eventually, they may find themselves in positions as team leads, project managers, and in some cases partners in the company. In these expanded roles they may be asked to make decisions that could impact the organizations for which they work. Importantly, practitioners who now find themselves in management are in a position to hire the next generation.

These hiring managers are pretty sophisticated about who they hire. While a degree in anthropology might have gotten you that first job in the past, it is no longer enough. While there is still an expectation that newly hired practitioners will learn on the job by "doing," expectations about what the new hire brings to the job have changed. Traditional training for a PhD in anthropology, like mine, can be strong in theory but lacking in method. For new practitioners there is a need for a more robust methodological toolkit. As one interviewee told me, "I wouldn't hire me out of school right now" (Mack & Squires 2011: 25).

In addition to training from traditional graduate programs at least at master's level, managers are now looking for people who can be flexible and adaptable to changing circumstances, who have a solid foundation in method, and who may already have some practical knowledge of working in an applied setting and experience of working in multidisciplinary teams. As one interviewee interviewed by Mack and Squires pointed out, "Academic training helps hone a vision and differentiates from someone without the academic training. It does not mean they cannot do it but we just have more practice at it" (2011: 25).

My career arc has followed this pattern. Over time I too became a manager in charge of large research projects around the world. But with promotion I found myself less involved in research and more in management.

Lessons Learned

The future role of ethnography in practice is still evolving. In the past it was the core skill that we brought to practice. Today anthropologists who want to go into practice can learn from those of us who "made it up as we went" and learned some lessons along the way.

1. The first lesson is to value the theory and methods of anthropology. These provide a foundation that can be adapted to a variety of situations. I have worked in educational consulting, business evaluation, new product development, and high tech. Educate yourself to provide the value that you will contribute to the workplace.
2. Before you seek your first job, gain field experience in an organization. Do a practicum or internship. Volunteer.
3. The setting and structure of the work environment is important. In large organizations anthropologists typically find themselves in the research group. Learn about your organization: its mission, hierarchy, leadership.
4. No matter the situation, collaborating with others in your group and throughout the company is a key skill.
5. The balance between research and organizational goals is a fine one. It can be an ethical challenge, so stay knowledgeable.
6. Don't underestimate the importance of a savvy, supportive boss, someone who understands the value of anthropology or is at least willing to learn.
7. Explore, learn, and contribute.
8. Finally, I recommend John Omohundro's handbook, *Careers in Anthropology* (1998) although written in 1998, for some basic "how to" ideas.

As increasing numbers of anthropologists have elected to work outside of the academy, the theory and methods that anthropology brings to practice have become better understood. Today anthropologists are actively recruited for their skills and knowledge. Future anthropologists will be hired into practice for our perspective on the world, our understanding of people and the system in which they live, rather than by a set of methods alone. As DePaula and colleagues have noted, "The transformation of our work practices, as aforementioned, did not happen by chance, we deliberately changed and adjusted them to match the ongoing changes in our organization" (2009: 14). Future practitioners can be more proactive in their career trajectory than the anthropologists who laid the groundwork for today's practice. It is no longer a "random walk" but a career choice with its own challenges and opportunities.

References

Briody, Elizabeth K. and Robert T. Trotter II (eds.) (2008) *Partnering for Organizational Performance: Collaboration and Culture in the Global Workplace.* Lanham, MD: Rowman & Littlefield.

Butler, Mary Odell (2006) "Random Walk." In Christina Wasson (ed.), *Making History at the Frontier: Women Creating Careers as Practicing Anthropologists.* NAPA Bulletin 26. Berkeley, CA: University of California Press for National Association for the Practice of Anthropology, pp. 20–31.

DePaula, Rogerio, Suzannne Thomas, and Xueming Lang (2009) "Taking the Driver's Seat: Sustaining Critical Enquiry While Becoming a Legitimate Corporate Decision Maker." *Ethnographic Praxis in Industry Conference Proceedings* 2009: 2–16.

Guerrón-Montero, Carla (ed.) (2008) *Careers in Applied Anthropology in the 21st Century: Perspectives from Academics and Practitioners.* NAPA Bulletin 29. Oxford: Blackwell.

Ikeya, N., E. Vinkhuyzen, J. Whalen, and Y. Yamauchi (2007) "Teaching Organizational Ethnography." *Ethnographic Praxis in Industry Conference* 2007(1): 270–282.

Jordan, Ann T. (ed.) (1994) *Practicing Anthropology in Corporate America: Consulting on Organizational Culture.* NAPA Bulletin 14. Arlington, VA: National Association for the Practice of Anthropology.

Jordan, Ann T. (2003) *Business Anthropology.* Long Grove, IL: Waveland Press.

Lombardi, G. (2009) "The Deskilling of Ethnographic Labor: Signs of an Emerging Predicament." *Ethnographic Praxis in Industry Conference* 2009: 41–49.

Mack, Alexandra and Susan Squires (2011) "Evolving Ethnographic Practitioners and Their Impact on Ethnographic Praxis." *Ethnographic Praxis in Industry Proceedings* 2011: 18–27.

Omohundro, John T. (1998) *Careers in Anthropology.* Mountain View, CA: Mayfield Publishing.

Pillsbury, Barbara (1995) "Lessons Learned in International Development: How Can We Apply Them at Home?" In E. L. Cerroni-Long (ed.), *Insider Anthropology.* NAPA Bulletin 16. Arlington, VA: National Association for the Practice of Anthropology, pp. 71–74.

Reed, Michael C. (ed.) (1997) *Practicing Anthropology in a Postmodern World: Lessons and Insights from Federal Contract Research.* NAPA Bulletin 17. Arlington, VA: National Association for the Practice of Anthropology.

Reese, William (2002) "Behavioral Scientists Enter Design: Seven Critical Histories." In Susan Squires and Bryan Byrne (eds.), *Creating Breakthrough Ideas: The Collaboration of Anthropology and Designers in the Product Development Industry.* Westport, CT: Bergin & Garvey, pp. 17–44.

Sabloff, Paula L. W. (ed.) (2000) *Careers in Anthropology: Profiles of Practitioner Anthropologists*. NAPA Bulletin 20. Washington, DC: American Anthropological Association.

Wali, Alaka (2006) "The Spiral Path: Toward an Integrated Life." In Christina Wasson (ed.), *Making History at the Frontier: Women Creating Careers as Practicing Anthropologists*. NAPA Bulletin 26. Berkeley, CA: University of California Press for National Association for the Practice of Anthropology, pp. 209–222.

Wasson, Christina, Mary Odell Butler, and Jacqueline Copland-Carson (eds.) (2011) *Applying Anthropology in the Global Village*. Walnut Creek, CA: Left Coast Press.

Williams, Holly Ann (ed.) (2001) *Caring for Those in Crisis: Integrating Anthropology and Public Health in Complex Humanitarian Emergencies*. NAPA Bulletin 21. Arlington, VA: American Anthropological Association.

Womack, Mari (1995) "Studying Up and the Issue of Cultural Relativism." In E. L. Cerroni-Long (ed.), *Insider Anthropology*. NAPA Bulletin 16. Arlington, VA: National Association for the Practice of Anthropology, pp. 48–57.

Chapter 7

Stress and Failure in Practice Work

Riall W. Nolan

In this chapter, Riall Nolan takes up a topic which is not usually discussed: stress and failure in the workplace. Because professional trajectories in the United States today can typically encompass a dozen different jobs and as many as three major changes of career, stress, setbacks, and occasional failures are practically guaranteed. Focusing first on stress (and burnout), Nolan provides some strategies for identifying stressors and dealing with them, up to and including changing jobs. Failure is a more serious matter than stress. After outlining some of the ways in which failure happens, Nolan provides suggestions for recovery, placing emphasis on the construction of a failure "narrative" which incorporates lessons learned.

Donald Schön (1983) presents an arresting image of the topography of the world of practice. He describes it as a wet and messy swamp, with a dry knoll rising from the center. Up on the knoll, problems are solved elegantly and cleanly, using research and theory. These problems, he says, are technically interesting but often irrelevant to humanity as a whole. In the swamp itself, problems are much more relevant and important, but they are also disordered, confusing, and difficult, resisting simple, neat solutions. Work in the swamp is uncertain, contested, insecure, and at times unproductive.

Practitioners work mainly in the swamp, not on the knoll. They encounter uncertainty, stress, and occasionally failure. These aspects of practice tend not to be discussed in the anthropological literature, probably for two reasons: (1) failure is not viewed very positively by our society; and (2) the realities of work in the swamp are largely outside the experience of most university-based anthropologists.

A Handbook of Practicing Anthropology. First Edition. Edited by Riall W. Nolan.
© 2013 John Wiley & Sons, Inc. Published 2013 by John Wiley & Sons, Inc.

This chapter is an attempt to look at stress and failure in a practitioner career in terms of what professionals can do to reduce stress and to recover from failure, should it happen. I'll begin with a short examination of career arcs today, move to a discussion of stress and burnout in the workplace, and conclude with some observations about professional failure and recovery.

Career Arcs in the World of Practice

We have very little longitudinal information on the career arcs of anthropological practitioners, but it's safe to assume that these career patterns resemble those for the US workforce as a whole, far more than they resemble the patterns of university-based academics.

Most American professionals change jobs several times during their careers. Hanna claims that professionals will change jobs perhaps seven times over a working lifetime (1998: 194; see also Falvey 1987: 140; Birkel and Miller 1998: 14). And this seems to be true for practitioners as well (see, e.g., Ervin 2000: 218).

Change is built into the nature of many practitioner jobs. International development professionals, for example, usually change assignments every few years, taking on new projects and perhaps moving to new locations. This can also be true for university administrators.

My own career arc illustrates both of these realities. Over a 40-year period, I've had three separate and distinct careers: first as a development planner, then as a university administrator, and finally as a full-time faculty member. During my years in development, I worked for five major employers for periods of time between two and four years, and a dozen other employers for shorter periods of time. I worked in six different countries for periods ranging from three months to four years. When I returned to the United States and began working as a university administrator, I worked at four different universities for periods of between three and six years, as a director, dean, and finally associate provost.

This career arc may be highly varied, but it is by no means unusual. It does differ, of course, from that of most academically based anthropologists, whose primary focus is on gaining tenure. There is considerable stress in academic life, and certainly failure, in particular with respect to tenure. But it seems clear that both the sources and consequences of stress and failure play out differently.

Practitioner careers, for many people at least, are actually a series of discrete projects, one after the other. The projects tend to be highly varied. If they are done for clients – as they often are – then each project needs to be successful. The costs of underperformance or failure can be high, up to and including the loss of future work. In this respect, the careers of many practitioners resemble those of concert performers. You may get away with one or two bad concerts, but eventually people will stop buying tickets.

The different projects themselves are often major transitions. Routines will change; professional roles and responsibilities may change, and with them relationships with others. And all transitions have the effect of closing off some options even as they open others. All of this will provoke stress of some sort, sooner or later, and perhaps even a significant failure.

Stress and Burnout

Stress is mental or emotional discomfort, which may also take physical shape. It is a response to external circumstances, but it is also a very personal thing. What one person finds stressful, another may not.

It's generally acknowledged that a little stress can be a good thing. It keeps people alert, focused, and motivated. It involves them in their surroundings. Culture shock, for example, can be stressful, but it is also useful in facilitating the process of cross-cultural learning and adjustment (see, e.g., Furnham and Bochner 1986).

At work, stress may accompany task overload, ambiguous or contradictory assignments, poor communication, interpersonal conflicts, anxieties about job loss, and so on (Wexley and Silverman 1993: 94–96). Stress may increase at times of organizational shifts or changes. At the early stage of their career, people may wonder if they've made the right choice, and if they're going to be happy and successful (London and Mone 1987: 162). Later on, they tend to worry about missed opportunities, boredom, or being in a dead-end job.

Certain jobs seem to bring more stress than others. "Professional helpers," as Veninga and Spradley (1981) point out, confront stress daily in their work. Police officers, social workers, relief workers, cancer ward nurses – these and others work in situations where they have little power to get in front of events, and little ability to actually "fix" their clients. They often face a variety of difficult and complex problems, for which there is often no easy solution. There may be little in the way of recognition, reward, or thanks for doing the job well. And often, in these types of jobs, as soon as one problem is dealt with, another appears.

But some level of stress will characterize almost any practitioner job. Practitioners are not unique here, but most of them are regularly entering new and unfamiliar cultural environments and developing reflective conversations in order to discover meaning (see Schön 1983). In effect, practitioners could be said to be entering the fieldwork situation over and over again with each new assignment. And some practitioner jobs – for example, development work, humanitarian assistance, and disaster response – can be very stressful indeed at times.

When stress is extreme, we speak of "burnout." Veninga and Spradley (1981) define burnout as characterized by emotional exhaustion, a loss of affect, and feelings of futility and powerlessness (see also Hanna 1998: 245). Burnout can be serious, with effects on physical and mental health. In addition to feelings of anger and frustration, people also may have less energy, and less resistance to illness. Burnout can produce absenteeism, inefficiency, and outbursts at work. At home, people may seek escape through drugs, alcohol, or domestic violence.

Responding to Stress and Burnout

Moving, changing jobs, getting married, having a child, losing a relative – all of these are major sources of stress, and they happen to most people. They are also temporary, and with time, even if one does nothing, stress usually diminishes. Other stresses related to the work situation, however, may be more permanent, and need to be dealt with. The first step is to identify and list the sources of stress. If you can identify the main stressors, then you can think about which ones might be changed, and how.

There are several things you might do to improve things at work.

- *Move things around*: you can shift – either vertically or horizontally – by identifying and seeking a different assignment within your organization which gives you more of what you're looking for. You can restructure your present job, negotiating changes with your boss or colleagues, to minimize the negatives. You can compensate, by finding and doing work outside your normal duties which gives you the satisfaction you need.
- *Manage relationships*: stress often arises from interpersonal relationships, so focus on using your people skills effectively. Dealing with differences of opinion and work style, negotiating outcomes, drawing the line tactfully when necessary – all of these things will help reduce workplace stress. Keep in mind that it is possible to work closely and happily with people who might never be your friends outside the office.
- *Manage time*: a lot of stress comes from overwork. Cultivate efficient habits, prioritize sensibly, and vary your routine. Try to learn new things as you go along; this will give you a feeling of accomplishment and will reduce stress at the same time.
- *Seek help through your network*: you're not the only person who's ever experienced stress; your friends and colleagues may have helpful suggestions and strategies which have worked for them. At the very least, they will be able to offer you support.

Outside work, find ways to make yourself happy and recharge your batteries. Having a happy and fulfilling home life will help a lot. Hobbies – that is, activities which are complex and time-consuming but have nothing much to do with your work – are a very effective way to take your mind off what's bothering you.

If you can't change what's bothering you at work, then try changing your perception of these things. Work on developing your patience and raising your thresholds. Don't react immediately to things which happen; don't rush to find solutions. Control your tongue; not every thought or opinion needs to be articulated. Pick your battles; not every issue requires you to weigh in.

Finally, if you have to, relax your standards. Many professionals hold themselves to very high standards, but perfection often gets in our way. Satisfaction, not perfection, should be your goal. Here's what one writer recommends:

> Adjust your career scoring system to more closely reflect those values that are meaningful to you. That doesn't mean lowering your sights or settling for less than you are

worth, but it does mean evaluating what you do best, what you can contribute, what effect you will have on others, and what of lasting value you may leave behind when your time in the ring winds down. (Falvey 1987: 184)

Above all, don't overreact. Stress – especially acute stress, as in a crisis – cries out for quick change, for decisive and dramatic action. Don't be knocked off-stride by stress, no matter how crazy things get. Do what you need to do right now, but don't let daily crises distract you from your long-term goals. Remember that you'll do better at reducing stress if you have a long-term strategy which helps you frame and prioritize daily events in terms of a wider set of goals.

Leaving Your Job

If none of this really helps, then consider your ultimate recourse: changing jobs. If you can't change the situation at work, and if it's still causing stress, perhaps it's time to leave. There are many reasons why a job change might make sense. You may have changed, and as you've changed you've simply outgrown your present job. You may long for new challenges which aren't going to come from what you're doing now. Perhaps your financial needs have grown, but your salary hasn't kept pace. You've mastered the basics, and now you're ready to move on.

Perhaps you're seeing the job now in a different way. The job which seemed so promising a few years ago may now look to you like a dead end. You've concluded that you're unlikely to advance, earn more, get more responsibility, or learn new things. There seems to be a general lack of challenge, future, or satisfaction. Perhaps the organization has values and practices which don't really mesh with how you think things ought to be. The work isn't really what you want to do, ideally. Your co-workers and you don't share enough of a common perspective for you to feel comfortable.

Your company or organization may have changed too. It may have been bought by another firm, reorganized, or "re-engineered." The job itself may have changed. Changes in the economy, demographic changes, and/or changes in technology – all of these might change the nature of what you do, and how you feel about it. The circumstances surrounding your work may have changed, for better or for worse. Perhaps you've started a family. Perhaps you've been offered – or denied – a transfer, promotion, or new opportunity. Your organization fails to win an important contract. A competitor takes away your most valued client. All of these things can act as triggers for change (see Hansen 1997: 220–221).

If you're considering a change, take stock before you do anything. You probably have a pretty good sense of yourself – your likes and dislikes, strengths and weaknesses. You probably also have a good sense of your field – where the opportunities and the minefields are. Look back at other jobs you've had that you've particularly liked. What made those jobs good? Look too at your less happy moments. What made those times unsatisfactory?

Use these previous experiences to develop a set of criteria for your next job. One writer suggests doing this in terms of six main categories: the challenge you seek; the location you'd like to be in; the level of responsibility you aspire to; the amount of money you need or want; the type of recognition or status you seek; and the degree of job security you need (Yate 1999: 182).

Leaving a job can be a big, scary decision. But don't stay if you are truly unhappy, or if you don't see any possibility of improvement. Many professionals are reluctant to change jobs because they feel that they owe loyalty to their present organization. If staying on suits your professional and personal purposes, then by all means do so. Otherwise, put your own interests first. One management writer puts it bluntly:

> Your strategic move should always be in your own short- and long-term interest. You have no obligation to an organization that is not wise enough to protect its investment in you. (Falvey 1987: 124)

If you do leave, then take care to manage your transition. Although we think of job change as a new beginning, what comes first is actually an ending – the ending of your current job. You may experience fear, anger, and a sense of loss, even as you feel exhilarated and energized. Acknowledging and managing these emotions is an important part of making a successful transition from one job or organization to another. You should take the time to say good-bye properly. This means not only saying good-bye to those individuals who have been important to you, but taking your leave in such a way that loose ends are tied up and old issues put to rest. And, of course, it goes without saying that it's hardly ever a good idea to burn your bridges, no matter how you feel.

Failure

Failure isn't something that's often openly discussed when we talk about careers. The American ethos doesn't really tolerate "losers" well, and we tend, like most people, to confuse an unsuccessful effort with an unsuccessful person (Ostrow 2001). Failure isn't always a bad thing, however. Engineers, for example, know the value of "destructive testing," where failure is sought. Systems analysts, computer programmers, and astronauts – to cite but three examples – are professionals with a keen interest in, and attention to, failure. In product design and development, there is a need to "fail fast" in order to avoid dead ends. Indeed, one of the hallmarks of successful leadership in most sectors is the ability to "embrace error" and learn from it.

We fail frequently, of course, when we attempt to innovate. Thomas Edison, apparently, tried an enormous number of materials in his quest to develop the light bulb. When questioned about this he is supposed to have said, "I have not failed. I've just found 10,000 ways that won't work."

But failure can be personally harmful, despite the fact that failure, for most of us, is an inevitable part of professional life. As Hyatt and Gottlieb point out:

The average American today will work for ten different employers, keep each job only 3.6 years, and change his entire career three times before retirement. *Woven into those statistics is a virtual guarantee: at some point everyone is going to fail.* (1993: 28; emphasis mine)

As these writers point out, failure is not an objective fact, but a subjective opinion, a judgment about events. Almost everyone will "fail" at some point. And all of them will be able to recover.

Failures should be distinguished from mistakes or setbacks. Mistakes are small failures, and we all make mistakes, every day, throughout our lives. Some we could have avoided if we'd given them a moment's thought. Others occur because we didn't know enough, but should have: we didn't think; we didn't know enough; we guessed wrong; we didn't do our homework.

All mistakes teach us something, and some mistakes teach us more than others. Mistakes are signposts on the road to improvement. I once worked with a man who had a plaque on his desk which read: "Good judgment comes from experience. Experience comes from bad judgment."

Failure, however, is a larger event, far bigger than a mistake. Failure usually involves a substantial loss of some sort, for example, of reputation, self-esteem, money, power, responsibility, access, or support. And this sort of failure has consequences. You lose the contract, or botch the assignment. You fail to get the job or promotion you wanted. You lose at office politics. You get fired. You get sued. Professionally and personally, failure is usually much more disruptive than a mere mistake; failure often closes off options, eliminates possibilities, and moves things in new, often unfamiliar directions.

The more professional you become, the more likely it is that you will fail at some point. Failure is often painful and sometimes very costly, but it can teach you a great deal. So the question is not how to avoid failure, but what to do with it when it happens.

Why People Fail

Failures occur for many reasons, some of which aren't about you at all. The market turns down, for example, or your company loses the big contract. Your boss gets fired, and your new boss doesn't think much of anthropologists, men, white people, folks over 30, and so on. These boil down to simple bad luck. Sudden changes might include new strategic directions, new policies or legislation, abrupt reductions in budget or other resources, and a more general category we might call *force majeure* – earthquakes, tsunamis, coups, epidemics, and other disasters. But in many cases, you *are* involved in whatever failed. Poor interpersonal skills are one common reason for failure. Being sensitive to others, listening to them, accepting and giving criticism well, working well with others, and being emotionally mature and steady – these are among the key people skills needed to keep a job and do it well.

Not paying enough attention to your surroundings is another. If you ignore crucial areas, if you don't do your homework well enough, if you can't distinguish good data from bad, or if you put your trust in unreliable sources, you're setting yourself up for failure.

Bad decision-making can also lead to failure. Perhaps you aren't familiar with some of the decision-making procedures and techniques you're required to know. Perhaps you panic. Perhaps you get overly emotional, and let your feelings override your common sense.

Bad strategy – or no strategy at all – is another cause of failure. Good managers know that they need to make small day-to-day tactical decisions continually within the framework of an overall long-term strategy. Bad managers often try to deal with everything, giving equal amounts of attention to trivial matters as well as important ones. They may confuse tactics and strategy – or not have a strategy at all – with the result that small, quick decisions lead eventually to larger problems and issues which were not intended.

Recovering from Failure

Recovering from failure involves analyzing – and then reinterpreting – what went wrong. Failure is a golden opportunity to understand more about how the world around you actually works. Mary Pickford is credited with saying "Failure isn't the falling down; it's the staying down."

The first step in recovering from failure is to look at the facts of the situation as objectively as possible. What happened first, and then what happened after that? Lay out the course of events as clearly as you can. Then put yourself back into the frame. How did you *feel* as events unrolled? What role did your feelings play in how you acted or reacted? What can you conclude about this? Finally, try to understand why things happened the way they did. You may need, at this point, to gather more information. You've been working up to here with what you yourself know, and what you feel. But it may be time now to tap your network, to talk with colleagues, or to go to the library, to fill in some of the blanks. By understanding why things happened the way they did, you are also trying to understand what you might have done differently.

This three-step analysis will help you frame this instance of failure so as to derive maximum benefit. Performers such as actors, musicians, athletes, and dancers do this all the time. They frequently deal with failure as they strive to improve. They make the past work for them, embracing failure in order to identify what needs to be done in the future. This process is also similar to that used by cross-cultural trainers in "critical incident analysis," helping people understand why certain things happen to them as they interact with an unfamiliar culture.

Once you've figured out what happened and why, you can proceed to create a personal story – a failure narrative – about this. Your story to yourself needs to be true and honest; it needs to explain what happened, why it happened, and what you took from the experience. The version of events which you have constructed to reinterpret, explain, and reframe your failure is primarily for your own benefit. Only part of your personal story needs to be shared, but what you share will be based on your personal story. It may help at this point to reach out to selected members of your network who know what happened and are willing to support you if necessary.

Eventually, as you reconnect with your professional community, you'll need to develop several slightly different public versions of your narrative for different audiences. Each version needs to be true – and seen as true – but it does not need to go into all the gory details. In your public narratives, you are in no way altering the facts of the case; rather, you are explaining these facts and situating them within a supportive context, in a way that will help you to learn, feel confident about yourself, and avoid making similar errors in the future (Ostrow 2001).

Some details of your story, for example, are known only to you, and do not need to be publicized. Other aspects of what happened, however, will already be known to others. Some of these may raise questions among your colleagues and peers, and so they should hear your version first, whenever possible and appropriate. Offer enough detail to make your case convincingly, no more. If the story is complicated, rehearse a version that you find acceptable. Anticipate questions and rehearse answers to them. Be careful how you discuss blame; few people like to hear someone run down their former colleagues. And be aware, throughout this process, of what the "word on the street" is about your situation.

At this point, you are well on your way to recovery. The process of recovery from failure may be slow, and will almost certainly be somewhat painful. It is important, throughout this process, that you not be too hard on yourself. You may indeed have made mistakes – even big ones. They are now in the past. Forgive yourself, forgive others, and move on. Find ways to boost your confidence, by taking on new projects, acquiring new skills, or establishing new contacts (DeMars 1997: 304–310).

Conclusion: Managing Your Work, Your Life, and Your Thinking

Understand that frustration, stress, setback, and failure are part of virtually any professional's experience, and they will probably be part of yours too at some stage. But understand too that there are things you can do proactively to minimize their frequency and intensity. And should failure happen, there are things you can do to minimize the effects, recover, and go on.

Always be aware of your professional options, even if you never exercise them. Monitor your field and what's changing within it through your network, and pay particular attention to changes which might affect you. Whether or not you *ever* experience failure, the ability to be flexible and mobile, either within your present organization or across organizations, provides you with a wide range of interesting opportunities, exposes you to new information, and is excellent protection against getting fired, laid off, or otherwise blindsided by sudden changes or shifts.

Having options will do one other important thing for you: it will put conventional workplace wisdom in its proper place. Being willing to move on means being willing to break with the prevailing pattern, and to some extent, therefore, with prevailing standards, values, and frameworks. Your ability – as a professional and as an anthropologist – to see beyond your immediate frame of reference frees you from overdependence on any one perspective or way of doing things.

As Louis Pasteur told us, "Chance favors the prepared mind."

References

Birkel, J. Damien and Stacey J. Miller (1998) *Career Bounce-Back!* New York: American Management Association.

DeMars, Nan (1997) *You Want Me To Do What? When, Where and How to Draw the Line at Work.* New York: Simon & Schuster.

Ervin, Alexander (2000) *Applied Anthropology: Tools and Perspectives for Contemporary Practice.* Boston: Allyn & Bacon.

Falvey, Jack (1987) *What's Next: Career Strategies after 35.* Charlotte, VT: Williamson Publishing.

Furnham, Adrian and Stephen Bochner (1986) *Culture Shock: Psychological Reactions to Unfamiliar Environments.* London: Methuen.

Hanna, Sharon L. (1998) *Career Development by Design.* Upper Saddle River, NJ: Prentice-Hall.

Hansen, L. Sunny (1997) *Integrative Life Planning.* San Francisco: Jossey-Bass.

Hyatt, Carole and Linda Gottlieb (1993) *When Smart People Fail*, rev. edn. New York: Penguin.

London, Manuel and Edward M. Mone (1987) *Career Management and Survival in the Workplace.* San Francisco: Jossey-Bass.

Ostrow, Ellen (2001) "Creating Possibility Out of Failure." *Chronicle of Higher Education.* At http://chronicle.com/article/Creating-Possibility-Out-of/45396/, accessed Aug. 28, 2012.

Schön, Donald (1983) *The Reflective Practitioner: How Professionals Think in Action.* New York: Basic Books.

Veninga, Robert L. and James P. Spradley (1981) *The Work/Stress Connection.* Boston: Little, Brown and Company.

Wexley, Kenneth N. and Stanley B. Silverman (1993) *Working Scared: Achieving Success in Trying Times.* San Francisco: Jossey-Bass.

Yate, Martin (1999) *Knock 'Em Dead 1999: The Ultimate Job-Seeker's Handbook.* Holbrook, MA: Adams Media.

Part II
Practitioner Bases

Chapter 8

Doing Anthropology – Full Tilt, Full-Time

Gordon Bronitsky

Gordon Bronitsky is an independent practitioner who works as a promoter of indigenous performers. In this role, he organizes performances and festivals around the world, bringing artists of all kinds across cultures to perform for others. Bronitsky provides us with a fascinating glimpse into this world, describing how he decided to do this type of work, and how his anthropology background helped him. He talks in detail about what you need to know to do what he does, and in particular, what you need beyond traditional anthropology training. The chapter concludes with a discussion of the things that make his work interesting and exciting, and offers us a few clues as to where he thinks his work may take him in the future.

Introduction

I am an anthropologist and I have established my own business working with indigenous peoples around the world in the performing arts and festival development. For the last 15 years, I have been founder/president of Bronitsky and Associates. Our firm, with offices in New Mexico and Germany, specializes in working with indigenous talent around the world in international cultural marketing of traditional and contemporary art, music, dance; fashion; film/video; photography; theater; and speakers and writers (Native languages and English). We also work with indigenous communities in festival development as an integral part of economic development across sectoral boundaries. And we've been doing this since 1994.

At Bronitsky and Associates, we see around us a world that is in many ways growing smaller, more connected, and more homogeneous. Groups and artists

A Handbook of Practicing Anthropology. First Edition. Edited by Riall W. Nolan.
© 2013 John Wiley & Sons, Inc. Published 2013 by John Wiley & Sons, Inc.

around the world want to preserve and develop their culture and heritage and voices on their own terms; others want to experience new ways of seeing the world. The audience for cultural diversity is wider than anyone has imagined so far.

In this chapter, I am going to explore how I got to where I am; what I needed to know (and didn't know when I started); some of the highlights of my work; and where I'm going from here.

We produced ORIGINS: First Nations Festival in May 2009, which brought indigenous theater companies and performers from the United States, Canada, Australia, and New Zealand to theaters and venues all across London.[1] We are now producing IndigeNOW! Indigenous Opera from Three Continents and Three Countries. In 2010 I served as a Fulbright Senior Specialist at Moi University in Kenya, in part to work cooperatively in the creation of an African theater festival. In May 2011 the Senior Curator at the Ethnographic Museum in Belgrade, Serbia was awarded a State Department speaker's grant to bring me into the country to assist in the development of a Balkans performing arts festival. In 2011 I also served as a speaker at the inaugural Royal Opera House Muscat Aspen Creative Arts World Summit in Muscat, Oman. And this is only a small part of the story, so let's begin at the beginning.

How Did I Get Here?

I grew up in Albuquerque, New Mexico, a state with an American Indian population of about 10 percent, one of the largest Indian populations of any state. I knew Indian people growing up, went to school with them, worked with them. By the time I was 12, I knew I wanted to study American Indians past and present – I wanted to be an archaeologist.

After an undergraduate degree from the University of New Mexico, I went to graduate school at the University of Arizona, again in anthropology. The focus of the department was on the totality of the human experience so I studied all of the traditional four fields of anthropology – archaeology, cultural anthropology, physical anthropology, and linguistics.

In 1977, PhD in hand, off I went. I taught at several colleges and universities as an archaeologist and anthropologist, usually teaching courses in all the basic fields and introduction to American Indian studies. I was on my way to tenure, a tweed jacket, and ivy – all the traditional accouterments of the professoriate. No marketing or business background for me – I was destined for academe.

And then two events changed my life. First, in 1984–5, I served as Senior Fulbright Professor at the Institut für Historische Ethnologie at the Johan Wolfgang Goethe University in Frankfurt in what was then West Germany. It was the year that changed my life. My teaching area was American Indians, and I lectured all over Europe and Israel on a broad range of American Indian and archaeological topics. In a sense, I saw the demand side of the equation of my future, and had a wonderful year.

And second, I was a professor in the Cultural Studies Department at the Institute of American Indian Arts in Santa Fe, the only American Indian-controlled institution of education in the arts in the United States, from 1987 to 1988. I was amazed by the breadth of its offerings and the talent of its students – here I saw what could be termed the supply side of the equation of my future.

For the next few years, I moved around a bit, enjoying the teaching but growing restless as I realized that working as a gypsy academic couldn't be sustained over a lifetime. I faced a choice – I could be an adjunct gypsy academic, teaching a course here and a course there, with no hope of a future, living on my knees. Or I could move on. So about 1994, I decided to plunge full-time into what I had been doing on a small scale for a few years. I had done further lecturing on Indians in Europe. I had talked with many Indians about their work and their frustrations at the narrow limits of what "everybody knows" Indians do.

It was a difficult decision. I couldn't go back and I wasn't sure where I was going, but I knew it was time to move on. I was divorced and my children had what they needed. I had some financial resources, and, perhaps most importantly, I had a network of family and friends who provided a safety net of emotional support, even when they (and I) were not always sure of where I was going.

The time was now. I dove headfirst into what was a totally new vision of my future. The first decision I faced was: what was my role going to be as a non-indigenous person working with indigenous artists and performers?

Cultural sensitivity is key to success in this business. American Indians and other indigenous peoples have had countless experiences with non-indigenous authors, writers, and performers speaking on their behalf. Those days are gone – if indeed they ever existed. Since the beginning of my work, I have reiterated that I am not indigenous, don't pretend to be, and don't play one on TV. This has meant that indigenous artists and performers have chosen the message, whether this message has been a traditional Navajo music and dance group, a Navajo fashion designer, or an Aboriginal Australian playwright (and I've worked with all three). My job is not to tinker with the message, adding a feather here and there. My job is and has always been *to turn up the volume*!

Another question I had to answer was: what was the nature of my business? There are plenty of anthropologists who are more knowledgeable than I will ever be about a particular tribe, region, or country. I decided to offer "one-stop shopping" to venues and booking agents around the world – whatever they wanted (or that I could suggest) in any performance medium, from any region or country, I would either know who did it or how to find it. As an example, I toured an Aboriginal Australian rock band to Russia. The organizers were quite pleased and then asked if I could help organize an international indigenous contemporary fashion show. This was the opportunity to prove that "one-stop shopping" was more than a slogan. Using the database of addresses for our e-newsletter *From All Directions* (now with 6,890 readers around the world), I contacted many indigenous artists, performers, and communities, asking about contemporary indigenous fashion. Many contacts later, the show was a success and I even have a web page of contemporary fashion for those who are interested in working with us to develop contemporary indige-nous fashion shows.[2]

I was especially fortunate that, shortly after I decided to follow my dreams, I met the Chinle Valley Singers, a very accomplished and professional group of traditional Navajo Indian singers and dancers. Traditional Navajo music and dance are very different from what everyone expects Indian music and dance to be – the flashy and individualistic music and dance of the Plains Indian powwow. Several people even told me I would never be able to do anything with them because they weren't powwow – and because most of the members of the group were women. But Linda Davis, the leader of the group, convinced me that they loved their music and were proud of Navajo music and dance, and that they wanted to see the world. How could I refuse? I didn't know where to start or whom to turn to for advice, so I began as simply as I could, learning about festivals, sending out masses of letters (I began in the days when people sent letters, rather than emails).

In response, I got an inquiry of interest from the organizers of Baltica in Estonia. Baltica is the major festival in the Baltic countries Estonia, Latvia, and Lithuania which rotates between them. I was delighted. There was a slight problem – they had never invited an American group and didn't have the funds to bring us there.

I did some research and found out about a program called Arts International, operated at that time by the National Endowment for the Arts. I learned what was needed and worked with the Baltica organizers to draft a letter of invitation from Baltica to the Chinle Valley Singers that I thought would work. They sent the invita-tion to me on their letterhead, I submitted it with the grant application – and we got funded.

When we got off the plane in Tallinn, greeted by the festival's welcoming com-mittee, I not only had a strong sense of satisfaction and accomplishment – I knew I was going to be able to make this work. As of today, I have toured the Chinle Valley Singers to Estonia, Latvia, the Philippines, England, the Netherlands, Italy, and Dubai.

As time progressed, I began to hear from more and more Indian performers, tradi-tional *and* contemporary – writers, theater-makers, modern dancers, rock bands – the quality and diversity left me amazed. I wondered why more people hadn't experienced these powerful and dynamic performers, or heard and seen their message.

What to do? I had to develop a marketing perspective: what value could I create for customers and clients? I had to focus my anthropological experience in new and innovative ways, in order to do new and innovative things. Where most anthropolo-gists seemed to focus on preserving traditional culture, I wanted to promote indig-enous performers. I was on my way.

What Do You Need to Know to Do This Work?

Cultural sensitivity and advocacy are absolutely central to my work. As an example, I toured the Chinle Valley Singers to a festival in the Philippines. The organizers asked the singers to bless the festival. They talked among themselves and came to me. They would agree to perform a blessing *but* it would have to be on their terms – no photography, no recording, no applause. I had to know this was a sufficiently important issue that I took it to the festival organizers and fought for it – and won. Blessing accomplished.

Personal sensitivity is important too. Whenever the Chinle Valley Singers tour to a country with beaches, they ask to visit the beach to perform a ceremony. I always make it happen – but I don't ask what it is, and I don't participate. In one country, our driver took us to the beach. The singers began their ceremony, and the driver began to walk over to the group. I told him that this was the time for us to take a stroll along the beach, and off we went.

Knowledge of what indigenous performers actually do is important – not just what "everybody knows" they do. Equally important is a commitment to fighting for indigenous performers to be heard, to educating venues and audiences about the depth and diversity of indigenous performance.

Recently, I received an email from an organization in Israel, proudly announcing that a Native performer would appear at their upcoming event. I did a little web research and found out the performer is actually not Native. I shared this with the organizers, only to be informed that this performer was "more oriented to Native spirituality" than many Native performers, and they weren't going to be "restricted by genetics." We had a lengthy discussion by email; at the end, I suggested to them that it would be something like asking Jews for Jesus to explain Judaism. And there it ended. Advocacy – working hard, fighting hard to get indigenous messages heard by as many people as possible, on their terms, in the best environments possible, to get past the trap of what "everybody knows" – that is the heart of what I do.

What Skills, Experience, and Other Qualifications are Relevant?

Advocacy is the core of my work – advocating for the full range of indigenous performance. But how to get these voices heard? I've been called a producer. I've been called an impresario. Both terms really mean "find the money." Creating and succeeding at this business has meant that I have had to learn many new skills and to develop a new worldview, neither of which was taught in graduate school.

I have had to begin at the beginning, listening and learning from community members to go beyond what "everybody knows" indigenous performance is. How do I go about this? Whenever I come to an indigenous community, I make it a point to do two things.

First, I ask local people this question: is there someone in your community who did something that made you say, "Wow, that's great!" I follow this up by explaining that I haven't said "traditional" or "contemporary," "visual" or "performance." What I want is "Wow." Indigenous people have grown accustomed to outsiders coming into their communities in response to perceived problems in the community – land loss, disease, substance abuse, spousal abuse, and more. My approach is radically different. I want to know what they consider the best they have, who they regard as outstanding performers and artists, without regard to the common anthropological emphasis on tradition (an approach I've sometimes referred to as "Keep 'em pure, keep 'em poor").

Second, I have learned how to say "Why not?" in the local language. This is a wonderfully open-ended question, which brings my passion and humor into play, while showing that I care about the community in my own way. They know and I know that I'm an outsider but an outsider with a strong interest in the best they have. Community members know their community and its performers better than I ever will, and I know international cultural marketing. It can be an ideal partnership of equals.

What Do You Need to Learn beyond Your Anthropological Training?

A successful practitioner needs to think very clearly about their passion: what do they find exciting about these artists and performers? Success also requires a very high degree of creativity and flexibility. How can the practitioner get others interested in the artists and performers? How can they find the funding to make ideas happen?

And it means knowing how to find out about money. When I began my career, I would receive letters from European venues, stating they would be "honored" to have American Indians participate in their festival. A few follow-up queries, and I learned quickly that "honored" is another way of saying they didn't have the funds. I realized that if I wanted the artists I worked with to tour, if I wanted the events I designed to happen, I had to figure out where to get funding.

It has meant drafting a letter of invitation for one of the groups I work with for the European festival so that they could then put it on their letterhead, sign it, and send it to the US embassy – and that worked. It has meant writing a statement for an indigenous performer (with their consent and review) about pride in performance, which they then successfully submitted to their national arts funding agency for travel funding. And it has meant figuring out what funders want. At the time of writing I'm in discussion with an Indian tribe which owns a casino and resort about hosting IndigeNOW! Indigenous Opera from Three Continents and Three Countries. In my meetings with tribal leaders and the CEO of their casino resort, I seldom discuss the beauty and power of indigenous opera. Instead, I focus on "heads in beds": the fact that this festival will draw an international audience to their casino resort, lifting them above the competition (there are four other tribally owned casino resorts within 60 miles) and will brand their casino resort as a unique destination.

I've had to learn how to publicize my work. Our e-newsletter, *From All Directions*, now has almost 6,900 readers but this is only a start. I can sort through the database by tribe, by genre, by country, continent, or city, and target mailings at the people who will be most interested. I have learned how to write press releases that work, and how to maintain good relations with media around the world. I've been interviewed by indigenous radio programs in Canada and Australia by people I've never met in person.

I've learned to create events that are interesting to the media. For example, when I toured the Chinle Valley Singers to Dubai, I produced the first Native-language broadcast from overseas *into* the United States by pre-arranging a long-distance call from the singers in Dubai to KTNN, the 50,000-watt voice of the Navajo Nation.[3] That certainly created a buzz in the Nation about the singers, about the event, and about my work.

Passion leads to goals and a long-term plan to achieve them – a business plan. These goals will help the practitioner decide which projects to devote considerable energy to, which projects to give only some effort to, and which projects to pass over altogether.

Passion will also help the practitioner develop a clear short statement – the "elevator introduction" that tells people concisely what the practitioner does and can serve as the basis for further discussion. For example, when I'm introduced, I always say, "I work with indigenous peoples around the world in the performing arts and festival development." If there seems to be some interest, my next statement is usually, "On the one hand, I work with a traditional Navajo music and dance group. They've toured overseas seven times. On the other hand, I also produced an international indigenous theater festival in London, bringing indigenous theater companies from Australia, New Zealand, Canada, and the US to London."

But passion also has to be held in check. I've learned the hard way that if people aren't interested in what I do, or simply don't understand it after these basic statements, further lengthy (and usually one-sided) conversation or a long concept paper won't help matters – and I should just let it go.

What Are the Most Interesting and Exciting Things Anthropologists Do?

Here again, I can only speak from my own experiences. I have been fortunate to have many memorable moments and exciting experiences, such as:

- the look on the faces of the Chinle Valley Singers as we emerged from the subway in Milan and they saw Milan Cathedral;
- Navajo designer Virginia Ballenger accepting the applause and bouquets from the audience after her one-woman show in Moscow;
- the excitement of the opening ceremonies for the ORIGINS festival of indigenous theater in London after so much hard work, grant-writing, telephone calls, and persistence;
- Aboriginal Australian playwright David Milroy speaking to Lakota students at Little Wound School, South Dakota;
- Sami playwright Harriet Nordlund interacting with a directing class at Winston-Salem State University, North Carolina;

- being honored by the Chinle Valley Singers at a song and dance in honor of their mother in Many Farms, Arizona, and step-dancing with members of the group as the rest of the group sang a song about my work;
- introducing a delegation of Siberian indigenous leaders to Navajo Nation president Ben Shelly in his office in Window Rock, Arizona;
- touring Mariachi Imperial de America in Armenia under the auspices of the US embassy;
- listening to Aboriginal artist and festival organizer Cathy Craigie speak at the Australian embassy in Mexico City about her feelings as she heard the prime minister of Australia apologize for the country's treatment of its Aboriginal citizens during the first Sorry Day.

Obviously, the list could go on and on.

What Additional Resources Are Available?

As mentioned previously, the first step is for the practitioner to really listen to their own passion – what is exciting about what they want to do. This passion, this direction, will then guide them to the sources needed to proceed further, whether it is literature and recordings about a particular kind of performance, or to seek information about funding, or to develop a business plan.

For me, much of my inspiration has come from indigenous artists and performers. When I find a work or a performer that excites me (and believe me, I just haven't been able to work with performers who don't), I immediately begin to think about "turning up the volume." Who would be interested? Who would fund it?

One of the directions in which I'm going is the creation of cultural or artistic exchanges between indigenous performers. For instance, I'm working on an indigenous fashion show featuring a Sami (Norway) designer and a Navajo designer from the United States. The concept will be to bring the Navajo designer to Norway for a collaboration and show in the Sami capital of Kautokeino, with a joint show under the auspices of the US embassy in Stockholm, followed by a joint show in Washington, DC under the auspices of the Norwegian embassy, finishing with a joint show at the Navajo Nation Museum in Window Rock, Arizona, the capital of the Navajo Nation. This enables both designers to build on their own already-existing audiences but extending the audience and building them up.

Where Am I Going from Here?

There is no "typical" pattern – at least there hasn't been one for my work. However, I do have a very clear idea of where I want to go. After 18 years in the business, I've come to know that indigenous performers, traditional and contemporary, are marginalized all the time. At any event or festival, there is usually just one indigenous performing artist, especially in the performing arts, and especially for contemporary performers. This marginalization often traps performers, audiences, and venues into the limitations of what "everybody knows" about indigenous performance and performers.

But where can audiences and booking agents and venues experience the range, the depth, the power of indigenous performance? In conversation with American Indian artists and performers, I often say that if I asked them where I could hear the best powwow music, or see the best arts and crafts, they could easily name 10 places off the top of their heads. But if I were to ask where I could hear the best indigenous hip hop, see the best indigenous theater, enjoy the best indigenous fashion, the answer is often just a shake of the head – who knows?

It is *not* because the fashion, the hip hop, or the theater isn't there. It's because there is no place to experience international indigenous performance on a regular basis. An American Indian play here this year, an American Indian modern music there next year – but nothing every year at the same time and in the same place, as is now widespread for traditional arts and crafts. And yes, several countries now have festivals and events which regularly showcase the best in their countries – The Dreaming in Australia, Planet IndigenUS and imagineNATIVE in Canada, Pasifika in New Zealand. These are all English-speaking countries and they have led the way. But what about indigenous performance from Siberia, or Mexico, or Peru? Or the United States?

As a result, I have decided that my goal now is to create an annual indigenous performing arts festival that will:

- be partnered from the beginning with an indigenous organization or community;
- showcase the best indigenous performing artists from around the world in theater, modern dance, music, fashion, film/video, photography, the written and spoken word;
- train indigenous young people how to run the festival and, eventually, take it over;
- introduce indigenous performing artists to the business, teaching them what an agent is, what constitutes a contract, for example, since many people come from isolated rural and urban communities where this information is difficult if not impossible to find;
- eventually serve as a performing arts showcase as well, introducing the best indigenous performers to venues and booking agents from around the world.

It won't be easy – it may not even be possible – but it's where I'm going.

Notes

1   See www.originsfestival.bordercrossings.org.uk.
2   At http://www.flickr.com/photos/gbronitsky/sets/72157631297596772/.
3   See www.ktnnonline.com.

Chapter 9

An Independent Consultant in a Business of One

Judy Tso

Judy Tso provides us with our second – and very different – account of life as an independent practitioner. She describes in detail what it is like to go into business for yourself, working in areas such as evaluation, management consulting, and training. She begins by outlining her background and her decision to work independently, then offers a frank and full discussion of the realities of working on one's own, highlighting both the issues and the opportunities. Much of the chapter is taken up with a discussion of building a client base and marketing services effectively. She concludes by offering suggestions on ways to continue to build your skills and experience, and emphasizes the opportunities and freedom that come from working on your own.

This chapter focuses specifically on being a sole proprietor or being in business for yourself. It will, hopefully, provide you with some important guidance as you consider whether this path is for you, and, if it is, what is the best way to go along this path.

Much of what I discuss is based on personal experience. For much of the first decade of my career, I worked for a small business or ran my own business. I went to college to study business and focused on two areas, multinational management and entrepreneurial management. After college, I started out working for a small consulting firm in the product development field. In my first position, I was responsible for marketing and communications work for the firm, writing a newsletter for clients. I was then was trained to be a facilitator of idea generation sessions (the firm's main service offering).

A Handbook of Practicing Anthropology. First Edition. Edited by Riall W. Nolan.
© 2013 John Wiley & Sons, Inc. Published 2013 by John Wiley & Sons, Inc.

Next, for nearly a decade, I ran my own firm from half-time to full-time in two locations. I began providing services that were similar to the work I had been doing at the product development firm, idea generation and/or running brainstorming sessions for companies. Along the way, I pursued a master's in applied anthropology at the University of Maryland. During the two years I attended graduate school, I ran my firm part-time. As I planned for the internship that was a part of my graduate studies, I was strategic about the type of internship I wanted to have and made sure that the internship experience would advance my consulting business.

For my internship, I conducted a program evaluation of two Baltimore Reads programs. I was able to use this experience to position and market myself in the area of nonprofit program evaluation. I wrote an article for *Practicing Anthropology* summarizing what I had learned from my internship.

While I was in the master's program, I started to diversify my offerings. I had always wanted to facilitate more strategic sessions, so I approached nonprofit companies that needed strategic planning work. I also offered program evaluation since I was formally learning qualitative research methods as a part of the master's program. I was deliberate in my choice of coursework, choosing a policy course and an evaluation course at University of Maryland, Baltimore County, in part because the students were older, more experienced with "real world" problems and the coursework was very relevant to the challenges of conducting evaluation in the real world. In addition, while I was pursuing the master's degree I also completed a coaches' training program at Coaches Training Institute.

When I began my master's, I thought that I would apply the degree back to product development work, specifically using the qualitative research background to do "voice of the customer" work (understanding the needs of consumers/ customers and designing products and services to meet those needs), but the master's program shifted my thinking a bit. Because I was in the community health and development track in the master's program, I studied issues of racism, equality, and so on. That reawakened a longstanding interest of mine in issues of social justice. How could I combine my experience with facilitation and my business experience with my anthropology training to address issues of diversity, equality, and fairness?

I began to explore how I could become a diversity trainer in a corporate environment. I began to pay attention to who I knew in my network who could connect me to the field of diversity training. I attended training with FranklinCovey and discovered that the trainer of the course also did diversity training. She connected me to the first firm I met in the diversity field. I began to conduct training for this firm and met some of the other trainers. One of these trainers connected me to a firm called JHoward and Associates, for whom I later became a trainer. (Already in this story you can see the importance of networking and keeping your radar on for connections.) I worked as a per diem consultant for JHoward. This was essentially a part-time position and I ran my own business in conjunction with the work. The training work provided a base of income, a bit of stability.

It is also important to note that my undergraduate degree was in business and I studied entrepreneurship in college. These classes gave me a basic foundation for writing a business plan, and for going into business for myself. I was also trained in basic accounting and finance, so had a background in the financial side of running my own business.

Running Your Own Business and Being Independent

First, I will disabuse you of any notion of romanticism associated with this path. While it is true that you are your own boss, you also bear the entire risk on your own if you fail. You will often work alone and must therefore be comfortable with solitude, and you will be responsible for all aspects of the business – networking, marketing, proposal writing, designing your website or hiring someone to do so, budgeting, invoicing and billing, paperwork, taxes, and so on. If you don't like all these aspects of running a business, you need to seriously consider whether you are suited for this path.

While at times you may hire someone to help you with a project if the budget is large enough, for the most part you will do everything yourself and there is no one to fall back on. Should you be wildly successful and build a firm, eventually you will have help for the tasks you don't like. You will receive no benefits and will need to buy your own health insurance, or if you have a spouse who is employed by a larger firm you will need to be covered by your spouse's plan. You will not get a paid vacation. If you go on vacation it is entirely on your own dime.

Having said all that, there is great freedom in being your own boss, and you can chart your own direction. If you are successful at gaining clients, you will likely be able to choose the organizations you want to work with and the kind of work you want to pursue. There will be no bureaucracy or approval processes to go through and once you make a decision, you can take action right away without delay. I don't think I fully appreciated how wonderful it was to make all the decisions and call all the shots. It is also very rewarding to decide you want to pursue a certain direction and to go forward and do it. There is no one to say no.

How to Break into the Business

There are easier ways to break into the business, and more difficult ways. Certainly, a common way to break into consulting is to go work as an employee for another consulting firm and learn the business, build a reputation, and build relationships with clients. If you own the relationship with the client, it is possible that when you leave the client may still want to work with you; and if you have a good relationship with the firm's owner, they may allow you to continue the relationship with that client. If you own the relationship and did all the work, there is a good chance that the relationship may end once you leave the firm and the owner may not be able to sustain it without you.

If you work for another consulting firm, you may be asked to sign a non-compete clause that prohibits you from contacting clients for a period of one or more years after you leave. If you hope to work independently, you will have to consider the impact of this clause. If you have not signed a non-compete clause, it is still a good idea not to burn your bridges. If you are parting on good terms, it is good to have a conversation with your employer and see if they will permit you to take some clients with you. Even if you do not have such a conversation, it is best to remain ethical and stay away from actively pursuing your former employer's client base. If you go work in industry, for example, for pharmaceuticals or hospitals, it is likely that you won't be prohibited from later working for a consulting firm.

You can also build the business from scratch. This will take an investment of time and you will need a financial cushion.

Navigating the Financial Territory

There are different strategies to be able to afford going into business for yourself. Do you have a partner or spouse who works, and can you rely on one family income for a year or two? Can you find a part-time job that covers your expenses while you build your clientele? If you are working in a full-time job, can you save enough money to live one year without an income in order to build your business?

My personal opinion is that the most difficult thing to do is to build a business while holding a full-time job. Once you start marketing, you need to be able to say yes to the work. If you are working full-time already, it is hard to accept the work. It is also hard to find time to market your firm while working a full-time job and, depending on the policies of your employer, you may be prohibited from running your own business while working for your employer. Of course, if you have lots of vacation time saved, it might be possible to do a job here or there.

Is Being an Independent Consultant Right for You?

The critical question to ask yourself is: do you like business development, marketing, and networking? Working as a business of one means you must be comfortable drumming up business, and the industry you are in is essentially the consulting business. Some people like to do the project work but don't like getting out there and networking, making new contacts, and building a reputation out in the world. If you don't like marketing yourself, you can stop reading this chapter now because it is the essential core to running your own business. When you are not doing the project work, you are marketing, networking, and writing proposals to land the next piece of work. Sometimes you find that doing the project work is all-consuming and you don't have time to market. The two can be difficult to balance.

Some have also posed the question: does anything about anthropology lend itself to being independent? I am not sure there is anything inherent in anthropology, but I will say that the ability to complete a graduate degree, and especially a PhD, means that you have learned to be disciplined, to manage your own time, and to work alone. These skills are useful for running your own business.

Also consider your personality. Can you handle long hours alone? If you need the company of others through the day to keep going, you will not thrive working independently.

Tax Status and Registering Your Business

One of the questions you need to answer is what type of tax entity you want to create for your firm. Some people choose a limited liability corporation or LLC, while others operate as a sole proprietor. When you are a sole proprietor, you do not have a tax designation that is separate from you as an individual. This also means you have no liability protection. If you are a sole proprietor you have the option of using your social security number as your tax ID or choosing an employer identification number (EIN). The IRS has a set of questions to answer to determine if you need an EIN.[1]

Each jurisdiction has different rules regarding registering your business. You will need to research the laws in your area. Do you need to fill out a form that lets the government know that you are "doing business as" Firm Alpha? Do you need to pay a fee? Do you qualify to be a minority-or women-owned business? If so, you will want to consider applying for certification as a minority-or women-owned business in your jurisdiction.

Liability Insurance

It is a good idea to consider liability insurance if you run a consulting business. While I have never had a problem, I chose to have liability insurance. If you were to have a dissatisfied client, liability insurance would give you some protection, especially if you operate as a sole proprietor.

Determine Your Core Set of Services

If you are considering this path, you will need to decide what your core set of services will be. Will you conduct qualitative research? Will you provide training? What services are you prepared to offer? Of course if you are studying socio-cultural anthropology, qualitative research is the main methodology. So you can offer variations on this work. You can conduct focus groups or interviews, write reports, and provide analyses.

Also, anthropology is a systems-focused discipline and it is likely you are a systems thinker either through training in anthropology or perhaps inherently. Not everyone is accustomed to big-picture thinking so anthropology can lend itself to such processes as strategic planning.

If you have had a career in another field before pursuing anthropology, perhaps you can offer your services to that field or industry. For example, if you worked in healthcare, you might be able to offer your services in the realm of culturally competent care or patient-centered care.

How to Build a Client Base

The consulting business is a referral business. You don't build a base of clients from advertising or direct mail. You build the base by having enough people work with you, experience your services, trust you, and respect you such that they are willing to say to others: "Hey, if you want an organizational assessment, call Jackie. She is the person you want to work with."

It is all about building relationships with people. People hire those they trust. If they receive your name from a person they trust, they are likely to have some trust in you from the beginning. Once you get to know your client and do a good job for them, you have a relationship and your client may refer you to others. One by one you will build relationships with individuals who become clients or consulting partners and over time more people can vouch for your work. Building and maintaining relationships is the key. Never burn your bridges, because even if you and your client part ways, you hope you have left enough of a good impression that they would refer you or, at the very least, not bad-mouth you.

You want to be the name that others pass along as the go-to person for the services you offer. Building a base takes time. It can take two or more years to build a base that will support one person. The actual income you make will be dependent on what type of clients you have and how many projects you can manage at one time. If you hire employees or subcontract work, you can handle more projects simultaneously, but will need to share the income with others. Nonprofits pay less and corporations pay more. Your hourly rate will also depend on the type of organization you are working for and what they can afford. Average hourly rates for consultants range from US$100 an hour to many hundreds of dollars. Some people work on retainers and provide a monthly rate. Others provide a project costing for the entire project that is built on an hourly rate but may include discounts for multiple hours.

Other Strategies for Deriving an Income

Beyond finding your own clients and building a base, there are other strategies to derive an income and reduce the financial risk of being without an income. One strategy is to link up to larger organizations that routinely need to subcontract people and subcontract your services to them. This can be with a medium-sized or a large consulting firm. I did this with JHoward and was able to derive a monthly income to supplement my own business.

Over the years more and more freelancing websites that seek to match consultants with work have sprung up. FlexJobs and Freelancer are some examples. While I have not used these particular sites, I have been part of databases or lists of consultants, and once in a while would receive a lead from one of them.

How to Market Your Business

Today because many people are their own brand, marketing means developing a brand for yourself and being known for a particular set of services or a particular expertise. The number one way to market is through networking.

Networking

Overall, networking is a key activity to undertake for a wealth of reasons. Not only is it a chief method for identifying and securing clients, it is also a critical method for finding colleagues to work with, for mentoring, and for professional development. By networking, I mean a set of activities that brings you into contact with more individuals. You can network in a number of ways:

- by setting up coffee or lunch with an individual;
- by attending networking or other meetings held by various organizations;
- by attending industry meetings;
- by offering to speak at a local meeting;
- by joining a board or committee of a local nonprofit organization; and
- by volunteering your time to set up association meetings or other events.

Going to industry meetings and conferences

It is important for you to attend industry and association meetings that are relevant to your field. So if you have worked with nonprofits, go to your state's Council of Non-profits meeting. If you are in the product development field, go to Product Development and Management Association (PDMA) meetings (www.pdma.org) or the Ethnographic Praxis in Industry Conference (EPIC) conference (http://epiconference.com). If you want to meet other anthropologists in the business sector, go to the EPIC meeting.

If you specialize in organizational development, go to the ODNetwork (www.odnetwork.org) meetings. If you go to industry meetings you can meet potential clients and start to build relationships. If you go to meetings targeting your consulting specialty you will meet potential business partners. For example, if you focus on market research, you will want to attend meetings such as the American Marketing Association meeting.

If you are focused on user-centered design go to the design conferences such as those run by the Industrial Designers Society (IDSA). If you are pursuing the healthcare industry, check out the 50 top medical meetings listed by the Healthcare Convention & Exhibitors Association.[2] One of the key organizations that runs conferences in different industries is the Institute for International Research (IIR), on whose website (www.iirusa.com) you can explore a list of meetings.

Meetings and conferences are great places to meet people, network, and introduce yourself to potential clients or business partners. Also, if you manage to get on the agenda of the meetings as a presenter, you have an automatic soft sales pitch. Meetings can be expensive so you will want to gauge which meeting will provide the most value to you and be selective.

As a consultant, speaking at a conference is a great way to showcase your expertise. Keep in mind that going to meetings will not automatically gain you new clients. It can take years before a potential client you met at a meeting calls you. In addition, some of the meetings you go to are for your own professional development, to keep you abreast of the field. At these conferences you may meet no clients but you will meet like-minded people who might become partners or mentors or people you can call on when you need advice.

Public speaking

Public speaking in general is a great way to market yourself. I began by speaking at various local business meetings for free and over time built that into a source of income. Many associations and local chapters of organizations are happy to have free speakers and, in return for your time, you get the opportunity to put your name out there, pass out your information, and meet some potential new clients or referral sources. For example, if you are targeting technology firms and are a woman, go to some of the Women in Technology meetings (www.womenintechnology.org) and then offer to speak at their next meeting. Contact your local alumni chapter and see if you can speak at an upcoming meeting.

Join boards and committees

Another great way to market yourself is to join a board or a committee of a relevant organization, industry association, or nonprofit. If you hope to develop business with nonprofits, join the board of a nonprofit you respect. Through attending board meetings and nonprofit events, you are likely to meet employees of other nonprofits, and the executive director of the organization you are helping will likely be open to referring you to other executive directors. You may even be able to offer some pro bono consulting to the nonprofit and ask for a testimonial in return. When you provide pro bono services, it is likely the organization will be open to referring you to clients who will be able to pay for your services. By sitting on a board and contributing good work, you demonstrate your trustworthiness and your competence. People will get to know you, and other board members may refer you.

You can also volunteer your time to help various industry associations. If you want to work with hospitals, then join a committee of the American Hospital Association. If you want to offer marketing research services, join the leadership of the local chapter of the American Marketing Association. Through all of these activities, you are seeking to build your reputation, to meet more people, and to make yourself known to your target market.

Create a web presence

Building that brand has become much easier on one level due to the Internet and social media marketing. You can write your own blog, tweet, and put your profile on LinkedIn, to name just a few ways you can promote yourself. You will want to market your expertise using every channel at your disposal.

I developed my own website and while I did not have a blog then, if I were to do so today, I would likely create one as it is one of the top ways to build Internet presence. Your web presence is essential for building credibility and your website functions as a brochure, but do not expect your web presence to yield business. It supports your marketing efforts; having a website alone does not generate business.

Building credibility through client testimonials

If you have testimonials from previous clients, post these on your website. Testimonials and recommendations are a powerful way to demonstrate your effectiveness to potential clients.

In addition to the website, I also sought to get my quotes placed in publications so I would appear in print in news publications and magazines as an expert. Whenever possible I would seek opportunities to write articles for business journals and other publications. Being able to send people copies of your articles is a simple way to demonstrate your expertise and boost your credibility.

Write a book

Writing a book is an excellent strategy for marketing yourself as you automatically become "the author of Book X," and being an author confers credibility. Also, when you are interviewed by newspaper reporters, they especially like to quote published authors. In addition, you can self-publish these days, so there is less of a barrier to becoming published. The reality of publishing now is that there is no real benefit to publishing with a big name publisher. If a large publisher agrees to publish your work (and most do not publish unknowns unless you get very lucky and have both an agent and a very powerful book proposal), they take the vast majority of the profit (you keep less than a quarter and they keep everything else). They also expect you to market the book for them.

By self-publishing you keep the majority of the income and it is not only an excellent way to market your expertise and services, but it also provides you with an additional source of revenue. The bottom line is that no one really asks who published your book. With "just in time" publishing options available today, you can publish as you go. You can sell e-books as well, which can be another source of income.

Marketing and business development through partners and partnerships

You may consider formal and informal partnerships with other consultants. There is a spectrum of relationships these days between consultants. You may choose formal legal arrangements; you may simply have a working arrangement whereby you call on colleagues to help you on client engagements; or you may find yourself called on to help your consulting colleagues. Because so many people are independent consultants these days, there is no need to build a firm or organization and take on the overhead of paying salaries to people. You can simply subcontract all the labor you need and for that given period of time those individuals work under your leadership.

Be clear about how partners present themselves and come to agreements before meeting with clients. In some cases you may ask your work colleague to refrain from mentioning that they work for themselves and at other times you may disclose to the client that you have brought in other firms or individuals to help.

So, in addition to hustling on your own for work, your ability to make partnership alliances or to build relationships with others is another key to building the business. I have sent work to others when I could not take it on or there was someone else more qualified and had other consultants do the same for me.

Diversifying Your Service Offerings

Offer a range of services. For example, in my business, I not only conducted program evaluations using my anthropological experience; I deliberately developed experience in diversity training, as it was an area I wanted to work in.

Over time you can add services to your offerings, but with consulting, people want credentials and credible experience. You must either be able to build and then cite the experience, or have a strong referral from someone who says, "I trust this consultant and vouch that they will do a good job for you." To add new services, it helps to find other consultants in the line of work you want to do and offer up your time to help them market or to be subbed on one of their projects. Once on the project, you can learn more about the line of work and gain some exposure.

To work with issues relating to diversity in the workplace, I met one owner of a diversity training firm and asked if they needed more people, and they were willing to train me and bring me in on several of their training contracts. This work led to my developing a relationship with another, even larger, firm and I became a trainer for that firm. With the second firm I worked as a per diem consultant. The firm would contact me when there was work and I would be paid for the work done. This was part-time work but it gave me a base income that I could count on.

If you can find one or two relationships with larger organizations that can provide a certain amount of work to you each month, it will provide you with some financial stability.

Keeping Fresh: Professional Development

When you work for yourself you also fund your own training department, meaning that if you want to be trained in a new area and to expand your skills, you have to pay for that training, that is, invest in yourself. I spent thousands of dollars after my graduate education (which already cost a significant sum) continuing to train myself. And this investment is absolutely necessary. You will need to update your skills constantly to keep up with the market. You will want to set aside a budget to continue to develop yourself, otherwise you will be rusty and no one wants to hire a consultant who is behind the times.

The Opportunity

What is the upside of being in business for yourself? As many people who move from the corporate space into the independent consulting space well know, they seek freedom. And freedom you will have. You get to decide what type of work you want to do, and once you persuade someone to hire you to do it you get to do that work.

Working for yourself provides great opportunity to explore different types of work and to follow your interests. I was able to transition several times into new lines of work and to reinvent myself. I went from product development consulting to nonprofit consulting and program evaluation, to coaching, to diversity training and public speaking, to cultural competency assessment. I pursued the training I wanted and sought out the business relationships I needed to do the work I was interested in doing. I would do work in the old space until I could establish a reputation in the new space.

It is important to keep in mind that you can decide to be independent at any point in your career. One of the most common junctures when people choose to go independent is after a long career with a larger organization (corporation, government, nonprofit, etc.). A period of downsizing might force them out or they may desire a change of pace and leave of their own accord. Individuals who have had a long career can draw on connections they have built over years as they build their business. Some even subcontract back to their old firm. This is a great option for both parties, as the organization doesn't have to pay benefits and the individual gets some income as a base for building the business. This is another good reason to go independent after a few years working for another consulting firm.

Finally, there are those who started right after graduate school. You can also oscillate, be independent for a while, work for someone else, and then be independent again. There are no hard and fast rules.

Next Steps on the Path

If you are considering this path, here are a few recommendations. Sit down and reflect on the following questions:

1. First, consider your personality. Ask yourself these questions: Do you like marketing and talking about yourself, as you will have to promote yourself to get business? Can you handle working alone, as many hours will be spent in a solitary environment? Do you enjoy networking?
2. Can you manage the financial aspect? Can you cover your own expenses for a period of time while you build your business? Can you take on part-time work? Do you have enough savings that you could spend to fund the ramp-up of your business? You need to create a budget of your expenses and determine how much monthly income you need. Overall the expenses necessary to start your business are not exorbitant; the main expense is paying your living expenses before you have any income coming in.
3. Do you have some projects under your belt and clients that will provide referrals? Prospective clients want to know that you done this type of work before.

Once you have decided to pursue this route, start writing a business plan to get your efforts organized. The Internet provides many samples of formats for business plans.

If you choose this path, it will be challenging and also rewarding. Enjoy the ride.

Notes

1   See http://www.irs.gov/businesses/small/article/0,,id=97872,00.html.
2   At http://www.hcea.org/research_top50.asp.

Chapter 10

How to Be a Self-Supporting Anthropologist

Grant McCracken

Grant McCracken, also an independent practitioner, offers us a fascinating glimpse into the construction of professional identity. McCracken's chapter is in essence a primer on how to think differently about one's anthropological persona, and how to present anthropology's perspective and insight to a variety of audiences. He draws implicit and explicit comparisons and contrasts between the roles he learned as an academic, and talks about how and why these roles changed and were enhanced in the process of working as a consultant, speaker, and writer.

I was sitting at my desk, sometime in the mid-1980s, when the phone rang. It was an advertising agency. "Why," they wanted to know, "is Chrysler selling more Jeeps in New York City than in Colorado?" Surely, they protested, a Jeep is an off-road vehicle created for the out-of-doors, not city life. The agency had tried everything: focus groups, surveys, strategy, brainstorms. Nothing helped. Free to "go a little crazy," they were now prepared to hire an anthropologist. I was their method of last resort.

I was so deeply conflicted about commercial work that when things kept coming undone – a canceled flight, a missed interview – I hoped very much that my colleague from the agency would consent to call the whole thing off. But, no, he carried on.

And on. And on. And this is the nature of commercial research. It's an exercise in improv. If one thing doesn't work, you try another. This reached its high point when, a few years later, a client said, "Look, just get on a plane and go. We'll figure out what we want you to do by the time you get to Shanghai."

A Handbook of Practicing Anthropology. First Edition. Edited by Riall W. Nolan.
© 2013 John Wiley & Sons, Inc. Published 2013 by John Wiley & Sons, Inc.

You Will Learn to Live with Ad Hocery

This sort of thing filled me with horror. I like planning. I like order. One of the reasons I care about ideas is that they give me a sense, and an instrument, of order. In some meetings, making things up as we went along made me wish to excuse myself, go to the bathroom, and throw up my breakfast.

But you get used to the ad hocery. In point of fact, you never say "no" to anything. (First, because you can't afford to and, second, because you don't know what you don't know – the project that sounds odd and unpromising might open up a new vista.) And, as it turns out, most things *can* get sorted out "on the way to Shanghai."

You Will Learn to Work in Shanghai

I don't know anything about Chinese culture. I made that clear. My specialty is American culture (if that) and no other. But, no, they insisted, we want the same set of eyes looking at the results in China, Brazil, India, and Mexico. My head, to say nothing of my breakfast, was spinning. I was no longer defined by my training, discipline, or expertise. I was now defined by the problem at hand.

You Will Learn to Ride Uneven Circus Ponies

My plan was to use my commercial work to fund my academic work. This meant a new versatility and the ability to perform quite different intellectual tasks, working out of sometimes conflicting paradigms at roughly the same time. In the early days, I found I could do one or the other, the anthropology or the consulting. Moving between the two was painful. The transitions were filled with "rough air." Or to use the metaphor that popped out of my mouth at one point, I felt like I was riding uneven circus ponies.

There is a more practical problem. You do a couple of projects and you spend the proceeds on a new standard of living which in turn obliges you to consult all the time, not just half the year. As anthropologists, we know how this works. Consumer expenditure has a way of ratcheting upwards. I call it the "Diderot effect," according to which a purchase in one category can set in train a change in other categories and an upward movement in one's consumer spending (McCracken 1988).

There will be moments when you veer in the other direction, back into your academic modality. I came to think of this as an "over-correction" too. The trick is to do both the academic and the industrial, learning to move back and forth between them, day to day, moment to moment. This gets easier over time, but the early days will be unpleasant and sometimes destructive.

You Will Learn to Live Simply and Wear a Rolex

The best way to solve the Diderot problem is to live simply. I haven't owned a car since I was 18. I dress simply, except when consulting, when I dress well. The semiotics are simple. Anyone who hires you is putting a small but not insignificant part of their career at risk. If you don't show up, if you don't deliver, someone (besides you) is going to pay for it. Dressing well is your way of saying, "I am professional, capable, reliable, and risk-worthy." Wear a Rolex when consulting (and only when consulting). It sends a message.

You Will Get Used to Being the Apostate

On learning that you are consulting, some people will never talk to you again. Really. A woman whom I knew when we were students at the University of Chicago simply walked away from our cocktail conversation – and never talked to me again. People will scorn you. A quite well-known Canadian anthropologist made a wise crack about ill-gotten gains. The hostility is marked.

In point of fact, if you use this hybrid consulting–academic model you won't make much money. All of your consulting money will be consumed by the academic half of the year. You will make roughly what a full professor does, perhaps a little better. But you won't have the benefits or the security of that position. But, not to worry, people will still go out of their way to scorn you as someone who sold out.

It's occurred to me that people might be right to scorn me, that I was wrong to undertake this career. I seek comfort in the idea that, with so many anthropologists converging in their opinions and interests, could it hurt to spring one or two of us on a different evolutionary course? I was happy to make my career that experiment. And if it failed, well, it wouldn't be the end of the world. I am realistic enough about my abilities to see that *this* failure would not cost the field a Malinowski or an Evans-Pritchard. The "opportunity cost," as the economists call it, would be small.

You Will Pursue a Curiosity Shaped Less and Less by the Professional Consensus

You are no longer subject to the scrutiny of "tenure and promotion" committees or funding agencies. You will go where your interests and the data take you. In my case, that meant, for instance, looking into "homeyness." This was the term which female heads of household would use to explain mantelpieces and decor choices. And when I asked them to expand on the term, they would give you that look that says, "Oh, come on. Surely that's self-explanatory." This is the moment you know you've hit something foundational. You have your assignment . . . or at least I had mine: to render a cultural account of homeyness. I didn't have to care that this was a topic that didn't interest the field of anthropology. I just needed to know that it was interesting to me. As it turned out, the American talk-show host Oprah was interested too (McCracken 2005).

One of the things that I noticed in the 1990s was how much mainstream culture was being produced "off license" by amateurs with new instruments and ambitions. It was as if the punk DIY conviction had seeped into the mainstream, or more probably that the cultural impulses that had produced punk had writ and moved on.

I wrote a book called *Plenitude* and published it online (McCracken 1997). No one much liked it. So I published it in hard cover and still no one took to it. I was so obsessed with writing and publishing this book that I had lost sight of consulting and when the book took a loss, I was suddenly in danger of losing my house. To complicate matters further, the book got excoriated in the Canadian press, and won no interest in the anthropological community. In sum, *Plenitude* proved a folly. Here too intercession from outside the community came to my rescue. Henry Jenkins, then at MIT, proved to be a fan of the book and that's how I came to have my connection with that institution.

But here there is another intellectual problem: how to manage your research career. Our professional identities have a way of navigating for us. They help identify what we care about, when to move on, and what to move on to. If you have disconnected yourself from this (to some extent) and you will have to figure out a bigger picture by dint of your own efforts.

You Will Learn to Supply Your Own Soap

Occasionally I see newly minted consultants on the plane. They are squirming in their seats. And I know exactly what has happened. The consultant said, not unreasonably, "Hotels supply soap, so I don't have to. That's one less thing to worry about." In fact, hotel soap, especially when added to altitude and alcohol, will strip your skin of moisture and it's not long before you are in a state of extreme discomfort. You should treat life on the road as a set of problems for which you cultivate a set of solutions. You should also have a support group, other consultants who supply advice and consolation (McCracken 2006a).

We return to the above theme: detached from the conventional topics, methods, cadences, and conferences of your discipline, you must now spend more time on self-government and self-invention. I tended to burrow into one topic and then another, leaving the larger view to take care of itself. As a result, the forces of disorder would rise around me, moving me to burrow more. I would be obliged then to course-correct, sometimes in an ill-advised, needlessly expensive way.

My advice: you will be advising managers; try acting like one.

You Will Learn to Manage an Embarrassment of Riches

Doing anthropology in your own culture is a classic "problem of plenty." There is never a moment of the day when you are not awash in data (McCracken 2006b,

2007b, 2010a, 2010b). But your consulting work will bring you still more data. You are charged with asking questions. And it is, of course, in the nature of ethnography that we don't know what we need to know so we must ask a great many general questions. This means we will collect a vast amount of data, only some of which matters to the client. The client will expect us to treat this data as confidential, but couldn't care less what we do with the rest of the data. We are free to collect and publish this for our own purposes (McCracken 2006c).

As and when ideas occur to you, you will want to blog them. This gives you a way of sorting them out. The ideas and insights that matter will rise to the surface. So will the ideas and insights that others care about. Your work now enters the public domain, and people have a way of finding the posts that interest them. Recently, I was moved to post on the TV show *Being Human* (McCracken 2011) and to remark on the similarities and differences between the UK and the US versions. This occasioned some 60 comments from readers, most of them thoughtful and, for me, illuminating.

I think of blog posts as messages in a bottle. They're a way to probe the universe. While I was busy with other things, smart people were gathering around a TV show. Now I know. I have written something like 1.5 million words on my blog. It has worked well as a way to solicit data and find friends. We can listen passively to contemporary culture, in the manner of the ham radio operator monitoring shipping lanes in the Bering Straits. But it's when we provoke the world a little that some of the best data are forthcoming. (This is the theme of my new book *Culturematic*: McCracken 2012.)

The advent of social media gives us way of exploring a very complex society. Anthropologists are good at intensive inquiry. One of our challenges is the extensive inquiry, the ability to reach across communities and see the diversity of the realities so profuse in number. Almost no one is paying attention to all these worlds at once. Journalists have tried (e.g., Fitzgerald 1986). Sociologists and novelists too (e.g., A. Wolfe 1998; T. Wolfe 1998). But there is work to do here.

It's worth pointing out that the new media have also contributed to the destruction of the "communities" and "worlds" that anthropology is accustomed to making the object of analysis. And this, for my money is where consulting gets really interesting. Now the data at hand force you out of familiar models into a frenzy of theory construction. I have been especially interested in the themes of multiplicity (*Transformations*: McCracken 2008b) and "cloudy" selves and groups (2007a, 2008a). And now the academic half of your enterprise proves valuable to the consulting half.

You Will Learn to Speak Plainly

Academics have a bad habit of needing to translate an idea or a problem into their own language before they can think about it. This is fine to do, but we are obliged to talk to the client in the language of everyday speech. This means using a prose style like the one I'm using now. This means being companionable in order to serve up meaning. A lot of the language in anthropology has what Silverstein (1976) would call meta-pragmatic objective, which means that it shows the learning, the seriousness, the sheer braininess of the speaker. But the price of this theater is high. We make it more difficult to talk to people outside the field. Obscure speech is not the most grievous error inflicted on the field by postmodernism, in my opinion, but it did have the effect of sealing us into a hermetic world.

You Will Learn to Talk about Culture

When the client wants to know what you do and why they should hire you, you may be inclined to say, "Well, I can tell you about culture." They will reply, "What's that exactly?" And now you have the daunting task of explaining that culture is, well, everything: all the categories and rules in our heads and all the things these categories and rules produce in the world. This is where the eyes of even the brightest clients begin to glaze over and you can tell they are thinking about that presentation they have to give at three. Time is short. Attention spans are stretched to breaking point. And you know that most consultants lead with a promise that is dead simple, effectively a short cut, "hot button," or "quick fix."

The trick, as I see it, is to find ways to talk about culture without simplifying it. My solution in one case was to say, in effect, "Listen, culture is complicated. You don't need to understand it completely any more than you do finance or operations. Hire a chief culture officer, and leave it to them." That was the plan behind my book *Chief Culture Officer* (McCracken 2009.)

More recently, I took another tack with a book called *Culturematic* (2012). Now my pitch is: "Look, you don't have to understand all of culture to build a little machine for making meaning. Here's how to build a Culturematic." You will create your own strategies.

You Will Learn that It's Not about You

Anthropologists insist on a moral vision and a moral voice. And this is a good thing. But I think we sometimes border on self-absorption. It can't always be about us. The moral, political, and epistemological issues matter and we must debate them. But they can't matter so much that this is all we do.

I was raised in post-Victorian Canada and a middle-church Protestant tradition where the message was "The self is an instrument for work in the world. Go do work in the world." But as I began to move my way out of the gravitational field of anthropology, I began to see that I was in fact a little spoiled, self-centered, self-regarding. Apparently I thought "I had got it" and they had not. This is a common affectation of the educated class. Indeed it's now epidemical.

But a "hipper than thou" conceit is unforgivable in the student of American culture. Naturally, it undermines your obligation to the client which is, for the duration of the contract, to treat their interests as your own. But I think it also betrays the intellectual opportunity. Anthropologists, when they are acting as anthropologists, are almost always most productive, I believe, when most credulous. When working in your own culture, you are especially well served when you are sincere and clueless – dare I say it, somewhat Canadian. When you insist that you "know better," you are supplying the assumptions you are supposed to be scrutinizing.

You Will Discover How Little You Know

I had been in the consulting business for a decade when the Harvard Business School called to ask if I wanted to come teach on a visiting appointment. I fancied myself a man of the world, someone who really "got" business. I was to discover how little I knew, sometimes, in front of 80 ferociously alert HBS students who, as they never tired of reminding me, knew quite a lot about business. In point of fact, my consulting experience had introduced me to a small piece of the puzzle. My university education in anthropology hadn't given me much more than the usual cautionary tales from the Frankfurt school. I am embarrassed to recall how limited my education and experience was.

It turns out that capitalism is a house of many mansions. There are an extraordinary number of ways to construct a market, to make and take things to market, to engage in acts of persuasion, to create exchanges, to build corporate culture(s), to invest, to innovate, and to respond to an increasingly turbulent world. To be sure, you will catch glimpses of the world according to the Frankfurt school. You will meet consumers addled by advertising and addicted to consumption. You will see the corporation driven by unworthy motives and craven people. You will meet monsters. But you will also see a world unanticipated by the received wisdom, the oral tradition within which anthropology "thinks" about capitalism. Indeed, these theories are so simplifying that when I hear them rolled out by an academic anthropologist, I think to myself, "If you were discovered saying this kind of thing about any other culture, you would be drummed out of the profession."

Capitalism is a deeply cultural enterprise. This has been on record at least since John Wheeler published *A Treatise of Commerce* in 1601. Wheeler's England was being transformed by the forces of commerce. Wrestling with this, he observed:

> there is nothing in the world so ordinary and natural unto men, as to contract, truck, merchandise, and traffic one with another, so that it is almost unpossible [*sic*] for three persons to converse together two hours, but they will fall into talk of one bargain or another, chopping [i.e., bartering], changing [i.e., exchanging], or some other kind of contract. (Wheeler 2004 [1601]: 129)

Natural? Probably not. Deeply cultural? Exactly so, especially for this Western culture, which is engaged in a search for what Lévi-Strauss called "that other message" (1968: 20). Wheeler concluded with a sentiment worthy of Ovid, that hero for the Elizabethan age: "All things come into commerce and pass into traffic" (2004 [1601]: 129).

The ceaseless circulation and exchange of meaning and value: this is the nature of the Western beast. Next to science, it is the way we go looking for "that other message." We've had glimpses of how we might think about this as a cultural system from Sahlins (1978) and Braudel (1973), but generally speaking it's as if the academic has imposed an embargo on this study (Carey 2002). The embargo lifts periodically, but only so that the anthropologist can excoriate capitalism for its failings. A dispassionate topic of this study is almost never forthcoming. That anthropologists should have talked themselves out of the study of this topic is – what's the word I'm looking for? – grim. It's grim.

After World War II, the corporation was the servant of managerial capitalism. It was preoccupied by hierarchy and defined by regulations that would impress a religious or military organization. That's mostly gone. The corporation is now flatter and less rigid. It reworks itself almost in real time. It is increasingly fluid, less something Weber would recognize and more and more an Ovidian exercise. This is a very large change but many anthropologists continue to insist that capitalism is ruled by men in the grey flannel suits.

The American family may once have been ruled by white picket orthodoxy but it now blooms with structural variation. The container in which it is sometimes housed, the suburban home, is now routinely rebuilt in the creation of a "great room" that has broken down the walls between dining room, living room, and kitchen. I know from my own research that the great room expresses a wish to create and accommodate new patterns of parenthood, childhood, food ways, and family time.

There is not a single word from anthropologists on this topic. Apparently, we assume the great room is yet another hollow trend in the consumer culture, a mere ornament of the McMansion, and the preoccupation of people mesmerized by the interior design magazine. Anthropologist, heal thyself. Simple prejudice has been allowed to flourish. Investigation has been forsaken, insight made impossible.

Using anthropological orthodoxy as a guide to American culture is a little like supposing that the place mat beneath your Denny's breakfast, and its hand-drawn city map, will serve you for the rest of the day. Wrong. This map is a miracle of self-absorption. It will only tell you where the other Denny's are.

You Will Learn to Maximize Your Strengths and Make Up Your Deficits

You come to the world of consulting with formidable powers of pattern recognition. They can throw virtually any problem at you and your anthropological training and experience will give you a way to think yourself through to a useful conclusion. Some of this advantage comes from the fact that you know how to think about culture. It may now be fragmented, decentered, distributed, and very, very complicated, but it is still for you "signal." Most of the people you will work with can only perceive it as "noise." For these people culture is a kind of dark energy of their professional world, invisible, mysterious, and finally inscrutable. That's why they will love you.

You will be tempted to suppose that this knowledge is sufficient. In point of fact, your knowledge of culture, powerful as it might be, is a small part of the larger proposition. And that's now your job: to see how many and how much of the other bodies and paradigms of knowledge out there you can master. Sometimes this is a simple matter of asking, and you will be charmed by how ready people are to tell you about their worlds. You can learn an astounding amount about "operations" over a beer. And you should. Some of these bodies of knowledge will require that you forsake some of your present assumptions and verities, and that, of course, make things much harder. Get started. You have miles to go.

If you are like me, and trained in a qualitative and interpretive anthropology, you will be especially tested by economics and any of the disciplines that use numbers to search for and capture complexity and scale. This won't come easily to you but it is, of course, bread and butter for many of the people with whom you will work. It is also, as you will eventually come to see, an essential way to understand this various and changeable world of ours. Happily, you have your anthropology to save yourself from your anthropology. You are, or ought to be, the master of free-form conversation, itself the perfect vehicle for discovering worlds constructed with assumptions at odds with your own. Anthropologist, unseal thyself.

References

Braudel, Fernand (1973) *Capitalism and Material Life, 1400–1800*. London: Weidenfeld & Nicolson.

Carey, John (2002) *The Intellectuals and the Masses: Pride and Prejudice among the Literary Intelligentsia, 1880–1939*. Chicago: Academy Chicago.

Fitzgerald, Frances (1986) *Cities on a Hill: A Journey through Contemporary American Cultures*. New York: Simon & Schuster.

Lévi-Strauss, Claude (1968) *The Savage Mind*. Chicago: University Of Chicago Press.

McCracken, Grant (1988) "Diderot Unities and the Diderot Effect." In *Culture and Consumption*. Bloomington: Indiana University Press, pp. 118–129.

McCracken, Grant (1997) *Plenitude*. Toronto: Periph.: Fluide.

McCracken, Grant (2005) "On Oprah." In *Culture and Consumption II: Markets, Meaning, and Brand Management*, Bloomington: Indiana University Press, pp. 6–16.

McCracken, Grant (2006a) "Advice to a Young Consultant." *This Blog Sits at the Intersection of Anthropology and Economics*. At http://cultureby.com/2006/06/its_easy_to_spo.html, accessed Aug. 28, 2012.

McCracken, Grant (2006b) "The Artisanal Movement, and 10 Things that Define It." *This Blog Sits at the Intersection of Anthropology and Economics*. At http://cultureby.com/2006/11/the_artisanal_m.html, accessed Aug. 28, 2012.

McCracken, Grant (2006c) "Ethnography and the 'Extra Data' Opportunity." *This Blog Sits at the Intersection of Anthropology and Economics*. At http://cultureby.com/2006/09/ethnography_and.html, accessed Aug. 28, 2012.

McCracken, Grant (2007a) "Cloudy Selves (navigational metaphors just in time for summer)." *This Blog Sits at the Intersection of Anthropology and Economics.* At http://cultureby. com/2007/07/cloudy-selves-n.html, accessed Aug. 28, 2012.

McCracken, Grant (2007b) "How We Say Hello in New England." *This Blog Sits at the Intersection of Anthropology and Economics.* At http://cultureby.com/2007/07/how-we-say-hell.html, accessed Aug. 28, 2012.

McCracken, Grant (2008a) "Tim O'Reilly, Now Shall I Compare Thee to a City State." *This Blog Sits at the Intersection of Anthropology and Economics.* At http://cultureby.com/ (2008)/01/tim-oreilly now.html, accessed Aug. 28, 2012.

McCracken, Grant (2008b) *Transformations: Identity Construction in Contemporary Culture.* Bloomington: Indiana University Press.

McCracken, Grant (2009) *Chief Culture Officer.* New York: Basic Books.

McCracken, Grant (2010a) "Ida Blankenship R.I.P." *This Blog Sits at the Intersection of Anthropology and Economics.* At http://cultureby.com/2010/09/ida-blankenship-r-i-p.html, accessed Aug. 28, 2012.

McCracken, Grant (2010b) "Why Do American Parents Call their Kids 'Buddy'?" *This Blog Sits at the Intersection of Anthropology and Economics.* At http://cultureby.com/2010/11/ why-do-american-parents-call-their-kids-buddy.html, accessed Aug. 28, 2012.

McCracken, Grant (2011) "Being Human: The UK and US Version." *This Blog Sits at the Intersection of Anthropology and Economics.* At http://cultureby.com/2011/04/being-human-us-and-uk-versions.html, accessed Aug. 28, 2012.

McCracken, Grant (2012) *Culturematic: How Reality TV, John Cheever, a Pie Lab, Julia Child, Fantasy Football . . . Will Help You Create and Execute Breakthrough Ideas.* Boston: Harvard Business Review Press.

Sahlins, Marshall (1978) *Culture and Practical Reason.* Chicago: University Of Chicago Press.

Silverstein, Michael (1976) "Shifters, Linguistic Categories, and Cultural Description." In *Meaning in Anthropology.* Albuquerque: University of New Mexico Press, pp. 11–55.

Wheeler, John (2004 [1601]) *A Treatise of Commerce.* Clark, NJ: Lawbook Exchange.

Wolfe, Alan (1998) *One Nation, After All.* New York: Viking.

Wolfe, Tom (1998) *A Man in Full.* New York: Farrar, Straus and Giroux.

Chapter 11

Becoming a Practicing Disaster Anthropologist

Susanna M. Hoffman

Susanna Hoffman's involvement with disaster began the day her own house burned down. In the course of this chapter she describes how this transformative experience led her to become an independent disaster consultant. Hoffman provides moving descriptions of how disaster manifests itself in human terms around the globe, as well as a comprehensive account of the various ways we respond collectively to these disasters, as a way of situating her own work and contributions. Her perspective as a highly experienced consultant practitioner who has nonetheless maintained an independent identity is particularly valuable and interesting.

An Unexpected Turn

I decided to become an anthropologist at the age of 14. I laughingly say that it was because, as a person who still characterizes her culturally bifurcated upbringing as akin to the split-screen segment in the movie *Annie Hall*, I wasn't sophisticated enough to become a psychologist. Psychologists, I calculated, were so evolved they could ask *why* they were the way they were. I was back at the *what*. And so I set out to study the *what*. What makes all the different people of the world, including my own disjointed lineages, so different?

As an anthropologist, I originally took to what was obvious, given my background. I concentrated on kinship and social organization. I also specialized in ideology and symbolism, and because I was interested in the depth of culture, I chose the long cultural legacy of Europe and the Indo-Europeans as my area. But a

A Handbook of Practicing Anthropology. First Edition. Edited by Riall W. Nolan.
© 2013 John Wiley & Sons, Inc. Published 2013 by John Wiley & Sons, Inc.

calling in life that may seem focused, even a sort of quest, when first elected can take unforeseen shifts and carry the voyager to destinations and purposes entirely unanticipated. It is as if you were to step into a river expecting to cross to the other side, but instead are buoyed to shoals you had not envisioned but which end up being far more fulfilling than you could have imagined. That is what happened to me.

On the evening of October 20, 1991 I received a call while thousands of miles away at a conference in Greece that my home and everything I owned had burned down in the Oakland–Berkeley firestorm. The fire was the largest urban conflagration in American history. It consumed 3,356 homes and 456 apartments, killed 25 people, and left 6,000 homeless. After a frantic two-hour drive and five flights, I arrived back home to learn two irrevocable things: my whole life had been turned upside-down and I was the closest thing to a laboratory experiment an anthropologist ever gets. I was standing in a pile of ashes 18 inches high that had once been my three-story house, three copies of my years of research, all my writing, my curriculum vitae, photos, library, coffee pot, and computer. I was also witnessing everything I had ever studied in anthropology unfold in front of my eyes. Exposed as if on a dissecting table were the nature of kinship and marital relations, the fragility of voluntary associations, the rise of political agendas, the eruption of health and psychological issues, the call of religion, the strength of place attachment, the mapping of time and space, the nature of identity, the many facets of conflict, the potency of unity, the facts of gender inequality, the rise of new linguistic terms, the creation of myth, the mightiness of history, the upshot of ideology, and far, far more.

I discovered yet something else. Countless people around the world were suffering or had suffered what I was going through, be it from fire, earthquake, tornado, hurricane, tsunami, eruption, drought, avalanche, meltdown, toxic spill, explosion, or creeping contamination, that such events occur on a continual basis, some sudden, some slowly amassing, and that, due to a myriad of factors, the numbers of people suffering from them was growing exponentially every year. The effects on people's societies and cultures were as great as on individuals. Indeed, the fabric of whole places and ways of living was often torn to shreds. As a consequence, my compassion and my wholehearted absorption were ignited. Practically overnight, I changed, and so did my anthropology. From being essentially abstract and theoretical, I undertook a humanitarian involvement the likes of which I could never have foreseen, nor could I have predicted the outcome. I embarked on a career that has made me more involved, ardent, and gratified than I have been before. I became a disaster specialist and a practitioner. It is now my life and how I make my living.

My feet still mired in soot, almost immediately, I wrote an article on what I was seeing anthropologically about the trajectory my fellow survivors and I were going through. That piece was picked up and published in a post-traumatic stress journal. Searching through the schedule of sessions at the next American Anthropological Association meeting, I found the almost singular anthropologist who was writing on the subject of disaster, Anthony Oliver-Smith. We joined forces and subsequently co-edited two books on the topic, each contributing a number of chapters we had personally written as well. As a result of those and other articles and speeches, I became the first recipient of the Aegean Initiative, a double Fulbright aimed at achieving a cooperative relationship between Greece and Turkey in response to their mutual earthquakes. From there I was invited to speak at numerous conferences and workshops. Now, a number of years later, I am called in to advise on disaster concerns for government and nongovernment agencies, institutes, and organizations worldwide. I address both national and international congresses and corporations. I go where disasters threaten or have occurred to confer. I have a website and founded my own disaster consulting business. Along with many locations in the United States, Greece, and Turkey where events have occurred, I have worked in India, Indonesia, Uzbekistan, Kazakhstan, and El Salvador.

More importantly, I have become an activist and advocate for the victims and survivors of disaster. They are of every color, sex, and sexual orientation. The come from every class, caste, economic sector, and political division. They live on every continent and adhere to an entire panoply of cultural traditions. They dwell in habitats from mud hut cluster to village to metropolis and, after an event, generally in camps. Most often the destruction they suffer is far worse than mine, with much death and injury along with loss. Their recovery takes far longer and is more arduous. Furthermore, disasters are growing in area, magnitude, and extent of harm. The aggregate of calamities happening annually has long been grievous, but it has magnified with burgeoning mega-cities, the movement of people to coastal areas, climate change, more and more people living on fault lines, hillsides, behind levees, and in other hazardous zones, and the tally of those impacted has likewise escalated. So have the concomitant costs.

In recent years a host of events have occurred, making it perfectly clear just how many places and people sustain life-altering calamities. Truly devastating catastrophes have taken place in Japan, Haiti, Chile, China, Indonesia, Fiji, Iceland, New Zealand, Australia, Thailand, and Louisiana and Missouri in the United States. Other events, which have attracted less attention, have occurred all across Central America, in Brazil, North Korea, Poland, Vanuatu, Tonga, Peru, Pakistan, India, and the states of Wisconsin, Texas, Oklahoma, and Mississippi. Some of the episodes have occurred where disasters are chronic, even predictable; others where catastrophes are intermittent or totally unexpected. Some have been a result of environmental triggers; others have been caused by human activity – though it is a mantra of disaster study that there is no such thing as a natural disaster, they are all human-caused at one level or another.

In every context in which I now ply my trade, my work and words are directed toward mitigating people's vulnerability and diminishing their plight. I have become a broker dedicated to aiding victims, steering agencies to appropriate solutions, resisting dangerous development, reversing the all too common re-victimization of survivors, and forestalling the global trends that are putting more and more people into peril. Rising from the ashes of my own catastrophe, I have evolved into a passionate and paid interceder not only for individuals involved in disaster, but for their cultures, their lifeways, perceptions, values, and ideologies. As well, I have become a mouthpiece, bringing the social and cultural insights derived from the upshot surrounding disaster into the scope of my chosen field. In a nutshell, I have never stopped being an anthropologist. I have merely turned my focus upon a critical and planetary problem rather than an academic one. The theories, the methodology, the analysis of my field have never disappeared from my work. Quite the opposite: they add to it and are necessary for it. In addition, what I contribute from my anthropology background has become vitally significant to those from other fields and disciplines involved with the same problems.

Why This Field?

You don't have to become a disaster anthropologist, or enter any other humanitarian field as I did, nor should you. I don't recommend it. Do not get singed, tumbled, buried, drenched, exposed, or starved in order to enter the vocation. It is entirely possible simply to choose disasters as a topic and field without experiencing one. I have colleagues who have become disaster practitioners because some catastrophe affected the site of their fieldwork. Others have entered the field because some event called upon them to go and give aid. Having become amazed or dismayed, they stayed with the work. Some were people in other employment with an anthropological degree or background when they witnessed the complexities of how a particular disaster happened and felt impelled to unearth the circumstances of others. In short, you can choose such an endeavor for many valid reasons. They range from those mentioned above to an emotion or drive that entices you, to witnessing the effects on someone or some place near you, or to an employment opportunity you have actively pursued or has fallen in your lap.

Nor is disaster the only humanitarian field a person wishing to become – or is offered employment as – a practicing anthropologist can embrace. Unfortunately, the needs and challenges in the humanitarian realm are all too abundant. It seems we live in a world where the image of Pandora's box, with all the evils inflicted on the human species, has been realized. The choice of which iniquity to tackle is legion. For example, besides disasters, there exist the perils of poverty, illiteracy, starvation, disease, deformity, conflict, genocide, climate change, environmental deterioration, exploitation, slavery, migration, and resettlement. And this is the short list.

On the other hand, there are many persuasive reasons to seek involvement in the field of disaster. As I mentioned above, calamities of various sorts occur on every location, fall helter-skelter on every people, and the number of events and of people affected is multiplying. The sorts of issues involved are anything but simple. They include almost every inquiry that might exercise the anthropological mind and, in their devastating wholeness, encompass all the matters other humanitarian efforts focus on, such as poverty, unemployment, illness, environment, and resettlement.

People experiencing disaster undergo more than the loss of belongings. They sustain marginalization, displacement, ghettoization, and privation. Temporary shelters often turn into permanent survivor settlements. Fickle agencies, like merry-go-rounds, tire of them. They brook the arrival of mobs of outsiders who grab all the emergent opportunities. Domestic violence rises. The poor and ethnic, often the most vulnerable to start with, suffer ongoing inequality. Economic restoration arrives only slowly and often not at all. Land lies in ruin; families are scattered. These destinies arrive with both fast-onset disasters, such as earthquakes and meltdowns, and slow-onset ones, such as drought and contamination. Disasters further entail corruption, political hegemony, neoliberal agendas, power struggles, contestation, sexual exploitation, violence, class and race snobbery, and media influence. In short, calamities offer the practitioner a veritable shopping mall of ills. Consequently, the angles that can be taken and possibilities that exist in disaster work are manifold. Then again, the other humanitarian domains involve equally complex morasses.

Due to the growing numbers affected worldwide, the employment prospects in disaster work have increased, as they have in every humanitarian domain. Ironically, this opening has occurred just as employment in the academic sector has decreased. Starting at the top with international institutions: the United Nations has a number of intersecting branches that deal with disasters and their consequences. The various commissions range from those handling immediate relief to those addressing long-term reconstruction. Others treat health concerns, all manner of economic rehabilitation, human rights and property infractions, forced migration, violence, and perennially entrenched encampment. Almost all other major international organizations, such as the World Health Organization, the World Food Organization, and the International Monetary Fund, similarly have branches that deal with catastrophes. In addition, almost every affluent country, the United States included, has an international arm of their national government that addresses foreign disaster aid. These include, for example, USAID, Disaster Aid UK, SPA from Italy, SIDA from Scandinavia, and so on.

Working alongside governmental departments, countless non-governmental organizations concentrate on disaster internationally. Most countries cannot recover without the help of civil society aid, nor can most nations alone afford the costs. Among the nongovernmental groups too many to list are the International Red Cross and Red Crescent, CARE, Doctors without Borders, World Vision, Catholic Relief Services and those of other denominations, Save the Children, AmeriCares, and Oxfam. Over 90 nongovernmental relief delegations arrived after the Ismet earthquake of 1999 in Turkey and over 400 in Aceh, Sumatra after the south Asian tsunami of 2004.

Each of these organizations tends to have a particular focus: a country (e.g., Kenya), a type of problem (e.g., rescue or building shelters), or a class of people (e.g., children or a special minority). Also there is a particular period when they enter the scene and length of time they stay. They clean up, construct everything from temporary shelters to permanent structures, do job training, and teach new skills. Some are secular, some religious-based. Dismayingly, some proselytize; most don't. Fraternal and sororal associations have long incorporated disaster help. Various professional groups, such as lawyers, firemen, police, and teamsters, have disaster response arms. Indeed, as the numbers of events and persons affected by calamity have grown worldwide, so have the number and kind of nongovernmental legations. In fact, they have proliferated. This applies to national and local organizations as well. Truth be told, there is funding along with altruistic gratification to be had in disaster. A further fact is that they all need advisers, organizers, field-workers, and technicians.

Internally within the United States, the Federal Emergency Management Agency (FEMA) is the most recognized and important governmental disaster responder, but it is by no means the sole authority dealing with disasters. Numerous other bureaus, including the National Oceanic and Atmospheric Administration (NOAA), the Department of Housing and Urban Development (HUD), the Agricultural Department, the Commerce Department, and the Forest Service, also offer programs and commissions in the field.

There exist numerous nongovernmental institutions that focus on disaster operating on a national level as well. Most famous and long-standing is, again, the Red Cross, but there are also many others, like the Salvation Army, the National Emergency Response Team, the Volunteers of America, and religious, fraternal, and professional delegations. The number is legion. Moreover, each state has a local disaster management office, as do most counties and cities. To top these off, each particular event, be it a tornado or a flood, gives rise to numerous newly formed aid agencies dealing with everything from rescue to rebuilding. Again, each of these requires personnel, experts, and organizers of many sorts.

Numerous for-profit organizations also enter the disaster picture. For a payment, they generally offer professional management services, tactics, debris removal, distribution of supplies, and the like.

They also vie for construction contracts. In addition – and to my mind the most important – self-help groups also arise from within the ranks of the victims and survivors. They often seek aid and advice. Consulting for them often becomes an altruistic gift. Nonetheless, it is part of what a devoted and passionate practitioner does; they also give.

Research grants come into play, and you do not necessarily need to have an academic position and an overseeing institution to receive them. However, you do need a background and reputation in the field. Support can be had from such quasi-governmental institutions as the Fulbright Association or numerous private research associations, but each does require a research proposal. Fraternal and other associations like the Rotary Club or Shriners often support individuals by providing certain kinds of help, but those too require at least an application.

Of course, you can always simply volunteer and in time, if you wish, work your way into a position with some establishment. Or, taking on a cause, you can form your own organization. Jodi Williams, who won the Nobel Peace Prize, started the International Campaign to Ban Landmines with just one person, herself. She called it "international" because she had a friend in England who said, "Sure, put my name on it." From that a mighty movement grew which reached around the world and continues to operate. All sorts of people start up aid organizations on their own.

Or you can do as I did, build a reputation from your academic and popular writings and from there generate work or launch a consultancy. In all honesty, though, I warn you that this route takes time, effort, and fortitude.

A person entering a disaster or another humanitarian field can have a particular geographic and cultural area in which they work, say Central America, especially if the region is one that sustains a chronic problem or calamities. Disasters tend to be embedded in certain environments and are repetitive features of life. Central America is a good example, for it frequently experiences earthquakes, hurricanes, mudslides, floods, and volcanic eruptions. However, entering the disaster field generally entails a commitment more to the topic than to the place. This is the most common approach for those of us from anthropology working in the domain. It offers a broader scope from which one can delve into any number of intertwined facets.

Disasters, as mentioned, offer a truly rich arena of themes. One of the advantages of humanitarian work is that, despite the seemingly one-dimensional face of each particular area, be it maternal health, genocide, water, or migration, none of these is actually simple. All are multifaceted. They are intellectually and compassionately profuse, which means they are rarely boring. Choosing the topic over a place allows leeway to explore and advise on many aspects. It means a career path that, rather than being narrow, can be quite broad and comprehensive. It can also involve working in many sites, not just one, a travel-seeking anthropologist's dream.

Personally, as well as having worked on many sorts of catastrophes and in numerous places, I advise, write, and speak on an ever growing number of issues. These include such things as outlining the stages of the disaster experience, analyzing whether a culture changes due to disaster, discovering hidden victims, and dealing with the many issues relating to gender. I've also worked on such topics as the return of old customs; new social structures, economics, and politics; how to develop effective disaster policy; and such esoterica as the influences of cultural ideology and imagery on disaster response and mitigation.

In the field of disaster – and the same holds true for a number of other humanitarian concerns – it has become clear in recent years how badly needed the training and perspectives of anthropology are. As more and more research has illuminated the ways in which natural and technological calamities develop, the theoretical and methodological pertinence of our particular discipline has become more manifest. Without question, anthropology as a social science is in a position to parse the totality of disasters in a way no other social science can.

Only anthropology takes into its reckoning the three planes that interface in catastrophe: environmental, biological, and sociocultural. The developmental and comparative perspectives of anthropological research also uniquely merge with disaster understanding. Disasters are the result of long, complex processes; they do not drop upon communities like bombshells. Their cultural, historical, and social phylogenies are manifold. Anthropology examines the small against the large, contrasts one society against another, and addresses social continuity as well as change – all central aspects of disaster. Added to these, anthropology contributes its keystone methodology – on the ground, down to earth, ethnographic fieldwork. It has become increasingly apparent that all disasters are local in their construction and local in their successful recovery. Not incorporating the local culture and survivor-driven recovery has led to chronic catastrophes, whose solution is anthropology's time-honored methodology. The theories and vehicles of analysis are crucial, but only ethnography truly elucidates how disasters are constructed, what recovery entails, and what the elements, often enshrouded, are that lead to a people's vulnerability.

In addition, anthropological study encompasses all the communities of the globe, including where most disasters take place. While North America experiences more wind events than any other continent, Asia sees the largest overall number of calamities. South America is chronically beset by a multitude of events, while fires rage across Australia annually, and Africa habitually endures horrific droughts. Meanwhile, seas and rivers are rising everywhere, with consequent land loss and flooding.

What It's Like: The Ups and Downs of the Flight

Humanitarianism has been covertly and overtly at the heart of anthropology from the beginnings of the field. From the earliest days, anthropologists were concerned with the disappearance of the many differing people around the world and their lifeways. They sought to preserve their customs, languages, beliefs, artifacts, and lives, considering the various peoples and their forms of existing equally valuable. The question of social justice has always underpinned that interest, and that question remains.

Working as a practicing anthropologist in the realm of disaster follows the same path. It entails saving people, their traditions, lifestyles, convictions, belongings, and habitats. It includes the justice of keeping them on their land, in homes of their choosing, and running their own lives. Formal charities started with the Byzantine empire, though undoubtedly the practice existed before. Now the concept of philanthropy and the foundations that exercise it have mushroomed. Political and moral shifts in philosophy and practice in recent decades have heightened the idea of our mutual obligation and the growth of social conscience.

All that is to the good. Unfortunately, one of the consequences is a growing shift in the structure of international and human-to-human relations that has resulted in a new hegemony of benefactor nations over recipient ones. The evolving situation brings to the fore a question: people may need our compassion, but do they need our power and patronage? Depending on the morality of the benefactor, the effects on the recipient can be dire. The only answer to the looming problem is the call for good practitioners.

The importance of being a disaster and practitioner anthropologist is undeniable at many levels. The bottom line is that disasters kill, and working to saving lives is crucial. Disasters destroy homes and communities and leave people devastated and impoverished. They are fearfully expensive in many ways, including in terms of human diversity and cultural legacy. How can we as both anthropologists and humans not turn our minds to helping? Disasters also have an urgency factor. The needs of the people impacted are immediate.

Besides the rewards of simple benevolence, there are other benefits to being a disaster practitioner. Inasmuch as I focus primarily on anthropology, part of what I enjoy about my work is that it encompasses learning far beyond my own discipline. I engage with many non-academic practitioners who come from dozens of backgrounds, including architecture, finance, politics, science, and energy. As well, the endeavor is by its nature interdisciplinary. I interact with geologists, meteorologists, seismologists, structural engineers, contractors, city planners, geographers, sociologists, and psychologists, and the wonderful socially minded who run outreach programs. I talk to the military, search and rescue personnel, firemen, and bulldozer drivers, along with local, national, and international government officials. I travel a great deal.

Generally, my efforts consist in giving talks and guidance to officials, more than working in the midst of the devastation, but not always. Usually I stay for days or weeks, sometimes for months. I set fees on a flexible scale, charging for time and effort, but also with compassion for organizations that cannot pay. I confess that, while I need to cover my living expenses, money has never been a great draw to me, and that is a choice a person contemplating practitioner work should consider. Positions in government and nongovernmental agencies are also not known for lavish remuneration.

There are drawbacks, of course. Employment in an organization or agency can produce a steady paycheck, albeit modest, but being an independent like me means that income is neither steady nor dependable. At various places I have worked, I have faced ethical dilemmas. I have encountered NGO staff who carried guns. I have clashed with some agencies that were more concerned with protecting themselves than the people they were assisting, although they were volunteers while the victims were indigenous. To me this was an unacceptable contradiction to anthropology's basic moral credo.

Governmental agencies are by and large bound by structured procedures that can be quite rigid. They also tend to involve a hierarchy of officials who say no before they say yes. Nongovernment agencies compete for uncertain donor dollars, and the competition can be quite fierce. They will sometimes only undertake high-profile projects, such as building hospitals and schools that will flaunt their name, rather than meeting the often mundane but crucial requirements of those in distress.

Often both government and nongovernment organizations overestimate the amount of territory they can service or the help they can provide such that they fail people. Other times they provide what they think is essential rather than determining what those they serve deem important. I experienced that myself. With my house in complete ruins, one well-meaning group provided me with a box of household cleaning products.

Finally, getting heard by those in authority, or seeking flexibility within a rigid top-down, predetermined formula, is often a fight. Agencies tend to find it easier to apply a single, cookie-cutter approach than to alter their relief according to the nuances of the culture. On-site managers in post-disaster rubble may see only their mission – to get supplies delivered, put up tents – without considering the broader picture. On one occasion I struggled to get a director to hire actual victims of the calamity to accomplish the tasks at hand rather than employ the unharmed outsiders who arrived on the scene. He was recalcitrant. He merely wanted to accomplish the tasks regardless of whom he used. Yet the victims of the calamity had lost all their livelihood and were destitute. Even when you are handing out pots and pans, economic help is part of the goal. Still, irrefutably, all agencies governmental and nongovernmental, and all the individuals working for them, have good intentions at heart.

The difficulties of getting into the work as an anthropologist are always somewhat challenging. We remain a small and frequently misunderstood social science. I cannot tell you how many people think I dig up old bones. From within my own discipline, I have been dismissed for being independent and not having an academic position. Those hiring me often hesitate because I cannot claim an academic title or institutional connection despite my publication record.

In disaster work, other larger branches of social sciences, sociology in particular, have risen to garner much of the opportunity and acclaim. Commonly, it is because their analyses are more quantitative than anthropology's more qualitative approach. With a stack of graphs and charts, their investigations seem more justifiably financeable to officials. Nevertheless, the value of the anthropological perspective is increasingly called for. Risk reduction and successful recovery cannot occur in the absence of cultural sensitivity, and we are the scientists who interact directly with people in such a way as to learn how communities actually function. Interestingly, the new head of the World Bank is an anthropologist and doctor, who before his new influential assignment had been employed by USAID, UNAIDS, and WHO.

All in all, the most satisfactory reward for being a practitioner in any sort of assistance program is still simply personal gratification. I am helping. I have advice to give. Everything, virtually every facet, of anthropology is important in what I do, and thus I stress getting a thorough grounding in all aspects of the discipline. Proverbial though it may be, the key to anthropological contribution is thinking outside the box. Embrace the subtle and flexible. Quite clearly, there are patterns and universals in all disaster scenarios. Yet each situation is different. Addressing the varying shades of difference is our stock in trade. If you are culturally attuned, you will see the solutions that make for success. In one instance in my work, where men and women alike wore cotton sarongs, the women had been stripped of economic viability by their calamity. I was able to have an agency bring in hundreds of treadle sewing machines. Granted, it was not the sort of employment that gave women a higher status, nor did it break the culture's gendered glass ceiling, but it did provide the women with cash income. In another situation, the agency I was advising was about to pull up all stakes when the government insisted we be accompanied by an armed escort, even to remote villages. I advanced the solution that the escort always be escorted. It required a rearrangement of assignments, but allowed the succor to continue.

Grab all the opportunities that come by; don't hesitate. Take the appointment even if it is under-compensated at first. Apply for the grant. Tact is always good, but don't forget to be the voice of the people. Often agencies have never heard that voice. And do provide the agency with feedback on their missteps.

Everything you learn could well have considerable significance for disaster professionals from every field, from academic to on-the-ground, so share. And take what you learn back to anthropology. There is a laudable change in academic circles emanating from the work of practitioners, particularly in the disaster sphere. In the last 20 years perhaps the most innovative concepts and perspectives in the discipline have come from disaster work, once a marginal study in the discipline.

Applied practitioners have introduced the notion of vulnerability and how many ills – including catastrophes – are socially constructed, often latently, often over time. We have begun to examine what makes a society resilient. These observations have crossed into mainstream anthropology. They have been borrowed and utilized in many branches. Disasters also expose all the issues I saw unfolding before me in the flames of the Oakland fire. Hurricane Katrina stripped off the cotton curtain that had obscured hidden social and cultural processes occurring in America. Calamities further reveal the connections between local hamlets to multiple levels of governance, while also exposing the stark reality of globalization. I believe this will be the story of practitioner engagement in every area. Practitioner fields are the wave of the future – not only in employment but in conceptual advancement.

Chapter 12

An Anthropologically Based Consulting Firm

Cathleen Crain and Nathaniel Tashima

Cathleen Crain and Niel Tashima are the founders and owners of LTG Associates, one of the most successful anthropology-based consulting firms in the US. They provide us with the background to their decision to go into business, and tell the story of how LTG grew and developed. Throughout the chapter, two themes get special attention: what's specifically anthropological about what LTG Associates does; and how and why Crain and Tashima have taken the business in the direction(s) they have. Along the way, they provide a fascinating description of what it actually takes to create and run a successful business. They conclude the chapter with a discussion of what it means to be a professional anthropologist, and what it means for practitioners such as themselves to engage with their discipline.

Introduction

In introducing our firm to those who do not know us, we use the following, or a variation:

LTG Associates is a minority-owned small business in its 30th year. LTG Associates is the oldest and largest anthropologically based consulting firm in North America. LTG's work centers on research, assessment, design, monitoring, evaluation, and support services. With experience in all 50 states, all territories and freely associated states of the U.S., and over 50 countries, we specialize in the development and conduct of health and human services programs, the content of policy, and the shape of communication. From multi-year contracts to short-term consulting assignments, LTG works equally

A Handbook of Practicing Anthropology. First Edition. Edited by Riall W. Nolan.
© 2013 John Wiley & Sons, Inc. Published 2013 by John Wiley & Sons, Inc.

well with quantitative and qualitative methods and demonstrates creative flexibility while maintaining quality standards and meeting goals and deadlines.

A mission-driven organization, LTG works collaboratively with organizations to plan, develop, implement, and improve services and systems. LTG's four main areas of practice are:

- Capacity development, support, and training for nonprofit, community service, and nongovernmental organizations. Areas of focus include assessment, program and system planning, development, infrastructure development, and monitoring and evaluation.
- Program design, monitoring, and evaluation.
- Program and policy research, planning, evaluation, and support.
- Program- and policy-focused convening and facilitation.

LTG uses a collaborative approach in all of our work, based on a strong belief that our work is an instrument of our client's improvement, and in the critical nature of partnerships and the inclusion of communities of interest and other stakeholders from the beginning of the work. Much of LTG's work has centered on the conduct of formative, process, and outcome research that focuses on the development and management of programs, the shape of communication, and policy that affects the lives of individuals and communities.

If you didn't hear anthropology in this narrative, consider the core skills and perspectives of anthropology, and read it carefully again. By reading this narrative, you will have learned briefly about our history, philosophy, geographic reach, skills, focus areas, and, by the way, that our work is based in anthropology. In this chapter, we will discuss how we came to run a consulting firm grounded in anthropology and both the joys and challenges of taking a road not only less traveled, but until recently, largely unknown. We will also reflect on what it takes to run a business no matter what its focus. Finally, we will reflect on where we see the potential roles for professional anthropologists in the future.

Who We Are

Cathleen became a professional anthropologist with the specific intention of working on improving access to and the appropriateness of healthcare services. Cathleen began her career in 1978 as an anthropologist/therapist at a regional substance abuse treatment center, after which she became director of research and evaluation for a prisoners' health project, then a consultant on health services, and, before LTG, in a series of positions in refugee health and resettlement culminating in a national position. Cathleen holds a master's degree in physical anthropology from McMaster University, a strong, four-field school. She was focused on becoming a professional anthropologist from the time she began training and determined that, while she was offered PhD programs, her master's had prepared her for a professional career.

Niel became an anthropologist and began his career focused on mental health issues, particularly with Asian Americans (AA) and Pacific Islanders (PI). One of his early positions was directing the first mental health services for arriving Vietnamese refugees in 1975. He then worked with community groups to organize community-based mental health services for Asian Americans and Pacific Islanders in several cities. He went on first to work in and later to lead national research on AA/PI mental health. Niel holds a PhD in psychological anthropology from Northwestern University; each of his universities has emphasized a four-field education.

Founding a Consulting Firm

We decided to create a consulting firm after having worked together on a large community assessment project. We both realized through that project that it was particularly rewarding but also especially comfortable to work with another anthropologist. We were both aware that it was not often that, as professional anthropologists working in our respective fields, we each had an opportunity to design and conduct work that was distinctly flavored by our discipline. We also understood from that experience that even though no one had prepared either of us to undertake real world projects grounded in anthropology, when we brought our skills to a project the shape, conduct, and outcomes were distinctly different. In a good way. In a way that has marked all of our work together for 30 years, even when nothing in the title said "anthropology." Our training as anthropologists in the four fields combined with our work in community-based organizations has informed much of our vision and LTG's development over the years.

As an organization, we have worked with all 50 states and in over 50 countries internationally. The two of us have worked across the United States and in the freely associated states and territories in the Pacific (American Samoa, Commonwealth of the Northern Marianas, Guam, Federated States of Micronesia, Republic of the Marshall Islands, and Republic of Palau). We have also worked across southeast Asia (the Philippines, Vietnam, Cambodia, Thailand, and Malaysia). We engaged in projects in Kenya, Tanzania, Tunisia, South Africa, and Zambia. Our skills as anthropologists have shaped our focus on crossing cultural boundaries and strengthened our approach to emphasizing local concerns and input. In much of what we have done, there has been a strong effort to bring various communities into the program, policy, or evaluation process so that participants can find their voices in our work together.

We began our firm as two practitioners and it has grown to multi-staff, multi-office operations. We have been in the fortunate position to have each other as partners in an endeavor which had no role model or plan to follow when we started. The ability to be able to constantly compare our perspectives and understanding in open conversation has been essential to our continued success.

Launching a Firm

We made the decision to launch a consulting group with absolutely no formal grounding in business – not the preferred or recommended preparation to ensure success. We would come to learn about such imperatives as business status, licensure, accounting, banking, taxes, employee benefits, labor law, and insurance. Over the course of the years we would employ or contract with accountants (inside and outside), bookkeepers, lawyers (business, labor, and procurement), insurance (health, disability, personal property, facilities, professional liability, valuable papers, and travel) and financial advisers, human resources professionals, real estate brokers, bankers, travel agents, and public relations and development consultants. While we are both four-field trained, neither of us can recall the courses that would have prepared us for the particular, complicated, and sometimes arcane challenges of developing and running a business.

But, before all of that, we had a vision that we as anthropologists, had something special to offer and that creating an organization that would allow us to shape projects grounded in anthropology would lead us to interesting places. And, oh the interesting places we have been! We have directed more than 200 projects and in many of them we have had the opportunity to actually do some of the work. Our projects have ranged from working with very small nonprofit organizations to working with some of the largest federal and international organizations. We have had contracts that have been the basis for the development of federal and international health programs and policies.

There have been three distinct but complementary major phases to our work together which illustrate the arc of developing and running our firm. In the next section we will discuss those phases.

Refugee and Community-Focused Projects

The projects

When we began LTG both of us had been working with refugee communities and that was the launching point for our firm's work. We conducted and provided technical assistance in community development across California and then nationally over a period of several years. Many of the projects were focused on assisting leaders of newly arrived communities to understand the American system into which they had come and to develop the internal structures to be able to help their own people adjust and thrive. Examples of the topics of the work that we undertook collaboratively with community leadership included:

- teaching Civics 101 so that community leadership could understand how to use the American systems to encourage community participation and to prevent their community from facing official discrimination;
- developing tools and aiding community leadership in navigating and negotiating with healthcare providers and systems to recognize traditional practices;

- developing tailored job training programs for new communities in such topics as medical assistance, court reporting, and, taxi driving.

But, most importantly, we provided willing, respectful, and available American translators and interpreters who enabled people to have discussions about the topics of central interest to them, even when the discussions never occurred directly. How will our children know who they are? How will the women develop job skills but still value our culture? How will we honor our culture but still adapt to the American ways and the demands of the support and service systems? Through this period we assisted at least 20 refugee community-based organizations and a number of related community-based organizations develop programs responsive to both funding availability and community-determined needs.

The anthropology

An essential anthropological facet of this early work was that we were not of the culture. We were interested outsiders who had no power over anyone and were not interested in owning anything that belonged to the people with whom we worked. We were respectful of the cultures the newly arrived communities brought with them and had knowledge of the culture in which they were living, providing the opportunity for interpretation to both sides. We had no purpose in the situation other than to assist everyone in being successful at understanding the other and working well together. As anthropologists we could ask the basic questions, "Tell me how that works in your culture," "Please explain how you would translate the American/English idea in your language/culture," or "Please help me understand how you experience this event."

The business

It was during this first phase that we began to understand some of the imperatives of the development of a business. While there were only two of us then, there were bills and taxes to be paid, insurances to be taken, and equipment to be bought and maintained. These imperatives resulted in our first internal hire, a bookkeeper, and our first consultant, an accountant. As we were to learn, the larger and more complicated our business became, the more people we would need to assist us in its running. Early on we made a simple decision that has continued to allow us to be a successful business: develop an administrative infrastructure ahead of need. This has meant and continues to mean developing administrative staff who can manage a business and understand those imperatives. At times this has meant more work for the two of us, but it has allowed the business to continue to be able to respond to new challenges.

HIV/AIDS

The second major phase began when we were asked to develop and conduct a community assessment of active, not-in-treatment, intravenous drug users in a metropolitan area to understand how their knowledge, attitudes, beliefs, and behaviors might affect their risk behavior for HIV. When asked if we could conduct the study and have a report ready in under six months, we said the words that have so often led us to fascinating and sometimes scary places: "Sure, we can do that."

We developed a method that was profoundly anthropologically informed and resulted in a deep and complex picture of the variety of peoples who used intravenous drugs. The method was seen by the Centers for Disease Control and Prevention (CDC) and we were asked to adapt it for four cohorts of HIV-prevention projects over the following years. We also provided technical assistance in community outreach to a variety of at-risk populations. The method is the community identification process (CID), eventually named an effective behavioral intervention (EBI) by CDC, and over 20 years later it continues to be taught by the CDC to those wanting to conduct behavioral change interventions. This first project begun in 1987, and the method development launched us into working in HIV and sexually transmitted disease (STD) prevention.

We have worked in HIV and STD prevention over the past 25 years both domestically and internationally, with CDC, with the Ryan White Care Act at the Health Resources and Services Administration, and with the World Health Organization (WHO). For the WHO we conducted a global, community-based HIV prevention evaluation and provided monitoring and evaluation capacity building to program grantees. While there were many other topics and projects that we worked on in this period, HIV/AIDs provided the most important arena for the use of anthropology.

The anthropology

The critical anthropological skills that were utilized in our HIV/AIDs work included the ability to learn how populations saw themselves, and what was important to them as communities that would inform the development of clearly focused prevention and treatment effective programs. The skills of anthropology allowed clinicians, researchers, program developers, and outreach workers to respectfully reach populations and not to define them by their risk behaviors. The employment of anthropologically based skills created a safe and replicable process for service providers and clinic staff to respectfully engage with a variety of communities and to value the community knowledge. The method also placed affected communities and individuals in direct contact with the health providers who would mediate their access to and the construction of prevention services. A clinician who received the training later became a provider of training to other agencies. The following is an excerpt of what she recently said about the method:

...we have used CID extensively in our training and it has been used, in turn, by well over 150 agencies doing STD/HIV prevention. The other three Behavioral Training Centers also teach PROMISE and incorporate CID so our work should really be multiplied several times to account for the true impact of this method. CID allows an agency's staff to learn from an insider's perspective about a community with which they are unfamiliar, and it builds real trust between the agency and the community that facilitates the delivery of HIV prevention messages and their adoption. Many times, after a CID training we have heard participants express enthusiasm for the technique and what they anticipate learning by using it. Later, we hear from agency staff that they now have gained access to a community that was previously closed to them.

The CID method is straightforward, easy to grasp, and highly effective in meeting its objectives of providing insider information to the agency conducting CID that can be used to provide highly effective programming and increasing mutual trust between the agency and the community on which to build that programming. Niel and Cathleen are to be highly commended for developing this important ethnographic method and documenting the steps so clearly that it can be adopted by agencies that are attempting to bring health messages to communities experiencing severe health disparities.[1]

While our interest is not in teaching non-anthropologists to be anthropologists, it is to make communities accessible to those who would serve them well.

The business

It was during this period that the business of the business grew and matured. We determined early in our development that it was important to bring management skills to the organization early both to ensure that it developed well and to keep us from experiencing many of the business problems that affect small businesses. A senior administrator, a human relations specialist, and an accountant formed the core of the management side of the business. As well, we began to work to develop project managers from among the social scientists who came to join the growing practice.

The development of coherent policies that would support the growth and development of the firm became a priority during this period. One of the most challenging aspects of any business is dealing effectively with personnel: being aware of the needs of those who work in the business, and understanding and adhering to the relevant laws and regulations. Both aspects of personnel management require focused attention, and in the case of laws and regulations bringing professional expertise into the firm, and actively engaging in affirmative management. LTG developed a personnel manual that responded to a broad variety of personnel policies and issues. This manual has continued to evolve over the years as we were confronted with new issues, could provide new benefits, and as new areas of law and regulations mandated changes.

Another important area of focus was in the continued development of sophistication in accounting and financial management. This is an area that too many small businesses fail to develop and which too often becomes a vulnerability. Finally, it was during this period that there was increasing pressure for the two of us to take on more managerial and less programmatic roles. We both have significant management roles in the life of the organization; however, we have both resisted becoming desk-bound. Individually and together, we continued to be active participants and managers of projects, likely to the detriment of the growth of the firm.

Monitoring and Evaluation

The third major phase of our careers and the work of our firm has been in monitoring and evaluation (M&E). Clearly, this phase is focused on tool and method rather than topically but it has utility across topics. The topics in which we have conducted M&E have continued to be based in health and human services. We have both conducted monitoring and evaluation and provided training and capacity building for evaluation to organizations, especially community-based groups. Our M&E work has ranged from local evaluations of small programs to multi-country evaluations of global programs. Local-level projects often focus on learning and improvement for the organization as well accountability both to the sponsor and to the community that the organization served. International M&E has included running two large global contracts that resulted in nearly 400 tasks being conducted in over 50 countries. These tasks are generally focused on program improvement and accountability.

Developing and providing capacity-building activities around M&E has been a particular focus. Adapting the tools of M&E to the needs of health and social services providers has been both a challenge and an especially rewarding part of our work. We have developed tools and methods for teaching and developing proficiency in basic M&E skills. In local projects, we have woven the teaching of methods into the conduct of evaluation. At the national level, we have provided capacity building to hundreds of federal grantees. And, at the international level, we have promoted the acquisition and use of M&E skills with both small community-based programs and with large, multinational organizations.

The anthropology

This tool-and-methods-focused phase has allowed us to emphasize the use of qualitative, and in particular, anthropological methods and perspectives in M&E. We have developed a reputation for being able to utilize mixed methods (quantitative and qualitative) and to produce highly credible and richly textured findings.

An important aspect of the M&E work has been to continue to promote two areas of focus that are of particular importance to anthropologists. The first area has been the careful delineation of cultural groups within a population of interest in health and human services. The second has been in ensuring that the authentic voices of populations of concern are represented in the deliberations and decisions that affect their lives.

The business

During this phase, the business functions grew with the size and complexity of the projects undertaken. Specialized bookkeepers to ensure the speed and accuracy of internal financial functions were needed to respond to the volume of work. Lawyers to advise on contract negotiations and to ensure contract compliance were needed. Specialists in international travel and insurances were required to support high-volume, complex travel in developing countries. Project managers to ensure the quality and timeliness of work became important staff additions for successful organizational growth. And recruiting, orienting, and managing hundreds of specialized international consultants to support particular tasks was an ongoing challenge.

During this period, which continues to the time of writing, we have continued to feel the pressure of being both managers and active, engaged social scientists. But the choices made have been our own and we choose to be the drivers of the content of our work as well as centrally engaged in the running of the organization. The increasing sophistication of our management staff and systems has allowed us to disengage with some aspects of the organization's functioning. Our financial systems are recognized as being of very high quality, particularly for a small business. Our contracts and personnel management systems are sophisticated and responsive.

Even with these talented people and well-developed systems, there continue to be daily challenges that require thoughtful responses; that means time and focus. In addition, the development of new work has never been a delegated function and consumes significant time, energy, and focus. Again, this retention of core functions has had implications for the growth of the organization.

So far, we have laid out what appears to be a very linear and well-planned development process. However, the current state of LTG has not come about as a result of an always well-thought-out plan. Within this apparently smooth arc, there have been many interesting and sometimes challenging paths and cul de sacs. When we were working with refugee communities the opportunity to develop methods to work with communities at risk for HIV/AIDS appeared and we followed that path. While working in HIV/AIDS we saw the potential to marry our skills with the tools of evaluation and followed that path.

The challenge always is to recognize possibilities for engaging new aspects of the universe and being proactive about outlining future potential. This is also where the critical attribute of good anthropologists, living with and working into ambiguity, becomes central. We have believed that our skills will help to advance the work at hand and found the way to create new possibilities. And we have always believed that being a professional anthropologist had the potential for fascinating challenges and the excitement of exploration and discovery.

Moving from topic to a tools-and-methods focus also proved to be a better long-term fit for us. It is easy to become immersed in a culture and each topic truly represented a culture. During our time spent working in those cultures, we developed a high degree of facility with the language and rules of each of the cultures. As anthropologists, we are "professional strangers" (Agar 1996) who explore the intricacies of cultures and, as professional anthropologists, we use the learnings to improve services and systems through a variety of methods. While clearly these topical cultures continue to evolve, the opportunity to explore new cultures decreases as immersion in a single culture grows. Anthropologists become identified with and experts on a specific culture, and that expertise begins to constrain their potential movement. We determined that having the flexibility to move across topics was an important aspect of our interest in trying to affect the shape and quality of health and human services, and moving from a topic to a tools-and-methods focus was a decision that we made to that end.

On Being Professional Anthropologists

We have never forgotten that it is challenging to be a professional anthropologist. We know this both because we are and because we employ numbers of professional anthropologists. LTG is an unusual place where we employ and generally appreciate the skills of anthropology. But the true future of professional anthropology lies in anthropologists being engaged across all the areas of endeavor where our skills can be useful. The arenas of potential engagement are virtually without limit if anthropology as a discipline helps new professionals and students to think creatively about their skill sets and their application. As we train young anthropologists, we must give them practical skills that are firmly grounded in our tools and theory. We must teach them about ethics, critical thinking, and discipline if they are to succeed. There must also be available role models that exemplify the best of the professional side of our discipline.

There is a joke that consultants ask to see your watch and then tell you the time. The meaning is that they don't bring something new to you, but rather tell you what you already know. One of the key challenges for anthropologists is to understand and be able to clearly articulate "the anthropological difference" that is, what we will be able to discern that others might not have known without our consultation.

Anthropologists are frequently poorly prepared to explain this. As a discipline, we tend to talk about our methods when asked what difference we can make, that is, we describe process rather than outcomes. Coming up with an accessible outcome answer is still challenging, but is likely more satisfying to the questioner.

One of the key outcomes that we as anthropologists offer is the ability to understand and synthesize a wide variety of cultural (read system, organization, etc.)

perspectives, levels, and functioning, and to understand them both from the perspective of the individual actor and as a cognitive whole. This also allows us to then understand where there is congruence or conflict in either or both of the articulated and the acted cultures. Simply put, we can then diagnose where the problems lie and the nature of them. We are then in a position to assist either in reconciling the disparate parts or in helping to define new methods of functioning (read systems, programs, rules). This is our singular difference. We are also culturally neutral when we are being good anthropologists; that is, we avoid taking sides or making judgments in a conflict or dysfunction: we recognize each perspective and articulate all in a balanced manner.

We have a companion challenge to continue to educate the public about the potential of anthropological engagement. Recognizing the potential markets for anthropological skills and developing campaigns to educate them and to promote the discipline will be foreign but necessary activities. Part of our commitment to the field is to be engaged as professionals in the discipline to promote the skill building, capacity development, and career options for new and young professionals. It has also been an important part of our engagement to work at a shared understanding of the potential of professional anthropology with other aspects of the discipline.

Early on, we decided that we should actively engage with the discipline of anthropology, out of a sense of professional responsibility and accountability. We have been engaged with the Washington Association of Professional Anthropologists and the Southern California Applied Anthropology Network over the years. More recently, we have been involved in both the Society for Applied Anthropology (SfAA) and the American Anthropological Association (AAA). We have worked as committee members and led committees for the National Association of Practicing Anthropologists (NAPA), a section of AAA. We have been deeply engaged in the formal and informal review of ethics in anthropology, from co-authoring the NAPA ethics statement to participating in the 2010 AAA Ethics Task Force. We co-led a 10-year NAPA ethics practicum from the 1980s to the 1990s and are reconstituting that effort through NAPA sponsorship.

Perhaps the most important work we have done is mentoring graduate students and new professionals. We continually engage with new or aspiring professionals about what a career in anthropology can look like and to show them that a professional career can be a first choice. We provide entry to networks of senior anthropologists and other professionals we know so that our networks are continually refreshed with new people, ideas, and perspectives. As LTG we have maintained a summer research assistant position to provide an individual with support through LTG to work as part of one or several of our teams and participate in the work of our projects. All of these activities come at a cost of time and money, but we have determined it is a small investment to make in our anthropological future.

LTG has been recognized by the WAPA Praxis Award four times, more times than any single organization in Praxis Award's history: three times with an honorable mention and once as the award winner. We consider all the awards a remarkable

achievement, for the Praxis is a biannual national competition for the best professional anthropological project. It is particularly gratifying to be recognized by our
colleagues. As anthropologists, we all too often work in worlds that do not understand what it is that we do, even as they appreciate the outcomes. We believe that
being in relationship with our discipline and with other anthropologists is important both for the growth and development of individual professionals and also for
the continued development of the understanding of and support for professional
anthropology.

Our experience has been one of stepping to the edge of projects, communities,
ideas, or experience and then believing that through our skills as anthropologists,
we can be successful in going into the unknown and developing an outline of how
to get from here to that imagined future. For 30 years we have been engaging the
unknown and outlining the future in our work. We have said yes more than we have
said no, we have gone places that have defied good sense, and we have had both
more fun and more heartburn than any six people should have. Our work continues
to take us in new directions that we could not have predicted but are excited to go.
Just ask us about programs like "Decent Care" or "Healthy People" and watch us
light up as we talk about new avenues to better health. And, even today, we say,
"Sure, we can do that," knowing that our skills as anthropologists and those of our
staff, will ensure that the outcomes are appropriate to the audience, move the needle
a bit in terms of change, and, on the best days, add learnings that we can share with
others.

Note

1   Anne C. Freeman, MSPH, Assistant Professor and Director, University of Texas, South-
    western Allied Health Sciences School. Quotation printed with kind permission of Anne
    Freeman.

Reference

Agar, Michael (1996) *The Professional Stranger: An Informal Introduction to Ethnography*, 2nd
    edn. San Diego, CA: Academic Press.

Chapter 13

Nongovernmental Organizations

Adam Koons

Adam Koons, with many years of experience in a wide variety of nonprofit organizations, gives us a broad look at the field in this chapter, describing both the types of NGOs currently operating, and the kinds of roles anthropologist practitioners play within them. Koons looks at the salient characteristics shared by most NGOs, and what this means for the kinds of work opportunities they provide. He offers tips and advice for breaking into this field, as well as some caveats for newcomers. Anthropologists, he says, are not hired for their anthropology; they are hired for what they can do. Nonetheless, Koons goes on to discuss in detail why anthropologists are a very good fit with the NGO sector. He concludes this chapter with a look at typical career patterns, and some thoughts on how the field is changing.

Characteristics of the Sector

NGOs are wonderful entities. They seek to help people. They are a good fit for anthropologists. There are even more types of nongovernmental organizations (NGOs) than there are types of anthropologists. It is almost shocking to realize their magnitude. For example, according to the IRS, there are 692,482 "public charities" and 91,447 "private foundations" that all qualify as NGOs. They can be very small, with a just few staff, modest budgets, and narrow foci – such as collecting used furniture in one American community to help poor households – or surprisingly huge, with billion-dollar budgets, seeking to address issues of poverty and education and nutrition on a global scale, with offices in over 100 countries and many thousands of staff.

A Handbook of Practicing Anthropology. First Edition. Edited by Riall W. Nolan.
© 2013 John Wiley & Sons, Inc. Published 2013 by John Wiley & Sons, Inc.

NGOs, or "nonprofits" as they are often called, cover a vast array of issues, missions, objectives, stakeholders, sizes, and structures that defy description in one chapter. Within any given type or category of NGO there are hundreds, and sometimes thousands, of individual organizations with their own culture and approach. Perhaps the broadest unifying elements are that they (mostly) seek to address perceived socially oriented problems or "causes"; their financial orientation is not for profit; and their staff are motivated largely by personal beliefs and attitudes rather than the pursuit of wealth.

Without apology, this chapter, and whatever generalizations and patterns it may identify, relies on my own personal experience and that of my colleagues. I have worked for a number of large NGOs focused on addressing issues of poverty, human rights, gender equity, health, education, food and nutrition, humanitarian assistance, and so on, in less developed countries around the world, and in some instances parts of the United States. Even this type of NGO is more numerous than one might imagine. There are 591 US-based "private voluntary agencies" registered with, and therefore eligible to receive funds from, the United States Agency for International Development, though many of these are relatively small and with limited scope.

It is important also to note that my own experience is with secular NGOs. However, a great many of the largest and oldest international NGOs are faith-based and connected to a particular religious denomination. Whatever their religious orientation, they all provide assistance regardless of race, religion, ethnicity, or political persuasion.

Collectively these are often referred to as the international development and/or relief NGOs (INGOs). In addition to American INGOs, a great many are based in other "developed" countries such as the United Kingdom, Canada, France, Italy, Germany, or Australia. There are also a substantial, and ever increasing, number of local or international NGOs in less developed countries that focus on issues within their own countries. These multitudes of NGOs represent a significant range of opportunities for anthropologists' involvement.

Breaking into NGO Work

In the United States, nonprofits employed 10.7 million staff in 2010, representing 10.1 percent of the workforce: 57 percent of the jobs are related to health care, 15 percent to educational services, and 13 percent to social assistance. It is interesting to note that 60 percent of the staff are women.

There are a number of entry points and approaches for anthropologists trying to break in to NGO work that correspond to the status of the job seeker. On the one hand, these are the kinds of prerequisites and "positioning" that lay the groundwork. On the other, they are the types of positions that may be available.

NGOs never advertise for "anthropologists." They advertise for people with the technical skill sets and experience they need for a particular assignment. Anthropologists are considered to be too academic, too theoretical, and too slow to produce work, such as an ethnography, sociocultural analysis, or a dissertation. NGOs seek pragmatic, action-oriented, results-driven, problem-solvers who work quickly and multitask. Unfortunately, that is not the image anthropology has normally conveyed. To work with NGOs anthropologists need to have the specific technical, geographic, and linguistic skills that are in demand. Though our anthropological perspective, tools, and perceptions are very valuable and relevant, they are demonstrated later, after we get in the door. Such skills are noted later in this chapter.

As with any other job, networking is fundamental. In this case it means seeking out and meeting NGO workers (including anthropologists) at conferences and meetings and through referrals. Meeting with them helps the job seeker to learn more about where they work and how the work is structured, as well as upcoming needs and opportunities. People one meets can also provide onward introductions and referrals.

And also, as with many other jobs, the old cliché about the benefits of being in the right place at the right time is very true. Learning through networks can alert you to when a particular topic is hot and which NGOs are focusing on it, or which field locations, like Ethiopia or Indonesia might need to scale up, and then – although it is not so easy and there are no guarantees – being there, in person, and ready to start.

Some ways to gain access

Volunteer Many NGOs use trained volunteers for particular assignments. This is an opportunity to gain valuable technical and field experience while also providing an inside track to networking and mutual familiarity within an NGO.

Internship or fellowship Many universities have relationships with particular NGOs, and alternately many large NGOs have specific programs that accommodate interns for several months. This is an opportunity for each party to understand the other and to explore, at close range, the possibilities for longer-term employment. Such possibilities can be identified by contacting NGO human resource departments, or directly through program staff.

Vacancy announcements NGO jobs are advertised in a number of places, including on NGO websites. The majority of these openings are for field positions that last from months to years and at differing levels of responsibility. Many – although not all – of these posts are "unaccompanied," meaning that the NGO will not support or sometimes will not allow staff to have their family with them during the assignment, even if it is for several years. It is often surprising to learn how many families accept such conditions, although I never have, and my family has always lived with me overseas. One of the more frequented sites for such announcements is that of the Development Executive Group at www.devex.com.

Consultant NGOs often need short-term, immediate, specialized technical knowledge and skills and bring in consultants for a few weeks or months. It is not unusual for these assignments to evolve into long-term consulting arrangements or full-time employment.

Some NGO Characteristics

NGOs almost universally depend on *donated funds*. Whether these are from good-hearted citizens, houses of worship, foundations, or governments, such funds are never guaranteed to be consistent or permanent. In fact, funding is guided by public sentiment and public knowledge, and often enlightened self-interest. And in tough economic times, spending on donations for the public good is very often considered an unaffordable luxury. Fortunately, the INGOs for whom I have worked receive the majority of their funding from the US government and so are a bit more stable financially, though even this changes according to prevailing politics.

Although a large amount of funding comes from the US government, it may be a bit of a surprise, and at the same time heartening, to know that in 2010 alone private donations to nonprofits totaled about $290 *billion* dollars. Religious affiliated organizations received 33 percent of those contributions, with another 14 percent going to educational organizations. Nonetheless, in 2011, 31 percent of smaller NGOs and 17 percent of larger ones received less than previous years and a large percentage reduced their operating budgets.

There are several implications of the funding uncertainty. NGOs tend to operate very economically, and some extremely frugally. Salaries are often (but not always) "modest." But more importantly, staffing also depends on *current* funds and the *current* number of funded programs, and so the number of staff that an NGO can afford in one year may change the following year, meaning that positions can be eliminated. But as large grants are awarded, positions can also increase. Job security, even with excellent performance appraisals, is uncertain. However, NGOs try very hard, and often successfully, to find ways to keep their most valuable staff.

Funding pressure also means constant pressure to replace funds that disappear owing to programs finishing. And most NGOs also want to increase their size and scope, beyond just resource replacement. Therefore *everyone*, in some form, is a fund-raiser and business development officer. Work is very results-driven and aimed at sustaining, replacing, or expanding existing programs, and at establishing programs in additional countries. Everyone is assessed on their output, production, and "deliverables." There is no coasting. At the end of the day, it's a business, but one that does "good" and is nonprofit.

Another issue related to the source of funds is *accountability* and, again, economy. The "public" that supplies funds for particular programs and projects is particularly concerned that they be spent as promised, that goals and targets are reached, and that resources flow as planned to "beneficiaries." The level of scrutiny and observation is high, and the amount of monitoring and reporting often exhausting.

A more hidden issue of the same funding circumstance is *ethics*. NGOs require funds to fulfill their mission and to stay in "business." But it is not unusual for those providing funds, especially the US government, to have their own agendas and their own policies. The issue then becomes whether those external agendas "tie" the much needed funds to guidance, approaches, and activities that the NGO does not entirely endorse. Each organization and each case is different, but the circumstance must be addressed when working for an NGO.

An irony of NGO work that is not usually apparent to outsiders is the *competition/ collaboration dichotomy*. In order to encourage the highest-quality program designs, funding donors explicitly require organizations to compete against each other for limited funds. Competition can be intense, with exhaustive information gathering, carefully guarded "technical solutions," analysis of competitor strengths and weaknesses, budget strategies, and key staff recruitment wars. NGOs are essentially fighting each other for the privilege to "win" funding awards that will allow us to help people. Yet it is clearly impossible for any agency to do everything, or to work in a vacuum. To actually accomplish our mission we must find complementarity, synergy, economies of scale, and shared or common techniques and information, instead of the substantial effort and expense of reinventing it every time.

So, in the field, during implementation of programs, and after funding decisions have been made and "winners" and "losers" are known, the time for competition is past, and NGOs collaborate and coordinate intensively. We could not operate any other way. The donors themselves require INGOs to collaborate and in most cases funding proposals must contain a detailed coordination plan. In fact, after doing this kind of work for a while, many of us actually know each other quite well personally, and we play this competition/collaboration "game" as part of the culture of our work.

Staff in NGOs are tremendously motivated and committed. This is not a job one does for the money, though the larger INGOs pay market rates for professional staff. Most have a deep passion for facilitating social justice and eliminating human suffering. Within and outside the large faith-based INGOs, staff are driven by their beliefs and values, ethics, and morals. While NGO staff are highly professional and consider their work as a deliberate career choice, NGOs are also a world populated by volunteers, on which many organizations depend. The volunteerism adds an additional element of contribution, self-sacrifice, commitment, and diversity that is refreshing and often re-energizing to the full-time permanent staff. In the United States alone, 62.8 million people volunteered part of their time in 2010. The NGOs for which I have worked have not used volunteers, but I have been around them a lot in collaborative settings and they are a powerful and wonderful element of the work.

Interestingly, a large number of Americans do not understand the nature of NGOs. In my experience, many people do not recognize the term "nongovernmental organization" or "NGO" and are equally unaccustomed to the term "nonprofit organization." Thus when I meet people (in less cosmopolitan settings) who ask what I do I have reverted to explaining that it is like a charity organization that

depends on donated resources and helps people. This often leads to what I personally have regarded as the "church lady" label, and results in questions like, "How
long have you been volunteering?" or "For which church are you a missionary?"
They are often surprised to hear that many of us do this full-time and professionally,
with advanced degrees and significant technical expertise.

INGOs are more structured than one might imagine. In the sense that they are
indeed businesses, and must be sufficiently organized to seek and manage funds
and undertake complex activities, they often have sophisticated systems, protocols,
templates, and processes. These have evolved over the years with far more software-
based and technologically oriented support than previously. It depends significantly
on the size of the NGOs, of course, but, for example, imagine the complexity of
managing fund-raising, finances, human resources, legal issues, and program implementation across a network of 45 foreign country offices (in places with inconsistent
support structures, technologies, and laws), and a headquarters of 200 people and
global staff of 5,000. No matter what responsibilities an anthropologist would have
within such an INGO, they would need to learn to adapt to and to utilize many of
these systems, and in some cases provide input to establishing, diagnosing, or
improving them.

Working for NGOs, particularly INGOs, is tough on families. NGOs tend to
leverage the staff commitment and tight budgets by expecting tremendous amounts
of output. Though NGO work is tremendously rewarding, the balance between
work and private life can be a serious challenge. My colleagues and I often work
12- to 16-hour days, and weekends. But not always. I travel about 30–40 percent of
my time, and often for 3–10 weeks (sometimes at very short notice), and although
this is certainly not true of everyone, it is also not unusual. And while traveling, the
hours are generally longer and the weekends shorter. The family joke is that when
they ask about the duration of my current trip I always say "three weeks" just to
have something to say. It is almost never three weeks. The other joke is that when
I get home from work by 7 p.m., or return home from a trip in only two weeks, my
family is often worried that it's because I've been fired!

Why Anthropologists Fit NGOs

Anthropologist practitioners are particularly well suited to NGO work in some
important ways. NGOs seek to solve human problems and improve people's lives.
It is impossible to do this without a very good understanding of the starting point
and the local definitions of what would constitute problem-solving or improvements. In changing people's conditions far more rapidly than culture evolves,
anthropologists in particular know the dangers, and are able to understand the
potential negative consequences, of even well-meaning activities.

NGOs all favor a "participatory approach" for working with local project participants in identifying, designing, and implementing projects, but overall the application
of such participation is inconsistent. Anthropologists are good at listening and

learning local perspectives, and at respecting local ideas, knowledge, and skills, and so can be invaluable assets in every phase of the "program cycle."

NGOs also all subscribe to the principle of "Do no harm" (i.e., the avoidance of negative side effects), so in designing, managing, and assessing programs anthropologists have the training, perspective, local access, and tools to understand how to cause the least harm. We are well suited to projecting and predicting the implications and consequences of particular strategies, approaches, and activities. We ask the right questions.

Because of the variety of technical topics ("sectors") covered by many NGOs, staffing tends to be very interdisciplinary. Anthropologists' capacity to fit into complex and diverse settings and to adapt quickly helps considerably. We are adept at observing and aligning with a variety of settings; learning how to behave appropriately, and this is useful in adapting to the specific corporate culture of NGOs headquarters, in the field office, and in the government ministries, communities, and villages in which NGOs work. And in some cases our personal experience of and expertise in particular regions, countries, and subgroups and their languages, will be directly useful.

Likewise, most INGOs are internally multicultural. Not only is it important to understand the various cultural contexts of our own "national staff" in countries as different as Sudan, Afghanistan, Colombia, and Indonesia, even our "international staff" based at headquarters or country offices, with whom we interact constantly, come from a wide range of countries. The US headquarters staff where I currently work are from over two dozen countries. Sometimes our lunch room sounds like a United Nations summit.

More concrete skills are also useful. Our ability to synthesize information and examine issues holistically, and sometimes rather extensive *writing experience*, make us good at drawing up grant proposals and reports. Our training in survey and interview research and in mixing qualitative and quantitative analysis lends itself to the types of program assessment, project monitoring, and evaluation activities that are so important to NGO work.

Going beyond Anthropological Training

Anthropologists are versatile and adaptable. Therefore they are able to learn, as I have, a number of additional (or revised) skills for the NGO environment.

Technical skills

Anthropologists are not hired for their anthropological skills. These are important, but they provide a framework or perspective and are not the basis for actual roles and responsibilities, or for recruitment. NGOs are focused on issues, topics, or technical "sectors." For example, anthropologists will need to have an understanding of such topics as human rights advocacy, program evaluation design and analysis, public health provision, refugee support, water and sanitation, small-scale agriculture, primary or vocational education, employment and livelihoods, democracy and governance, to name just a few.

This is a key issue. Anthropologists need not have a second degree in such topics, but they need to be sufficiently familiar with some of them to help design strategies and programs, or to manage or evaluate them. They need to understand the basics and the terminology. But this is not tremendously daunting; many of us in our previous research or academic study did indeed gravitate toward particular technical issues. In my case it was gender dynamics and knowledge acquisition in rural agricultural systems in Cameroon. In NGO terms this was "rural agriculture," "training," "gender issues in livelihood systems," "West African community dynamics." The anthropology we have done is all transferable to the type of work INGOs do. It requires learning a bit more about how a topic is treated in actual development projects. Even new technical topics, of which we have little prior experience, can be mastered using the multitude of books, studies, reports, and other materials that exist.

Speed

NGO work is always to a deadline, and the deadlines are often very short. There is little opportunity for time-consuming in-depth analysis, and no time for extensive surveys or research. The quality must be high, but the time allocation is short. Funding proposals for many millions of dollars must often be started, and completed, within a month, including all the field research, strategic development, budgeting, and writing! The pace is hectic and fast. Sometimes there are a lot of 14-hour days and seven-day weeks for sustained periods. Some people are able to adapt to it, but others cannot and drop out. It is not always like this, but one must be prepared because such periods are not infrequent.

Multidisciplinary teamwork

Teams are assembled to do everything from field assessments to proposal design, from drafting to program evaluation. It is not difficult for most anthropologists to learn to work closely with colleagues whose technical background, jargon, style, and experience are very different. It is part of the fun of this kind of work. And, of course, conflicts and differences occur, and must be addressed to ensure the team completes its tasks.

Precision responsiveness and compliance

This skill seems so obvious. Yet my colleagues and I have found that it is not necessarily common among academics and social science researchers who transition into this type of work, as they are often more accustomed to defining their own parameters according to research interests, personal perspectives, or evolving situations. However, when designing projects that seek funding, for example, donors usually prescribe very specific conditions and requirements for the way we present our strategies. These must be met precisely, without deviation; that is, we must interpret what they want and give it to them exactly as they have prescribed. Likewise, programs are funded on the basis of a set of carefully monitored, measured, and evaluated "deliverables," quantitative targets, or qualitative impact objectives, and so sticking carefully to the plan, which is not always easy, is required. Deviations and flexibilities must be negotiated and agreed.

Management

There are numerous opportunities for management of staff, programs, departments, initiatives, and so on in NGOs. Management is both a skill and an art, and it must be deliberately and carefully learned if it is to be practiced well. Although, depending on career choices, it may not be necessary to develop management skills, if it is there are ample training and guidance resources to assist with the process, as well as the potential for receiving certification in professional project management.

Marketing, public relations, representation, diplomacy, and negotiation

Though not exactly synonymous, all of these skills represent the kinds of capacities and abilities that professional NGO staff must be adept at when interacting with the "outside" world. I have had to use every one of these skills numerous times. For example, meeting with potential donors becomes a marketing exercise in the benefits of funding your (rather than another) organization. Meeting the media in the field during a crisis or for a human interest story requires discussing issues clearly, interestingly, and without jargon. Being the only staff member from your organization at key coordination meetings requires both broad knowledge and understanding of the "message" the organization has carefully chosen to convey to its peers, donors, or professional technical community. Or, for example – as happens not infrequently – convincing a foreign government not to tax imported humanitarian goods at commercial rates so they can be used to help their own citizens, requires diplomacy, tact, and negotiation skills, as well as tremendous patience and frustration tolerance. As does convincing a government – without panicking – not to throw your agency out of the country because another Western organization has been caught handing out Christian Bibles to Muslims!

Stress control

As noted earlier, the hours are often long and exhausting, intercultural misunderstandings can occur, funding is uncertain, and, above all, one is frequently dropped into new settings and needs to adapt immediately. These are all stressful factors. I could add to them the type of work I do now in disaster relief and emergency response, where trauma, chaos, tragedy, and urgency come together. If we add working in war zones, we have a great recipe for extreme stress. Just a few days working amid the horrors of Darfur or the Haitian earthquake could lead to meltdown. Those of us who have survived many years doing this kind of work (not only in relief but in NGOs overall) have found our own personal methods and techniques to relieve stress. And I have seen many people leave this kind of work, to do something "calmer."

NGO Career Patterns

NGO career paths vary according to the starting point, personal preference, and predisposition. A new graduate would start at a different level than an experienced mid-career person. Additionally, some may want to focus on the operational or technical side while others prefer to progress through the management levels. Some may want to live and work mostly overseas, while others may choose the hectic life and more management-oriented character of headquarters. In smaller NGOs, with a smaller hierarchy, one person may play a variety of roles and wind up as a jack of all (NGO) trades.

On the *technical* side, consultants and junior and senior program officers may help design programs, assessments, and baseline surveys or plan implementation strategies that are culturally and socio-economically appropriate. Or they may participate in or lead the monitoring and evaluation of programs. They may also undertake policy analysis and advocacy, or design public education campaigns.

On the *management* side, anthropologists can serve as deputy project managers or project managers, if they have sufficient technical sector knowledge, combined with administrative and management skills. Their skill level and past performance and experience can lead to management of very large and complex projects, involving hundreds of staff with budgets worth millions of dollars. Likewise, it is possible to serve as a deputy country director or country director, responsible for every single aspect of the organization's work in a particular country. The same is true for headquarters positions in management of departments or divisions.

The opportunities for an anthropologist within NGOs are basically the same as for any other NGO staff member. They are limited only by personal preference and skills and experience, not by discipline. An anthropologist could become an NGO vice president, president/CEO, board chairman, or founder. But they cannot, because of the necessary skill set, become, for example, chief financial officer, audit director, or human resources director.

In my own career I have worked for six NGOs (as well as the US government and some for-profit development companies). As I've gained experience, my various roles in NGOs – mostly located in developing countries – have included research assistant, technical analyst and adviser, social science researcher/adviser, monitoring and evaluation officer, program design officer, program manager, regional program manager, country director, and headquarters-based technical department director. Yet even in a large NGO, in my current management position as Director of Relief and Humanitarian Assistance, I still actively undertake every one of the range of skills and capacities described above. I plan field assessments, represent the organization at coordination meetings with the US government and other NGOs, lead project design strategy exercises, draft proposals, and provide feedback and review of proposals that others write, including those from other departments, and undertake many other tasks.

It is interesting that the NGO "base" is very fluid in two major ways, at least within its international development oriented part. Staff tend to move around a lot between NGOs. People change organizations in order to change locations (i.e., particular foreign countries or headquarters locations), and they change type of organization, according to opportunities for increased or different kinds of responsibilities. They also sometimes move from NGOs to for-profit development firms, to government bodies that fund and manage the resources and design the programs, or to one of the United Nations agencies, and then back again a few years later. Some veterans alternate between assignments overseas and those at headquarters countries.

The number of people doing this kind of work is not very large, and over time one gets to know quite a few of them. Many of us have had the same peers, on a global scale, for a long time. Consequently, when you run into someone you have not seen for a few years – perhaps the last time you saw them was in Khartoum, Sudan three years ago – by chance at a meeting in Dhaka, Bangladesh, the first question is usually "So, who are you working for these days?"

NGOs Are Exciting, Fun, and Rewarding

The most gratifying aspect of the work is that we get to help people directly and then see the results. Everything else is an element of that process. The bottom line is the visible linkage between what we do and the positive effects on people's lives and conditions. It sounds corny or trite, but it is the primary motivator that enables us to push through the stress, frustration, exhaustion, and tedium of the work.

Consequently, by far the most exciting and fulfilling of my activities throughout my NGO work is *meeting the people* affected by programs in which I am involved, in their communities and homes, schools, and clinics. I listen to them. I try to see who they are and how they live, try to understand their needs and our impact on those needs.

I also invite them to ask me questions, and make it a two-way interaction. They are often interested and curious about the NGO overall, or about me and my family. I have taken my wife with me on a number of field trips, even to Darfur, and this has clearly added an important element of "humanity" to the visits: I am not just a foreign aid worker who parachutes in; rather, I am a person with a family, doing this job far from home.

I often make such visits at different stages, before, during, and near the end, of projects, and so can see the changing conditions even more clearly. There have been a number of times I have had to address hundreds of people and make formal speeches (complete with battery-powered loudspeakers), alongside local dignitaries. In all honesty, being the central attraction and being treated as a VIP take a bit of getting used to. It is not what anthropologists normally seek, but it is also, I must admit, fun.

Also related to being in the public eye are other tasks that, depending on one's personality and one's position and job, are challenging, interesting, and exciting. For example, I have been filmed, taped, and interviewed for the media over the years, usually in the field, during crises such as the Darfur crisis, the Haiti earthquake, Hurricane Katrina, the Horn of Africa famine, and so on. At such times I have been tasked with representing my organization in particular, and NGOs and aid work in general, and this affects public perception, which in turn can influence funding and even policy. Those who periodically do such PR are usually given media training.

In relation to public representation, I have also given a number of professional papers at conferences – including anthropological conferences – about my own work and that of my organization, and it is at these times that I try to frame what I do in anthropological terms and examine the sociocultural basis or implications for the work.

Conducting training, on a number of topics, is another task that has been very interesting, particularly when the curriculum also needs to be developed. It is an opportunity to reflect, research, and examine what to convey to build on past success and lessons learned and to avoid mistakes. Interacting with motivated, inquisitive, mature participants is very stimulating.

Project design is at the technical heart of the job. It is the reason we meet people, as described earlier, in order to try to help them. This is where the topical skills (such as food security, water systems, sanitation, conflict resolution, etc.), local knowledge and understanding obtained through preparatory needs assessments, global past experience, anthropological perspective, and interdisciplinary teamwork all converge. Being a part of or leading a team, designing a new project, determining technical solutions, identifying activities, determining participant criteria, setting key qualitative and quantitative targets and indicators are is very exciting. Whether the project will be funded or not depends on the quality of the design process. And if it is funded, design determines whether or not the project will deliver the intended results and benefits to the people involved.

This job consists of roughly equal parts stress and excitement. There are also, of course, a great many things we do that are not at all exciting or stimulating. But they come with the territory, and do not belong in this chapter. They are certainly more than made up for by the interesting tasks.

Some Recent Changes

The way we help people is changing. Anthropologists have always recognized the importance of the knowledge, skills, perspective, and investment of local people in logically and rationally managing their own decisions and resources. This is a rather crude oversimplification, but in poor countries people have often lacked access to more efficient and effective technologies, knowledge of such techniques, and access to the financial resources to utilize these approaches and technologies. All too often, they also lack adequate institutional support systems to help them with these things.

The greatest paradigm change in recent years, which has gained strong momentum very recently, is that of shifting the capacities as well as the resources to local entities, whether they are local governments, or local NGOs and civil society. This has created the need for much greater local-level capacity building, a greatly enhanced level of partnership between international and local actors, and a focus on creating truly local and sustainable "ownership." Anthropologists are well placed to help with this bridging and transfer process. We can understand both sides and help find approaches that satisfy these newly focused objectives.

The way we support our work is changing. Economic constraints, competing priorities, and changing politics and policies have made dependence on the same large-scale donors, such as national governments, less consistent. Consequently, NGOs are networking more to diversify their resource base and to seek funding from a wider range of contributors, including foundations, individuals, religious groups, and corporations, for example. The size of individual grants and contributions is smaller, and the amount of time and effort needed to inform and educate, negotiate, and report to these sources is far greater, as well as the financial and administrative effort. The consequence is that limited staff have to spend more time obtaining funds, which reduces the time and effort available to utilize the funds. Staff have to work harder at a wider variety of tasks that are not directly related to program implementation. In a nutshell: staff work harder.

We need to justify and prove our work more carefully now. With very good reason, donors of every sort want assurance that their valuable funds are being spent well, and that intended and promised results are achieved. NGOs, more than ever before, are being held accountable for their work. On the one hand there are increased financial audits and increased diligence regarding the use of funds. On the other, and more to the point, is the task of demonstrating clearly and reliably that we are helping people sufficiently, and doing it appropriately according to a number of commonly agreed standards.

Therefore, organizations are significantly increasing their capacity, expertise, and rigor in monitoring and evaluation (M&E). M&E is something that anthropologists in this domain have always been particularly involved with. Our ability to identify appropriate indicators, and to collect, measure, and collate quantitative and qualitative data into a cohesive analysis is key to the kind of M&E that is increasingly being required.

Chapter 14

Multilateral Governmental Organizations

William L. Partridge

Multilateral government organizations are large, powerful, and highly influential in the development arena. William Partridge offers us a chapter discussing in detail the culture of one such multilateral, the World Bank, and provides us with a fascinating account of his activities there as an anthropologist. He begins with a look at how the bank is set up and structured, moves to an account of how he became involved with it, and then provides several detailed and concrete examples of the kind of work he did and the challenges he encountered. He concludes with some thoughts on the kinds of contributions that anthropology can make in organizations such as the World Bank.

This chapter discusses the challenges of practicing anthropology in multilateral governmental organizations. It is based largely on my experience working on the staff of the International Bank for Reconstruction and Development (IBRD) and the International Development Association (IDA), usually referred to together as the World Bank,[1] as well as on numerous short-term consultancies to the Inter-American Development Bank (IDB) and the Asian Development Bank (ADB) and on my service as senior adviser to the United Nations High Commissioner for Refugees (UNHCR) in Colombia. While there are differences in the cultures of these institutions, they share broad similarities in structure and organization, the skills they require to be effective, and the professional challenges they offer. Nevertheless, the following reflections are mostly derived from my experience in the World Bank.[2]

A Handbook of Practicing Anthropology. First Edition. Edited by Riall W. Nolan.

Structure and Function

Multilateral organizations such as the World Bank are owned and governed by their member countries. The IBRD has some 187 member countries today represented on its Board of Governors and Board of Executive Directors, and the IDA some 171 member countries. The boards have ultimate decision-making power within the organization on all policy, investment, and membership issues. The members include high-income countries such as Germany, Canada, France, which are not eligible to borrow from the World Bank, and developing countries which are eligible to borrow such as Ecuador, Tanzania, India, and Vietnam.[3]

The IBRD lends to low-income countries at market interest rates. The money it lends is raised through the sale of its bonds or is borrowed from international money markets to finance development projects in transport, agriculture, energy, water supply, health, education, governance, and other sectors. The IDA provides interest-free loans to the 80 poorest countries in the world. This is made possible by contributions from richer donor countries, including those that have "graduated" from IDA eligibility such as Turkey and Chile.

The World Bank only finances part of the total costs of a development project, sometimes as little as 20 percent. Its borrowers must obtain the remaining finance from commercial banks, such as Deutsche Bank or Banco Santander, the export guarantee agencies of industrial countries, and private sector investors. The World Bank maintains a staff of around 9,000 professionals – engineers, economists, educators, financial analysts, ecologists, anthropologists – who conduct field appraisals or evaluations of proposed loans that seek to ensure they are sound and will yield the benefits promised. Commercial banks, export guarantee agencies, and private investors do not maintain international staffs to conduct such field appraisals and thus value the World Bank's lead in making their investment decisions.

The World Bank insists upon borrower governments adopting widely accepted international standards for the contracting or procurement of works, goods, and services; labor health and safety; environmental impact assessment; cultural property; land acquisition and involuntary resettlement; indigenous peoples; and public consultation and participation.[4] When borrower governments sign project legal agreements with the World Bank, these have the force of international treaties, superseding domestic statutes and practices, thereby providing a measure of reassurance for other investors as regards reputational risk.

Entering the World Bank

My work at the World Bank grew out of my research on the social and cultural impacts of involuntary resettlement. The filling of the reservoir of Mexico's Aleman Dam, constructed on the Papaloapan river in the mid-1950s, forced some 20,000 Mazatec indigenous people to abandon their homes and farms. They were provided new homes and farmlands in five different resettlement sites by the government of Mexico. When I visited them in the mid-1970s four of the five new settlements were complete failures. One was successful.

Prior to their resettlement, the Mazatec had been independent small-scale peasant farmers, marketing coffee, maize, sesame, and other cash crops to urban markets. But the inhabitants of the four failed settlements had been impoverished: they had lost the replacement farmlands they were allocated, education and health conditions were dismal, and they had been reduced to wage labor on neighboring plantations and cattle estates. In contrast, in the successful settlement the Mazatec had retained their lands and were producing surplus maize, plantain, mango, citrus, sugar cane, and other crops sufficient to permit investments and/or savings in the form of livestock. They enjoyed levels of income, education, and health significantly higher than those of neighboring communities who had not been resettled.

How can one explain the dramatically different outcomes? This became the focus of my research, which continued through 1977–8 with support from the National Science Foundation. Without my being aware of it, the published research results were read by staff of the World Bank, Inter-American Development Bank, World Health Organization, Organization of American States and others (e.g., Partridge and Brown 1982, 1983; Partridge et al. 1982; Partridge 1984). They were aware that involuntary resettlement operations caused by hydroelectricity, irrigation, water supply, transport corridor and other large-scale infrastructure projects were almost always failures, leaving the displaced people impoverished. This was the opposite of what was supposed to be the purpose of a development investment in the first place.

I began to receive requests to consult on resettlement operations in projects underway, to speak at seminars and training courses at headquarters offices, and to participate in the preparation of new projects. Between 1983 and 1985 my time was increasingly absorbed by consultancies for these multilateral government organizations and I increasingly postponed academic pursuits to concentrate on practicing anthropology.

Critic and Gadfly

Two examples will illustrate what that work was like.

*   In India the Maharashtra Composite Irrigation III project was underway, displacing and presumably resettling over 18,000 people from land flooded by the storage reservoir. The World Bank had received protests claiming that displaced farmers had not been resettled on new lands, but the government of India claimed that 90 percent had been provided with land to replace that flooded. I was sent to investigate. Not speaking Hindi or Maharati, I recruited Professor L. K. Mahapatra (University of Orissa) who had studied resettlement disasters elsewhere in India and who agreed to assist me in a field survey of the affected villages. I paid his fees and expenses from my consulting fees. We surveyed 13

of the 20 affected villages. We found that only 5 percent of farmers had received compensation sufficient to buy replacement land; a full 95 percent were made landless and impoverished. Back in Washington my report resulted in disciplinary measures for the team leader responsible for the preparation, appraisal, and supervision of the project. The World Bank department responsible requested that the government of India take corrective measures to help the victims in regaining their lost lands, to which the government responded by ignoring the request. By then the loan had been entirely disbursed and the bank staff felt they had little leverage left to force the issue. The affected people were left impoverished.[5]

- The Inter-American Development Bank contracted a comparative analysis of a successful resettlement project, the Arenal Hydroelectric Project resettlement in Costa Rica, and what they considered a failed resettlement operation, the Chixoy Hydroelectric Project in Guatemala, for the purpose of advising on establishing an IDB resettlement policy. After presenting my findings at an IDB seminar in Washington, I was asked by the World Bank, which together with IDB had co-financed the Guatemala project, to present the analysis of the Chixoy experience to the staff of the department responsible for Guatemala. The presentation reported the human disaster that was resettlement at Chixoy: two years after the reservoir filled, I found 3,700 Maya huddled in temporary shacks just above the reservoir margin, their corn fields, fruit trees, and pastures under water, who were surviving by selling off their livestock, but had no schools, no potable water, no roads. The World Bank team responsible had not once visited the resettlement operation, and the unfolding disaster was never mentioned in the team's supervision reports to management over the previous four years. The bank project team in attendance was incensed; they angrily defended themselves and attacked me. At that point a man stood up in the rear of the room, who turned out to be the vice president for the Latin America and Caribbean region, and said: "What we have here is a fuck up, and I want it fixed." He then left the room. The fix turned out to be holding up a new loan to the government of Guatemala until they signed a legal agreement incorporating a resettlement plan designed to restore the lands, production systems, and livelihoods of the affected Maya. I was asked to help prepare and appraise the new plan in the following months.[6]

These and other consultancies for multilateral government organizations convinced me that one could practice anthropology in such institutions, that there was need and scope for making positive contributions, and that there were managers and staff willing to use empirical findings to make better decisions. In 1986 I was invited to work as a full-time consultant by the World Bank's social policy adviser, Michael M. Cernea, a sociologist from Romania and the first non-economist social scientist hired by the World Bank. It was a one-year contract but I accepted without hesitation, resigned as chair of the Anthropology Department at Georgia State University, and with my family's support moved to Washington, DC.

The following year, when the World Bank created its first Environment Divisions in each of its regional vice presidencies, I was offered and accepted a permanent staff position as anthropologist in the newly formed Environment Division for the Asia and Pacific region. I soon learned that working within the institution would be unlike what I had experienced as an external consultant.

Staff Member

My anthropological training had been in Latin America, I was fluent in Spanish, and had 15 years' research experience in Latin America. So it may seem a bit odd that I would be hired by the World Bank initially in the Asia and Pacific region. What that tells you is that the bank hired me not because I was a cultural or regional expert but because I could help them solve a problem. That problem was most pressing in the Asia and Pacific region, where there were a score of ongoing resettlement operations, all of them failing, and many more in the pipeline. Bank management couldn't care less whether I were an anthropologist or a Martian – what they wanted was someone who could help member governments come up with workable resettlement plans.

My role had changed from being a gadfly and critic of bank management and staff actions or omissions, independent and with no responsibility for decision-making, to being a member of the staff responsible for making decisions. Now I was to work directly with the engineers, lawyers, and other civil servants of member governments – ministries of public works, secretariats of agriculture, electricity corporations, departments of irrigation – to correct past errors and avoid future ones. In that role I was to confront opposition from my government counterparts ranging from polite indifference to undisguised hostility. Many viewed forced resettlement as a kind of "collateral damage" which was an unavoidable cost of development and, moreover, the exclusive prerogative of government. And opposition from government counterparts translated into opposition from some bank staff, many of whom resented having to share scarce bank budgets historically monopolized by economists, engineers, financial analysts, with anthropologists, environmental scientists, and other "new guys on the block."

To be viable, an involuntary resettlement operation must fit a country's legal, regulatory, and policy framework, specifically, the statutes governing land acquisition, compensation, and resettlement. My anthropological training had not prepared me for legal research. Some of my greatest allies were found in the bank's legal department. They guided me to the relevant statutes in India, Indonesia, Nepal, Philippines, China, and so on, which became my nightly homework.

I quickly learned that the majority of country legal frameworks for land acquisition, the major cause of involuntary resettlement, are entirely silent on the resettlement and re-establishment of displaced people (Shihata 2000). Yet member countries and the bank staff had to comply with the World Bank's operations policy on involuntary resettlement issued by its Board of Executive Directors representing all member countries.[7] That operations policy explicitly requires: (1) avoidance or minimization of resettlement where possible, and (2) where resettlement cannot be avoided, the formulation and implementation of a resettlement plan designed to improve, or at least restore to pre-project levels, the livelihoods and standards of living of people displaced by the project. Thus a major part of my work became helping draft and negotiate resettlement policy frameworks and plans – their designs, staffing, and financing – to re-establish affected people socio-economically.

Opportunities Discovered

Much of my work involved shuttling between projects, sometimes alone but usually as part of a bank team, to supervise, prepare, appraise, and monitor and evaluate resettlement operations. I was in the field about 200 days a year. Most countries in which I worked had well-developed faculties of anthropology, and I made it a priority to recruit in-country colleagues to work with me. Typically I would disappear for a week or two into the villages affected by a project, accompanied by my in-country anthropological colleagues, while my fellow team members remained in the capital city conversing with government officials. Consequently, my findings from the field often did not match the information conveyed to my colleagues by our government counterparts. And this usually meant rather tense meetings in the capital city and back at headquarters. With the support of bank management, and sometimes despite resistance from bank staff, we saw the first generation of solid resettlement and re-establishment plans incorporated into projects and, most importantly, into legal agreements between the bank and its borrowers.[8]

Equally important was contributing to the operationalization of the World Bank's resettlement policy. Michael Cernea was the principal author of the bank's operations policy on involuntary resettlement issued by the Board of Executive Directors.[9] While the policy was explicit regarding the risks of impoverishment and the overarching objective of involuntary resettlement operations to restore lost production systems, housing, infrastructure, and so on to avoid impoverishment, it was less explicit regarding how to achieve those objectives. One of my first assignments, therefore, was to design and write up guidelines of what steps bank staff and governments should take to comply with the policy, what were the component elements of a workable resettlement plan, and what actions were required to achieve the policy objectives. That guideline was included as an annex to Cernea's landmark *Involuntary Resettlement in Development Projects: Policy Guidelines in World Bank-Financed Projects* (1988). Its basic message was: Because forced resettlement destroys a previous way of life, all resettlement operations must be designed and appraised as development projects. This and other technical materials we produced became the basis for a series of training seminars and workshops for bank staff, managers, and consultants in the coming years. The feedback from staff and consultants regarding accumulating experience was an ongoing process of learning that contributed to our refinement of the policy and its reissuance by the board in 1990 and again in 2001.

An additional responsibility was identifying and recruiting anthropologists from the member countries of the World Bank who could strengthen our capacity. When I was appointed environmental assessment manager, and later chief, of the Environment and Social Development Unit of the Latin America and Caribbean region, most of my staff were Greek, British, and US nationals. Few spoke Spanish or Portuguese and most knew little of the societies in which they were working. There existed a belief in the bank that staff should not work in their own countries or region in order to remain "objective." I believed the opposite – to be effective one had to know the society, its language, and system of governance. So I began to hire high-caliber Latin American professionals, eventually assembling a team of 23 sociologists, anthropologists, environmental engineers, biologists, ecologists, and economists from Brazil, Colombia, Ecuador, Costa Rica, Chile, and so forth.

Finally, a fourth area of activity was reviewing proposed bank loans to ensure that they were in compliance with the institution's involuntary resettlement, environmental assessment, and indigenous peoples policies. When the board of directors created the environment and social development units in each regional vice presidency, it also instituted a process of mandatory screening and technical review by environmental and social specialists of future lending operations. This gave our small Environment and Social Development Unit unprecedented influence in decision-making. More than once we found project preparation to be incomplete – institutional capacities weak, technical designs questionable or absent, social impacts denied or ignored, financial management systems nonexistent – or even in violation of bank policy. More than once bank management backed us up and sent the project back to the drawing board. Such review responsibility also represented a tremendous workload for the few environmental and social specialists then employed, and fueled our recruitment of more. In the space of five years the number of environmental and social scientists in the bank grew from a handful to more than 200 professionals.

New Challenges

The Environment and Social Development Unit's arena of responsibilities extended considerably beyond involuntary resettlement. We provided the experience and expertise to ensure that a formal environmental assessment (EA) was carried out for all projects that entailed significant social and/or environmental impacts.[10] A core element of the EA process is prior and informed consultation with and participation of stakeholders likely to be affected and, especially, local communities that would suffer direct or indirect negative impacts (Partridge 1990, 1994; Davis and Partridge 1994; Partridge et al. 1998).

In that regard, a particularly difficult and sensitive challenge was prior and informed consultation with indigenous populations of the Americas, who were structurally excluded from the dominant societies due to ubiquitous language, culture, and race discrimination. Consultation with indigenous peoples, much less their participation in EAs, or for that matter in development projects of any kind, was unprecedented in Latin America and the Caribbean. Only Canada and Mexico had evolved mechanisms, instruments, and processes, albeit incomplete and flawed, for including indigenous peoples to any extent in the development process. Throughout the rest of the Americas indigenous peoples remained voiceless, invisible, isolated, and impoverished.

While we began by insisting on consultation and participation in the EA process, our larger agenda quickly moved to involving indigenous communities in the design, staffing, implementation, and monitoring and evaluation of all development projects affecting their territories, natural resources, and cultures. The push back was strong and immediate. Bank staff were aware that borrower governments of the region almost always represented only the dominant and profoundly racist segments of their societies, and they did not relish attempting to redress this deeply rooted inequity.

We had three powerful allies in the struggle to direct bank investment towards indigenous communities. First, in the 1990s the indigenous communities themselves were rising up to demand their right to "development with identity" (Partridge 1990; Davis and Partridge 1994; Partridge et al. 1998). In some cases they achieved voice and representation peacefully (Ecuador), in others their efforts were violently repressed (Guatemala). But the tide could not be turned back.

Second, the international community, including the United Nations and human rights nongovernmental organizations, mobilized in support of the indigenous movements. We were able to secure a major grant from the Swedish International Development Agency (SIDA) to conduct consultations with indigenous organizations. We used it to finance a series of workshops with indigenous communities (costs of travel, lodging, meals for indigenous leaders and in-country anthropologists) in 11 countries of the region. In these workshops we invited them to propose development projects for their communities and we promised to put those proposals on the table with their governments. We followed up with further visits by international and in-country anthropologists to help them formulate their proposals in forms and formats the bank could act upon.

Finally, our indigenous development initiative was strongly endorsed by the regional vice president, Shahid Javed Burki of Pakistan, and his chief operations adviser, Myrna Alexander of Canada. Without this high-level support and the efforts of in-country anthropologists we would not have been able to overcome the resistance both within the bank and in member governments. Within two years we shepherded through the first generation of bank loans to indigenous organizations in Ecuador, Mexico, Argentina, Guatemala, and Peru. Recognizing the significance of this initiative, the vice president then took the decision to hire a sociologist or anthropologist in each of the resident offices of the bank throughout the region to help target bank investments to benefit the structurally excluded: Afro-descendants, indigenous, ethnic minorities, and other communities trapped in the informal sector of a country's economy.

Final Reflections

Practicing anthropologists bring to multilateral government organizations the capacity to analyze the myriad stakeholders, countervailing forces, and vested interests of a society which perpetuate the structural obstacles that exclude the poor and vulnerable. But analysis is merely the first step. Overcoming such obstacles always entails going beyond the normal functioning of government institutions. It is not that government institutions do not function well, but that they do so only for their clients. The excluded are not and have never been their clients. Reaching the poor and those at risk of impoverishment entails designing innovative mechanisms, processes, and instruments that permit the flow of services, goods, and works to those who have never had access to development resources. It means going beyond business as usual to challenge and correct the institutionalized social exclusion that perpetuates persistent poverty.

Practicing anthropologists in multilateral government organizations depend upon empirical field investigation. It is only through *in vivo* field investigation that the institutionalized structural obstacles that perpetuate poverty in any given society can be addressed. While anthropologists on the staff of such organizations do not conduct lengthy ethnographic research, they identify, recruit, and commission in-country anthropologists who have conducted in-depth investigation, who are familiar with the languages and cultures of their societies, and who manifest an ethical commitment to people's participation in the development decisions that will affect their lives. The latter have the requisite knowledge and skills to tailor development interventions to defeat structural social exclusion, and the former have the job of involving them and making it stick.

Notes

1   The IBRD and the IDA comprise two institutions of the World Bank Group. The World Bank Group also includes the International Finance Corporation (IFC) which provides loans and equity to private sector investment in developing countries, the Multilateral Investment Guarantee Agency (MIGA) which underwrites losses caused by non-commercial risks in developing countries, and the International Centre for the Settlement of Investment Disputes (ICSID) which provides international facilities for conciliation and arbitration of investment disputes.

2   Initially as anthropologist in the Environment Division of the Asia and Pacific region, then as principal anthropologist and environmental assessment manager, and later chief

of the Environment and Social Development Unit for the Latin America and Caribbean region, and finally as lead anthropologist for the Latin America and Caribbean region.

3　Countries are eligible for IBRD lending if per capita income is below US$10,000 per annum. Countries are eligible for IDA lending if per capita income per annum is less than US$2,000. These thresholds are updated annually.

4　The World Bank was the first multilateral governmental organization to formulate policies on involuntary resettlement, indigenous peoples, and environmental assessment, policies which have today become international standards.

5　Professor Mahapatra and other social scientists in India, with support from colleagues in the multilateral governmental organizations, continued working to influence governments at the national, state, and local levels to assist these displaced people and others in other similar projects to regain their lost livelihoods.

6　While the Guatemalan Electricity Institute which owned the Chixoy project agreed to the new plan at the time of appraisal, the lawyer for the government succeeded in excluding any mention of it in the legal agreement for the new loan. The government of Guatemala consequently ignored the agreement entirely (see Partridge 2006).

7　The World Bank's Operational Policies 4.12 and 4.30 on "Involuntary Resettlement" can be found in the *Operational Manual* (World Bank 2012). The text of these two policies may be found online at http://go.worldbank.org/GM0OEIY580 and http://go.worldbank. org/96LQB2JT50 respectively.

8　Forced resettlement is always perceived as a disaster by displaced people. But human communities are not homogeneous and neither are their responses to disaster. Generally, the elite take their money and leave, rather than be subjects of a government resettlement program. At the other end of the spectrum, some of the most vulnerable will fail for lack of capacity to take advantage of the investments in resettlement programs. Most others, however, often discover a silver lining in the disaster. The effect of the exit of corrupt elites – large landowners, commercial middlemen, shopkeepers, moneylenders – is like taking the lid off a boiling pot. The capable, hardworking majority are liberated to make the most of new opportunities represented by the resettlement investments, opportunities that would previously have been captured entirely by the corrupt elite (see Partridge 1989).

9　Cernea was assisted by anthropologists Thayer Scudder (California Institute of Technology), who had studied the disastrous Kariba Dam resettlement, and David Butcher (Edinburgh University), who had documented the equally tragic Akosombo Dam resettlement in drafting the policy statement.

10　This policy became the World Bank's Operational Policy 4.01 on "Environmental Assessment." It can be found in the *Operational Manual* (World Bank 2012), at http://go.worldbank.org/K7F3DCUDD0.

References

Cernea, Michael (1988) *Involuntary Resettlement in Development Projects: Policy Guidelines in World Bank-Financed Projects*. World Bank Technical Paper 80. Washington, DC: World Bank.

Davis, Shelton H. and William L. Partridge (1994) "Promoting the Development of Indigenous People in Latin America." *Finance and Development* (Mar.), 38–41.

Partridge, William L. (1984) "Relocalización en las distintas etapas de desarrollo de los emprendimientos hidroeléctricos." In Francisco M. Suárez, R. Franco, and E. Cohen (eds.), *Efectos sociales de las grandes represas en América Latina*. Buenos Aires: Organización de los Estados Americanos y Naciones Unidas, pp. 151–182.

Partridge, William L. (1989) "Involuntary Resettlement in Development Projects." *Journal of Refugee Studies* 2: 373–384.

Partridge, William L. (1990) "The Fate of Indigenous People: Consultation and Coordination Can Avoid Conflict." *Environmental Forum* 7(5): 29–30.

Partridge, William L. (1994) *People's Participation in Environmental Assessment in Latin America: Best Practices*. LATEN Dissemination Note 11, Latin America and Caribbean Technical Department. Washington, DC: World Bank.

Partridge, William L. (2006) "The Guatemala Chixoy Project Resettlement Disaster." Paper presented to the American Association for the Advancement of Science workshop on "Reparations and Resettlement." American School of Social Research, Santa Fe, NM.

Partridge, William L. and Antoinette B. Brown (1982) "Agricultural Development among the Mazatec: Lessons from Resettlement." *Culture and Agriculture* 16: 1–9.

Partridge, William L. and Antoinette B. Brown (1983) "Desarrollo agrícola entre los mazatecos reacomodados." *American Indígena* 43: 343–362.

Partridge, William L., Antoinette B. Brown, and J. B. Nugent (1982) "The Papaloapan Dam and Resettlement Project: Human Ecology and Health Impacts." In Art Hansen and Anthony Oliver-Smith (eds.), *Involuntary Migration and Resettlement*. Boulder, CO: Westview Press, pp. 245–263.

Partridge, William L., J. Uquillas Rodas, and K. Johns (1998) "Including the Excluded: Ethnodevelopment in Latin America." In *Annual World Bank Conference on Development in Latin America and the Caribbean 1996: Poverty and Inequality*, vol. 1. Washington, DC: World Bank, pp. 229–250.

Shihata, Ibrahim F. I. (2000). "Involuntary Resettlement in World Bank Financed Projects." *In The World Bank in a Changing World: Selected Essays*. Dordrecht: Martinus Nijhoff.

World Bank (2012) *The World Bank Operational Manual*. Washington, DC: World Bank. At http://go.worldbank.org/DZDZ9038D0, accessed Sept. 4, 2012.

Chapter 15

Tools for Gauging Success in the Corporate Sector

Tracy Meerwarth Pester

Tracy Meerwarth Pester worked for many years in the research and development division of General Motors. She offers a fascinating account of what it was like to be a member of a multidisciplinary team, working on a variety of projects. In addition to describing the work itself, she offers detailed reflections on how General Motors considers and responds to internal and external forces, and how this impacted the work she did. She became particularly interested in how one develops an independent assessment of one's personal and professional success in a largely impersonal corporate setting, and provides us with several concrete criteria which she found useful in this regard.

Introduction

I am writing this chapter from the standpoint of an anthropologist who has worked in the corporate sector for over seven years. My anthropological experience is primarily based in research because I spent seven years as a contract researcher at General Motors' Research and Development (GM R&D) labs in Warren, Michigan. I was a member of a five-person research team situated amongst 500 other R&D workers from various backgrounds, including computer science, operations research, mathematics, physics, and metallurgy.[1]

My anthropological work at GM was applied. Our team used ethnographic methods and our understanding of culture to help individuals in the organization resolve problems and gain new insights into aspects of their work generally. Our value to the organization stemmed from our ability to convey new knowledge in

A Handbook of Practicing Anthropology. First Edition. Edited by Riall W. Nolan.
© 2013 John Wiley & Sons, Inc. Published 2013 by John Wiley & Sons, Inc.

the form of books, recommendations, games, models, workshops, presentations, and research papers that would ultimately help GM enhance its relationships with its partners, customers, and fellow employees.

During my tenure, I worked on three high-visibility projects that yielded numerous internal papers, two books (Briody and Trotter 2008; Briody et al. 2010), and one US patent.[2] We learned how to build more successful partnerships, how to create and sustain a better manufacturing organization by building better GM and United Automotive Worker (UAW) relationships, and how to design R&D office space that inspires creativity and productivity. In 2008 our group, comprising both contract and full-time GM employees, was laid off when GM was forced to make some drastic cost-cutting decisions. Unfortunately, our projects ended and many of us have pursued employment or continuing education elsewhere.

My motivation for writing this chapter is threefold. First, I hope to inform practitioners going into the field of business anthropology of some salient characteristics of organizations that may influence their work. Second, I hope to demonstrate how developing personal metrics can help focus the practitioner in a corporate environment of change. Finally, throughout the chapter I weave some thoughts on what I would have done differently to prepare myself for my career in business anthropology. While the insights in this paper are derived from my experience as a corporate anthropologist, my hope is that they represent and are applicable to other areas of applied work.

Forces Exerted on the Organization and You

I'll begin with a discussion of some salient characteristics of the corporate sector. These are by no means complete; however, they emerge at the forefront of my experience at GM R&D. Each corporate "field" experience is different, but there are some similarities across traditional companies, not-for-profits, and family businesses.

My team and I did not operate in a cocoon, but in the context of a host of internal and external forces acting on the organization and subsequently on us. No matter how smart or how dedicated we were to our work, we were still subject to the complex ebb and flow of internal and external forces. As you can imagine, this leads to a very rewarding, dynamic, and daunting corporate experience.

Looking back, I underestimated the degree to which GM was focused on change and my role in that change process. In graduate school we dedicated time to cultural theory and the methods enabling the study of culture. I guess I believed that my job at GM would follow the graduate school model. While having the tools to study culture was critical, I felt less prepared to tackle the practical issues of culture change facing an organization. A general sense of the obstacles to culture change, and the tools to aid in that transformation, are some things I wish I had known more about prior to entering my first practitioner experience.

External forces

Whether you work for GM, a nonprofit organization, or a family business, external factors such as political and economic forces will exert pressure on that organization. Companies are very sensitive to market changes and therefore to the topics you will be pursuing. GM is a public company and must answer to its shareholders. Because of its sheer size and its products, the company enters into discussions with larger economic and political players such as the US government and the UAW. GM is also competing for car production on global platforms, which leaves it susceptible to major market changes in costs associated with manufacturing materials (e.g., aluminum, steel) and innovations in how to power the vehicles they produce (e.g., oil, hydrogen, E85). Businesses such as GM have a global reach. As a result, GM has to plan to produce and manage workers living and working in different countries with a whole host of additional work requirements.

This means that there will be factors influencing your work that you as an employee in the organization may not immediately see. Some you will begin to understand on your own and others will be less obvious. For example, in a smaller company your projects may change in line with local legislative changes, how many grants are accepted, or where family members are willing to invest their resources. Because of GM's sensitivity to the economic environment, management's responses to our projects and recommendations would change to adapt to the political and economic climate. It's not that they didn't value our work; rather, they were faced with determining how to use our findings within the broader context of business. With that said, it is worth taking time to "connect the dots" between your work and the external pressures and opportunities your company faces while you are working for them. Specifically, they will play a part in what projects you work on, the budgets you will have (or not have), the customers you will work for both within and outside of the organization, and, yes, whether or not you have a job.

Internal forces

Internal corporate forces are at work as well. As I said before, one of the most salient processes at GM was culture change. Broadly speaking, in all of our projects there appeared to be a desire to change from an "old" way of doing things to a "new" way. For example, when we studied organizational partnerships we were trying to understand how best to transition to a more relationship-based way of working with a variety of university and for-profit businesses to ensure continued success. In our examination of R&D office space in Bangalore, India and Warren, Michigan we were capturing features that would enhance spatial design for better productivity. All of our projects were about getting relationships and business units from one place to a perceivable better future place.

This desire to be dynamic, to move forward toward a new desired outcome, pervaded the organization. One of the interesting aspects of being part of culture change is that the interest level in your work can be unpredictable depending on who is at the leadership helm. Typically, leaders of companies come from diverse backgrounds and are hired because of their specialties and approaches to strategy, change, and the like. For example, the head of GM R&D had a strong physics background and was particularly interested in our scientifically based cultural approach to exploring problems. He was inspired by a report written by Elizabeth Briody, GM's resident anthropologist, and following several face-to-face meetings he would go on to sponsor three major projects for us. Perhaps our projects and success would have taken a different course had GM R&D had another leader. Similarly, Troy Clarke, the president of GM manufacturing in North America was motivated to build better relationships across the table between GM and the UAW based on what he witnessed in a Mexico City automotive plant. He saw the value in working on the relationship component of global manufacturing and was curious as to how culture played a role in building a better manufacturing organization in the United States. This means that your research could go in and out of favor depending on who is leading and their strategic approach.

Culture Change and the Corporate Organization

Because all organizations are dynamic and presumably desiring to be better at what they do, it is worth understanding what the company thinks and projects about where they are and where they are going. This was very apparent in our work through the intersection of various historical paradigms. Paradigms are defined as points of view, ways of thinking and acting. In the case of GM, a paradigm would be a codified (e.g., formalized) way of conducting business. GM was founded in the 1900s, since which there have been numerous changes in the way they organize workforce responsibilities and define production work methods.[3] These would appear in company literature, presentations, speeches, and the stories employees told.

What I have learned is that each organization you will be a part of has an approach that it follows, and that it changes over time. This intersection of historical paradigms came through very strongly in my work in GM's manufacturing plants when we were trying to understand what made an ideal automotive plant culture. Many employees were supportive of the new work style proposed by management, while others embraced paradigms proposed years before that they referred to as the "old" way of doing things. They conveyed these tensions through storytelling. The desire to continue with the old way of doing things while being encouraged to do something new can be referred to as the "legacy" or "founder effect" in family businesses. The original way of doing things may have a strong following even as the leaders seek to improve on the direction of the founder or owner who built the business and who may have moved on long ago or even passed away.

Knowing that these different paradigms exist gives you a starting point from which you can see patterns of culture change at work. Changes in company points of view can have an impact on the products and systems you study. Attached to these paradigms are emotions and memories, and employees often have important things to say during the change process.

The Art of Practice

As I mentioned earlier, I believe what could have served me better before entering the corporate sector was a better understanding of culture change and of the art of being a practitioner in that change process. I say this only because businesses often hire us to make a case for changes with the data we report and, in many instances, ask us to lead that change process. It is worth learning how to locate and investigate culture because that is the foundation of the work we do, and for practitioners in business, culture change is very much part of the work they do.

As I see it, the practitioner needs to be aware of the fundamentals of culture change and be well practiced in the art of communicating those findings to the stakeholders of the project. For example, in our Ideal Plant Culture project, which was focused on creating a more productive automotive plant culture, we identified several traditional cultural obstacles to culture change including the acceptance or resistance to change, processes of learning a new culture (acculturation and enculturation), and ethnocentrism (the belief that your way in your culture is the best way, compared to other cultures). It was easier for the two other anthropologists on our team, who together had 60 years' experience, to identify these barriers. During the next phase we were to make recommendations for ways to move past these obstacles. Important questions that we asked ourselves as practitioners were: What are the enablers for change? How can we design ways in which employees learn to manage these barriers to change? And what are the appropriate formats for teaching to take place? As you can see, these were all ways in which we needed to "operationalize" our research on culture change.

This takes me to my point about the art of being a practitioner. The processes of applying cultural theory to real problems – that is, being able to match well-documented cultural issues to interventions and recommendations in the drive for change – is an area that I feel could have been more important in my graduate experience. The key is recognizing that recommendations must be made in formats that "fit" the organization and are relevant and appropriate in nature and form.

Organizations are complex systems and many things must be considered when we try to influence change. One of my suggestions to graduate programs with an applied focus is to expose practitioners in training to real life scenarios that require critical thinking. For example, some thought should be given to who will hear your ideas,[4] in what order, and what form this information should take. You may need to determine what factors influence whether this will be done face to face, in a group, or over the Internet. Furthermore, will you pass on your recommendations in the form of workshops, a physical report, a computer model, or all of them, and what are the reasons for choosing one over another?

Another question to consider is what boundaries you have as a practitioner. Perhaps research is your primary job and training is ancillary. How will you navigate the requests you get from leaders to run the training with your paid position as researcher? You must also ask yourself how long you as a practitioner want to be involved in the roll-out phase, and whether you want to formalize the recommendations so that you can hand them over to appropriate leaders to take over? In this case you may need a plan to ensure that someone champions the knowledge you have generated so that what you have done does not fall by the wayside. The process of matching recommendations in an appropriate and relevant way is a skill that I would have found beneficial before my work at GM. It is my feeling that graduate programs focusing on applied work are well situated to provide this scenario-based training.

The Nagging Question that Remains

It goes without saying that my experience at GM was fulfilling and fun in terms of intellectual development, personal growth, and a sense of camaraderie. I frequently look back fondly on the experiences I shared with others. Perhaps the one nagging question that remained when I was laid off was how to gauge my success. In other words, I was faced with the question of how, as a practitioner, one achieves a meaningful and productive work life, as well as who defines that.

For the most part, I believe those who are employed to do knowledge-based work are looking for meaning in their work beyond financial compensation. We certainly don't become anthropologists for the money. How did I come to ask the question of how success and meaning are evaluated? First, I was never formally evaluated as a researcher in the form of reviews and/or progress reports.[5] This was the perk of full-time GM colleagues. Second, there was an unpredictability as to whether our findings would be supported or not. Oftentimes our material was readily adopted and stakeholders would support new projects, but, for what seemed like no apparent reason, other recommendations never got through the pipeline even though a substantial amount of money had been allocated to the research. As a result, I was unsure of how my success and impact could actually be measured. How could I as a practitioner be evaluated apart from other practitioners on my team?

What I have learned from posing this question is that I would have sold myself short if I had looked back on my experiences through the conventional corporate metric lenses such as salary reviews, compensation, and pay packages. I don't mean to say that these are not important; they certainly are. It's just that traditional metrics offer a limited reflection of a practitioner's success. For example, traditional metrics are organizationally driven and organizationally specific and tend to be more short-term in nature. Traditional metrics are also limited in their measurement of how the practitioner is directly benefitting the organization, which may or may not be what the practitioner elects to be *their* professional priority. Quarterly and annual performance reviews typically evaluate the practitioner's latest projects that are completed or will be completed in the near future. Overall, traditional job metrics do not offer a holistic representation of practitioner's true value.

How to Gauge Success as a Practitioner

What I have found helpful is to establish personal metrics in parallel with traditional metrics. Personal metrics help you gauge your progress by measuring yourself on your own terms as you move through different jobs to build a career as an applied anthropologist. My experiences at GM were the building blocks for my career. It set the foundation for my professional development on many different levels. I have learned that defining your own metrics will serve you way beyond your immediate corporate experience as you develop yourself in the field.

The great thing about developing metrics on your own is that you have choices. Managers and colleagues do not define them for you. Believe me, there is much time ahead to be judged by others in terms of the work you are doing! Personal metrics help complement the judgment you will invariably receive from others. Personal metrics are dynamic in nature, changing as you move to different organizations. Defining what makes you successful *in your own eyes* is important because there are many forces beyond your immediate control as an employee. The process of comparing your current situation with your personal benchmark may help to keep you focused on things that are important to you as a practitioner.

Keep in mind that I established my metrics *after* I left GM, but they serve me as I move forward into new job arenas. They were important tools that came from my corporate experience, and I want to pass them on as a best practice. Interestingly, the three metrics I developed pertain not to corporate anthropology specifically, but to learning more about culture and to enhancing the explorative and investigative process. I ask myself the following questions: (1) Is my education as a practitioner being enhanced? (2) Is my understanding of culture being enriched? (3) Am I imparting cultural knowledge to others?

Is my education as a practitioner being enhanced?

The first question I ask myself is: Am I taking the right steps to enhance my education? To me education includes both mentorship and hard skills that you acquire in school and on the job.

My interest in applied anthropology began in college. I went to Bucknell University where I was inspired by a class taught by Professor Tom Greaves.[6] I caught the anthropology bug from the thrill of the investigative process and the satisfaction when community members adopted our team's suggestions. After college, my interest in anthropology gained momentum as I returned to my family business. Working in sales, I remember one particular meeting where a German supplier of engineering products was describing the purchase of a Korean company. He said that the Koreans "were just not doing things our way" and that it was a stressful adjustment.

Something in me wondered if there was a part of anthropology dedicated to understanding the workplace. It was then that I decided to contact Tom to have a conversation about my future.

Tom assured me that there was a field of study called business anthropology and
that there were key figures in the field I should contact. I think my decision to contact Tom and eventually to speak to Elizabeth Briody at GM helped inspire and direct
me toward a job I loved. Both Tom and Elizabeth were leading practitioners in applied
work, and their decisions and stories helped legitimize my vision for what I wanted
to do in the corporate world. I underestimated the degree to which these individuals
would help me sift out what I thought my interests were and set me on an initial career
trajectory. That said, it is worth attending conferences (e.g., American Anthropological
Association, Society for Applied Anthropology), signing up for the National Association for the Practice of Anthropology's (NAPA) mentoring program, and just
learning who the leaders are in your field of interest. I have never come across a practitioner in our field who is unwilling to provide guidance and support.

My desire to work on real life problems led me to the applied track of study at
Northern Arizona University in Flagstaff, Arizona. Three classes served me well for
my corporate practitioner experience: Methods, American Culture, and Internship.
It is important to be able to produce research reports and presentations while under
strict deadlines and time constraints. We were taught how to communicate anthropology to audiences while under pressure and exposed to criticism, and that was a
valuable skill I took into my corporate work. American culture class helped me to
think critically about patterns that are manifest in our own backyard, thus helping
me identify storytelling as a way of conveying a desired culture at GM. American
corporations reflect facets of American culture whether they or not are transparent
and that class inspired me to dig more deeply to uncover these patterns.

NAU's commitment to getting students trained, into and out of a successful
internship, and into the field was apparent in their well-structured internship preparation class and post-internship experience. Regardless of your area of study, professors were intent on connecting you with individuals in their network who might be
useful in promoting your career. With this solid background and practice (e.g.,
research projects, teaching assistantships) in data collection, analysis, and data presentation, I hit the ground running when I joined GM.

That said, you should visit programs where you wish to study, interview the
faculty, talk about the classes and their connections outside of the university environment. Oftentimes the strength of strong *and* weak ties will serve you well as your
continue your education.

Is my understanding of culture being enriched?

The second question I ask myself in evaluating my success as I move forward is: Do
I leave projects with a deeper understanding of culture? Specifically, am I challeng-

ing myself to test new techniques, uncover cultural patterns that may not be as obvious, and look at culture from different vantage points? Hopefully, most of the work you get to do will feed your curiosity for the human condition.

One successful approach in my fieldwork experience was to explain my role in the change process to participants. Sometimes the practitioner must manage workplace anxiety when "studies" are initiated in corporate environments. This may take the form of conversations or of more formalized workshops. Workshops can serve to explain the fieldwork process to larger audiences and offer participants opportunities to ask questions. In one of my earlier fieldwork days, a female metalworker asked if our findings would lead to job cuts. I had not considered this possibility in preparing to speak with her, but her concern was legitimate. Perhaps she had heard of or witnessed this outcome at first hand and was concerned about the impact of our project on her future. I realized that not being empathetic to her concerns would probably affect my conversations with her and other individuals in the plant. I told her that I did not know what form our recommendations would take, how others would use them, and how they would directly affect her job, but that my purpose was to share her experiences to inspire positive change. I wanted her to know that our intent was to improve her experience, but that we would not have ultimate control over the outcomes. Conveying this intent went a long way toward our developing a mutual respect for one another and subsequently led to better communication during the fieldwork process.

Part of the excitement gained from practitioner work is recognizing the lenses through which you can begin to understand culture. The ease of speaking to individuals during the data collection stage led to some innovative ways to help encourage the change process. For example, our team designed a video game using storytelling as a basis for understanding what choices employees could make in order to accomplish work in a plant environment.[7] The game was based on an observation and some follow-up interviews regarding an actual event on the plant floor. Data, in the form of stories and grounded experiences, helped us understand obstacles to and enablers of change. We developed scenarios using people's work decisions and relationships based on examples of good and bad behavior. Points were accumulated based on the decisions they made in the game, which ultimately tallied a relationship score and a work process score.

I found the creative, investigative process to be very rewarding as it is a conduit to new knowledge. Developing the game was a challenge because we had to translate our knowledge of plant culture into a game format that conveyed the cultural reality. For example, we had first to determine what inputs to assign to the relationship and the work process gauges.[8] We then had to assign an appropriate weight (on a scale of 1–10) for each input based on character decisions. Distilling the inputs and assigning weights to behavior to depict realistic character responses necessitated a thorough and critical understanding of culture. The game was ultimately successful as it heightened awareness of and tips for conflict resolution, assessing and improving collaboration skills, and learning from best practices.

Am I imparting cultural knowledge to others?

The last metric I would like to discuss is related to the passing on of cultural knowledge. This is a priority for me because I was inspired by the stories of other practitioners. I recognize that there are ways of exposing others to cultural knowledge inside and outside of the corporation. I touched on workshops previously, which are a great way to assemble individuals from across work groups inside the organization to get a sense of what you do and how you approach things. Don't assume that others know what and how you study. Workshops challenge you to speak to different audiences of people and shed light on insights you have gained. This kind of public experience and visibility has the potential to highlight the anthropological approach in your workplace.

You can also help others learn from your work, and you can learn from others' work, by making a commitment to publish and present papers at anthropology meetings such as the SfAA and the AAA annual meetings. Here you get the opportunity to present to your peers and to field questions about your work and its relevance to anthropology generally. Elizabeth Briody and I presented for seven straight years on a variety of GM projects and at each meeting we met new practitioners. These exchanges helped us clarify our ideas and, we hope, helped others with issues they were encountering in their fieldwork.

Conclusions

The corporate world is dynamic and the practitioner's experience can be both exhilarating and daunting. Although this chapter is written from the standpoint of a practitioner working in a business setting, I feel that all practitioners are exposed to culture change whether they are studying it or work in its wake. Given changes in leadership, market forces, and budgets, it is often unclear whether we have been successful in the projects we undertake.

I argue that personal metrics should be established by practitioners and used in parallel with traditional corporate metrics. Traditional metrics vary significantly from personal metrics in terms of direction, duration, and scope of impact, and therein lies their value. Personal metrics can serve as a reliable guide in a sea of often unforeseen forces. They are dynamic and can be customized to personal experience. Personal metrics reflect short- *and* long-term practitioner goals, which are not only project- but also career-specific.

Notes

1 Our team size varied over the seven years. At its height, there were eight of us, four anthropologists, two operations engineers, and two student interns.

2 "System and Model for Performance Value Based Collaborative Relationships." Oct. 9, 2007. Patent number US 7,280,977 B2.
3 Briody et al. (2010) goes into greater detail about these changes at GM.
4 It is helpful to find key individuals, teams, and work groups that will work as advocates to help champion your project and the work you do.
5 It is possible that the principal investigator evaluated me on our projects, but I cannot be sure. I have a hunch that the contractors, such as myself, were evaluated on the basis of how well or poorly our whole team was doing.
6 Another student and I were trying to understand why a large community park in the university's town was being underutilized. This project taught us how to plan a project, get out and interview community leaders, and come up with suggestions on how to improve the park's standing in the community.
7 Elizabeth K. Briody, Tracy L. Meerwarth, Robert T. Trotter II, and Randombyte Software, *ExplorePlantCulture* (PC game, 2008).
8 Relationship inputs included job empathy, support, and relationship health. Work process inputs included role effectiveness, recognition of effort, and task responsiveness.

References

Briody, Elizabeth K. and Robert T. Trotter II (eds.) (2008) *Partnering for Organizational Performance: Collaboration and Culture in the Global Workplace*. Lanham, MD: Rowman & Littlefield.

Briody, Elizabeth K., Robert T. Trotter II, and Tracy L. Meerwarth (2010) *Transforming Culture: Creating and Sustaining a Better Manufacturing Organization*. Basingstoke: Palgrave Macmillan.

Chapter 16

Working for the Federal Government

Shirley J. Fiske

Shirley Fiske draws on nearly two decades of experience with federal agencies to describe what practicing anthropologists do in them. She outlines the types of opportunities which exist in government service for anthropologists, and describes the career path of a public servant, with particular attention to the internal politics of the bureaucracy. She gives a detailed account of her own job and talks about what skills and qualifications are most useful, and what else a practitioner needs to learn in order to be successful. She concludes her chapter with some thoughts on how practitioners can maintain an independent voice within the federal bureaucracy, while at the same time advancing successfully through the ranks.

Introduction

The executive branch of the federal government in Washington, DC was my workplace and home from home for 17 years of my life, to which I added another seven years in the legislative branch as a Congressional adviser. That makes a total of 24 years working for the government, since the legislative branch participates in the same civil service framework and there is a permeable seam between the two branches. In this chapter I will concentrate my comments on life in federal agencies rather than in Congress,[1] since most anthropologists work for the government in that context.

Despite the public's overwhelmingly negative opinion of government employees in national opinion polls and recurrent scandals such as the "over the top" General Services Administration conference in Las Vegas, my experience in the federal gov-

A Handbook of Practicing Anthropology. First Edition. Edited by Riall W. Nolan.
© 2013 John Wiley & Sons, Inc. Published 2013 by John Wiley & Sons, Inc.

ernment was very positive. During my tenure at the National Oceanic and Atmospheric Administration (NOAA) I sensed that my fellow colleagues felt that it was a privilege and an honor to work there. Perhaps it was because NOAA was a relatively "new" agency, having been created in 1970 by President Richard M. Nixon; and perhaps because the agency culture interpreted its work as a "white hat" agency, on the right side of public issues – warning the public about tornados, hurricanes, and severe weather; protecting marine mammals; and mapping the oceans, among other things. Public service was seen as a positive career choice where one could make a difference.

As you would imagine, describing one's experience working for the federal government is a bit like the blind person describing the proverbial elephant – it all depends on where you are and what you touch and sense. There are differences between national headquarters and regional offices. There will be differences in agency mission and culture that have dramatic effects on employment experience (domestic regulatory agencies vs. agencies that do development assistance). As I describe the kind of work I do, it is important to keep in mind that variability is contextually and structurally driven – by one's agency's mission and by where you are hierarchically and functionally within the agency (Fiske 1994; Hamada and Sibley 1994).

Overall, there are many positive things about a career in government, including the personnel benefits such as employer-supported health care, a good salary,[2] civil service protections, and the ability to identify, refine, and ameliorate public issues and public policy that affect broad swaths of the American public. Anthropologists have a love–hate relationship with the government and policy process: they want to be part of them, but they don't want to be part of them if it means being employed by the government. I hope that when you have read this chapter you will see that such arguments are not black and white or cut and dried, and that you can be part of the government and policy process without surrendering your anthropological calling card.

Do Federal Agencies Hire Anthropologists?

Again on the theme of interagency variability, some agencies seek out and hire cultural anthropologists. The US government's Office of Personnel Management provides the designation 0190 for "general anthropology." Agencies such as NOAA, Department of the Interior, Smithsonian, Bureau of Indian Affairs, and National Park Service advertise specifically for anthropologists or ethnographers. The Centers for Disease Control (CDC) and other agencies like National Institutes of Health (NIH) advertise for behavioral scientists. See Abbott-Jamieson and Clay (2010) for a good look at the kind of work that anthropologists do in the National Marine Fisheries Service (NMFS). If the vacancy announcement is for a behavioral scientist or a social scientist, anthropological skills may be appropriate, depending on the job description. Other agencies such as USAID do not hire by disciplinary specialty, but by their own specialties, such as "agricultural development specialist," and anthropologists have to tailor their experience to what is advertised in the job announcement.

A frequent job announcement for the federal government will call for individuals with skills as a "policy analyst," "program analyst," or "evaluator." Anthropological skills and background are very appropriate for these types of jobs if you emphasize your research skills (both qualitative and quantitative) and your ability to analyze issues holistically. But, again, you will need to tailor your skills and to market them appropriately. The Peace Corps recently hired an anthropologist to be an evaluator of their programs worldwide; you can see the advantages that an anthropologist brings to an international effort such as the Peace Corps, where people deal daily with people from and issues that arise in different cultures. As another example, an agency like the US Environmental Protection Agency (EPA), with highly focused regulatory functions, will be looking for social scientists or communications people to help improve their relationship with regulated entities, such as utilities, manufacturing plants, or communities at risk, from American Indian communities to communities near highly regulated petrochemical plants.

What's a Typical Career Path?

Assuming you make it through your probationary period and you continue to like what you do and are evaluated positively by your boss, there is a career path for you. As a social scientist or anthropologist with a master's degree, you will probably start off as a GS-11 or GS-12, the entering point for the professional series. With a PhD in anthropology you may be hired at a GS-13 or GS-14. You may start off as an evaluator, a program analyst, a social scientist, or an anthropologist, and later in your career be asked to assist in running a program, move up in the analytical support series, or work for a higher-level program manager. As an analyst, your career path generally goes up only to a GS-14 or GS-15 at the top, so if you want to continue in the government you have to be promoted and take on a different job title, or compete internally for a different job that has more management responsibilities. There will be a number of training opportunities available to you, in management, or more in-depth training in your particular issue areas, or an upward mobility opportunity, depending on your agency. Basically, you will be assigned greater and greater responsibility, your scope of work will increase, and you will be promoted.

In my agency people were often hired as a scientist in a laboratory or a science unit, of which there are many across federal agencies from the Department of Energy (e.g., Oak Ridge National Laboratory) or NOAA (e.g., NMFS labs). Individuals hired at this level were considered "bench scientists," working on actual research projects which they developed and managed. Their career paths ultimately took them into management, as they were promoted, leading to the typical complaint, "All I do these days is manage *other peoples'* research!" Quite a few anthropologists are working for federal government research enterprises across the nation, from Seattle (Battelle and NMFS) to Oak Ridge to Sandia national labs. Anthropologists are in a good position to compete for behavioral scientist and social scientist positions.

A career in development agencies (USAID) and the foreign service can include substantial amount of time spent in developing countries, particularly if you are in operations. One anthropologist was promoted to the highest levels and became country director for a South American country, then was asked to take on another region of conflict, Afghanistan. Another colleague was based in Washington, DC but spent time in the field in Africa on her upward career path. The career paths in development are slightly different than those in the rest of the executive branch.

As you continue on a career in the federal government you will be asked to represent your agency as a spokesperson for a program, an issue, or a constituency. Being asked to speak for the entire agency is one of the "rungs" on the human resources career ladder and is valued by the civil service personnel system. You will spend a lot of time in interagency meetings on cross-cutting issues, like healthcare reform or climate change. It means that you are trusted to be able to deal with increasingly national issues across agencies and increasingly high-ranking private and nonprofit sector leaders, such as university presidents, association directors, foundation directors, and the media. You know that your star is rising when you are assigned to media training – either that, or you're in big trouble. And you know that you have great responsibility at a high level (or you're in big trouble) when you are asked to provide testimony to Congress.

As you are promoted you will probably be asked to step into a management role. Your boss may leave federal service, or more likely retire, and you may need to compete for the position or be promoted internally, which is what happened in my case. Responsibility was continually aggregated under my oversight ("piled on"), as was responsibility for personnel to manage a number of programs. Eventually you will reach a career threshold (which a handful of anthropologists have crossed) on training for the Senior Executive Service (SES). If you cross that threshold and into SES status, you will be in a world of management, with greater responsibility (and endless budget cycles). You will be part of the highest cadre of trained professional government managers, and you may be asked to serve your agency anywhere that the Secretary needs you to work, that is, you work at the discretion of the Secretary.[3] One anthropologist who has made that transition and now works at the Government Accountability Office relates his career story in a chapter on careers in the federal government (Fiske 2008b).

The above is the normative career path for professionals in the federal government – increasing responsibility for management and program direction leading to the invitation to join the elite federal corps of professional managers. But be aware that it does not always work this way. Alternatively, and more likely, you may decide that you like what you are doing and not aspire to climb the management ladder, or you may prefer to be in the field and outside the "Beltway," and transfer to a regional office. Some anthropologists have moved from one bureau to another to find a comfortable fit. You may be in a situation where a program is undervalued and underinvested and suffers benign neglect to the point that you have to get out from under the job. You may see an egregious or illegal set of activities undertaken with public funds (defense contractors come to mind here), and become a whistleblower.

A career-changing event can occur when an office, or worse, an entire division, is "riffed" (abolished) when a new administration comes in, as happened shortly after I joined NOAA. Every presidential election can bring a new set of political appointees ("Schedule Cs") who set out to infuse their political philosophy throughout their agency according to the presumed mandate of the last election (and the leadership mandates of their "bosses" at the White House). And many times, those changes include reorganizing the agency to meet their objectives: setting up a new, user-oriented service, or closing certain offices in remote locations (hard and costly to keep operating). Sometimes the reorganizations mean closing offices at headquarters.

A seasoned bureaucrat offered me a piece of advice – part of federal organization culture – that was directly on target since I worked in an office that answered to the Administrator (Under Secretary) of NOAA:

> "Stay high enough to make the job interesting, but not high enough to be vulnerable."
> He followed with the explanation, "Don't get too close to political appointees." I was
> starting work on a special project for the Undersecretary [a political appointee]. And
> I appreciated this advice from a veteran of over 20 years of federal service, although
> at the time I did not fully understand the warning and assumptions it contained. (Fiske
> 1994: 95)

His admonition was prescient. When a new Administrator was confirmed a few years later, our policy office was dissolved and we were, basically, all fired, which is what "riff notices" are all about. Fortunately, I had been working on several projects that allowed me to do pretty thorough intra-agency networking. As an anthropologist, I knew that networking provides resilience in times of turbulence, maybe even survival – a skill that most anthropologists know about and do well. My position was picked up in another part of NOAA (the research arm) where they knew my capabilities as a social scientist. This turned out to be a most valuable career move in NOAA – moving farther down into the organization (away from political appointees) and into a part of NOAA that provided research programs to meet national needs. For a fairly recent and thorough treatment of careers for anthropologists in the federal government, I unabashedly refer you to my chapter on federal careers in the NAPA careers publication (Fiske 2008b).

A Day in the Life: What It's Like to Do What I Do

Much of my time as a federal official is spent trying to convince people to do things, using leadership, social pressure, and negotiating skills. As a program manager and program officer I have to make things happen even if it comes out of their "hides" with no new money, and sometimes to try to convince other offices to do new things that they've never done before, like initiating a new direction for fisheries marine extension, or holding a national workshop on seafood safety, or providing educational training for marine teachers.

At other times I am on the other side – people above my pay grade at a higher organizational level try to convince me to get on board or participate (with the always limited resources of our program) in earmarked mandates where we have little choice but to figure out how to do it without spending too much of our hard-earned core appropriations. A good example in the Clinton administration was Vice President Al Gore's initiative to develop a participatory global program which involved students and teachers in classrooms or educational settings that spanned every continent and subcontinent taking simple observations like temperature, precipitation, wind speed and direction, and so on and sending their observations up to satellites where they were compiled and then accessed by classes and teachers across the globe. This GLOBE program created a global capability and learning opportunity.

I wear a number of hats. I am responsible for managing a small number of support staff and colleagues who are professional staff. I have to evaluate their performance accomplishments and their plans for each year relative to their and the organization's goals. I build cases for promotion and for hiring. There is a certain amount of human resources work and training, particularly when you reach higher grades in the government. I run national programs. A good example of a program that was very successful, again in the educational realm but at a graduate level, is national fellowship program for master's and PhDs in marine sciences and marine-related fields (including a number of anthropologists over the years), who do a year-long fellowship on "The Hill" (with Congressional committees and personal offices) or in federal agencies.[4]

In addition, I manage the "outreach" division for my office, the National Sea Grant College Program. We call it the "Outreach Team," and I am the "team leader." Together, the functions of communications, marine extension (modeled after US Department of Agriculture's agricultural extension service), and education activities from K-12 or public education, are combined into one unit. Now, this is an interesting management conundrum – how do you bring leadership and visibility to a national program of marine extension, communications, and marine education when you do not have a direct-line relationship with any of the actors?

In fact, I managed a network of professionals distributed in coastal colleges, universities, and communities across the United States – from Eastport, Maine to Honolulu, Hawaii – none of whom answered to me, but we were all knit together by the same funding source and a common understanding of the goals of the program tempered by state objectives and different disciplinary backgrounds. What it says in my job description is that I "provide leadership" to this virtual organization – by providing guidance on priorities, funding, reviewing, creating subgroups and new networks, and generally being trustworthy and inspirational. I am also expected to maintain close ties with my profession and professional organizations, which in my case is anthropology; others in the office maintain ties to the American Geophysical Union and the American Meteorological Society). The multidisciplinary genius of the program was embedded in its authorizing legislation – a fact for which I am eternally grateful, and one of the reasons I can recommend federal employment so strongly.

I spend a lot of time reviewing programs, research, and outreach initiatives that we fund and getting peer review groups to review them, and building capability in the national system. Sometimes I end up negotiating over funding levels with deans, program directors, and even university presidents. I also spend a good amount of time in the field – my favorite part, because programs are always seem to be housed in gorgeous coastal areas: marine institutes on Sapelo Island in Georgia, Bodega Bay in California, Penobscot Bay in Maine. This is where I meet with constituents of the program who are seafood processors and fishermen, coastal residents and communities, and nonprofits concerned with the quality of their watersheds, coastal and ocean water, and their communities.

Relevant Skills, Experience, and Qualifications

What skills, experience, and other qualifications are particularly relevant in the federal sector? In general, good writing, communication, and general analytic skills are important, not only in the government sector. Of the skills sets in anthropology, I personally found my knowledge about research methods and practice to be very valuable and used it almost continuously in my career in the executive branch. By "research methods and practice" I refer to the mix of methods, from ethnography to survey research and evaluation, to analysis of data, to the peer review processes of social science and science. A second skill is the ability to understand communities and issues holistically and from the ground up, that is, to keep in mind how people live their lives and are affected by federal policies.

Beyond Anthropological Training

What kinds of things will a practitioner need to learn beyond their anthropological training to work effectively out of this base? Certain concepts and knowledge are more specific to the federal government sector, and a practitioner should have a good understanding of these, for example, applicable federal laws and their amendments that relevant to a particular agency and office (e.g., the National Environment Policy Act, the Historic Preservation Act, the Affordable Care Act). It may be important for you to be familiar with the rule-making process, the Code of Federal Regulations, and how the civil service works.

Also important, and specific to working for the federal government, is the ability to understand and use (and sometimes generate) a federal budget. Understanding the role of Congress vis-à-vis your agency and how to interpret and make the most of it is another important skill. The mission and culture of your agency will shape its relationship with Congress and Congressional committees. The chair of committees that have jurisdiction over your agency, and the appropriations committees that oversee your revenues and often add earmarks, are important to know and monitor, depending on where you are in the agency.

Issue knowledge is an important knowledge base. There will be a body of information and knowledge of the area in which you work, for example health disparities, rural development, micro-enterprise, carbon offsets, environmental quality, health care, ocean policy, or fisheries management. Management skills are not exclusive to the government sector, but it is worth noting that in the CoPAPIA survey, the two most frequent descriptors of people's jobs were "education/outreach" and "administration/management" (Fiske et al. 2010); and when respondents were asked about additional skills, management and project management ranked high.

Practicing anthropologists find themselves with jobs where management skills are valued and yet not generally included in anthropology curricula. In fact, most of this knowledge it is learned on the job.

Ethics, Research Transparency, and Confidentiality

Anthropologists have raised a number of concerns about the work of their colleagues in the federal government, particularly the ability to undertake critical analysis and whether government-sponsored research could be used to harm the community under study. Although some academic anthropologists may believe that working for the government (or any "client") strips anthropologists of their ability to invoke critical thinking, the situation is much more nuanced than that.

If you are considering a federal career, you need to be aware of where you are in the agency, what your research will be used for, and ensure that appropriate ethical and legal standards are in place or invoked. Generally, transparency of research objectives and the sharing of information with the public is a goal that is consistent with anthropological ethics (as articulated by the Society for Applied Anthropology and the American Anthropological Association) and government accountability. However, if you are working in an agency that conducts studies on human subjects (and that includes public health and disease agencies, land management agencies, and environmental agencies, as well as the Department of Defense[5]), you may face challenges meeting the anthropological ethical standards while responding to the laws and producing "court-defensible" documents for lawsuits. The Freedom of Information Act (FOIA), for example, allows the public to request documents and reports that may contain sensitive information on sacred religious sites or about individuals and families. Muriel Crespi, chief ethnographer in the National Park Service, has written persuasively about the tensions between the two conflicting forces – the need to protect human subjects and the freedom of public information – for archaeologists and anthropologists (Crespi and Mattix 2000).

With respect to independence of thought, the review procedures for written documents and public presentations range from very secure (classified) to quite open, depending on where you work, the type of work you are undertaking for the agency, how high up you are in the food chain, and the topic on which you are publishing or speaking.

You may recall the extreme case under the George W. Bush administration, where Dr. James Hansen, a prominent National Aeronautics and Space Administration climate scientist and climate change advocate, was literally prohibited from making public speeches. Similarly, I would expect there to be strong restrictions on what you can write or say if you work for any of the intelligence agencies or the military. In the CDCs, the federal agency mandated to deal with public health issues, every article that is written by CDC scientists and behavioral scientists (including anthropologists) undergoes multiple levels of peer review – as stringent as a peer-reviewed journal article – before it can be published, ensuring scientific integrity. There are also "concurrence" processes in many agencies requiring successive levels of higher political review on some reports and certainly testimony to Congress. In some agencies the only level of concurrence needed is one level above yourself, your boss.

My "corner" in the federal bureaucracy did not require extensive concurrence on scientific papers and presentations (such as anthropological association meetings, or scientific unions like the American Geophysical Union) in part because we were an extramural research program. However, internal reports (e.g., an evaluation of a NOAA program) were generally reviewed by NOAA management one or two levels above me. Other line organizations of NOAA that funded surveys or human research in-house took great care to ensure the confidentiality of individuals, among other things. The highest-level managers in NOAA had their speeches and testimony written by the offices of public affairs or Congressional affairs; they were not at liberty to say just anything they wanted, but had to adhere to ritual language norms about appropriations. For example, they could not say that NOAA needed bigger appropriations to get something done.

My experience is that expectations for review and editorial control are highly variable across agencies and sometimes in different units within agencies; and that, despite the theoretical concerns, anthropologists in the federal government continue to write articles about programs and communities that can range from being highly critical of their agency's policies and relationships with communities, to supportive and thoughtful critiques.

Here's What I'd Tell You

You're part of a large system – you need to understand it formally (organization charts) and in terms of how things really work (your own ethnographic insights) – including the dimensions of power, authority, and collaboration. You can't always control your trajectory through time and space, and you can't always formulate your own research agenda. You aren't an individual anthropological researcher from academia in the old school sense. You may be buried in a slow-moving and under-funded effort way down in the bureaucracy. Your work will be much more partici-patory and iterative, with a lot of feedback loops. It is more consultative, unlike the academic model.

You may have to make compromises as part of a team – generally, editorial deci-sions, negotiations over funding, and, in the worst cases, ethical challenges. You need to be aware of the intended use of information you produce and of the anthropo-logical ethics codes to "do no harm." On the positive side, you have many opportu-nities to affect decisions and policy, and to make a difference for social change – which sometimes takes decades – and the quality of programs and policy that underlie social change.

One piece of advice I found useful is to *find your niche and your unique specialty and make yourself indispensable.* I filled a niche as the "social science conscience" of my agency. It was an informal designation that I didn't realize until one day someone described me using the phrase. As a niche group, anthropologists have tended to forge new programs, sometimes centered on anthropological insights, in agencies that add to their understanding of the social and cultural nuances and the com-plexities of public issues, the need for greater inclusion of public voices, and the definition of community and community well-being. Two examples come to mind, but there are a handful of others that I have described elsewhere: the development of the ethnography program in the National Park Service (Crespi 1998/9; Wray et al. 2009); and the development of social science capacity in the NMFS (Abbott-Jamieson and Clay 2010).

Don't stay buried in the organization too long: actively seek out ways to create networks and relationships throughout the agency both horizontally and vertically: this is very important, for political reasons both inside and outside the agency. Use external allies effectively – "up, down, and out" – as I refer to it. Building ties hori-zontally helps share costs for mutual efforts. Build alliances that can be important for accomplishing objectives; and, clearly, you will ultimately need your own man-agement support from above for budget initiatives or other activities. Building these kinds of networks is probably intuitive for most people, but it is important to pay attention to it. "Outside" relationships, sometimes neglected, are equally important – via external advisory committees, site visits, field visits and training, and grants and contracts with other social scientists and stakeholder groups. Sometimes these may be fraught with friction. Outside relationships can be very important vis-à-vis Congress[6] and top management; but, depending on the issue and agency, there can also be potential lawsuits by environmental groups or landowners (for example) which require delicate maneuvering. Nonetheless, look for opportunities to relate to external groups, especially if they can be potential allies.

You may feel quite alone in your federal job – perhaps not so much archaeolo-gists, but cultural applied anthropologists, who are often the only one in a bureau or even a small agency – or you may be dispersed throughout a very large agency. I would stress the importance of joining professional organizations and being part of the network of conversation or contact. I have been a long-standing member of the Washington Association of Professional Anthropologists (WAPA), a local practitioners' organization (LPO), but I recognize that not all areas have LPOs. Our major professional organizations have sections and interest groups that are valuable in generating networks of inclusion. If you are a government anthropologist, check out FedAnthro, a voluntary listserve of federal anthropologists in the Washington area. If you are at CDC in Atlanta, you have probably already been in touch with the central nodes of the anthropological network there (Fiske 2008a). As more and more anthropologists enter the government sphere, the opportunities for connections are increasing dramatically.

The above nuggets of cultural knowledge derive from my experience and collegial and friendship networks with other anthropologists who also work or have worked in the government sector. To return to my earlier caveats, my experience may not mirror the career of other federal anthropologists and it has to be seen in its context of the agency where I worked and the type of work I did; there are likely to be any number of anthropologists who have had different types of work and different interpretations, particularly in development assistance and foreign service. I have tried to excerpt some of the commonalities of experience to give students and young professionals enough information to help make a decision as to whether it might be right for them. I've also tried to give them a sense of the opportunities in government employment, as well as a discussion of some of the anthropological concerns about this type of work.

Notes

1 The legislative branch is exciting, with a lot of "bang for the buck" and opportunity to influence policy and legislation affecting the public at large. But that's another story.
2 Government executives and the Office of Personnel Management, however, consistently point out that government salaries do not match private sector counterparts.
3 This is also a typical way to get rid of political appointees who have burrowed their way in by converting to the civil service before their president leaves. An agency head will tell one of these people, an "SESer" (member of the Senior Executive Service), that they have to move to some corner of the country where they would not want to go. Ultimately, these members of the Senior Executive Service are the top managers, the heads of major operating units and divisions who run things for the political appointees (and intermingle with them organizationally, that is at similar levels).
4 The Sea Grant Fellows Program, later renamed the Dean John A. Knauss Fellows Program by Congressional mandate to honor a renowned oceanographer and former Administrator of NOAA.
5 This chapter does not cover military and intelligence employment, and the issues surrounding them, for anthropologists, which are covered in Chapter 21, by Kerry Fosher and Frank Tortorello.
6 It should be noted that executive branch managers are usually restrained from talking directly to Congress, particularly with regard to appropriations. But from my vantage point, within both executive and legislative branches, there are numerous ways to work around the prohibitions using informal means and venues.

References

Abbott-Jamieson, Susan and Patricia M. Clay (2010) "The Long Voyage to Including Socio-cultural Analysis in NOAA's National Marine Fisheries Service." *Marine Fisheries Review* 72(2): 1–33.

Crespi, Muriel (1998/9) "Seeking Inclusiveness." In *Common Ground: Archaeology and Anthropology in the Public Interest*. Washington, DC: National Park Service, pp. 12–14.

Crespi, Muriel and Carla Mattix (n.d.) "Negotiating Ethical and Legal mazes in the Federal Workplace." *Park Ethnography Program*. At http://www.nps.gov/ethnography/mandate/negotiating.htm, accessed Aug. 31, 2012.

Fiske, Shirley J. (1994) "Federal Organizational Cultures: Layers and Loci." In Tomoko Hamada and Willis E. Sibley (eds.), *Anthropological Perspectives on Organizational Culture*. Lanham, MD: University Press of America, pp. 95–119.

Fiske, Shirley J. (2008a) "Anthropologists and the Public Health Agenda." *Anthropology News* 48(6): 51–52. doi: 10.1525/an.2007.48.6.51.2

Fiske, Shirley J. (2008b) "Working for the Federal Government: Anthropology Careers." In Carla Guerrón-Montero (ed.), *Careers in Applied Anthropology in the 21st Century: Perspectives from Academics and Practitioners*. NAPA Bulletin 29. Oxford: Blackwell, pp. 110–130.

Fiske, Shirley J., Linda A. Bennett, Patricia Ensworth, et al. (2010) *The Changing Face of Anthropology: Anthropology Masters Reflect on Education, Careers, and Professional Organizations. The AAA/CoPAPIA 2009 Anthropology MA Career Survey*. Arlington, VA: American Anthropological Association.

Hamada, Tomoko and Willis E. Sibley (eds.) (1994) *Anthropological Perspectives on Organizational Culture*. Lanham, MD: University Press of America.

Wray, Jacilee, Alexa Roberts, Allison Peña, and Shirley J. Fiske (2009) "Creating Policy for the National Park Service: Addressing Native Americans and Other Traditionally Associated Peoples." *George Wright Forum* 26(3): 43–50.

Chapter 17

Anthropologists Working in Higher Education

Dennis Wiedman

Not all anthropologists working in universities are academics. Many are administrators, doing a wide variety of interesting and important jobs. Dennis Wiedman has been one of those practitioners for many years, and in this chapter he describes some of these non-academic roles within the university structure, and talks in detail about his own administrative career. He then looks at some of the most significant administrative functions within the university, and explores how anthropological training can contribute to these. He concludes his chapter by offering thoughts and advice on career transitions, the pros and cons of administration, and the need to stay connected to the discipline.

Introduction

What is it like to work in a college or university, not as a professor with teaching and research responsibilities, but in the wide array of employment roles that are required to run a university? Many anthropologists have had long and successful careers in the many employment roles in higher education: from program coordinators and center directors, to academic provosts and university presidents. Professors primarily have teaching, research, and service assignments, whereas anthropologists can fill many other employment roles vital to the educational success of students and the university enterprise. In many communities, colleges and universities are the largest employer in the geographic area and the employer with the longest continuous history. There are dozens of jobs in a university for every one faculty

A Handbook of Practicing Anthropology. First Edition. Edited by Riall W. Nolan.
© 2013 John Wiley & Sons, Inc. Published 2013 by John Wiley & Sons, Inc.

member, jobs specific to the tasks and functions necessary to the fulfillment of the university mission and goals.

An anthropologist employed in higher education with an applied/practitioner perspective can thrive professionally while having a personally fulfilling career. In many cases, anthropologists have become leading figures with powerful budgetary, policy, and planning responsibilities. For example, Yolanda Moses, president of the American Anthropological Association from 1995 to 1997, served as president of the City University of New York/City College from 1993 to 1999, as well as chair of the Board of the American Association of Colleges and Universities, and president of the American Association for Higher Education. At each of these levels she was a champion for women and minorities in higher education (García and Moses 2000). With effective anthropologists employed in these roles, the discipline of anthropology can influence the future directions and lives of students, employees, and communities for generations to come.

Anthropologists have a long history of contributing to the analysis of human and organizational problems, yet they pursue employment positions to implement those perspectives and findings infrequently. This chapter is about the ways a person with anthropology training and an anthropological perspective can succeed in enhancing a university as an organization, a workplace, a knowledge creating and disseminating institution. Anthropological training provides anthropologists with a meaningful and usable set of skills to work in universities. This chapter will emphasize how the anthropological perspective of holism and the concept of "culture," combined with ethnographic writing skills can facilitate evaluation, planning, and policy development – three critical functions that are necessary for the success of any unit within the university.

Practical Anthropology Perspectives and Skills

Rather than being narrowly trained in a specific set of skills, we anthropologists have a holistic perspective that allows us to conceptualize the role of an organizational unit within the overall social institution and to better understand the changing demands placed upon it and the changing environments within which it must operate. Our understanding of "culture" and human diversity enables us to conceptualize, observe, and explain how diverse people in a workplace can enhance quality while adapting to social processes and changing environments.

As experts in human behavior, we can work with a wide array of people and even take the proactive role of culture change agents. Ethnography, the foundation methodology of cultural anthropology, is greatly valued in university roles that require written reports, grants, policies, marketing copy, web page content, and rapid communication using email and media. Our ability to observe people and systems enables us to make good observations, and to write up our recommendations for systems improvements and enhanced efficiencies. These reports are most important in relation to program improvements and justifications for funding.

A proactive way for a practicing anthropologist to influence organizational change is to become involved in university committees, task forces, and special projects that address critical issues. These are often places within an organization where social structures are changed and cultural themes modified, resulting in new plans, polices, procedures, organizational units, and employment roles. If you can demonstrate that your anthropological skills are useful in these settings, you may be given further responsibilities and opportunities for leadership.

Applying Anthropology Perspectives and Skills

Beginning in 1986, I was asked to coordinate the accreditation of Florida International University's transition from a comprehensive to a doctoral granting university. FIU was a young, public, urban university, which had opened its doors in 1972, offering upper division BA degrees and a few master's degrees to the Miami metropolitan area. By 1986 it had begun to offer doctoral programs which required accreditation as a doctoral granting institution by the Southern Association of Colleges and Schools (SACS).

Working with the provost, graduate dean, and department chairs of these doctoral programs, I helped the university attain this new level of accreditation, setting it on the road to adding a wide array of doctoral programs. In 1988, as associate director, I began the university-wide 10-year self-study for reaffirmation of accreditation, coordinating hundreds of organizational units. After successfully leading the reaccreditation in 1990, my organizational and analysis skills were recognized when I was asked by the provost to join the Provost Office to help manage the Division of Academic Affairs. I then worked in the Provost Office for over a decade from 1990 to 2004, leading academic planning, policy development, accreditation, and program evaluation.

During this time I helped guide the university's development from a comprehensive college of 17,000 students to a research-extensive university of 33,000 students, serving one of the most culturally diverse student bodies in the country (46,000 students enrolled in the fall of 2011). During the 14 years I worked in the Provost Office, accrediting agencies mandated the implementation of ongoing planning and evaluation, and the state legislature called for increased accountability with the formulation of written plans, goals, and measurable outcomes, policies, and procedures (Wiedman 1992).

Throughout these years, while I was considered an administrator, I consciously maintained my professional identity by introducing myself as an anthropologist – a practicing anthropologist. Describing this experience in the *Anthropology Newsletter* in 1994 (republished in 2001), I described the value of anthropology in this way:

> If one views anthropology as the study of humans in all their complexities throughout time and in all places, then anthropological theories and methods should be replicable and useful in any human situation, not only among exotic and distant peoples, but in our own society and institutions as well. (Wiedman 2001: 99)

University Employment Careers and Job Functions

There are many careers and jobs for anthropologists within universities. An understanding of the common social structure and organization of universities enables a person to gain employment more purposefully. Every college and university in the United States has similar divisions, departments, and organizational structures. For instance, an organizational unit with staff specifically devoted to supporting students, their organizations, and their activities is often called the Division of Student Affairs. Other common organizational units would be the Office of Development, for relating with contributors; the Division of Research, which facilitates faculty research; Alumni Affairs, which works with the college's graduates; and Academic Affairs, which manages the faculty and degree granting units. Institutional Research maintains information about the university, providing critical information for the president and other decision-makers, and responds to external governmental and accreditation requests. Business and Finance handles financial issues and manages the resource allocation system. The university president guides the overall direction of the university and is responsible for its operations.

An array of other divisions are based on the university's situation and vary greatly from university to university. For example, if there is on-campus housing then there is a Student Housing division. If there are sports programs, then there is an Athletics Division. According to the mission of the university, various centers and institutes perform research and service. Centers are highly variable in the ways they may be organized within a university, for example, they may be within Academic Affairs or other divisions, or report directly to the provost or president. Units relating to international studies, study abroad, or minority student support are particularly welcoming of anthropologically trained staff.

The names of these organizational units, and how they are structured within the university differ from one university to another. However, there are basic functions required of every university to manage the budget, personnel, faculty, students, buildings, and external affairs. The functions that must be accomplished for a university to be fully functional have accompanying employment roles and tasks with associated job titles and descriptions. A college or university is a highly structured social organization with many employment statuses, titles, and job descriptions that are standard across all universities. The titles president, provost for academic affairs, vice president for development, vice president for student affairs usually designate those responsible for each of the major divisions within the university.

There are innumerable ways an anthropologist can become integral to the functioning and management of a university. Anthropologists bring a set of skills and perspectives that are unique and highly valued by leaders of organizations, especially universities.

Typically, a person who advances to the higher ranks within a university is excellent at managing budgets and personnel, regardless of the academic field they are trained in. Over the past few decades, with the commercialization of education, universities have moved toward the business model of management (Bok 2003). This trend encourages the employment and advancement of the person trained in business management who focuses on setting up systems of control, accountability, and profitability, and organizational structures to manage people and resources. With a business perspective, they devote enormous time and effort to budget allocations and personnel issues.

The College Administrator's Survival Guide (Gunsalus 2006) provides real life cases and examples, insights and tools, in dealing with dilemmas of academic management such as handling complaints, negotiating disagreements, responding to accusations of misconduct, and managing difficult personalities. Although these consume the majority of the director's time in every unit within the organization, it is only with careful attention to systematic planning, evaluation, and policy development that an organization can better meet its goals and objectives. It is in these areas that an anthropological perspective provides a career advantage.

Access to Positions in Higher Education

There are many different points of access to positions in colleges and universities. Undergraduate students engaged in student organizations and clubs become familiar with the rules, bureaucracies, and cultures within a university. Student internship and work study opportunities allow insight into the inner workings of a unit. Positions open up to those with a bachelor's degree, especially if they have shown their experience and knowledge of the unit's responsibilities. It is possible to find a reasonable position in higher education with an MA in anthropology, especially if the person has experience in that type of unit through internships, or even volunteering.

Once employed, you can enhance your career advancement by taking courses related to the job. Some universities offer tuition-free courses for employees taking job-related courses. It is possible to earn advanced degrees while working full-time in this way. In universities with PhD-granting anthropology programs with an applied anthropology emphasis, it is even possible to design PhD-dissertation-quality research related to the university. Many universities with schools of education offer EdD or PhD degrees in higher education administration.

As noted earlier, universities are highly stratified; therefore advancement to the higher levels of university administration usually requires a PhD. There is a glass ceiling for those with less than a doctoral degree. This is especially true of Academic Affairs where faculty and degree programs are located. Even so, those with an anthropology BA or MA can find a lifelong career in higher education. Most universities are hiring a greater proportion of part-time adjunct teachers than tenure-track faculty. PhD adjuncts, who engage in an array of university functions other than teaching, are more likely to be recognized for their applied skills and to move into full-time university employment. Those who can write research and program grants are highly sought after in universities. In specialized centers and institutes which are dependent on continuing grants and contracts anthropologists can continue for their entire careers.

Anthropologists attaining a tenured faculty position who have an applied or practitioner perspective can transition to influential administrative roles such as center directors, deans, and provosts. These mid-career shifts entail less teaching and research responsibilities, with significantly more authority to guide program and organizational culture changes.

Although a university's social structure appears to bound by tradition, rigid, and highly stratified, especially those with histories that go back hundreds of years, these organizations must change and adapt to external circumstances. In this era of student consumerism, Internet teaching, budget restraints, and calls for measurable outcomes and accountability, universities must adapt or lose their student enrollments, faculty quality, and alumni support (Altbach et al. 2011). Once a person has a staff position and has participated in and observed the daily and annual operations of the unit, they can begin to influence changes that affect the proper functioning of the unit.

Every interacting group of people has a "culture," and every unit within a university has its unique culture that reflects the larger culture of the university. Aspects of verbal discourse, symbols, cognitive themes, social relationships, material objects are communicated and experienced within the context of this culture by employees and others who deal with them. Becoming an agent of cultural change in such a setting, or even directing the change, is a role which anthropologists are particularly suited to playing.

Planning

There are numerous roles that anthropologists with a cultural perspective can play in influencing the planning process. From the organizational culture perspective, the university consists of subsets of individuals interacting within networks of communication and exchanges which exhibit distinguishing traits. Cultural manifestations are thus elaborated as members interact to confront similar problems and, as they attempt to find solutions, they devise and employ strategies to be passed on to new members. These can be viewed as subcultures, each with its own cognitive paradigm, language categories, dress codes, expected behaviors, and so on. Anthropologists have the skills to organize information, symbols, and people in ways that influence the allocation of resources and facilitate change in directions consistent with the goal of the university (Wiedman 1990).

For example, during the 1990s, as the lead academic strategic planner I facilitated the planning process for the development of the university's strategic plan, which set out the direction of the university into the twenty-first century. Working with the president and vice presidents, and facilitating broad-base discussions among faculty, staff, students, and external constituencies over many years, I coordinated the development of "Reaching for the Top," the university's strategic plan which outlined the steps needed for it to be recognized as a top public, urban research university, and formulated the academic and management themes that prioritized future programs and allocation of resources (Wiedman 1996).

Applying cultural theme theory, now known as cognitive schema theory, I purposefully refined specific words and phrases that would clearly communicate shared meanings and motivate future behaviors. Five academic themes guided the development of academic teaching, research, and service programs; two management philosophies led the ways in which administrative units strived to excel. To provide an example: working with the health faculty, we formulated the "health" academic theme and a vision for the university's future health programs, including a new medical school. By serving on the medical school concept committee for several years, I helped develop a conceptual basis for the planned MD degree and medical school which opened in 2009 with a specific mission and curriculum for educating community-based, culturally sensitive physicians to serve south Florida's diverse demographics. One of the first faculty employed by the FIU medical school was a medical anthropologist.

In the 10 years from 1988 to 1998, the university grew from 17,000 to 30,000 students, from a balanced multicultural institution where no one group held the majority to the largest producer in the United States of BA and MA Hispanic degrees. Minority students increased from 57 percent to 77 percent, while minority faculty only increased from 29 to 31 percent. With this demographic change in the student body, it was important for the management philosophy of "diversity" to express that differences between people are celebrated as a source of rich creativity and innovation. Following the development of the diversity management philosophy, extensive initiatives and programs focused on faculty, staff, and students to create an inviting campus environment and a curriculum and pedagogy responsive to the diverse constituencies (Wiedman 1999).

To enhance your professional skills, you should seek specialized training whenever possible. I was trained by the National Center for Higher Education Management Systems to link strategic planning, budgets, and information systems. In my role as strategic planner for the university, of utmost importance were my skills in quantitative and qualitative data analysis, experience with the computerization and management of vast amounts of information, and my ability to identify external environmental factors and historical trends as the basis for future forecasts.

Evaluation

Anthropological training in ethnography and multiple research methods provides a strong foundation for participating in and leading a university's evaluation and assessment activities. Every unit in the university is increasingly being called upon to document the outcomes of their efforts. From teaching effectiveness, to meeting the major goals of the entire university, employees devote significant time to program outcomes and evaluation. Over the past two decades the trend toward a business model for university management has been significant and pervasive. Every unit now needs to have specific goals and mechanisms in place to measure outcomes of their budgets and personnel efforts. Significant time is now devoted to fulfill these demands for annual assessments and written reports.

Accreditation and the state legislature's demands led to the formulation and writing of plans, goals, measurable outcomes, policies, and procedures. In this young university accreditation forced academic subcultures to develop written traditions, thus making explicit what was implicit when orally communicated. The ethnographic skills of the anthropologist assisted in helping units to consciously recognize and then record their regularized behaviors. From an anthropological perspective, we can better understand the influence of accreditation in forcing organizations to shift from oral to written traditions, and the subcultural and organizational responses to accrediting agencies' demands for systematic planning and evaluation (Wiedman 1992).

A university is required to undergo a regional accreditation self-study every 10 years. I served as the associate director of the university's reaffirmation of accreditation by the Southern Association of Colleges and Schools for two accreditations (1990 and 2000), and was the university accreditation officer for more than a decade. The accreditation assessment entailed a two-year self-study by every unit in the university and the mobilization of practically every member of the faculty and staff. In 1990 SACS had recently changed the accreditation criteria to include institutional effectiveness, and few schools had conducted self-studies under this new requirement, which called for ongoing planning and evaluation. I viewed it as an opportunity to direct culture change: a shift from present to future thinking, from crisis management to strategic management, and from oral to written traditions (Wiedman 2001).

Policy Development

In the development of written policies and plans, ethnographic skills are invaluable in documenting behaviors, beliefs, and practices. FIU, being a relatively young university, primarily communicated orally without written procedures. My ethnographic skills at recording behaviors, compiling historical documents, and interviewing people about how things work empowered me to become the compiler and editor of the first set of undergraduate and graduate policy manuals. It is an understanding of social structure, social organization, and culture change that facilitates the building of a consensus for approval of policies and procedures. Each of the hundreds of policies needed to be reviewed and approved by multiple levels of people from the faculty, faculty senate, deans, to the provost. Understanding linguistic and cognitive processes allows for the creation of words and symbols for the development of workable policies and the portrayal of a shared future vision built on acceptable cultural themes (Wiedman 1990).

Management Culture

Anthropologists who recognize the similarities and differences between organizational and management cultures can be more effective in solving human problems by influencing decision-making and policy development. Over recent decades, American businesses, organizations, and institutions have undergone similar transitions to increase productivity and efficiency through "strategic planning," "best practices," "strategic management," and "total quality management" (TQM), to name but a few programs. These global management cultures greatly influence local-level organizations and universities.

These can be viewed as management fads, but they can also be seen as sociocultural adaptations to a changing environment. They have come at a time in our history when the invention and diffusion of electronic information technology are revolutionizing the communication patterns, decision-making, and authority structures of the workplace and of organizations. Strategic planning is a conscious, purposeful effort to influence the future. To be successful at these efforts, we must consider the organization's external environment, especially the political, economic, and demographic context. The holistic perspective enables the anthropologist practitioner to excel at identifying and assessing the importance of these macro influences as well as the micro processes of human interactions and beliefs (Wiedman 2000).

Information Dissemination

When the Internet became a reliable infrastructure for communication, I took on, in addition to my other roles, that of developing the Academic Affairs web page. This first administrative web page in the university enhanced the wide distribution and discussion of plans, policies, and organizational information. What was once only on paper or verbally communicated could be available to the entire university community. Building a broad consensus of university members from various levels in the university, together with a wide dissemination of this information through the Internet, enabled the dispersal of information in ways that were once possible only to those in power, thus helping to reduce social inequalities and disjunctures. Hopefully, from these experiences you can see how an anthropologist can organize information, symbols, and people in ways that influence the allocation of resources and facilitate organizational culture changes.

Career Development and Transitions

Higher education positions are similar from university to university, facilitating career moves between universities over the years, each time increasing your responsibilities and income. Basic university functions in almost every university have similar employment titles and descriptions with related professional organizations, conferences, and publications. The *Chronicle of Higher Education* is the primary location for university employment announcements. The *Chronicle*'s section on "Academic Life" has a plethora of information about how universities really work (http://chronicle.com/section/Advice/66/). *Inside Higher Ed* has a section titled "Advice" which also contains a lot of good information (http://www.insidehighered. com/advice).

For long-term career development it is wise to attend the yearly conference associated with a professional group, to be a presenter at the conference, and to be an active committee member or elected officer. This enables you to keep abreast of the state of the art in the field, to bring back best practice information to your job, and to build networks of experts you can call upon for advice. The Association for Institutional Research (http://www.airweb.org/pages/default.aspx), for example, is the world's largest professional organization for this professional group, with more than 4,000 members focusing on providing educational resources, best practices, and professional development opportunities. Student Affairs Administrators in Higher Education (http://www.naspa.org/) is the leading association for the 12,000 student affairs professionals which provides professional development, policy advocacy, and substantive research to inform practice for members serving a variety of functions and roles working within housing and residence life, student unions, student activities, counseling, career development, orientation, enrollment management, racial and ethnic minority support services, and retention and assessment.

By being active and engaged in the professional organization related to your job title, you can bring recognition to your university, improve your understanding of the common issues facing those in your career, and enhance the quality of your own organization. By attending conferences, making presentations, and serving on committees you become nationally recognized, enhancing your employability within your university and also increasing your opportunities for moving to another university for career advancement. Some professionals build a reputation in a specific area, enabling them to be asked to come to a university to improve operations quickly. As consultants, or as full-time employees, these change agents do not have the historical baggage that sometimes prevents tough decisions from being made.

Benefits, Drawbacks, and Awkwardness

University staff positions are full-time, year-round, with employee sick leave and annual leave benefits. Faculty positions are usually for nine months, without pay during the summer. These university staff positions with consistent year-round employment are highly valued by professionals with families and children.

Annual employee evaluations are now standard operations within universities for staff and faculty at all levels. While faculty are evaluated on their teaching, research, and service assignments, staff evaluations are based on the specific goals and outcomes of their particular units. Staff positions do not normally recognize teaching, research, and publications as part of employee evaluation. Therefore, the anthropological practitioner desiring to remain active in their field of teaching and research will have to do this over and above the defined job responsibilities. A way to do this is to teach at least one course a year for the anthropology or a related department. This experience enables you to understand the current student body and keeps you current on the literature and trends in the field. As for anthropology practitioners in other employment fields, employers do not usually reward employees for publications or activities in professional anthropological organizations. Unless they take a personal interest in continuing their membership in such organizations, practitioners gradually lose their identity as anthropologists and take on the identity of their job position. Some attend anthropology conferences for a short time, soon realizing that these forums do not meet their professional development needs or relate to their job requirements. For those who do want to continue to participate in anthropology as a profession there are several organizations where higher education employees may find a home. Within the American Anthropological Association there is the Council on Anthropology and Education (CAE), the Society for Anthropology in Community Colleges (SACC), and the National Association for the Practice of Anthropology (NAPA). Each of these has sessions at the annual meetings of the American Anthropological Association and publications in *AnthroSource*. If you do not find sessions and publications within these sections of the AAA, you should become a change agent within the section by organizing sessions on topics of interest to you and by mobilizing others in higher education with similar interests. For example, for those who do university program evaluation, within NAPA there is the Evaluation Interest Group which organizes events, publications, and sessions by those employed as evaluators in many employment fields. The Society for Applied Anthropology (SfAA) also has many ways for someone employed in higher education to continue their professional affiliation and identity. If you do not stay engaged in your academic profession, it is unlikely that you will be able to transition to a faculty position with teaching, research, and service assignments.

A drawback that is often awkward for academics is that most of what is produced by a staff member will not have your name on it. It will be disseminated under either your boss's name or that of the unit as a whole, often with no acknowledgment of authorship at all. This is counter to the emphasis that faculty place on the authorship of a product. In a unit staff position, you will be paid for your contribution to the university and unit; individual recognition comes only with continued employment, career advancement opportunities, occasional employee recognition awards, and most importantly salary merit increases.

Conclusion

Anthropologists who recognize the similarities and differences between organizational and management cultures can be more effective in solving human problems by influencing decision-making and policy development. These experiences illustrate how practicing anthropology in a university can be a meaningful and fulfilling life pursuit, especially if you can study specific issues, make program and policy recommendations, and then lead an organization to address them.

References

Altbach, Philip G., Patricia J. Gumport, and Robert O. Berdahl (eds.) (2011) *American Higher Education in the Twenty-First Century: Social, Political, and Economic Challenges*, 3rd edn. Baltimore: Johns Hopkins University Press.

Bok, Derek (2003) *Universities in the Marketplace: The Commercialization of Higher Education*. Princeton: Princeton University Press.

García, Mildred and Yolanda T. Moses (eds.) (2000) *Succeeding in an Academic Career: A Guide for Faculty of Color*. Westport, CT: Greenwood.

Gunsalus, C. Kristina (2006) *The College Administrator's Survival Guide*. Cambridge, MA: Harvard University Press.

Wiedman, Dennis (1990) "University Accreditation: Academic Subcultural and Organizational Responses to Directed Change." In T. Hamada and A. Jordan (eds.), *Crosscultural Management and Organizational Culture*. Williamsburg, VA: Studies in Third World Societies, pp. 227–246.

Wiedman, Dennis (1992) "Effects on Academic Culture of Shifts from Oral to Written Traditions: The Case of University Accreditation." *Human Organization* 51(4): 398–407.

Wiedman, Dennis (ed.) (1996) *Florida International University: Reaching for the Top*. Miami: Florida International University.

Wiedman, Dennis (1999) "Celebrating Diversity at FIU: A Role Model for the Future of U.S. Higher Education." *Journal for the Art of Teaching* 6(1): 37–46.

Wiedman, Dennis (2000) "Best Practices Compared to Strategic Management and Total Quality Management: A New Paradigm or an Incremental Change in Management Culture." *High Plains Applied Anthropologist* 20(2): 146–152.

Wiedman, Dennis (2001) "Directing Organizational Culture Change through Strategic Planning and Leadership." In P. Sabloff (ed.), *Careers in Anthropology: Profiles of Practitioner Anthropologists*. NAPA Bulletin 20. Washington, DC: American Anthropological Association, National Association for the Practice of Anthropology, pp. 99–103.

Part III
Domains of Practice

Chapter 18

Methods and Approaches

Mary Odell Butler

How, from a methodological standpoint, do practitioners approach their work? It's too broad a question, of course, but Mary Odell Butler manages, in this concise and focused chapter, to get to the core of things. She discusses the role of theory in practice work, drawing on her own experiences, and how she learned to use theory in her work and to explain it to others. She then discusses the types of methods that she has found most useful, placing particular stress on the need for teamwork, collaboration, and multidisciplinary thinking. She concludes her chapter with a discussion of some problem areas of particular concern to practitioners, such as ethics and confidentiality.

I approach this chapter with considerable humility. It is a kind of hubris to attempt to describe methods and approaches in the practice of anthropology. The field is as broad as anthropology itself. And the approaches that we use are even broader, moving as they do into interdisciplinary studies. I know only what I know. What I say here will almost certainly leave out approaches to practice that are important and frequently used by practitioners of anthropology. No matter how carefully this chapter is vetted by my colleagues in this volume, some of you will find that it falls short of your own experience. I can only ask your forbearance, and welcome your comments.

But we are all anthropologists and we share a core understanding of how the world works and the best ways to find out about this. Often people come to us for help because they recognize – explicitly or implicitly – that we have mastered something that will help them in their own work. Another reason for laying some of this

A Handbook of Practicing Anthropology. First Edition. Edited by Riall W. Nolan.
© 2013 John Wiley & Sons, Inc. Published 2013 by John Wiley & Sons, Inc.

out is that many of us – at least those of us who did not go through graduate programs in applied or practicing anthropology – aren't sure exactly how what we do fits into practice. In this volume, the effort to put anthropological theories and methods into a practice context is useful, even if it is necessarily incomplete.

What do we mean by "approach"? I mean a fairly flexible combination of theories and methods that are combined to achieve a specific objective. When approaches are used in practice, obviously they refer to this combination applied to a practical situation defined by an organizational or client need. In this sense, research in anthropological practice is distinguished from the research that we all did, at least as part of our graduate work, which is intended to arrive at answers to problems defined with reference to the theoretical questions posed by scholars. Seldom will organizations pay for answers that are strictly academic in the sense that they are interesting from some perspective. People buy research in practice because the answer to a research question is needed or useful in some way. It is the purpose of the research or the use to which results are to be put, rather than a body of theory and method – an approach – that distinguishes practice from any other kind of anthropology (Patton 2005; Copeland-Carson et al. 2012).

When I began in anthropology in the early 1970s, I was a follower of Marvin Harris – a cultural materialist and logical positivist. I believed that most things could be explained by adaptation to a system of interacting forces normally driven by the material conditions of life. As a graduate student, I was labeled by some the departmental Marxist, although at that stage of my life I didn't understand Marx well enough to earn the label. I would like to think that my approach has become more nuanced since then – in fact, I know that it has. But this phase of my thinking taught me to approach things scientifically.

This has been a huge advantage in the public health evaluations that I have done for the past 25 years. As a program evaluator, I assess how public health programs are performing and make recommendations for their being continued or discontinued, reduced, modified, or expanded. Time and money ride on what I and my colleagues do. Evaluation must be scientific, carefully linked to evidence, and credible to those who use its results to do things. I have found a booming market for the application of ethnographic theory and method to evaluation. Understanding the perceptions of public health initiatives by the people they are directed at is critical to their success or failure. In the final analysis, public health action is the result of negotiation between the views of providers and those of recipients of programs as to what constitutes good health and what steps are acceptable in its pursuit. Still it's evaluation, and to do it we must become expert at building bodies of evidence.

Finally, I was an undergraduate pre-med major and I have worked mostly (but not exclusively) in public health. Although I have tried to incorporate other people's experience, my examples tend to come from this perspective.

In the sections that follow, I will discuss some of the theoretical approaches and the methodologies that I have found useful in my own practice of anthropology. I hope that by the end of this discussion not you will be able to apply anthropological methods and theories to practice. Many of you already know how to do that better.

Thinking Anthropologically: The Role of Anthropological Theory

Few concepts have caused me, my clients, my students, or my colleagues more difficulty than this idea of theory. Theory was the central concern of my training in anthropology – cultural theory, biocultural theory, theories of change, theories of dissemination and the adoption of innovation, theories of religion and economics, political economy and human diversity, grand theory and (presumably) "ungrand" theory. I found all of this fascinating even if I did wonder from time to time how I would know the right ones to use when the time came. One of the things that was never explicitly addressed in those days was how to use theory to find out things about how humans functioned to build their lives into coherent systems of understanding. Absent this grounding in experience, theory became a rather fuzzy idea that is difficult to use as a tool in doing anthropology.

I have resigned from the debate about what theory is and is not. As I use it, theory is simply a guide that explains to you and to others what you are exploring in the effort to produce an understanding of what people are doing, how, and why. It is the way that you believe that the elements of a human system articulate to produce some kind of result, whether it is a nuclear test ban treaty or a babysitting cooperative. I recognize that the systems approach may not be universal, and that others would use other words to express this, but let's try to avoid a theory of theories. Suffice it to say that, if you can't identify what you are looking at, you can't develop knowledge. And for practitioners of anthropology, knowledge of human life is what we produce.

Theory should never be confused with truth. I once believed that theoretical eclecticism was the great enemy of clear thinking. After all if you can change your theory with the situation, theory can never be falsified (Harris 1979: 287). This is a model of science that I have left behind as I have learned more and more about how messy human life can be. Sometimes theory emerges like a shadow rising up from deep water, creating "aha" moments that lead to new and improved ways of seeing things. Sometimes it is more recalcitrant and has to be hammered out through experience and argument. Theory can be developed at many levels of complexity within and across societies; it can be adjusted and modified as more accumulated information becomes available. It can even be discarded if a better one comes along.

One kind of theory that we engage as practitioners is the whole idea of culture. In my area and in a lot of others, cultural and sub-cultural disjoints turn out to be a significant part of what we are called to clarify. What one group of people considers sound public health practice, another considers an unwonted intrusion into their civil liberties. One example of this is the controversy surrounding the vaccination of pre-adolescents against human papilloma virus (HPV). HPV vaccination neutralizes a set of viruses that are known to be an important cause of cervical cancer. HPV infection often occurs in the early years of sexual activity and can stay in the body for decades before it becomes active. Testing for HPV at any age is costly. The disease itself can be prevented by vaccinating both boys and girls at puberty before they become sexually active (MMWR 2007, 2011). But campaigns to implement HPV vaccination programs are controversial. What public health officials see as a proven way to protect people from a form of cancer that can be deadly, some parents may consider a way for the state to make promiscuous behavior "safe" and even normal (Krishnan 2008; Walloo et al. 2010). The only thing anyone can do in this situation is to work toward a better mutual understanding of the problem – a negotiation across cultures. Failing this, the immunization program will fail and a number of unvaccinated young people will face infection with the omnipresent virus as adults, if not in their teen years.

Part of the problem with the culture concept is that everyone thinks they know what it is and often they have a definition that has worked for them for a long time. When you start talking to people, you begin to see that their definition may be effective, partially effective, or flat out wrong in terms of day-to-day action. People confuse culture with language, ethnicity, area of residence, urbanicity. This wouldn't matter in the least if they weren't trying to use the idea of culture as a tool to achieve some desirable outcome. The health literature is full of examples of cultural mistakes in reaching out to people with health services and public health interventions (see, e.g., Fadiman 1997). In many of these cases, failure to understand the mosaic nature of culture, the role of acculturation in immigrants, the difference in the patterning of the cultural mosaic socio-economically or politically can become a prescription for misdirection of worthwhile efforts.

This is not to say that anthropologists have a special lease on the culture concept. You don't need to be an anthropologist to use this concept effectively even if the concept is different from ours. We are not struggling for correctness of theory. As anthropologists who have thought a lot about culture, it is not our job to force our definition of culture on people from other disciplines. But it is incumbent on us to broker a shared culture concept by bringing these various visions out and making sure that people converge on a shared idea, at least shared enough to achieve what they have set out to do. This is true whether the "others" are colleagues on interdisciplinary teams or clients from other disciplines. As you may have noticed, it also applies to other anthropologists. Otherwise why is there so much noise about culture at AAA meetings?

Ethnography is the methodological and theoretical nexus for cultural anthropology, incorporating both a theory of how culture works and a method for discerning and documenting it. Many professionals consider ethnography to be a method. And it certainly is that (see below). But ethnography is also a theoretical stance (see, e.g., Atkinson and Hammersley 1994; Fetterman 1998). Ethnography as it is practiced in anthropology and elsewhere privileges the perspective of participants in a cultural interaction of some kind. Whether we do it consciously or not, our training as anthropologists tells us that the ultimate end of ethnography is to comprehend the perspective of the "insider," whether that insider is a Trobriand islander or an Arab American woman seeking breast cancer screening. This comes from the idea that culture is relative, based on who you are and where you are. Your goal then becomes untangling these cultural understandings so that an outsider can see the inside. The whole issue of perspective and whose perspective you need to have is far from a universal concept in the science of other disciplines. Very often others will believe in the "truth" of points of view rather than in culture as a negotiated space. Yet very often, it is clashes of perspective that are the focus of our work.

When I first became a practitioner, I worked hard to eliminate the terms "emic" and "etic" from my working vocabulary. I had come to use them as ordinary words, as in: "Well, given the lack of culturally competent medical care in their neighborhood, etically they have no services." I got really tired of the look people gave me. I have had to put them back at least into my professional vocabulary because they are so useful that many disciplines other than anthropology and linguistics have begun to use them – psychology, social work, ethnomusicology, nursing, medicine, education, and many others (Schwandt 2007). As you may remember, this set of terms marks perspectives in some situation: *emic* being the perspective of the participant and *etic* being the perspective of the outside observer (Pike 1954; Harris 1968). A lot of the time, what I have done in practice is capture the emic perspectives by doing ethnography, then translated this to an etic perspective that makes sense to my clients.

This theoretical stance relative to human life is thus very important. However, it must be used with some subtlety. There are normally multiple emic perspectives, and assembling them into an emic portrait of a community may not be straightforward. Most experienced ethnographers have had the experience of arriving at an understanding only to realize that they hadn't really arrived there at all. In my own graduate work one of my professors used to set up a scenario in which you solved the ethnographic problem fairly easily because most of your informants told you pretty much the same thing. And when you had it all figured out and reported it to your informants, one man stepped forward and said, "I do not agree." What do you do then? You go back to the drawing board because clearly you have missed something key in your ethnography. But many people, trained in other ways of thinking, view the lone dissenter not as indicative of a problem but as an outlier to be disregarded.

Like many anthropologists, I see culture as a system embedded in a context partly made up of overlapping systems. This is also part of our preparation as anthropologists. Traditionally anthropologists have sought holism in their view of culture and a respect for the context in which people operate (e.g., Radcliffe-Brown 1952). Today holism and context have become more sophisticated as chaos theory and complex adaptive systems have refined our understanding of system dynamics. Chaos theory, for example, teaches us about the phenomenon of patterning at boundaries (Gleick 1987). Complex adaptive systems have moved beyond the (sometimes tautological) application of adaptation to change to refine our understanding of the multiple context in which systems evolve (Lansing 2003).

Finally, we bring to our careers an understanding of how to use the idea of community and communities to build theories about culture. As Tip O'Neill, the late speaker of the US House of Representatives used to say, "All politics are local." O'Neill was, of course, talking about what motivates Congressmen to compromise in ways that may not be optimal for their constituencies. But everyone, whether they are the queen of England or a mine worker in South Africa, is always fitting themselves to the conditions that have a proximate effect on their lives. In the practice of anthropology, where the stakes in your results may be high and not very explicit, an understanding of what communities are, how they overlap, and how conflict within and between communities work is critical. From the Yanamamo on, we have all spent a lot of hours trying to understand culture conflict.

We are theoretically well prepared to live in the multidisciplinary, applied world of anthropological practice. We carry our own set of theoretical orientations that have proved to be useful in what I am trying to stop calling the "real" world. And we respond to other kinds of theoretical models, often drawn from other disciplines, because our anthropological perspective has taught us that we must move beyond looking at a thing itself to understand that everything that ever occurs occurs in a context that is dynamic. We use concepts like *diachrony* and *synchrony* (simultaneity and separation in time), emics and etics, the imperfect translation of culture to behavior, the situational nature of human life.

Doing the Work: Methodological Approaches to Practice

I have found the methodology of practice to be pretty much what it was in all of the previous anthropology I had done. You may need to adapt it to budget or time constraints, but I don't find that I've developed anything methodologically revolutionary as part of my practice. It is true, however, that we adapt methodologies to particular contexts of practice. In this section, I would like to describe what I have found to be most useful in the anthropological toolkit as applied to practicing anthropology and some of the ways that I have fine-tuned methods to meet the specific – if not unique – needs of this kind of anthropology.

Very often clients are looking for ethnography when they first consider anthropology, whether or not they are aware that this is what they need. Ethnography as method incorporates a holistic, multi-method way of uncovering how a defined community uses culture to manage community life. A very important characteristic of ethnography is holism, meaning that ethnographers try to look at the phenomenon of interest embedded in its context. The ethnographer wants all of the information that they can possibly obtain in order to build the richest picture possible of the experience of the community. Specific methods include open or semi-structured interviews, informal conversations, participant observation, direct observation, document abstraction, mapping, and anything else that provides information. Ethnographic work almost always involves chasing down leads and discovering the unexpected.

Traditionally in anthropology, fieldwork involved total immersion in the daily life of the studied community. We can seldom do that these days in practice or in academic research. It is too costly and anthropology itself has moved theoretically and methodologically beyond the "lone wolf" approach. Moreover, not all anthropology is ethnography and not all ethnography is done by anthropologists. There is, of course, some variation in how ethnography is done in different disciplines, but the method is similar enough across disciplines so that interdisciplinary "team" approaches are possible. And as practitioners, we must learn to do this. Effective practice must move beyond debates about who owns what tools. The methodological trick here is to define things well enough so that everyone understands the domain being studied.

You must become expert not only at conducting open-ended interviews but at explaining how they work to others who have never learned to do this. Open-ended interviews are both a desirable and undesirable thing from the point of view of non-ethnographers. People can readily understand using this technique in an exploratory way, that is, we're not sure what we want to know and are trying to develop a map for more intensive study. But, in my experience, nothing makes clients as nervous as this. The kind of open discussions that anthropologists like to do are difficult mentally. You have to hold the "instrument" (usually a set of topics) in your head while listening to responses, remembering what you haven't asked yet, assessing the respondent's affect at various points in the process, and capturing the information. There is an element of art in good ethnographic interviewing, although I seldom say this to clients who aren't used to the idea of ethnography. They already worry that it isn't very "scientific." Also in my experience a lot of perfectly well-trained social scientists don't understand a critical rule in ethnography: "The person who talks the most learns the least." Controlling the opening up of ethnographic interviews is subtle. You need to stay in a designated domain without stifling new information. The best way to lose emerging data is to talk over it.

You don't always get to do a lot of participant observation in practice, although this varies a lot with the kind of practice you are talking about. In my case, everyone knows that I'm an evaluator and what I'm there to do. The closest I ever get to real participant observation is sitting in on meetings (which does give me an opportunity to understand how people negotiate things) or being an appropriately dressed fly on the wall in a clinic setting. Other practitioners spend a lot of time doing this.

Finally, we need to become expert at building data analysis and inference from qualitative data. Everything I do has to be evidence-based. This is a critical concept in both public health and evaluation. The building of evidence and the linkage of evidence to conclusions happens in careful analysis of qualitative data. This is time-intensive, expensive, and worth every cent. I usually insist that interviews be taped and transcribed verbatim prior to analysis. I didn't have this luxury in the past, but now I do. So I demand it.

Partners Can Help Us Do It Better

We aren't the only people who use these methods and theories. Most practice – at least in anthropology – involves work in interdisciplinary teams. In my career, I have collaborated with psychologists, epidemiologists, physicians, psychiatrists, economists, historians, sociologists – the list could go on and on. In collaborating on projects in multidisciplinary teams, we all have a piece of the approach though we may view it differently. I have learned a lot from other people this way. We all put in our piece of the puzzle, integrate the pieces, and create an approach that is stronger because it brings so many strengths to the table.

For example, case study designs build understanding by thorough investigation of a contemporary phenomenon in its real life context using multiple methods of data collection (Yin 2009: 18). Case studies are part of many disciplines and there are fairly well-developed ways of doing them. Ethnography fits beautifully into this multi-method approach because ethnography also emphasizes finding out everything you can from as many sources as you can. But good case studies require expertise to cover all of the bases. In all disciplines, much of the expertise involved lies below the surface rather than being directly visible from the activities you can observe. I can do a cost-effectiveness analysis by reading up and feeding data into a formula. But I will not necessarily do it the same way an economist would. I need the education and experience of other kinds of minds.

Quantitative analysis is similar. For reasons related to my own history, I do this fairly well, but professionals in this kind of work will always do it better than I do. Usually I have been in a position to bring in the statisticians and mathematicians I need. But their work cannot be independent of mine if we are doing ethnography. I once convinced a federal agency to accept me as a statistician, but I have tried never to forget that this doesn't mean I *am* a statistician.

Policy analysis considers the implications and effects of a proposed policy on people who are in some way affected by that policy. The effects, of course, vary. Compiling the perceptions of multiple people with an interest in policy decisions (in evaluation we call them "stakeholders") is one more form of ethnography. But others – political scientists and other "policy wonks" – are usually important in understanding who the stakeholders are and how policies reverberate through governmental and social structures.

Problem Areas

There are some things that are always problematic when multiple disciplinary perspectives pull together to get something done. These may not seem like theoretical or methodological concerns. Yet they require considerable expertise to navigate successfully. There are several issues that crop up in just about any study I have ever been part of. Some of them are presented below.

Uncertainty about research design – especially the unit of analysis – comes up a lot. What is being observed? Is it a population? A community? A social organization? Several social organizations? All of the above? One of the things I have found most often to be at the bottom of difficulties in getting agreement on research design is disagreement about what is to be studied. We tend to assume that the unit of analysis is a community or some culturally specified group of people working together in a social organization. Psychologists tend to assume that the unit is the individual reacting to some kind of context, often a society (social psychologists). Epidemiologists and demographers assume it is a population. You're probably starting to get the idea. These assumptions about what we will study are an unending source of disagreement about research questions, instrumentation, data collection methodology, the content of informed consent, analysis. The design goes much much more smoothly if these sources of disagreement are ironed out first rather than making uncertain compromises that may later confound analysis of the data. Hash it out at early meetings.

Confidentiality, informed consent, and data ownership are issues that also need to be resolved before any research involving human beings is undertaken. Many people misunderstand the protections that are necessary (and not necessary) in ethnographic and other qualitative work. They either fail to recognize the danger to people should their confidentiality be compromised or go to the other extreme and say that no qualitative data collection can take place because confidentiality can't be ensured. (The latter are likely to be sitting on institutional review boards) In evaluation this is an especially difficult issue because programs tend to be carried out in small worlds where people are recognizable from subtle clues in the data. And the stakes in terms of people's careers are high. Release of any of the data is problematic. I never quote people I have interviewed in evaluations and I am very careful about attribution of statements to categories of respondents (e.g., "One health department head in an urban area told me . . ."). It doesn't matter if a reader guesses wrong. The damage is done in any event.

It is very important for us to be familiar with the ethical stances of our own professional organizations and of those of members of our team. We must learn how to "sanitize" data by removing identifiers and any cues we can find. We should always err on the side of caution in protecting our respondents. This can be a special issue for work done under government contract. Practitioners working under contract are working as agents of the clients, which means that they own the data we collect. This is specified in every contract I've ever seen. This didn't occur to me until it became an issue on a project where the very participation of individuals on an HIV coalition would have been dangerous to their position in their communities. Yet the client wanted the raw data. That was when I learned to clean data. It is best if you negotiate confidentiality issues at the beginning of a project. If your client will not commit themselves to protecting the respondents, then you shouldn't agree to collect the data.

Conclusions

So what does this all mean? First of all, the tools that anthropologists bring to the table – our theories and methods – are important to the practice of anthropology. We do not in any way abandon these outside of the academy. We are still anthropologists. We aren't the only people who use these ways of understanding what people do. We shoot ourselves in the foot when we pretend that we are. I have heard academic anthropologists worry that "everyone who calls themselves an ethnographer can get a job as one." I don't worry about this. Whatever context I'm in, I'm using anthropology as effectively as I can. If my partners learn something about how we do ethnography, that's good. If you can teach them, then teach; if they can teach you, then learn. Or do both. Either way, everybody wins.

We should be very humble about our own ability to practice someone else's profession. Traditionally, when anthropologists went alone to do ethnography in remote places, they were never fully prepared for what they might need. With no access to libraries and colleagues, we learned to become statisticians, economists, psychologists – whatever we needed to do. I am of this generation and I do not know to what extent this is true now with a different model for fieldwork and the resources available online. But it is practice that has taught me that I don't know what other specialists know. And I try to let people from other specialties do their jobs no matter how strident the urging of my brain to get in there and make sure everything fits the way I think it should. It usually works out just fine.

References

Atkinson, Paul and Martyn Hammersley (1994) "Ethnography and Participant Observation." In Norman K. Denzin and Yvonna S. Lincoln (eds.), *Handbook of Qualitative Research.* Thousand Oaks, CA: Sage, pp. 248–261.

Copeland-Carson, Jacqueline, Mary Odell Butler, and Christina Wasson (2012) "Global–Local Connections: The View from Applied Anthropology." In Christina Wasson, Mary Odell Butler, and Jacqueline Copeland-Carson (eds.), *Applying Anthropology in the Global Village.* Walnut Creek, CA: Left Coast Press, pp. 7–20.

Fadiman, Anne (1997) *The Spirit Catches You and You Fall Down.* New York: Farrar, Straus and Giroux.

Fetterman, David (1998) *Ethnography: Step by Step,* 2nd edn. Thousand Oaks, CA: Sage.

Gleick, James (1987) *Chaos: Making a New Science.* New York: Penguin.

Harris, Marvin (1968) *The Rise of Anthropological Theory.* New York: Crowell.

Harris, Marvin (1979) *Cultural Materialism: The Struggle for a Science of Culture.* New York: Random House.

Krishnan, Shoba S. (2008) *The HPV Vaccine Controversy: Sex, Cancer and God.* Westport, CT: Praeger.

Lansing, J. Stephen (2003) "Complex Adaptive Systems." *Annual Review of Anthropology* 32: 183–204.

MMWR (2007) "Quadrivalent Human Papillomavirus Vaccine: Recommendations of the Advisory Committee on Immunization Practices." *Morbidity and Mortality Weekly Report* 56(RR-2): 1–24. At http://www.cdc.gov/mmwr/preview/mmwrhtml/rr5602a1.htm, accessed Aug. 29, 2012.

MMWR (2011) "Progress toward Implementation of Human Papillomavirus: The Americas, 2006–2010." *Morbidity and Mortality Weekly Report* 60(40): 1382–1384.

Patton, Michael Quinn (2005) "The View from Evaluation." In Mary Odell Butler and Jacqueline Copeland-Carson (eds.), *Creating Evaluation Anthropology: Introducing an Emerging Sub-field.* NAPA Bulletin 24. Berkeley: University of California Press.

Pike, Kenneth (1954) *Language in Relation to a Unified Theory of the Structure of Human Behavior*, vol. 1. Glendale, CA: Summer Institute of Linguistics.

Radcliffe-Brown, Alfred R. (1952) *Structure and Function in Primitive Society*. London: Oxford University Press.

Schwandt, Thomas (2007) *Sage Dictionary of Qualitative Inquiry*. Thousand Oaks, CA: Sage.

Walloo, Keith, Julie Livingston, Steven Epstein, and Robert Aronowitz (eds.) (2010) *Three Shots at Prevention: The HPV Vaccine and the Politics of Medicine's Simple Solution*. Baltimore, MD: Johns Hopkins University Press.

Yin, Robert K. (2009) *Case Study Research: Design and Methods*, 4th edn. Thousand Oaks, CA: Sage.

Chapter 19

Practitioners Working in Health

Suzanne Heurtin-Roberts and Martha Hare

In this chapter, two practitioners working for two different federal agencies draw on their extensive experience to give us an overview of how anthropology relates to the domain of health and medicine. They begin with short personal background stories describing how and why they became involved with the field. They follow this with a detailed examination of what anthropology brings to health and medicine, with particular emphasis on the government context in which they both work. In order to be effective, it is essential that the practitioner understands the nature of this bureaucratic context. They conclude with a discussion of the importance of teamwork, and of the differing disciplinary perspectives implicit in teamwork, perspectives which offer anthropologist practitioners opportunities as well as challenges.

The views expressed here are the authors', and do not reflect the views or policies of the National Institutes of Health/National Cancer Institute.

In this chapter we intend to explore practice in the field of health, give our personal stories of how we got to where we are, and describe some of the issues and challenges involved as well as the rewards. We suspect that anthropologists in practice positions frequently ask themselves what practice *means*. We've formulated some thoughts about the question, none of which are completely satisfying responses. The best we can do is to share observations, lessons learned, and some insights we can offer to any anthropologist who may be, or wish to be, similarly engaged. Please remember that these are the thoughts of two medical anthropologists and are not

A Handbook of Practicing Anthropology. First Edition. Edited by Riall W. Nolan.
© 2013 John Wiley & Sons, Inc. Published 2013 by John Wiley & Sons, Inc.

to be read as a definitive description of anthropological practice in health or in the context of government.

Both authors currently work in government health agencies and have done so for some time.[1] We have assumed numerous roles, occupied various locations within hierarchies, worked on widely different projects, engaged in diverse tasks, and seen our power and influence fluctuate across time and contexts. For the most part, we've worked in bureaucracies. We'll begin with our stories.

Suzanne Heurtin-Roberts's Personal Story

I was an asthmatic child from a very young age at a time when asthma treatment was not well developed. I spent much of my childhood in a hospital oxygen tent. This made an exceedingly strong impression on me, and I became fascinated with all things medical. I planned to go to medical school, but also loved the social sciences. In college I caught the anthropology bug. After a BA in anthropology with lots of biology courses, I did a master's in sociology, still focusing on health. But I missed anthropology's broad holistic perspective on humanity. I decided I could combine my interests in health and anthropology as a medical anthropologist.

I didn't want to be an academic. Rather, I wanted to do something applied, practical, and active, although I didn't really know what that might be. One of my professors became so frustrated with my insistence on action that I was told perhaps I should get a degree in social work instead. So I did, as part of a postdoctoral fellowship in mental health services research, after receiving a doctorate in medical anthropology. Still, both sociology and social work have greatly influenced me. Sociology in particular has informed my thought relative to working in the context of organizations, especially bureaucracies. Anthropology, sociology, and social work have made me exquisitely conscious of the nature of my work context: the United States and its government, a powerful, affluent nation with a large working and under-class, a focus on the individual, and many injustices. As a researcher and provider (social work), I've spent a good bit of time in clinical settings such as hospital clinics, inpatient and outpatient mental health programs, and hospital geriatric and psychiatric units. This has also broadened my perspective.

After my postdoctoral work, I took a faculty position in a school of social work in Washington, DC. I took it because it was offered and also because an academic career seemed to be a natural progression after training in anthropology. I taught for several years, always representing myself as a combo anthropologist–social worker. In 1997 I received an unexpected phone call from a federal sociologist asking if I would come to interview for a position in disease prevention among "special populations." She was looking for someone who had a deep understanding of culture and behavior, and who had knowledge of both qualitative and quantitative research. A mutual colleague had put her in touch with me. I was encouraged by family and colleagues to try it as a brief learning experience. I left my academic position in 1998 and, almost 15 years later, I am still with the federal government.

As a public servant I have been able to have an influence broader than I think I could have had as an academic. I've worked with smart, committed people. There always seems to be another critical project to take on.

Martha Hare's Personal Story

Like that of my co-author, my career has been varied, with several major influences on its trajectory. I was trained in the critical tradition, with an initial focus on eth-nomedicine, and my career has focused on real world issues, in particular cancer prevention and control, health disparities, and delivery of service. An undergraduate anthropology major, I obtained a bachelor's degree in nursing before returning to anthropology in graduate school. In many ways, my decade in patient care and community health served as field experience – although relatively brief, these years were highly formative. They gave me the opportunity to negotiate the culture of a large urban medical center's pediatric floor, that of a community health agency in inner city New York, as well as several brief experiences including a semester in rural India. Although my dissertation was concerned with the use of Chinese medicine by urban non-Asians, I was deeply influenced by my mother's experience as a cancer patient undergoing experimental treatment which was successful for many years.

After completing graduate school I found that my hybrid status was highly mar-ketable, allowing for entrée to public health clinics where I conducted most of my applied practice as a government-funded program evaluator in a large research firm. When I transferred to a position within a federal government agency, my hybrid status led to positions as a research administrator in nursing science and in cancer health disparities.

On Practice

What does it mean to practice anthropology in health? And do we mean practice or praxis? Although the terms are frequently used almost synonymously, in fact they differ. Praxis has been defined in many ways and attributed to numerous thinkers. The concept's origins can be traced to Aristotle's thinking of action that adheres to ideal standards of behavior; Marx and Gramsci used it to mean action that liberates the oppressed and transforms the social order (see Warry 1992 for an excellent discussion of praxis). However, as Warry notes, praxis originates from a philosophi-cal or theoretical base; he argues for the need for a two-way dialogue between theory and action (Warry 1992: 156).

In this chapter, our actions are described as examples of practice, not praxis. Certainly we attempt to locate our activities within theoretical contexts, but we make no claims about theoretical contributions. Practice stated intuitively can be seen as the action of employing knowledge, theory, and/or methods to meet a particular goal or objective, or, even more informally, "making anthropological knowledge useful" (Chambers 1989: 17). That is, we put anthropological theory, knowledge, and methods into "practice" to achieve a desired end.

Framing Anthropological Practice in the Medical Health Domain

Medical anthropologists practice in numerous settings reflecting both the employment opportunities available and the diversity of anthropological training. In the early days of the discipline, roughly from the 1970s through the 1990s, the majority were trained as cultural anthropologists, some with additional coursework in ethnomedicine, epidemiology, public health, psychology, and perhaps the sociology of biomedicine. Others were trained as biological or nutritional anthropologists. Increasingly, medical anthropologists may avail themselves of training in bioethics, biomedicine including genetics, and other biological sciences. Outside of academia, the practicing anthropologist is often in the situation of helping the employer or funder know what is relevant to the problem under consideration. These include (1) human behavior as the confluence of biological, social, and cultural influences; (2) understanding groups and patterns, structures and processes, not just the individual; and (3) policy insights and recommendations.

Medical anthropology can be seen as a melding of anthropology's holism with the science demanded by medicine (Womack 2010: 2–3). This creates both opportunity and tension in the role of the practicing anthropologist, whether in private practice, government, foundations, community organizations, or elsewhere. A major challenge to the practitioner is maintenance of a professional identity as an anthropologist in settings that may lack a realistic knowledge of an anthropologist's core set of skills and values. Increasingly, anthropologists are employed in settings which require the input of multiple disciplines. This reflects a need for transdisciplinary approaches to resolve complex issues. A *multidisciplinary* approach brings many disciplines to bear on a problem; an *interdisciplinary* approach, or collaboration between disciplines, uses components of more than one discipline; while a *transdisciplinary* approach leads to the creation of a new consciousness (Holmes et al. 2008). In reality, not every issue requires a transdisciplinary consciousness, but practicing anthropologists would do well to position themselves to work in a continuum of collaborative endeavors.

And so, the question turns to what we actually *do* all day. With reference to our own experience, we will consider medical anthropological practice as a government worker. Much of government work, whether or not it is health-related, revolves around programs. Unless its mission is regulatory (as with the Food and Drug Administration, or FDA), a health agency uses programs (organized, purposefully structured actions) to achieve its outcomes, with overarching goal of health maintenance or improvement. This means engaging in activities such as program conceptualization and implementation, funding, management, evaluation, investigation, and cessation and closing out, among others. These activities are not always clearly delineated or differentiated, and a single worker is frequently responsible for more than one activity.

As an example, at a health-research funding agency, Heurtin-Roberts was part of a team developing the concept for a research program to investigate processes leading to health disparities. The team of physicians, psychologists, epidemiologists, and the anthropologist, developed the concept and published it as a request for applications (RFA) so that researchers could apply for funding to conduct the research. Throughout this process, Heurtin-Roberts relied upon her medical anthropological knowledge of community health and action research, ethnic and professional culture, contemporary US society and politics, as well as human biology and human variation to contribute to the concept. She also used field anthropology training to understand work group interactions and social and organizational processes, and to manage her own (ethnic and professional) interactions cross-culturally.

Heurtin-Roberts was assigned as program director to the majority of the resulting research centers. Much of this work was administrative. This meant she was responsible for overseeing funding, making some funding decisions, managing the program, overseeing center budgets and activities, evaluating logistical and scientific progress, and looking out for any misconduct. Her earlier experience of anthropological research and its management prepared her for much of this work, but not at the level of complexity this program required. Managing an interpersonal, inter-research center, and inter-agency relations, was perhaps the most difficult. Anthropological theory and knowledge helped her to understand the source of many of the problems and good field-worker behavior helped with the human aspects of the job. However, some business or management education would have helped greatly.

When Hare found herself dealing with similar issues administering a multi-site research study, she added skills in negotiation to her toolkit. Based on the model developed by Fisher and colleagues (1991), these skills center on the concept of negotiation on principle, not on winning or losing. The anthropologist is trained to gather information by interviewing, observing, and listening. In real life situations, whether public health, biomedical institution, community organization, or government agency, the culture usually demands assertiveness and even active defense of a position. In administrative settings, this is critical in order to demonstrate leadership. Through the use of good negotiation skills, Hare was able to elicit the best approaches for dealing with a number of research-related issues and to work with individuals from varied disciplines toward a successful conclusion.

This administrative role is quite a different one from that of knowledge producer or broker. The latter, probably more comfortable, role for the anthropologist, involves the production, communication, and translation of knowledge. Administration, however, involves employing knowledge to carry out an intervention, which traditional anthropology has been less comfortable with. Indeed, anthropologist Karen Hanson, recounting her career in social service administration, noted her move away from the role of anthropologist as knowledge producer to anthropologist as knowledge user (Hanson 1988).

The practicing anthropologist must also learn to be comfortable with a leadership role in which they make decisions for a group or organization. At the same agency discussed above, Heurtin-Roberts led a working group on behavioral research and health disparities that included an anthropologist postdoc and intern (MacPhee et al. 2005). The three anthropologists adopted a participatory approach to the group, with the intention of being democratic and inclusive. Over time it became increasingly clear that the group was reluctant to provide input or to decide upon action. After much reflection the anthropologists realized that they had been taking on the role of ethnographers, that is, they had been observational and refraining from intervention. Heurtin-Roberts learned the unusual lesson (for an anthropologist) that she was in charge – she had the power, authority, and responsibility to act and make decisions – and that group wanted her to lead. Leadership and decision-making are not commonly taught in anthropology.

What Does the Medical Anthropologist Bring to Potential Employers?

In quasi-academic settings (e.g., research organizations, government agencies, foundations), anthropologists often work closely with other behavioral or social scientists. Critically trained anthropologists can find the theoretical frameworks and models upon which sister sciences build their inquiry to be static or linear, yet these models are often popular in studies for determining healthcare policy or directions in practice.

Behavioral strategies have largely been based on models derived from health psychology using an individualistic approach that fails to account for the relationship of individual actors with their environments and social contexts. Examples are numerous, such as the health belief model (Rosenstock 1974), social cognitive theory (Bandura 1986), theory of planned behavior (Ajzen 1991), and Prochaska's transtheoretical model (1979) which examines an individual's readiness to change or to stop a harmful behavior. Anthropologists have also relied on models that were highly individualistic, such as Kleinman's explanatory models (1981) with attempts to broaden the approach to include sickness behavior, or the social dimension of illness (see Hahn 1995 for a discussion of theories of sickness and healing, along with some practical applications).

The social–ecological model, which came from psychology (Bronfenbrenner 1979) is particularly consonant with anthropology in that it illustrates the many intersecting domains of human action. In 2009 Pasick and colleagues offered a critique and response for conducting research in communities experiencing disparate health conditions, such as Philippine migrants.[2] The approach offered by this team made use of three major domains: relational culture, social capital, and transculturation and transmigration (or maintenance of cultural identity across national boundaries). This was done to overcome the focus on individual actors to the detriment of the numerous asymmetrical relationships affecting health behaviors.

For anthropologists working in administration, evaluation, design, planning, and policy, it is important that they understand the organizational and systemic context in which they operate. Certainly management and business have their own theoretical literature, and reviewing these may be helpful. However, anthropological theory and method bring additional value to the business model of organizational work and support an *anthropological* practice. If an employer wanted only a business approach would they have hired an anthropologist to begin with?

Classic theories of structure and organization (Firth 1951; Radcliffe-Brown 1958), as well as symbol and meaning embodied in social action and structure (Geertz 1973) seem basic to the understanding of organizations. Sociologist Max Weber's analysis (1967) still provides a solid basis for understanding the bureaucracy. It is also important to place our work in the context of healthcare systems, biomedicine, and broader, political-economic global systems, casting a critical eye over all (see Baer et al. 1997; Farmer 2003; Waitzkin 2011).

Components of the practicing medical anthropologist's toolkit will vary by employment and by particular application – research, policy development, management, and so on. The bedrock of anthropological training for those educated in the four fields or predominantly cultural programs is excellent, rigorous qualitative research skills. Although not all practicing anthropologists will engage in research, the more literate they are in a variety of qualitative software packages, the more marketable they are professionally. This should include packages for coding data and text analysis (e.g., ATLAS.ti, NVIVO). The ability to use geographic information systems (GIS) is in high demand for conducting needs assessments, situation analyses, surveillance, and other applications.

In the fields of health and medicine, it is unthinkable that an anthropologist could function without a basic knowledge of statistics. By far the greater part of health research conducted and published involves statistical analyses. You do not need to be fluent in statistics, but you must at the very least be literate enough to understand health and medical literature and able to communicate meaningfully with your non-anthropologist colleagues about that body of research. Although most large organizations have statistical analysts, the practicing anthropologist needs to have a basic knowledge of one or more statistical packages should they conduct analyses on their own, but more importantly, they need to speak the lingua franca of most health-related research.

All practicing anthropologists need to be able to write for a variety of audiences, such as funding agencies, the public, the media, and colleagues or supervisors. The ability to write clearly and succinctly, without jargon or embellishment, is critical. Closely related is the ability to make compelling presentations for a variety of audiences. Outside of anthropological academia, the culture expects presentations to include, at a minimum, eye-catching PowerPoint slides. This is a skill that cannot be overemphasized. In addition, some practitioners will be called upon to communicate with the media. It is the anthropologist's responsibility to ask for questions in advance, to think through how to make points succinctly, and to stay on message during the interview. Communicating with the public can take many forms. Anthropologists speak to policy-makers, funders, community leaders, and community members. Each type of communication requires thinking through the major points to be made and can involve the use of different materials. The material communicated can be research findings or results, discussions about future projects or community needs, or interpretations of data. Whenever possible, communication should be interactive.

Potential Problems

Interdisciplinarity and team science

Much of the anthropological worldview is interpretivist, interactionist, and holistic. Most of science, including behavioral science, is pragmatic and post-positivist or positivist (see, e.g., Crotty 2010 for a recent explication of epistemologies within social research) Practicing anthropologists need to understand that other disciplines may operate from different epistemological origins. The anthropologist must develop communication, education, and diplomacy skills in trying to negotiate differing world views, paradigms, and methods. This is a problem not only for anthropologists but for many disciplines in the increasingly transdisciplinary research world.

Team science is increasingly the norm in health and medicine as technologies allow us to address more complex problems and more than one discipline is needed to handle that complexity. The days of "lone ranger" research in health and medicine are pretty much over except perhaps for dissertations. Anthropologists must adapt to working effectively and productively with others even though there will be differences in theories, methods, and resources needed.

Even if positivism is not the mode of training for all scientists, large-scale funders prefer studies that have clear measures in the belief that this will lead to clear policy recommendations or interventions. The anthropologist is trained to understand context, whether through the analysis of culture through ethnography (Womack 2010: 1), the analysis of propositions within a case study (Yin 1989), the community's responses obtained through community-based participatory research (CBPR), or simply embedding community-focused measures in survey studies.

Unfortunately, much of what we as a profession see as necessary to the full understanding of a situation is thought by others to be confounding. Fortunately, with recent statistical techniques, the anthropologist can work with interdisciplinary teams to develop research reports and policy statements that incorporate analyses of the relationship of the focus of the study (or results of hypothesis testing), with an analysis of the impact of contextual factors. The major reason why stripping data of context is so compelling is that the resulting outcomes can be generalized to larger populations.[3] An exciting innovation is the use of meta-synthesis (Sandelowski and

Barroso 2007). Like meta-analysis, a meta-synthesis synthesizes findings from a large number of qualitative studies of a particular phenomenon, such as the health-care needs of HIV-positive women.

Definitions of race and ethnicity

Another area of confusion is in the categorization of human groups, in particular as races or ethnic groups. It is imperative that a practicing anthropologist be pre-pared to cope with areas of conflict in creative and honest ways. This includes negotiation and compromise, as well as educating colleagues, supervisors, and funders. Anthropologists hold a nuanced view of race, recognizing that categories used in the United States reflect social and historical forces.[4] Even when loosely related to biological markers, genetic admixtures are shifting due to migration and changing patterns of reproduction. Furthermore, the term "Caucasian" has become acceptable in scientific literature, even though it is a non-scientific throwback to a racist past.[5]

In the United States, the Office of Management and Budget (OMB) developed five major categories of race (American Indian/Alaska Native, Asian, Native Hawaiian or Other Pacific Islander, Black/African American, and White). Only two categories of ethnicity are recognized, Hispanic and non-Hispanic. Federal funding requires the use of these categories. One use of the data is to demonstrate progress in over-coming disparities in health as noted in differences in morbidity, mortality, and survival between members of various populations in the United States with a history of prior injustice. Thus the current system reflects a real need to track the health experience of major population groups.

At the same time, biologists are increasingly aware that genomic differences within and between populations may be due to genetic ancestry, a much more refined concept than race. Due to admixtures, it is very difficult to predict the likeli-hood of a particular genetic profile for any phenotype. The bottom line is that no discussion of race and ethnicity is simple, and the anthropologist needs to under-stand and communicate *both* sociohistorical and biological knowledge. Using race as a quick way of determining genetic ancestry is not acceptable, but avoiding the subject can place populations at risk of falling further behind in health disparities.

Cultural competence

Cultural competence is an example of a concept that the practicing anthropologist encounters. Initially a way of ensuring that public agencies incorporate knowledge of the culture of clients, students, and patients in order to improve service, educa-tion, and health care, the concept has proven problematic. Based on a static notion of culture, cultural competence avoids more nuanced and historically grounded approaches to the communities with whom many anthropologists practice. CBPR practitioners such as Wallerstein and Duran (2003: 41) recognize the impossibility of competence, preferring the term "cultural humility."[6] The anthropologist may be able to provide an even more nuanced alternative that raises awareness of culture as dynamic (Hare and Villarruel 2007), and of competence as a process rather than a discrete set of skills based on specific attributes of an ethnic group or community.

Conclusion

For the anthropologist who wishes to practice in the area of health and medicine, opportunities are plentiful. Public health organizations, health or science consulting agencies, NGOs, nonprofits, development firms, state and local health agencies are just a few settings to consider. The website of the American Public Health Association (APHA) has a section called "Public Health Career Mart" which lists numerous types of positions open nationally and internationally. Academy Health, a national organization focused on health services and policy research also has a similar feature called the "Career Center." It is not necessary to be a member of either organization to access these pages.

For the anthropologist who is interested in working for the federal government, the USAJOBS website is the place to start (www.usajobs.gov). There has been a move to post all federal positions on USAJOBS, but some positions may not be advertised there. It is wise to go directly to the website of any federal agency, since some still have their own employment systems.

Finally word of mouth and networking are always important in any job search. Hiring is fundamentally about human relationships and behavior, with which the anthropologist should be comfortable. For the anthropologist interested in health and medical practice, the future looks good.

Notes

1   In this chapter, we will only state that we have worked in the federal government and in what sort of agencies we have worked. We will not name particular agencies or individuals. Although we don't think anything in this paper is particularly controversial, it is much simpler this way.

2   The impetus for the research summarized as "Behavioral Constructs and Culture for Cancer Screening" came from the late Dr. Sabra Wooley, a medical anthropologist who served at the National Institutes of Health/National Cancer Institute. The disciplines represented in the research include anthropology, epidemiology, psychology, nursing science, and others, with one individual sometimes representing more than one discipline.

3   The anthropologist, of course, has a broader methodological repertoire than can be discussed in this chapter. See, e.g., de Munck and Sobo (1990) for a treatment of both quantitative and qualitative approaches to fieldwork.

4   See www.understandingrace.org/.
5   "Caucasian: a non-scientific term invented by German physician Johann Blumenbach in
    1795 to describe light-skinned people from Europe (and, originally, from western Asia
    and North Africa as well) whom Blumenbach mistakenly thought came from the Cau-
    casus Mountains. The term became synonymous with 'white'" (http://understandingrace.
    org/resources/glossary.html, accessed Sept. 4, 2012).
6   Wallerstein et al. (2005) cite Tervalon and Murray-Garcia (1998: 118) who define cultural
    humility as "'a lifelong commitment to self-evaluation and self-critique' to redress the
    power imbalances and 'develop and maintain mutually respectful and dynamic partner-
    ships with communities.'"

References

Ajzen, Icek (1991) "The Theory of Planned Behavior." *Organizational Behavior and Human
    Decision Processes* 50: 179–211.
Baer, Hans, Merrill Singer, and Ida Susser (1997) *Medical Anthropology and the World System:
    A Critical Perspective.* Westport, CT: Bergin & Garvey.
Bandura, Albert (1986) *Social Foundations of Thought and Action: A Social Cognitive Theory.*
    Englewood Cliffs, NJ: Prentice Hall.
Bronfenbrenner, Urie (1979) *The Ecology of Human Development: Experiments by Nature and
    Design.* Cambridge, MA: Harvard University Press.
Chambers, Erve (1989) *Applied Anthropology: A Practical Guide.* Prospect Heights, IL: Wave-
    land Press.
Crotty, Michael (2010) *The Foundations of Social Research: Meaning and Perspective in the
    Research Process.* Los Angeles: Sage.
de Munck, Victor C. and Elisa. J. Sobo (eds.) (1998) *Using Methods in the Field: A Practical
    Casebook.* Walnut Creek, CA: AltaMira Press.
Farmer, Paul (2003) *Pathologies of Power: Health, Human Rights, and the New War on the
    Poor.* Berkeley: University of California Press.
Firth, Raymond (1951) *Elements of Social Organization.* London: Watts.
Fisher, Roger, William Ury, and Bruce Patton (1991) *Getting to Yes: Negotiating without
    Giving In*, 2nd edn. New York: Penguin.
Geertz, Clifford (1973) *The Interpretation of Cultures.* New York: Basic Books.
Hahn, Robert A. (1995) *Sickness and Healing: An Anthropological Perspective.* New Haven:
    Yale University Press.
Hanson, Karen J. (1988) "Anthropology and Policy in Social Services Administration." In
    Karen J. Hanson (ed.), *Mainstreaming Anthropology: Experiences in Government Employ-
    ment.* NAPA Bulletin 5. Washington, DC: National Association for the Practice of
    Anthropology, American Anthropological Association, pp. 28–39.
Hare, Martha L. and Antonia M. Villarruel (2007) "Cultural Dynamics in HIV/AIDS Preven-
    tion Research among Young People." *Journal of the Association of Nurses in AIDS Care*
    18(2): 1–4.
Holmes, John H., Amy Lehman, Erinn Hade, et al. (2008) "Challenges for Multilevel Health
    Disparities Research in a Transdisciplinary Environment." *American Journal of Preven-
    tive Medicine* 35(2S): S182–S192.

Kleinman, Arthur (1981) *Patients and Healers in the Context of Culture*. Berkeley: University of California Press.

MacPhee, Marybeth, Suzanne Heurtin-Roberts, and Chris Foster (2005) "Traveling the Uncharted Path of Leadership in Federal Anthropology." *Practicing Anthropology* 27(3): 25–28.

Pasick, Rena J., Nancy J. Burke, Judith C. Barker, et al. (2009) "Behavioral Theory in a Diverse Society: Like a Compass on Mars." *Health Education and Behavior* 36(S1): 11S–35S.

Prochaska, James O. (1979) *Systems of Psychotherapy: A Transtheoretical Analysis*. Pacific Grove, CA: Brooks/Cole.

Radcliffe-Brown, Alfred R. (1958) *Method in Anthropology: Selected Essays*. Chicago: University of Chicago Press.

Rosenstock, Irwin M. (1974) "Historical Origins of the Health Belief Model." *Health Education Monograph* 2: 328–335.

Sandelowski, Margarete and Julie Barroso (2007) *Handbook for Synthesizing Qualitative Research*. New York: Springer.

Tervalon, Melanie and Jann Murray-Garcia (1998) "Cultural Humility vs. Cultural Competence: A Critical Distinction in Defining Physician Training Outcomes in Medical Education." *Journal of Health Care for the Poor and Underserved* 9(2): 117–125.

Waitzkin, Howard (2011) *Medicine and Public Health at the End of Empire*. Boulder, CO: Paradigm Publishers.

Wallerstein, Nina and Bonnie Duran (2003) "The Conceptual, Historical, and Practice Roots of Community Based Participatory Research and Related Participatory Traditions." In Meredith Minkler and Nina Wallerstein (eds.), *Community-Based Participatory Research for Health*. San Francisco: Jossey-Bass.

Wallerstein, Nina, Bonnie Duran, Meredith Minkler, and Kevin Foley (2005) "Developing and Maintaining Partnerships with Communities." In Barbara A. Israel et al. (eds.), *Methods in Community-Based Participatory Research*. San Francisco: Jossey-Bass, pp. 31–51.

Warry, Wayne (1992) "The Eleventh Thesis: Applied Anthropology as Praxis." *Human Organization* 51(2): 155–163.

Weber, Max (1967) "Bureaucracy." In *From Max Weber*. London: Routledge & Kegan Paul, pp. 196–244.

Womack, Mari (2010) *The Anthropology of Health and Healing*. Lanham, MD: AltaMira Press.

Yin, Robert K. (1989) *Case Study Research: Design and Methods*, rev. edn. Newbury Park, CA: Sage.

Chapter 20

International Development

Mari H. Clarke

Clarke, a long-time development practitioner, gives us a comprehensive look at the domain of development anthropology. She begins by noting some of the important shifts and changes in the development agenda, and then moves to a description of the main organizations involved in development work today. Specific sectors of development are noted, both by topic and by region. Clarke discusses in detail the types of roles anthropologists play in development work, and illustrates her points with numerous examples from her own work and experience. She concludes the chapter with thoughts about how practitioners can break into the field, and what it is likely to look like in the future.

Development Anthropology Past and Present

Is anthropological engagement in development an "uneasy relationship?" (Lewis 2005). Are development anthropologists reinforcing ethnocentric, dominating models of development (Escobar 1991)? Is development "anthropology's evil twin" (Ferguson 1996)? Or is development anthropology based on strong ethical principles? Does it provide a "moral narrative," giving voice to the voiceless with stories drawing attention to their plight (Gow 2002)? Are development anthropologists advocates for sustainable development and growth with social justice (Horowitz 1989) – who promote "putting people first" (Cernea 1991)?[1] The line in the sand in debates about the evils and virtues of development anthropology is largely between university-based critics and those engaged full-time in development agencies.

A Handbook of Practicing Anthropology. First Edition. Edited by Riall W. Nolan.
© 2013 John Wiley & Sons, Inc. Published 2013 by John Wiley & Sons, Inc.

For over 40 years, I have strived to help humanize the ever changing development paradigm through my work for bilateral and multilateral development agencies, nongovernmental organizations, and private consulting firms.[2] Rather than critiquing development from the outside, I chose to facilitate its transformation in small ways as an internal organizational change agent, in large part by raising awareness of the sociocultural and gender dimensions of development to influence policies and programs.

The development agenda has changed dramatically over the past half century with technological development, escalating globalization, and geopolitical transformations. I entered international development at the beginning of the 1980s, during the Cold War era, joining the Program for International Training in Health (INTRAH) – a US Agency for International Development (USAID) maternal and child health and family planning project for Africa and the Middle East. A decade later the Berlin wall came down. After completing a PhD in anthropology, I joined the Office of Women in Development at USAID as an on-site consultant. During my first year on the job, I co-chaired a session at the 1989 American Anthropological Association (AAA) meetings on "New Directions in Foreign Assistance and New Roles for Anthropologists," including social dimensions of macroeconomic policy reforms, environmental sustainability, microenterprise development, gender, and urbanization.

The twenty-first-century development agenda has moved from cold war to wars on drugs, crime, terrorism, and gender-based violence. In an increasingly interconnected world, we are addressing global issues such as HIV/AIDs and avian flu, human trafficking, terrorism, climate change, and associated acceleration of natural disasters. We are striving to meet the Millennium Development Goals (MDGs) with a target date three years away. The global financial crisis that developed in 2008–9 has brought into question assumed "truths" about liberalizing economies. The electronic revolution of information sharing through the Internet and the use of cell phones facilitates activities such as banking, business, education, health care, social networking, and even revolution, as well as government surveillance. Anti-corruption, governance, transparency, corporate social responsibility, and conflict mitigation have entered the development agenda.[3]

Development Anthropology's Domain Structure

There are various types of development organizations in which development anthropologists can play many different roles Development organizations are typically structured by sectors and regions.

Types of organizations engaged in development

The major players in international development include the United Nations (UN) organizations, the multilateral development banks (MDBs), bilateral donors, various

US government departments,[4] international nongovernmental organizations (NGOs), private foundations, private think tanks, government-funded institutions, university-based development centers, for-profit and non-profit consulting firms, and multinational corporations. These organizations offer opportunities for consulting, full-time and part-time employment, and many also offer funding for development-related projects and research. I have worked for or collaborated with nearly all of the types of organizations.

Each organization has its own culture, structure, spheres of activity, and set of acronyms which development anthropologists need to absorb very quickly. My work in the Office of Women in Development in USAID provided me with a crash course on development organizations because of the UN conferences on women, donor coordination on gender and development, and collaboration with the US Census Bureau, the US Women's Bureau, and the US Department of Labor. I quickly learned "AIDspeak" – the many acronyms and terms used in meetings and memos.

Multilateral development banks

MDBs, such as the World Bank and the Asian Development Bank, provide loans to client countries. Unlike the bilaterals, which provide funds and implement the development programs directly, MDBs conduct due diligence in the preparation, appraisal, and supervision of projects, but the borrower countries conduct social and environmental assessments and baseline studies, and implement projects. Countries are often reluctant to invest borrowed money in "soft" programs addressing gender and other social issues. Skilled negotiation is required to keep these issues on the table when leaders are focused on concrete structures, such as superhighways and hydropower dams, to demonstrate their achievements to constituents.

Rather than broader engagement in project design, MDB anthropologists are often channeled into social safeguards – assessments and action plans preventing negative impacts of development on indigenous people, and others who are displaced or resettled.[5]

It is more difficult for Americans to attain full-time employment at the World Bank because of quotas to ensure equitable access for applicants from developing countries. It is much easier to find short-term consulting which can lead to longer-term and, occasionally, permanent employment.

Bilateral agencies

Bilateral agencies are affected by the foreign policy agendas of their governments. Government funding comes attached with priorities for development spending. Agency leaders are often government appointees. USAID, for example, reports to the Secretary of State, who appoints the USAID administrator, who appoints heads of bureaus. Under this political overlay are career civil service and foreign service staff, as well as country nationals in field offices. Various contractors manage implementation of projects and provide technical support. Security clearance is required for work in USAID and many other government agencies.

Nongovernmental organizations

Nongovernmental organizations conduct a wide range of programs in different countries and sectors. They range from well-organized structures to loosely knit entities. In many contexts NGOs have political affinities and agendas. Many rely on private donations; this enables them to pursue their own agendas and to lobby governments. This independence requires significant fund-raising efforts. NGOs must respond to the oversight of their board of directors, so its composition is very important.

Advocacy groups

Many NGOs and other nonprofit organizations and networks advocate for action on environmental, human rights, and other issues. They lobby international policy conferences, governments, and donor agencies and use various media to educate the public as well as policy-makers relying largely on private funding. Anthropologists David and Pia Mayberry-Lewis and Evon Vogt founded Cultural Survival in the 1960s, when extraction of resources in Amazonian and other remote areas began, with devastating effects on indigenous peoples (http://culturalsurvival.org). The organization lobbies for indigenous peoples' rights to land, languages, and culture. Lobbying the UN with indigenous groups over many years led to the adoption of the UN Declaration of Indigenous Rights.

Private think tanks and university-based development institutes

Private think tanks and university-based development institutes provide anthropologists with opportunities for development-oriented research. The University of Manchester's Institute for Development Policy and Management conducts policy research on a range of issues. Anthropologist Caroline Moser is leading research on violence in cities, asset accumulation, and adaptation to climate change. She studied related issues for two policy think tanks, the Brookings Institution in Washington, DC and the Overseas Development Institute in London.

In the US, the Bureau for Applied Research (BARA) at the University of Arizona conducts research and outreach activities to help local communities determine their own sustainable livelihood activities, using a livelihood security approach. They focus on the decision-making processes of households and communities within the context of larger political, social, and economic institutions in Africa, the Middle East, and Latin America using quantitative and qualitative methods.

Working within university-based institutes can enable development anthropologists to keep one foot in the academic world, teaching students and conducting research, while applying anthropological theory and methods outside the academy. Keeping such organizations afloat and re-energized with new generations of staff requires ongoing fund-raising, applications for contracts and grants, and recruitment and mentoring of young professionals.

Private consulting firms

Several anthropologists in the Washington, DC area have founded and managed for-profit and nonprofit development consulting firms.[6] There are many other "beltway bandits" seeking contracts for development work. Even though I sat in the Office of Women in Development at USAID with secret-level security clearance, I was employed by a series of consulting firms through technical support contracts. I have also done numerous short-term assignments for various firms. I joined in a results report team assisting USAID Albania in compiling evaluation and other data to report on outcomes of development projects. I traveled to Afghanistan with a scoping team for a bid on a USAID girls' education contract and assisted in drafting the proposal.

Multinational corporations

A few anthropologists work in multinational corporations that recognize the need to respond to increasing stockholder pressure for corporate social responsibility. Although I was not employed by any corporations, when I directed the USAID-funded US–Egyptian Education Secretariat, I networked with software firms, promoting public–private partnerships with the Ministry of Education. Based in London, Carolyn McCommon guided Rio Tinto's long-term sustainable development planning (with time horizons of over 20 years) to mitigate the negative impacts of mining operations on communities for several years. Another anthropologist works on community relations for the OK Tedi copper mine in the highlands of Papua New Guinea. Ayze Kudat, who retired from the World Bank, now consults for oil and gas corporations, conducting social impact assessments for pipelines and associated construction and developing resettlement action plans.

Development Sectors

Even though the lives of ordinary people in rural and urban areas are multi-sectoral, most international development agencies and programs are carved into sectors such

as agriculture, health, education, transportation, mirroring the line ministry structures in their own countries and those receiving assistance. The World Bank orga-
nogram includes sector-based "anchors" offering technical support and state of the
art knowledge. The United Nations System contains sector-specific agencies such as
the Food and Agriculture Organization (FAO) and the World Health Organization
(WHO).

Working as a development anthropologist in specific sectors requires a solid
understanding of the issues, methodologies, and terminology of the disciplines and
agencies involved. To do this, some anthropologists pursue another degree in fields
such as public health, education, law, and environmental sciences. I added a master's
degree in education to my academic credentials which provided a foot in the door
of international development. However, after entering, I needed to quickly learn
about maternal and child health, family planning, and population dynamics to help
develop technically sound training materials. My training in anthropology and
education provided a framework that facilitated my ability to learn the "language"
and "culture" of other disciplines quickly.

My work on gender and development has included assignments on micro-
enterprise, labor markets, agriculture and natural resource management, land
tenure, forestry, climate change, girls' education, social safety nets, transport, water
and sanitation, energy, urban development, mining, and information communication technologies. Each assignment was a tremendous learning experience in which
I dived into the literature on the sector and gender issues within it, attended seminars and workshops led by experts in the fields, and asked questions. To understand
and communicate effectively about barriers to women's access in different sectors,
it is essential to understand the nitty-gritty of those sectors.

For the past six years I have worked on gender and infrastructure at the World
Bank – largely in transport. I leaped at this opportunity because infrastructure was
long assumed to be beneficial to all, which made it difficult to build the case for
addressing gender issues. Investments in infrastructure and potential human
impacts are huge and are growing.[7] This year, for example, I assisted transport
engineers in Vietnam in developing training materials on routine maintenance for
women in rural communities. This required an understanding of technical considerations such as types of road surface, camber (upward curvature toward center of
road), different systems for drainage, and bioengineering (using vegetation to
reduce erosion).

Regional Structures

Many development organizations are also structured by region. The World Bank
has vice presidencies for sub-Saharan Africa, south Asia, the Middle East and north
Africa, Latin America, and East Asia and the Pacific which oversee investments in
those regions, facilitated by field offices in client countries. Regional vice presidencies are divided into country desks and sectoral departments "mapped" to the

anchors. There are United Nations economic and social commissions for each region. Bilateral agencies, such as USAID, and larger international NGOs also have regional bureaus and overseas field offices.

An in-depth understanding of regional development issues is essential for development anthropologists. Some anthropologists focus their development work on the country or region where they did their dissertation research. Many move on to pursue opportunities in new countries and regions, as did I. When Albania opened up after the death of Enver Hoxha, my knowledge and research with Greek Albanians in the Balkans gave me leverage to assist USAID Albania in conducting a gender review of the project portfolio. I also participated on teams from Land O'Lakes in assessing the dairy industry, Aid to Artisans in evaluating the artisan business development program in Hungary, and the Land Tenure Center (LTC) in conducting a comparative study of Serb and Albanian land tenure in Macedonia.

When new opportunities arose, I did not restrict my work to the Balkans and eastern Europe alone. Instead I immersed myself in literature on the social and political context and gender issues in each new region and country in which I worked. Thus far this has included Afghanistan, Albania, Egypt, Ghana, Guinea, Hungary, Jamaica, Kenya, Latvia, Macedonia, Mongolia, Nepal, Papua New Guinea, Peru, Poland, Senegal, Sierra Leone, Turkey, and Vietnam.

Fluency in widely spoken languages is a valuable asset in international development, less so in languages spoken by fewer people. I have not used language in development work, but my ability to read French was essential for a recent assignment synthesizing several studies on gender and transport in the north Africa and Middle East region, since the Tunisia materials were in French. Development work in Latin America requires fluent Spanish reading, writing, and speaking skills. Many agencies provide language training before posting staff to a new country.

Roles for Anthropologists in International Development

Whatever the type of development organizations, my experience has been that anthropologists have opportunities to play many different roles in international development over their careers.

Research and evaluation

Anthropologists are involved in designing and conducting research on, and evaluations of, development impacts on different groups of people at various levels – national, sub-regional, municipal, community, and household. Often the actual research is conducted by local researchers who need training in qualitative and even quantitative research methodologies and may have limited capacity in data analysis. As educated elites, some of them do not value the perspectives of less educated people.

In 1998 I led a team of six Albanian women researchers from Tirana Agricultural University on a gender baseline survey for a USAID forestry project. We drove around the countryside at a time when other teams were not allowed to leave Tirana due to civil unrest. I insisted it was important to conduct the survey in Albanian, not through translation. The researchers had strong quantitative skills but no experience in qualitative research. I provided training, including interview role plays. During the survey pilot body language suggested that the most senior researcher was telling the rural people what their answers should be. One of her colleagues, with experience in participatory approaches, confirmed my observation and assisted in coaching her colleague to listen to local people. When we analyzed the data, the research team struggled with the analysis of open-ended, qualitative responses. I provided articles on qualitative analysis and showed them how to compare and contrast the findings. I prepared the final report (Clarke 1999).

Technical support to donor agency teams and government agencies

Anthropologists also work with donor agencies and country governments to provide technical support on the sociocultural dimensions of development policies and projects. In 2001 I conducted a gender assessment of the project portfolio review and developed a gender action plan for USAID Nepal. They had dropped a strategic objective for women's empowerment due to budget cuts and wanted to ensure that gender would be addressed in the project portfolio. I arrived two weeks after the massacre of the royal family by a nephew. Maoist control was rapidly expanding in the countryside, particularly among *dalits* (untouchables) and women. I met with project teams and traveled to sites of the women's empowerment, maternal and child health, and community forestry projects. I found that the onus of gender mainstreaming had fallen on the women's empowerment project which would soon end. Agriculture, health, environment, and other teams did not view gender as their responsibility. I prepared a report that highlighted gender achievements and gaps, proposed key actions to spread ownership of the gender agenda across teams, and conducted a half-day gender workshop for staff (Clarke 2002).

Project design

There are various ways in which anthropologists contribute to project designs, ranging from comments on project concept notes to leading project design teams. Anthropologist Scott Guggenheim was task team leader for the World Bank-funded, billion dollar Kecamatan Development Project (KDP), covering more than 20,000 villages in Indonesia.[8] Local-level institution ethnographies in 48 villages tested new thinking on social capital and explored why glowing reports of development outcomes were not matched by results on the ground. The studies found that community-owned projects performed better than government or NGO projects and had higher participation of the poor. KDP changed the project paradigm from technical assistance delivery to provision of block grants to communities linked with facilitated planning, simple management procedures, and rules promoting transparency. Although KDP did not always reach the poorest of the poor, it increased women's participation in decision-making, reduced community tolerance for corruption, revived village and *kecamatan* meetings as governance and conflict-resolution forums, and ethnic groups that negotiated in these meetings were less likely to join disruptive disputes. The presence of anthropologists "sitting in the belly of the beast" enabled the translation of ethnographic findings into innovative project designs and mechanisms (Guggenheim 2004: 30).

Project and organizational management

Some anthropologists have moved into management positions ranging from chief executive officer (CEO) to project manager, that is, they have shifted from doing analytical work to supervising it. Peter Benedict was a mission director for USAID. Tony Barclay served as CEO for Development Alternatives Inc., with 2,000 staff in 60 countries. Describing her experience as founder and CEO of Pacific Women's Health Institute, Barbara Pillsbury (2008) stressed the need to let go of her role as a technical expert and focus on her management responsibilities. After managing several projects, I realized that the burden of bureaucratic aspects of project management (budget preparation, negotiations with the client, staff recruitment and evaluations, reporting on project results, arranging the logistics of events) and my desire to do analytical work outweighed my satisfaction from playing a leadership role.

Training

Training and facilitation is another role that some anthropologists play. This requires building skills and knowledge in adult learning theory and active learning (discussed in Chapter 29). In 2002 I worked on a social impact team to develop training materials on community-level fiduciary management for the World Bank. Fellow anthropologist Rolf Sartorius and I conducted training for World Bank procurement officers who were very concerned about financial due diligence for community-driven development and funds that provide grants directly to communities. I later pilot-tested the materials in Jamaica, co-training a dynamic group of local NGOs with a World Bank fiduciary management team.

Strategic planning

Strategic planning, a systematic process of envisioning a desired future, and translating this vision into broadly defined goals, measurable performance objectives, and a sequence of steps to achieve them, takes place at many levels from global down to individual offices and projects. While working with the USAID Office of Women and Development, I drafted a background paper on mainstreaming gender in the restructuring of the agency. I also joined a team assisting USAID Senegal in developing a results framework with strategic objectives and indicators for its country program. I participated in CEDPA's (Centre for Development and Population Activities) development of a new mission statement and vision. Currently I am providing input on gender issues for the World Bank's new water strategy.

Policy dialogue

Policy dialogue resolves regulatory and policy differences between stakeholders through facilitated meetings to develop or influence policies or regulations at various levels. In 1994 I participated in a delegation to a preparatory conference for the Fourth UN World Conference on Women as a technical expert. There was endless word-smithing of the joint resolution in line with the political policies of different countries. NGOs tried to lobby the delegates while they were listening to the debates. We had to resolve differences within our own delegation as well. The Department of Labor opposed changing national accounts to include the unpaid care economy, while the Office of Women in Development supported it.

Interagency coordination

Coordination is challenging at any level but very exciting when dialogue leads to interagency collaboration. When I directed the US–Egyptian Education Secretariat, we facilitated US–Egyptian, US, and Egyptian public–private partnerships through exchange visits, high-level sub-committee meetings, and expert working groups and workshops on workforce development, education practice and new technologies, and nutrition and education. On the Egyptian side, we had an office in the Ministry of Education, and coordinated with the Ministry of Foreign Affairs, the Egyptian Business Council, and the Alexandria Business Association. On the US side we worked with USAID Cairo, the USAID Education Office in Washington, DC, the US Department of Education, the US Chamber of Commerce, and various US for-profit and nonprofit organizations working on education and workforce development. The Egyptian bureaucracy was extremely top-down in decision-making, which was not an easy match for collaborative partnerships with US groups and companies. The very political nature of the Secretariat made it challenging to move beyond dialogue into action (DevTech 1997).

Advocacy

There is a long tradition of anthropologists serving as advocates for the people with whom they work. Less visible is the advocacy that goes on inside development agencies making the case for attention to human needs, differences, and the importance of giving them as voice. Anthropologist Mac Chapin is co-founder and director of the Center for the Support of Native Lands which focuses on the protection of biological and cultural diversity by assisting indigenous peoples in preserving their natural and cultural heritage through participatory mapping. In Central America Chapin helped indigenous peoples retain lands that developers claimed to be uninhabited. Chapin has collaborated with indigenous peoples on mapping projects in Central and South America, Africa, and New Guinea (see www.nativemaps.org; Chapin and Threlkeld 2001).

Fund-raising

Most anthropologists apply for funding for research or other projects. International development project stakes are higher, particularly in US government contracting which involves large consortiums of firms and NGOs. Even within MDBs it is often necessary to apply for bilateral trust funds for social research and pilot activities that client countries won't fund through loans. Most of the work I have done for the World Bank over the past three years was funded through trust funds awarded on the basis of proposals I had written (my fund-raising for CEDPA is described in Chapter 29).

Entry Points for Anthropologists in International Development

Networking and self-marketing

Networking and self-marketing and essential. Cultivate faculty and fellow graduate connections, join professional organizations, attend talks and workshops, join social networks, participate in e-discussion groups, and stay in touch with former clients in development organizations. Networking is the only way through which I have secured jobs and consultancies. My initial entry into international development was through former graduates of my instructional design program. My dissertation adviser provided the connection for my first World Bank consultancy through his graduate school classmate, whose friend at the World Bank was looking for someone to do a literature review on survival strategies of the poor in Kenya. That connection led to introductions to other World Bank staff and my current work in gender and transport many years later.

Search the Internet for information about development agencies and opportunities. Sign up with free development job clearing houses. Groups such as Devex (www.devex.com) and DevNetJobs (www.devnetjobs.org) list job opportunities and do not charge job seekers. A modest membership fee with Devex entitles you to participate in social networking happy hours with employers in international development.

Experience

Experience of working in development organizations is very important – the more experience, the better. If paid opportunities do not immediately appear, volunteer, pursue internships, or assist in university-based international development contracts. You can volunteer for longer stints overseas through faith-based groups, the Peace Corps, or international NGOS listed in the online InterAction roster. The World Bank has special programs to attract promising young professionals.

Résumé

Your résumé must reflect experience and expertise that are relevant to development work. Begin with your development-related experience and skills. Move degrees and research to the end. If you have publications, indicate that you will provide them on request. Each time you pursue a different consulting or employment opportunity, it is important to fine-tune your résumé, highlighting the experience and skills which are most relevant for the positions sought.

Additional degree or skills training

An additional degree or skills training in a development-related field opens up avenues for entry into development work. Consider a master's or higher degree in a development-oriented field to complement your anthropological skills and knowledge (international relations, education, public health, environment, law, business, conflict resolution). This broadens your networks and strengthens your résumé. Web-based degree programs are reducing the cost and logistical challenges of weaving in additional education while still working.

Elevator pitch

Prepare a two-minute "elevator pitch." This should clearly and concisely state your key skills, experience, and professional goals. Use this speech to market yourself during conversations after meetings and workshops, during cocktail parties, in the hallway or the elevator.

Informational interviews

Conduct informational interviews with development anthropologists. Find practitioners working in areas of interest to you, and arrange to meet with them. Seek advice and additional contacts. Do not push for job opportunities. Doing so could alienate the interviewee rather than impressing them enough to pass on your résumé to a colleague or call you in the future when they are looking for a consultant. Before the interview, conduct internet research on the agency and the work of the anthropologist as a basis to craft thoughtful questions. Read an article they have written. Look at the strategy and programs of the department in which they work.

Practitioner organizations

Join and actively participate in practitioner organizations. These include anthropological groups, such as WAPA, SfAA, NAPA, and relevant sector-specific sections of the American Anthropological Association (medical, legal, education, environment, etc.) and international development organizations such as the Society for International Development (SID) and InterAction (a coalition of NGOs), as well as professional associations in sectors in which you work, such as the International Health Section of the Public Health Association.

Opportunities in the Near and More Distant Future

In this chapter I have described a variety of opportunities for development anthropologists to make a difference in international development. The experience of these practitioners needs to feed into broader anthropological thinking as well. In their analysis of global anthropological practice, Carole Hill and Marietta Baba argue that the future of anthropology is "rooted in the theoretical and methodological issues that are emerging in the frontiers of practice" (Hill and Baba 2006: 201). Promising areas of work in international development in the near future include climate change, conflict and post-conflict settings, transparency and social accountability, innovative applications of information communication technologies, infrastructure, and corporate social responsibility. In an increasingly globalized world, the application of experience from work in developing countries in donor countries with growing multi-ethnic populations is also very salient. For the distant future it is important to stay attuned to changing global trends because development issues will change, probably in dramatic ways, as they have in the past.

Notes

1   There are already numerous accounts of the history of development anthropology from the colonialist days to the present so I do not address it in this chapter. See Hoben (1982); Ferguson (1996); Moran (1996); Nolan (2002); Edelman (2005); Lewis (2005); Mosse (2012).

2   For more details on my career path and my approach in development anthropology, see Clarke (1991, 1996, 1998, 2006, 2012), and Chapter 21 in this volume, "Working on Cross-Disciplinary Teams."

3 For further discussion of anthropology in a globalizing world see Edelman (2005), Inda and Rosaldo (2008), and Wasson et al. (2012).
4 In addition to the Department of State, and within it, the US Agency for International Development, a number of other government agencies are engaged in international development research and technical support on global issues such as the Departments of Commerce and of Agriculture, Labor Centers for Disease Control, and the Census Bureau.
5 Social safeguards cover indigenous peoples and displacement and resettlement. There is also an environment safeguard. Based on an independent evaluation group (IEG) evaluation of safeguards, the World Bank is engaged in a process of updating and consolidating the environmental and social safeguards. See http://go.worldbank.org/5442CH02G0.
6 Examples of international development consulting firms founded and managed by anthropologists include Cultural Practice (Deborah Rubin and Deborah Caro), LTG Associates (Cathleen Crain and Niel Tashima), Heartlands (Shirley Buzzard), and Social Impact (Rolf Sartorius and Pat Hanscom).
7 For more discussion on the development aspects of transport and other infrastructure see Clarke (2012).
8 Kecamatans are the administrative sub-districts, which are composed of 20 to 50 villages.

References

Cernea, Michael (1991) *Putting People First: Sociological Variables in Rural Development*, 2nd edn. New York: Oxford University Press.
Chapin, Mac and Bill Threlkeld (2001) *Indigenous Landscapes: A Study in Ethnocartography*. Arlington, VA: Center for the Support of Native Lands.
Clark [Clarke], Mari (1991) "Humanizing the Development Paradigm." In John P. Mason and Mari H. Clark (eds.), *New Directions in U.S. Foreign Assistance and New Roles for Anthropologists*. Studies in Third World Societies 44. Williamsburg, VA: Dept. of Anthropology, College of William and Mary, pp.13–26.
Clarke, Mari (1996) "Development Anthropology: Assessing Anthropology's Impact." *Development Anthropologist* 14(1–2): 20–31.
Clarke, Mari (1998) "On the Road Again: Consulting in International Development." In Paula L. W. Sabloff (ed.), *Careers in Anthropology: Profiles of Practitioner Anthropologists*. NAPA Bulletin 20. Washington, DC: American Anthropological Association, pp. 71–74.
Clarke, Mari H. (1999) *Gender and Participation in Natural Resources Baseline Survey: Albania Private Forestry Program*. Washington, DC: Chemonics International.
Clarke, Mari (2002) *Gender Assessment and Gender Action Plan of USAID/Nepal*. Washington, DC: Development Alternatives. At http://pdf.usaid.gov/pdf_docs/PNACE616.pdf, accessed Sept. 10, 2012.
Clarke, Mari (2006) "Pursuing International Development with a Gender Lens: Reflections on a Nonlinear Career Path." In Christina Wasson (ed.), *Making History at the Frontier: Women Creating Careers as Practicing Anthropologists*. NAPA Bulletin 26. Berkeley, CA: University of California Press for National Association for the Practice of Anthropology, pp. 32–54.
Clarke Mari (2012) "Engendering Transport: Mapping Men and Women on the Move." In. Christina Wasson, Mary O. Butler, and Jacqueline Copeland-Carson (eds.), *Applying Anthropology in the Global Village*. Walnut Creek, CA. Left Coast Press, pp. 57–92.

DevTech Systems (1997) "Completion Report: US–Egyptian Education Secretariat." Prepared for USAID Cairo.

Edelman, Marc (2005) *The Anthropology of Development and Globalization.* Oxford. Blackwell.

Escobar, Arturo (1991) "Anthropology and the Development Encounter: The Making and Marketing of Development Anthropology." *American Ethnologist* 18(4): 658–682.

Ferguson, James (1996) "Development." In A. Barnard and J. Spencer (eds.), *The Encyclopedia of Social and Cultural Anthropology.* London. Routledge.

Gow, David (2002) "Anthropology and Development: Evil Twin or Moral Narrative." *Human Organization* 61(4): 299–313.

Guggenheim, Scott (2004) *Crises and Contradictions: Understanding the Origins of a Community Development Project in Indonesia.* Jakarta: World Bank. At http://siteresources. worldbank.org/INTINDONESIA/Resources/Social/KDP-Crises.pdf, accessed Sept. 4, 2012.

Hill, Carole E. and Marietta L. Baba (eds.) (2006) *The Globalization of Anthropology.* NAPA Bulletin 25. Arlington, VA: American Anthropological Association.

Hoben, Allan (1982) "Anthropologists and Development." *Annual Review of Anthropology* 11: 349–375.

Horowitz, Michael (1989) "Development Anthropology in the 1990s." *Development Anthropology Newsletter* 30(9): 3.

Inda, Jonathan and Renato Rosaldo (2008) *The Anthropology of Globalization.* Oxford. Blackwell.

Lewis, David (2005) "Anthropology and Development: The Uneasy Relationship." *LSE Research Online.* At http://eprints.lse.ac.uk/archive/00000253, accessed Sept. 20, 2012.

Moran, Emilio (ed.) (1996) *Transforming Societies: Transforming Anthropology.* Ann Arbor: University of Michigan Press.

Mosse, David (ed.) (2012) *Adventures in Aidland: The Anthropology of Professionals in Development.* New York: Berghahn.

Nolan, Riall (2002) *Development Anthropology: Encounters in the Real World.* Boulder, CO: Westview Press.

Pillsbury, Barbara (2008) "Applied Anthropology and Executive Leadership." In Carla Guerrón-Montero (ed.), *Careers in Applied Anthropology in the 21st Century: Perspectives from Academics and Practitioners.* NAPA Bulletin 29. Oxford: Blackwell, pp. 131–151.

Wasson, Christine, Mary Odell Butler, and Jacqueline Copeland-Carson (eds.) (2012) *Applying Anthropology in the Global Village.* Walnut Creek, CA. Left Coast Press.

Chapter 21

Military and Security

Kerry B. Fosher and Frank J. Tortorello, Jr.

Kerry Fosher and Frank Tortorello are both anthropologists working for the Marine Corps, but with different jobs. From their two perspectives, they offer a look at the issue of role and identity for anthropologists in military organizations, and how these affect professional decisions. The chapter focuses particularly on how military organizations think and act – with particular reference to the Marines – and what this implies for how anthropologists work within them. Fosher and Tortorello look at both challenges and opportunities here, and provide a wealth of "travelers' advice" for practitioners considering the military option.

The views expressed in this work are the authors' alone and do not represent the position of the United States Marine Corps or Professional Solutions, LLC.

Introduction

There are many issues confronting cultural anthropologists considering work within a military organization. Within the confines of a short chapter, we had to choose to address one subset and merely point to some of the others. We settled on issues related to role and identity, as those underpin decision-making for all the others. The majority of the chapter is, therefore, dedicated to our experiences with setting goals and shaping our roles and work context. At the end, we have included a small section of "travelers' advice" pointing to some issues that appear to have been common stumbling points for anthropologists entering this domain.

A Handbook of Practicing Anthropology. First Edition. Edited by Riall W. Nolan.
© 2013 John Wiley & Sons, Inc. Published 2013 by John Wiley & Sons, Inc.

The authors are cultural anthropologists working within the same organization, but with different positions, responsibilities, and goals. As described below, the work context and expectations in military organizations constitute a powerful shaping force that can influence your ability to control your work and your professional identity. We present our insights separately in hopes that that the different ways we address the topics will help the reader sense how small variations in point of entry, positionality, and intent can yield different work experiences, opportunities, and obstacles.

Fosher did her field research among first responders in the Boston area during the time of the September 11, 2001 attacks and subsequently worked for a research center focused on homeland security issues for three years. She began working directly with military organizations in 2006, pursuing her goals from different positions in the US Air Force and Marine Corps. Roles for anthropologists during this time were not well defined and she worked broadly across policy, training and education, and intelligence. She currently runs a research group in the Marine Corps' Training and Education Command.

Tortorello conducted his field research with active-duty US Marines training to be instructor-trainers in Marine Corps Martial Arts. He completed one course as a trainee and returned for a second course as a guest instructor-trainer. He began working with the Marine Corps' Training and Education Command in 2010 as a contracted researcher. His research covers topics such as assessing the impact of culture training on Marine missions, understanding how Marines conceive of resilience and steadfastness, and developing general cultural concepts to assist Marines in global deployments.

Setting Goals, Shaping Conditions

Kerry Fosher

The last several years have seen renewed debate over the roles that anthropologists fill when working with military or intelligence organizations, the ethical challenges associated with such work, and its potential impact on other anthropologists and the discipline as a whole. While initial writing and discussion centered on the controversy surrounding the US Army's Human Terrain System, there are now several books that capture a broader, although still partial, range of the kinds of work anthropologists do in military organizations, as well as discussions of the ethical challenges (Price 2004, 2008, 2011; Peacock et al. 2007; Albro et al. 2009, 2012; Fosher 2009; Lucas 2009; Kelly et al. 2010; McNamara and Rubinstein 2011).

These texts don't cover all the roles or considerations, but they are a place to start. The most significant piece of advice I can provide to somebody considering working with the military is: *Do your homework.* Read these accounts and perhaps reach out to the authors. Read historical accounts of past times when the military and anthropology intersected and what some of the problems were (Deitchman 1976; Price 2004, 2008, 2011).

My own goals and trajectory were formed during a time when new roles for anthropologists in the Department of Defense (DoD) were still in flux. To be clear, there were already many anthropologists in military organizations, faculty in military universities, archaeologists doing cultural resource management on bases, analysts and program managers in a range of organizations. However, the rapid increase in military interest in anthropology, coupled with the slow pace of formal institutional change, meant that we had greater freedom than anthropologists had only a few years before to work with employers to shape job descriptions and working conditions. That window of opportunity is closing as formal job descriptions are created, organizations no longer perceive anthropologists as scarce resources for whom concessions must be made, and there are increasing expectations that anthropologists will conform to normal roles and the working conditions of civil service or contract employees. This has some serious implications, described later in the section.

My initial goal was to incorporate contemporary anthropological theory into the cultural training and education being developed for military personnel. Within the first year, as I learned more about the institutional context, this goal broadened. I came to see that one of the most important things anthropologists can do is to try to integrate contemporary theory, methods, and critique across a broader range of topics and problems, to try to shift the way military personnel think about and consume science, especially social science. DoD bias toward technological solutions is fairly well known. Attitudes toward what counts as science have been shaped by a long relationship with "hard" sciences and the approaches those disciplines take to the scientific method, standards of evidence, what constitutes acceptable measurement, and how problems are framed. It has also been shaped by budgetary and accountability processes favoring solutions that can be purchased and, most importantly, quantified so organizations can easily report back to Congress how funds have been expended. As one might expect, the convergence of these influences makes it difficult for organizations to design, implement, and sustain programs where the outcome is an improvement in the less tangible knowledge or skills of military personnel rather than a piece of technology that can be counted.[1]

I believe that helping military organizations shape their questions using a broader range of disciplinary thinking and making qualitative assessment more accessible remain two of the core challenges anthropologists can confront in this domain of practice. However, they are challenges that require the ability to influence the thinking behind the decisions, which in turn requires access. There are formal ways military services structure their science and technology objectives and request research projects. Perhaps more importantly, there are informal conversations with leaders and project managers where you can help them incorporate new ideas, as they help you understand the messy formal and informal ways the organization consumes science.

Working toward this kind of broad, long-term goal means being willing to accept that your influence may be invisible and unacknowledged. The latter means you have to accept that you may not be able to demonstrate your successes to government colleagues or fellow anthropologists, which can create professional challenges.

Regardless of the goals you have and how they change as you work with a military organization, understanding how to navigate role expectations and professional identity issues is critical. As suggested above, new roles for anthropologists were being created as I came into the domain. Anthropologists were sought rather than having to seek employment. I wasn't job hunting when I first started talking with the services about these issues. Consequently, I gained a great deal of information about different organizational contexts and leaders prior to considering taking a job within one of those contexts. I was able to choose organizations where I felt there was the greatest degree of potential flexibility to help me reach my goals, ensure I could maintain the American Anthropological Association's (AAA) Code of Ethics, and stay connected with the discipline.

Positions for anthropologists in many military organizations are now more formalized, but there is still room to shape the job and working conditions. Doing that from a purely external standpoint isn't likely to work. If you don't know the personalities of individual military leaders, you may not know what it means that a new colonel is about to take over an organization. If you don't understand the relationships and tensions between military, civilian, and contract workforces, you'll have a hard time assessing how you can be best positioned to achieve your goals.

Many organizations do not even interview candidates for jobs. The hiring process is completed by a human resources office or contracting company outside the organization. New employees in military organizations may never meet anyone with whom they'll work until their first day. Right now, this is particularly true with positions for cultural subject matter experts and analysts. As far as most federal civil service hiring processes are concerned, you are being hired to perform the functions listed in a particular job description. At that level, only the job description and whether your résumé checks the right boxes matter. Your suitability for the work environment, your strengths and weaknesses, your goals, whether or not the organization is set up to allow you to perform the listed duties – none of these things matter. So, unless your goal is simply a paycheck, you will need help to choose wisely.

Even when you know the organization and the people, there is a lot of room for misunderstanding. Potential employers may think they can provide freedoms or protections that, in fact, they cannot. This has been the case for a number of anthropologists who were promised time to write and publish but found that the organization could not make it work. In other cases, employers simply may not understand what your expectations are. I was astonished that I was expected to work a rigid schedule and to fill out mounds of paperwork if I needed to make the tiniest change. I was also taken aback when, until I set some clear boundaries, an organization expected to be able to control what I wrote and said in scholarly venues. I didn't understand why civilian personnel seemed to feel little obligation to live up to what I had been promised by their military leaders. It never occurred to my new co-workers that I would be surprised by these sorts of things, which are taken for granted in many civil service positions.

Sometimes these misunderstandings can be easily resolved. However, they can also be quite serious and have long-lasting effects on your life and career. It's safest to approach any discussion about a job with the military as a cross-cultural encounter. Don't take any of your assumptions for granted. Spend a lot of time finding out what they expect of you, how much autonomy and authority you will have, and where your goals fall in their list of priorities. Also spend time asking questions about whether or not the organization is actually structured so that you can conduct the work in the job description. If you're being hired to do research, is there an institutional review board available to review your proposals? If one of your responsibilities is to influence policy, is your job positioned in the organization in a way that ensures that you will be allowed to attend policy meetings and act on behalf of the organization? This may seem absurd, but these discontinuities are common in the civil service. Both of my job descriptions in Marine Corps organizations have held me responsible for things I was not initially positioned to influence.

You want your official position description to match your actual work as closely as possible. This is in part because of the hiring process mentioned above. You can reshape an entire organization, change national policy, or cure world hunger, but if your position description says you're a junior analyst, when you apply for a new job you'll be processed as a junior analyst. More importantly, in large organizations, you eventually come to be perceived in terms of your billet and level by co-workers rather than in terms of your anthropological identity. This is not dissimilar to cross-cultural encounters where your interlocutors choose the characteristics about you they find most salient – female, white, unmarried, scholar, or American – according to their logic and values. Whether in the field or at a job, being put in a box not of your own making, and being told that your own box is irrelevant, can be unnerving.

Also realize that your relationship to the organization requires constant monitoring. Slow changes and institutional drag will begin almost immediately. There often is a "honeymoon" period during which you will see the best, most open, and flexible side of the organization. Over time, sometimes despite everyone's good intentions, your presence becomes less exciting, handshake agreements made in interviews are forgotten in favor of official paperwork, and people start expecting you to conform. Change can happen fast as well. The military leadership in such organizations changes on a regular basis and you cannot assume that whatever agreements you had with the last leaders will be seen as valid by the new ones. A shift in budget, program decisions, or foreign policy can change the priorities of the organization and the expected function of your position. Therefore, positionality is never about crafting or attaining the right job at the right level or ensuring that you get things in writing. It's a constant dance.

The above account focuses on warnings about working with a military organization and you may be left with the sense that it is not worth the risk. For some, it may not be. In my case, it continues to be worth the struggle in spite of all the issues above and others. The work has brought me into partnership with Marines who have provided some of the most intellectually challenging and fascinating conversation (sometimes argument) I have experienced. It has allowed me to see the inner workings of and the role of human agency in institutions that are often opaque to anthropologists looking in from the outside. Over time, it has afforded me the opportunity to see the impact of small changes I have helped make on the way people understand problems and think about solutions. These changes are never as fast or as comprehensive as I would like, but thus far they have been worth the effort.

Frank Tortorello

By the fourth year of my nine-year doctoral program I had decided to pursue employment with the military (as a civilian US government employee) rather than a tenure track teaching position. Kerry Fosher's report of the shrinking number of general service (GS) positions is accurate. By the time I earned my doctorate in 2010, new federal hiring for the military was frozen. I ended up applying to be a consultant in a private company contracted to provide research to the US Marine Corps. The opportunity to work with Marines outweighed my concern about doing anthropology as a business endeavor because it allowed me to use the knowledge I had gained in writing my dissertation, which focused on how Marines train to be courageous.

I can best put some sense of the concern I had about working as a consultant[2] into context, offering the pros and cons of university versus consultant positions. For me, the pros of potential long-term stability via tenure, the clarity of copyright, and the freedom to choose and pursue research topics were offset by the thought of potentially spending seven years chasing tenure only to be rejected. Fellow scholars have related horror stories of ideologically motivated, personality-driven tenure processes. My personal experience with grant applications revealed similar dynamics at work among those charged with awarding grants.

Conversely, the cons of having to be concerned with office politics, "serving two masters," that is, answering to both a consulting company supervisor and a government client, the lack of long-term stability in employment, and potentially giving up my freedom on copyright and research topics was made up for by the pros of good pay, the immediate availability of a position, and the chance to work directly with Marines. These pros and cons express my personal values and thinking. There are many more, and many ways to weigh them relative to one another.

There are important dynamics to be aware of in the consulting world. Your firm's willingness to sponsor your application for the different levels of security clearance can impact your future both professionally and personally. Consulting companies balance service to the client with cost control and this impacts decisions about what professional development activities they will support, the expectations they might place upon your time in terms of developing new business opportunities for them with the government or military, as well as the time allotted to you for illness or vacation. For example, sick days can come out of the same pool of hours as vacation time, which you earn over time (you are not awarded a bucket of hours upon your start date as with many higher education institutions). The more you are ill, the less vacation time you have. If you have children, you can use up all your earned paid time off quite quickly.

Having had significant professional experience in both corporate recruiting and collegiate career services, my approach to getting a job was to network. Applying to positions by posting résumés online is ineffective in my view; my advice is to find *people*, not *positions*. To find military anthropologists, locate their publications and read them, meet them at conferences, ask them about their writing and their views, ask them for advice, and review your pros and cons with them.

One of the more challenging situations that I've faced as an academic, researcher, and consultant is being confronted by very different views of "research" among members of the military, government, and consulting communities. They tend to envision research relevant to people (as opposed to vehicles or weapons) as ultimately producing numerically based insights into the mysteries of human behavior. Often the type of research these communities are exposed to and prefer is when a topic like "unit cohesion" is "explained" in terms of regression analyses of quantified qualities such as a "trust," or when the act of suicide in military populations is looked at in terms of the impact of a biochemical entity like cortisol.

Ethnographic methods of research are difficult to promote against this view, and can be puzzling because they do not result in charts, graphs, tables, or other visual cues. These visual cues are often seen as the "proof" that the conclusion offered by researchers is based not only on "real" science, but on appreciable, clear causal chains. Community members tend to expect, then, that research results will be – or ought to be – factual, stable, clear, identifiable, monolithic, and direct. The notion that "real" science counts only what is countable goes a long way toward ensuring its own irrelevance by failing to take seriously the idea that what counts may not be countable. Human social life falls into the latter category for me.

If you share this kind of view, you should be prepared to have conversations with key government and military personnel not only about what counts as evidence in ethnographic research, but also about getting community members to understand the amount of time it takes to do research. Such conversations are made more difficult by the inability to guarantee clients a viable answer to a research question, no less what the answer might look like or whether an answer might end up requiring more research. So far, the best way I have discovered to get ethnographic research onto the agenda of Marine Corps leaders is to offer them a way to make better sense out of what they themselves do, and what they see Marines doing and hear Marines saying. This not just a descriptive act; it is explanatory as well. I see the work as offering Marines other ways to articulate who they are, and as in all other areas of anthropology, you had better know your host community well before venturing into this territory. The danger is that you'll substitute your own conceptions and meanings for theirs, and they're experts at identifying this kind of mistake.

The "what counts as proper research" challenge is intimately bound up with the culture of the Marine Corps. "Advanced planning" for the Marine Corps is pegged at 72 hours. One can easily imagine how a one- or two-year ethnographic research project would sound to a Marine general (this appears to reflect the Corps' structuring of itself as a "quick reaction" force – the activities of the corps over the past decade in Iraq and Afghanistan is, technically, an aberration). As if these issues were not enough, there can be a general sense that contractors are not worth very much in achieving goals. There are good and bad reasons for this that considerations of space prevent me from addressing. In this light, your ability to actually conduct research can depend on your ability to recognize when it is better to advise rather than criticize, adapt rather than argue, and assist in making bad situations a little bit less bad rather than seeking to change them. I should emphasize that both sides of these action continua are welcome in the Marine Corps. The art is knowing when, where, why, how, and with whom.

There is a critical caveat to what I have said so far: All of it is inflected by a particular relationship with the Marines made possible by Fosher. Housing a research unit within the corps is a novel idea and one that is still in its infancy in terms of the Marines figuring out what they can do with us or learn from us. Working on Marine Corps Base Quantico on a daily basis provides a great opportunity to interact with Marines which is not available to most contracted social science researchers. "Hallway conversations," those personal interactions outside of structured meetings that are noted in sociological literature as important means for organizational functioning, are frequent occurrences. Bumping into Marines you can discuss ideas with, gain insights from, ask for feedback, get advice from, and so on is invaluable in learning the culture of the corps. So it is quite possible that in other cases your consulting company's project manager may be the primary person interacting with government and military clients. It may be incumbent on you to have the conversations noted above with your project manager instead of with government or military clients directly.

A final point about the culture of the corps that shapes the experience of a researcher. Like all communities, Marines have a complex sense of themselves that can be appreciated in terms of a linguistic frame or border. The border is permeable to some things, people, and ideas and not others, at least not without hard work. This is captured in the term "marin(e)izing," which means translating, *not* "dumbing down," a concept or practice into a Marine idiom. That idiom is exemplified by the term "operational." For me, negotiating the border – getting ideas across if not accepted – has meant many hours of thinking through how anthropological knowledge can be presented to Marines as "useful" or "efficient." This does not necessarily mean the notion of helping them be more efficient killers. Killing is never simplistic or simply utilitarian for Marines despite their promotion of that very idea. Current, serious concerns in the Marine Corps that suggest a need for anthropological research focus on how and why Marines can be better diplomats, ethicists, communicators, stress reducers, citizens, spouses, mothers, and fathers before and after deployment, critical thinkers, language users, team members, problem-solvers, motivators of self and others, decision-makers, leaders, and a host of other identities.

Travelers' Advice

There are a few things mentioned in the above section that are worth drawing out as specific topics for investigation by those considering work in a military organization.

Clearance

Getting a security clearance may mean you are required to have your publications reviewed even after you leave government.

Copyright

While some organizations do not strictly enforce it, federal copyright law means that anything written using government time or resources is owned by the government. You may find that you have to do your scholarly writing at nights and weekends, keeping a strict distinction between the two parts of your professional life.

Voice

Academic freedom is inverted in government. Unless you specifically state otherwise, you are assumed to be representing the position of your organization. This can complicate your ability to participate in scholarly venues unless you clearly stake out boundaries and are vigilant in maintaining them.

Participation in the discipline

Working with the military is likely to remain a controversial topic in anthropology. If you want to continue to participate in an anthropological association, you need to have a solid understanding of the debates and be willing to engage substantively. You must be willing to critique and be critiqued.

Conclusion

We have tried to outline some of the issues related to position and identity that are relevant to anthropologists working in military organizations, many of which are shared with other domains of practice. Some can and should be revisited as your goals and work environment change. Others, such as the decision to seek a security clearance, can have permanent repercussions. Because of the history of relations between anthropology and the military, both real and apocryphal, the boundary between this kind of practice and traditional academic positions is less permeable than with other domains. While both of us feel that what we have learned and been able to accomplish in military organizations has been worth managing the challenges, our accounts, taken together with other descriptions in the literature, show that this is not a decision to be made quickly or alone. Discussions with anthropologists working in government, academia, and other fields are essential before you start and as a permanent part of your decision-making process.

Notes

1   See, e.g., my note on discourses of buying and becoming (Fosher 2008), and Cohn's (1987) classic article on technological discourse.
2   The terms "consultant" and "contractor" are interchangeable in my case, since my consulting firm had been contracted by the government to do certain kinds of work.

References

Albro, Robert, James Peacock, Carolyn Fluehr-Lobban, et al. (2009) *AAA Commission on the Engagement of Anthropology with the US Security and Intelligence Communities (CEAUS-SIC) Final Report on the Army's Human Terrain System Proof of Concept Program.* Washington, DC: American Anthropological Association.
Albro, Robert, George Marcus, Laura A. McNamara, and Monica Schoch-Spana (eds.) (2012) *Anthropologists in the Securityscape: Ethics, Practice, and Professional Identity.* Walnut Creek, CA: Left Coast Press.
Cohn, Carol (1987) "Sex and Death in the Rational World of Defense Intellectuals." *Signs* 12: 687–718.
Deitchman, Seymour J. (1976) *The Best-Laid Schemes: A Tale of Social Research and Bureaucracy.* Cambridge, MA: MIT Press.
Fosher, Kerry (2008) "Practice Note: Defense Discourses." *Anthropology News* 49(8): 54–55.
Fosher, Kerry B. (2009) *Under Construction: Making Homeland Security at the Local Level.* Chicago: University of Chicago Press.
Kelly, John D., Beatrice Jauregui, Sean T. Mitchell, and Jeremy Walton (eds.) (2010) *Anthropology and Global Counterinsurgency.* Chicago: University of Chicago Press.
Lucas, George R. (2009) *Anthropologists in Arms: The Ethics of Military Anthropology.* Lanham, MD: AltaMira Press/Rowman & Littlefield.
McNamara, Laura A. and Robert A. Rubinstein (eds.) (2011) *Dangerous Liaisons: Anthropologists and the National Security State.* Santa Fe, NM: School for Advanced Research Press.
Peacock, James, Robert Albro, Carolyn Fluehr-Lobban, et al. (2007) *AAA Commission on the Engagement of Anthropology with the US Security and Intelligence Communities Final Report.* Washington, DC: American Anthropological Association.
Price, David H. (2004) *Threatening Anthropology: McCarthyism and the FBI's Surveillance of Activist Anthropologists.* Durham, NC: Duke University Press.
Price, David H. (2008) *Anthropological Intelligence: The Deployment and Neglect of American Anthropology in the Second World War.* Durham, NC: Duke University Press.
Price, David H. (2011) *Weaponizing Anthropology: Social Science in the Service of the Militarized State.* Oakland, CA: AK Press.

Chapter 22

Anthropologists at Work in Advertising and Marketing

Timothy de Waal Malefyt

Timothy Malefyt brings his years of professional experience with advertising into this chapter, beginning with a thoughtful and insightful discussion of what advertising is today, and how it differs from the past. He then goes into detail about how and why anthropological training is an advantage in this environment, while at the same time highlighting the significant differences between the work of practitioners in advertising and the work of their academic colleagues. Malefyt then spends some time looking at how practitioners can get started in the field, and concludes with some thoughts on where advertising and marketing are likely to go in the future.

As an anthropologist who has worked in advertising for over 15 years, I share my experience and observations of working in the trade in hopes of encouraging interested anthropological practitioners and students to pursue a satisfying career. In this chapter I will discuss the vast changes underway in marketing and advertising that increasingly call for a more consumer-centric understanding of consumption, which is well suited to an anthropological approach. I will also discuss how anthropologists might likely break into this field, what everyday work in advertising is like, what one might expect on the job, as well as compare and contrast the similarities and differences between academic colleagues and anthropologist practitioners and other non-academic professionals. Finally, I will discuss the future direction of a burgeoning new field called business anthropology, which calls for more anthropological input into marketing and advertising practices that help focus corporate responsibilities on fair and equitable marketing practices toward consumers, as well

A Handbook of Practicing Anthropology. First Edition. Edited by Riall W. Nolan.
© 2013 John Wiley & Sons, Inc. Published 2013 by John Wiley & Sons, Inc.

as the ethical issues anthropologists may face and the ways they can increasingly shape corporate discourses to achieve better practices for consumers today.

Vast Changes in the Marketplace

Advertising and marketing are intrinsically related, but there are marked differences. Advertising is the communications component of the broader mix in marketing, which includes brand and product pricing, packaging, brand innovation, and promotions. Both advertising and marketing have become more important in the age of branding, writes Naomi Klein, where their role has changed from delivering simple product information to building an image around a particular brand-name version of a product (2000: 6). Indeed, even in the last decade, since Klein noted the rise of the brand, marketing and advertising have experienced vast sea changes. With the advent of the Internet, online blogs, Twitter, Facebook, and mobile apps, information about products and brands circulates in record time, and consumers who purchase products and brands have greater awareness of social issues. Consequently they can exercise greater control by turning off or tuning out advertised brands and marketed messages they don't like.

The old ways of advertising and marketing, such as fixating on messages that push products to consumers, are no longer sustainable. Rather, new approaches call for building lasting relationships with consumers. The focus in marketing is on providing people with products and brands that add value to their lives, rather than just selling goods. This means that for marketers the emphasis has shifted from one-way terminal interactions, to establishing ongoing "dialogues" that extend and continue relationships with consumers (Lury 2004; Arvidsson 2006; Malefyt 2009).

Advertising is also more effective when it doesn't "preach" to the consumer, but rather includes them in a relationship of mutual meaning-making. Advertising account planner Jon Steel writes that the best and most effective advertising involves consumers, both in the communication of advertised messages and in the subsequent development of marketing campaigns. He asserts that

> Advertising works better when it does not tell people what to think, but rather allows them to make up their own minds about its meaning. They participate by figuring it out for themselves. (Steel 1998: 6)

In other words, advertising is stronger when it does not arbitrarily "push" the manufacturer's intended "meaning" of products and human situations that an advertiser or marketer prefers, but rather builds on and expresses both consumer-derived and manufacturer-intended meaning.

This kind of interaction develops relationships with consumers by accurately representing target users or a relevant situation that consumers can identify with, in concert with the communication of a brand benefit. Without accurate consumer representation, advertising can miss an opportunity to build relationships with consumers. In ethnographic work I conducted on the Cadillac automobile brand, we found that iconic Led Zeppelin music, along with dramatic driving scenes, matched to a tagline of "Break through," resonated more with boomer consumers in the United States, rather than the calm, tranquil scenario of the new Infiniti luxury automobile. This comparison is illustrated in an article comparing the successful Cadillac automobile advertising campaign in the early 2000s with a failed Infiniti automobile advertising campaign in the 1980s (McCabe and Malefyt 2010).

Increased emphasis on building relationships with consumers means that corporations also have to be more transparent with their advertising, product effectiveness, and quality. Marketing experts Philip Kotler and John Castilone argue that transparency in business is no longer an option, but a necessity to maintain integrity: "honest and authentic behavior in a company's business dealings are now one of the most important factors in gaining and maintaining customer and stakeholder loyalty" (Craven 2009: 2). Companies cannot get away with coercive business practices or poor product quality and survive. For instance, most recently, the esteemed Apple corporation has come under scrutiny following reports that its suppliers in China employ sweatshop conditions, forcing Apple to respond by revealing its long guarded manufacturers' identities and calling for investigations into fair working conditions (Porter 2012).

With changes in increased corporate transparency and consumers seeking more information to confirm their choices, the post-purchase cycle of consumption is far more valuable today. What consumers feel and say about a brand to their friends and colleagues *after* buying something is much more likely to affect a brand than persuasive advertising alone. For instance, more than 60 percent of consumers of facial skin care products conduct online research about the products they buy, and discuss with others their feelings after they purchase them (Edelman 2010: 67). Advertising and marketing seek to pique the interest of interested buyers so that they pursue additional ways to invest in a brand or product, and perhaps persuade others to do the same.

The Anthropologist's Advantage

How might an anthropologist fit within this environment and how do they add particular value? As mentioned, corporations produce the products or services that, it is hoped, consumers desire and buy. Much of what anthropologists do in advertising and marketing is develop research that gives shape, voice, and image to how consumers use brands in their lives. Anthropologists conducting ethnographic research for marketing firms or in advertising agencies are particularly adept at understanding the multiple ways in which consumers derive unspoken satisfaction from the brands and products they use. Anthropologists employ a holistic approach to understanding culture that is especially useful in this regard. When corporate anthropologists take a broader view of consumers and apply this to the network of cultural systems and relations in people's lives, they help make sense of seemingly disparate actions by consumers in terms of a larger whole. For instance, in a study we conducted on cooking for a soup company, we discovered that when consumers, such as mothers in families, express creativity by making daily decisions of what to feed their families for dinner, we noted the interconnections between the ways they rely on their cell phones, Internet, and mobile devices to keep track of family wishes, changes in individuals' schedules, coupon offers, and last-minute recipe searches. While brand categories in an advertising agency or a marketing firm may keep brand and client categories distinct – in this case, a food company and a telecommunications company – the integration of these experiences into a seamless whole is how consumers naturally live their lives. This is why an anthropological perspective, which cuts across arbitrary marketing categories and reveals the way people normally behave, is such an advantage in business.

Furthermore, because of their holistic perspective, anthropologists in business can explain the meaning behind consumer behavior that often appears contrary or paradoxical. Consumer insights are not always easy to discover, since consumers cannot always articulate what they want and need. But anthropologists, by training, have learned to observe and to listen closely for broader patterns of behavior, and to look for a unifying logic between apparent contradictions in what people say. For instance, during another project conducted for a packaged goods client, I interviewed a staunch environmental supporter in her home. She discussed her passion for "green" products which she was keen for others to share. Yet I was surprised to observe that she also drove a large, gas-guzzling sport utility vehicle, which was apparently at odds with her environmental concerns. Probing further, I tried to discern a unifying logic. The respondent said that she used her vehicle to car-pool her own and other children, and admitted that she felt most "protected" in a large vehicle. Her passion for the environment was also expressed in generalized concerns of "protection for the planet" as well as for her family. Anthropologists notice such apparent contradictions and look for the internal logic that connects two separate domains into a unified whole.

As cultural experts in a business organization, anthropologists also bring together broader cultural perspectives within specific ethnographic assignments from clients. There is great value in anthropologists conducting research that connects current cultural trends with specific client goals in ethnography. This leads to what Grant McCracken (2009) proposes as greater integration of cultural leadership in corporations. This is a critical advantage that corporate anthropologists can offer advertising and marketing enterprises. Anthropologists can help investigate and interpret trends and consumer perspectives to better inform corporations, for example, about consumers' attitudes to and beliefs about health and wellness, in order to improve the marketing of a corporate food product.

For instance, the slow food movement today is a trend that arose in reaction to the growing propensity for eating fast food mindlessly. It is also a movement about slowing down in general, raising social awareness, and encouraging consumer activism to keep traditional food ways intact outside the control of multinational agribusiness (Hamilton 2009). Health and wellness is a consumer trend that converges with other cultural movements, such as concern over global warming, diet and obesity, fair trade, energy consumption, fair labor practices, and so on. These movements spread rapidly through social networking on the Internet and politicize the call for better food practices from manufacturers. Anthropologists attuned to these cultural movements can better inform corporate agendas and business practices, so as to align the marketing of food with consumer trends. Thus, in conducting consumer research on eating habits anthropologists may incorporate how food choices in restaurants and home cooking are shaped by larger trends, even as respondents may not explicitly mention these trends or even be aware of the choices they are making.

As companies seek to develop closer interactive relationships with consumers in order to achieve product improvements, anthropologists in advertising agencies and market research firms have greater influence in shaping corporate discourses and marketing practices to meet consumer expectations. Thus, recognizing the value of anthropological fieldwork in identifying and explaining culturally significant domains and trends is a vital first step toward improving the knowledge practices within advertising agencies and corporations, now and in the future. Anthropologists can have a greater impact in shaping corporate marketing plans when they work alongside corporate clients *within* advertising agencies than they do when working *externally*, as consultants or hired vendors. Anthropologists working as insiders have substantial responsibility for shaping corporate ideologies and consumption agendas toward more beneficial ends.

Everyday Work in Advertising Is Different from Academia

Everyday work for anthropologists in advertising means focusing on the client's brand and the business of the companies. Anthropologists may conduct ethnographic research for various clients on what motivates consumers to use these brands; they may investigate current trends, such as food movements or social activism among different populations such as among teens or boomer couples; they may contribute to strategic thinking in an advertising pitch; they may help manage staff and develop client relationships. Since the marketplace is always in flux with new consumer trends, the launch of competitive products, and changes within a particular corporation, each day brings new challenges.

Corporate anthropologists carry out their daily assignments by working closely with other members in an agency, such as account planners (the research part of agencies), account supervisors (the client relations side of agencies), and occasionally writers themselves (the talent who develop advertisements). As such, a corporate anthropologist's day-to-day responsibilities are distinct from those of their counterparts in academia.

University professors often occupy specialized domains of expertise. Academic anthropologists typically work on their own. They choose a topic of interest, investigate their people, and write a report (book, paper, or article), which they then present to a mainly academic audience. In addition, academic anthropologists in colleges and universities conduct ethnographic research through observations, interviews, and taking field notes, which are later formulated into narrative documents that provide a testament to their work. George Marcus explains the academic process: "Textualization is the heart of the ethnographic enterprise, both in the field and in the university setting" (Marcus and Fischer 1986: 264). Even when academics gather collectively at conferences, they read papers to one another. The *text* is the primary means of communication and representation of others and of ideas in academia.

In contrast, most communication and representation for corporate anthropologists in advertising and marketing takes place discursively in meetings. Anthropologists working in advertising and marketing frequently attend workshops and meetings where they listen to, or present to, others (Malefyt 2003). They work on new business, as in crafting and delivering a pitch, and maintain current client relations, for example by preparing research reports, debriefs, and briefings (Moeran 2006). While meetings may function to disseminate information, they also present a frame for strategic interaction and performance. For instance, ad agencies continually try to impress other corporations (new and current) by managing impressions in presentations (Goffman 1959). As Brian Moeran states, frequent presentations are not so much like theatrical performances, but rather more of an organizational behavior (2006: 70). Performance in presentations helps to manage and deliver the two most important elements of the relationship that agencies have with clients: handling the everyday concerns of a corporate account and delivering new creativity. These two vital aspects of agency life often require special internal rituals in meetings that help resolve conflicts and maintain the status quo (Malefyt and Morais 2012: 35–46).

Another area where corporate anthropologists in advertising and marketing differ from their academic counterparts is where difficult, even ethical, issues arise in their daily work. For instance, working on a lemon-lime soft drink project for a global beverage company, we developed a marketing and advertising strategy based on associating the benefits of the soft drink with fulfilling the longing for connection and security.[1] We conducted ethnographic interviews with young men and women in their twenties who were heavy users of the brand, to better understand their emotional connection to the lemon-lime soft drink category and this brand in particular. We focused on the transitory life stage of this audience. Our research hypotheses suggested that humor and laughter played an important role in young people's lives, easing their anxieties about transitioning to adulthood. We then used these insights about the importance of "stress relief" in humor and laughter to develop an advertising campaign for the brand. We formulated a marketing strategy that aligned the brand's "light-hearted" lemon-lime features – bubbly, clear, and sweet – with imagery associated with overcoming difficult situations, using humor as a suggested means for consumers to lighten up, feel de-stressed, and move forward in life.

As an anthropologist I questioned the ethics of using people's insecurities and ambivalences in facing life transitions for the purpose of a marketing campaign. American consumers are free to choose; they can accept or reject marketing messages based upon their evaluation of the advertising promises made (Beeman 1986). Nevertheless, is it ethical when marketers and researchers draw on people's emotional sensitivities in clever, light-hearted ads to promote their product, which in truth cannot replace real human relations? Advertising increasingly seeks to position brands using emotional imagery rather than by providing rational information, to make messages more personal and less subject to popular criticism (Malefyt 2007). Ethical issues such as this are common in marketing and advertising, and never present themselves in simple black-and-white choices. And for this very reason anthropologists can make a difference by working within these structures of power to help shape and mold discourses that affect consumers in their daily purchases.

How to Start a Career in Advertising or Marketing

Interested anthropologists and students of anthropology can break into this field without marketing or advertising experience. They can promote themselves in résumés and through executive recruiters as qualified to study various dimensions of people in culture. While actual field experience in conducting ethnography is helpful, it is no longer the catchword in marketing that it once was. This is because ethnography has become a standard practice in market research today, conducted broadly by many marketers in the field.[2]

The idea of "decoding" brands for their symbolic and emotional meaning to consumers is very attractive for many advertisers and marketers. Marketers are continually seeking to explain why people do the things they do, especially in ways that may help to clarify contradictory behavior, as mentioned before. An anthropologist's understanding of the symbolic functions of rituals in culture, and of the various uses of language, systems of exchange such as gift exchange, and performance in culture, can offer a different view of consumer behavior. Such anthropological insights are what advertising and marketing firms are looking for today.

Furthermore, anthropological studies that can help explain the rise in social marketing will be most vital for advertising agencies and market research firms. Anthropological and sociological perspectives on the ways people connect through social media (Facebook, YouTube, Twitter, LinkedIn, Pinterest, etc.) are especially valuable (Turkle 2011). In the last five years, we've seen what is referred to as Web 2.0, or the rise of social media. Since the mid-2000s, applications for social network patents and mentions of social media in books have grown exponentially. New models of social media show that our thoughts, tweets, and inside jokes texted to others are themselves the raw material that have become monetized as social material. It's not that Facebook and Twitter finally allow people to be social, but that these new media are wholly dependent on others for sociability (Childress 2012). People rely on technology to discuss with friends and family first-hand what happens in their lives, and this is of interest to marketers and advertisers.

Nevertheless, anthropologists seeking work in advertising agencies and marketing firms should not limit themselves only to anthropological or cultural analysis. Anthropologists entering the advertising and marketing industries need to educate themselves in the manners, customs, and especially the particular language of business.

They should actively seek to understand the roles and responsibilities of their business subordinates, peers, and superiors in other domains. They need to grasp corporate marketplace agendas and financial goals, know the competition, and become proficient in the language of business. They should be cognizant of corporate philosophies and comprehend how their particular assignments impact and are impacted by the larger business enterprise.

Anthropologists who work in advertising, for example, should not only know the components of a creative brief, the one-page document or blueprint that provides consumer insights and strategic brand direction for creative talent to work from (Steel 1998). They should also be skilled in crafting one and be aware of where the brand they advocate stands in the marketplace relative to other brands and how their client plans to build market share (Malefyt and Morais 2012). Through these efforts anthropologists will connect their research and insights more effectively with the aims of their advertising and marketing partners. And, equally importantly, they will maximize their value to a corporation or advertising agency.

Future Directions

The rise of anthropology as a valued discipline in the corporate world is spreading and there is growing demand for cultural experts. This news is encouraging and, hopefully, will inspire more anthropologists to seek employment in the marketing and advertising industry. Still, problems arise from working in the corporate world as a result of misconceptions over what anthropology is as a discipline and what it can offer business practices. For one, many marketers continue to conflate ethnography with anthropology. Both are assumed to be interchangeable as approaches, where anthropology should be seen, more broadly and analytically, as a means of recognizing larger patterns in human behavior.

Second, business often perceives ethnography to be more valuable than other research methods for zeroing in on consumers' unarticulated desires, and assumes that what is said in the context of home, work, or while shopping is unquestionably true. However, much of the analytical thinking that accompanies anthropologists' use of ethnography is still underutilized or misunderstood in marketing and advertising. This is because anthropology asks a set of questions that are different from those specific to a brand or a marketing strategy (Sunderland and Denny 2007). Anthropologists often step back to look for the larger pattern in explaining the inconsistencies of consumer behavior.

Anthropology in the corporate setting still needs to move beyond the singular and limited use of ethnography as a methodology. This will lead to richer contributions by anthropologists in corporations, particularly those anthropologists who are skilled at understanding the larger impact of culture on a range of business practices. McCracken (2009) has strongly advocated anthropologists taking on greater roles within corporations as chief culture officers (CCO). While this ideal for high-level executives is admirable, more industry jobs are available to professionally trained anthropologists and others with an anthropological sensibility at middle levels of management. Responsibilities could entail gaining a deeper understanding of a company's target consumers, and of emerging cultural trends and their impact on brands and targets, and linking these trends to societal beliefs and values that affect consumption. Internal corporate anthropologists, such as Elizabeth Briody (in her work for General Motors), would also contribute to a better understanding of internal corporate operations and tensions between groups. Anthropologists employed as corporate insiders are better suited to understanding the business goals of an organization from within, and can contribute actively to the crafting and managing of business strategies. In this role, anthropologists become integrated into the corporate fabric and ultimately have more direct management responsibility, as opposed to the supportive research and advisory roles that anthropologists employed as outside vendors typically have.

In the future, more anthropologists will traverse back and forth across what now exists as a divide between those who practice anthropology in advertising and marketing research (and other businesses) and academics who study consumers and consumption (Malefyt and Morais 2012). Now is the moment to bring together a range of mutual interests and understandings of the same subject matter. This conversation will be aided by a greater attention to theory in business anthropology studies, as advocated by Maryann McCabe (2011). Even as academic literature in recent years has shifted to include discussions on the nature of capitalism, consumption, and globalizing forces – topical to both anthropological practitioners and academics – too often academic anthropology stands apart, failing to acknowledge the work and ideas of practicing anthropologists, and vice versa. More anthropologists are needed in business, including advertising and marketing, to fill the ranks in conference meetings and thus increase cross-channel discussions.

The rise of the Ethnographic Practice in Industry Conference (EPIC), the continuing efforts of the Society for Applied Anthropology (SfAA), and other conference proceedings, as well as two new business anthropology journals (*Journal of Business Anthropology* and *International Journal of Business Anthropology*) show greater receptivity to anthropology in business settings. There is still a need for a higher level of mutual intelligibility and for greater communication and acceptance between academic and practice discussions on anthropology, consumption, and consumer research. This will increase knowledge exchange between academic and practice vocations and lead to career advancement for new MAs and PhDs. Careers that cross-pollinate academia and business are desirable; they need not be mutually exclusive professions.

Finally, anthropology as an interdisciplinary endeavor will likely continue to adapt to business formats and economic models to gain further acceptance in advertising and marketing. Feinberg anticipates that the future of anthropology will continue its "cross-disciplinary hybridization," a tendency, he notes, which already marks the history of some of anthropology's greatest contributors: Boas trained in physics and geography; Malinowski studied math and physics; Firth earned an MA in economics; Mead majored as an undergraduate in English and psychology; Geertz studied philosophy (Feinberg 2009: 4). Anthropology is adaptable as a social science, as an expression of humanism, and as a form of social critique. It will be equally important for anthropology to adapt to advertising and marketing in ways that will demonstrate its potentially greater usefulness as a global business model and as a way of mediating culture between producers and consumers (Malefyt and Morais 2012). This will require those working as anthropologists in marketing and advertising also to adapt to new situations, to incorporate new learnings, and to be more flexible in their outlook.

Conclusion

Anthropologists working in advertising agencies and marketing research firms can and should influence corporate ideologies and the perceptions of consumers by encouraging ethnographic fieldwork and other research that directly impacts corporate practices in the production of products and services. The fieldwork experience of anthropologists among consumers of a brand or service can often enlist those corporate clients themselves to join in the process of observing and interacting with users of its brands. When the anthropologist involves corporate clients in becoming participant observers in research, the latter will grow in their understanding of the impact of their brand in consumers' lives. This mode of mediation with clients through guided ethnography can lead to better ways to manufacture and market a wide range of brands and services. In this regard, the task and responsibility of anthropologists working in advertising and marketing research is not only to gather more compelling research of consumers' lives for their clients' brands, but also to foster and build strong relationships between corporate clients and their consumers. Better-informed clients in corporations are then compelled to make better products for their consumers. Greater interaction, contestation, and integration of ideas give rise to more ways to influence one another's perspective. This results in more positive outcomes for all.

Working as an anthropologist in advertising and marketing can be rewarding when one sees how ideas become manifest in marketing plans and communication efforts. This can improve corporations' understanding of their potential clients and how they represent them in their advertising messages. The desire in advertising and in corporations for new ideas that resonate with consumers makes the work more interesting and valuable to both marketers and consumers. And this is the part that is so fulfilling about working as an anthropologist in advertising. Helping to create advertisements and marketing plans that tap into some consumer truth can be quite inspiring. These are the moments when it is very fulfilling to be part of something that makes a difference.

Notes

1   See the chapter on ethics in Malefyt and Morais (2012: 121–135).
2   See Malefyt (2009) for a discussion on the rise of corporate ethnography.

References

Arvidsson, Adam (2006) *Brands: Meaning and Value in Media Culture*. London: Routledge.

Beeman, William O. (1986) "Freedom to Choose: Symbols and Values in American Advertising." In H. Varenne (ed.), *Symbolizing America*. Lincoln: University of Nebraska Press.

Childress, C. Clayton (2012) "All Media are Social." *Contexts* 11(1): 54–55.

Craven, Alistair (2009) "Chaotics: An Interview with Philip Kotler and John A. Caslione." Emerald Group Publishing. At http://emeraldinsight.com/learning/management_ thinking/interviews/pdf/kotler_caslione.pdf?PHPSESSID=klfigsjtjp0lghd8hdvv 9if993, accessed Sept. 4, 2012.

Edelman, David C. (2010) "Branding in the Digital Age." *Harvard Business Review* (Dec.), 63–69.

Feinberg, Richard (2009) "Bridging Science and Humanism: Thoughts on the Future of Anthropology." *Anthropology News* 50(9): 4, 8.

Goffman, Erving (1959) *The Presentation of Self in Everyday Life*. New York: Doubleday.

Hamilton, Joslyn (2009) "What the Slow Food Movement is Really About." At http:// www.examiner.com/article/what-the-slow-food-movement-is-really-about, accessed Sept. 4, 2012.

Klein, Naomi (2000) *No Logo: Taking Aim at the Brand Bullies*. New York: Picador.

Lury, Celia (2004) *Brands: The Logos of the Global Economy*. London: Routledge.

Malefyt, Timothy de Waal (2003) "Models, Metaphors and Client Relations." In Timothy de Waal Malefyt and Brian Moeran (eds.), *Advertising Cultures*. Oxford: Berg, pp. 139–163.

Malefyt, Timothy de Waal (2007) "From Rational Calculation to Sensual Experience: The Marketing of Emotions in Advertising." In Helena Wulff (ed.), *The Emotions: A Cultural Reader*. Oxford: Berg, pp. 321–338.

Malefyt, Timothy de Waal (2009) "Understanding the Rise of Consumer Ethnography: Branding Techno-Methodologies in the New Economy." *American Anthropologist* 111: 201–210.

Malefyt, Timothy de Waal and Robert J. Morais (2012) *Advertising and Anthropology: Ethnographic Practice and Cultural Perspectives*. Oxford: Berg.

Marcus, George and Michael Fischer (1986) *Anthropology as Cultural Critique*. Chicago: University of Chicago Press.

McCabe, Maryann (2011) "Business Anthropology, the Future and Pursuit of Theoretical Directions." In Robert Guang Tian, Daming Zhou, and Alfons van Marrewijk (eds.), *Advanced Readings in Business Anthropology*. Toronto: North American Press, pp. 281–285.

McCabe, Maryann and Timothy de Waal Malefyt (2010) "Brands, Interactivity, and Contested Fields: Exploring Production and Consumption in Cadillac and Infiniti Automobile Advertising Campaigns." *Human Organization* 69: 252–262.

McCracken, Grant (2009) *Chief Culture Officer*. New York: Basic Books.

Moeran, Brian (2006) *Ethnography at Work*. Oxford: Berg.

Porter, Eduardo (2012) "Dividends in Pressing Apple over Labor." *New York Times* (Mar. 7), B1, 5.

Steel, Jon (1998) *Truth, Lies and Advertising: The Art of Account Planning*. New York: Wiley.

Sunderland, Patricia L. and Rita M. Denny (2007) *Doing Anthropology in Consumer Research*. Walnut Creek, CA: Left Coast Press.

Turkle, Sherry (2011) *Alone Together*. New York: Basic Books.

Chapter 23

Anthropology in Design and Product Development

Crysta Metcalf

Crysta Metcalf begins her account of working as a design anthropologist – a job she never intended to find – with a short sketch of how she got there. Embedded within that story are insights into how one's anthropological training can be used in multiple ways, as well as observations on what it's like to work primarily with non-social scientists. Metcalf describes her work in a team of designers in considerable detail, and talks about how the overarching corporate culture both enables and constrains the work she and her team are able to do. Throughout her chapter, Metcalf stresses teamwork, synergy, and transdisciplinary thinking as the keys to successful performance.

I am what I would call a design anthropologist. I didn't start out this way, nor did I ever have the intention of ending up in this field when I was in graduate school. This chapter is about what it means and what it's like for me to be a design anthropologist working in new product development and high tech innovation.

Today, I am the director of interactive media research within Motorola Mobility's Applied Research Center, and I lead a cross-disciplinary team of social scientists, computer scientists, engineers, and designers. The team studies how people interact with media, how they interact with each other around media, and how they communicate through media. We do this to create feature and design guidance for the next generation of compelling media products. I have worked in applied research in Motorola since 2000, on a variety of projects utilizing team-based, transdisciplinary methods for technology innovation.

First, let me say that while I did not start my education with an intention to become a design anthropologist, I am very glad I ended up here. I love my job, and

A Handbook of Practicing Anthropology. First Edition. Edited by Riall W. Nolan.
© 2013 John Wiley & Sons, Inc. Published 2013 by John Wiley & Sons, Inc.

I love working on teams with people in other disciplines. It hasn't always been easy, and of course nothing is always fun, but I wouldn't trade what I'm doing now for any of the things I thought I would do when I was starting out.

When I started out I simply knew that the various anthropological theories of how humans behaved with one another were intriguing, that studying people seemed much more interesting and difficult than studying chemistry, and that I was passionately drawn to the discipline. I changed my major from chemistry to anthropology and was immediately intrigued with the idea of using anthropology to solve real world problems. I was studying at the University of South Florida, one of the first universities in the country with an anthropology department that was exposing students to the concept of applied anthropology. I didn't know it then, but this would significantly affect the trajectory of my career.

In my last semester I had a senior seminar class with Dr. Gilbert Kushner that exposed the students to various ways of applying anthropology. We read parts of volume 10 of *Practicing Anthropology* on "Anthropology and International Business," guest-edited by Elizabeth Briody and Marietta Baba (1988). It caught my interest and soon I was reading the NAPA Bulletin authored by Baba (1986) which described how the discipline of "Business and Industrial Anthropology" came about. Studying organizations to understand organizational culture and its influences on organizational behavior fascinated me. If we understand how organizations work, we can change what they do from the inside, I thought.

I wrote my final paper for the class on business anthropology, focusing particularly on Brian Burkhalter's (1985) contention that business is not immoral as much as amoral and Hendrick Serrie's (1983) argument that an anthropologist working in business can direct organizational change toward longer-term commitments to the communities those organizations are in. I decided to attend Wayne State University to study under Marietta Baba and Elizabeth Briody, and to become a business and organizational anthropologist.

Interestingly, except during my dissertation, I never really practiced business and organizational anthropology. For my dissertation I studied how organizational culture influences the adoption and use of information and communication technologies. Once I had defended my thesis, and was trying to figure out what I wanted to do, it just so happened that a friend of mine, who was working at Motorola, overheard a research manager say that he needed an anthropologist on his team. His team did user research for new product innovation throughout the Motorola product line. He wanted someone who had experience of studying people using qualitative methods. All the people on his team were experienced in quantitative methods, but none had expertise in qualitative methods, and he wanted to be able to do both types of research. I thought that having an influence on what products a company makes would be interesting; after all, new products can create positive change in the world. I had studied the use of information and communication technologies for my dissertation, and so I applied – and got the job.

That was the end of me being a business and organizational anthropologist, and the beginning of my path to turn myself into a design anthropologist. At that time there was no university in the country that had an anthropology program in design anthropology, I didn't even know the term; I just said I was an anthropologist working in product design and development. And I started learning how to apply my anthropological knowledge and skills in a new way. As an aside, I wish I had known Christina Wasson at the time: the year was 2000 and she was working and publishing on design anthropology in the Chicago area (Wasson 2000). It would have helped immensely to have someone to talk with about translating anthropological research for new product development.

This story is significant in two ways. It illustrates the fact that anthropological training can be used in ways quite different from how a newly minted anthropologist might first conceive of planning a career. But more importantly, it highlights a significant challenge in applying anthropology in organizations that are primarily composed of non-social scientists.

I was hired for my methodological training, *purely* for my methods knowledge. Indeed, when I was first hired I brought various theories into our team's discussion of research questions, methods, and analysis. It was clear that this was not only unwelcome, but that my insistence on bringing theory into the discussion could jeopardize my career. Quite frankly, no one was interested, and they labeled me an "academic" when I started talking theory – the death knell in the organization I had just joined. "Academic" meant "not applied" and therefore not useful.

I became a methods geek – learning far more than I had in graduate school (see a list of additional readings at the end of the book). Theory had to come in under the radar – I didn't talk or write about it, but used it in my research design and data analysis. Later in my career I would speak about the importance of anthropological theory in cross-disciplinary research at the American Anthropological Association annual meetings, but in the company I still keep the focus on methodological rigor.

So what is a design anthropologist anyway? There are many definitions – as many as there are definitions of design, and as many as there are things that can be designed. I like to think of it as using anthropological theory and method to create new products. Design anthropologists who are helping to develop new products may be involved in defining hardware features (color, materials, shape, etc.); or they may be involved in designing interfaces (What is the first thing that someone sees? How does this look? Where is it placed? What is the workflow and navigation? And so on); or they can be involved in defining what features and functionality should be included in a particular product. They can be working in the field of architecture, organizational planning, medical equipment manufacturing, the automobile industry – wherever something to be used by humans is being designed, an anthropologist can contribute.

I design communication and media technologies (cell phones, tablets, and TV infrastructure are the most common examples), and I work almost exclusively at defining what features and functionality should, or should not, be developed, with some of my work influencing software interface design. Because my team is located in the research arm of Motorola Mobility we are not designing the next product to be released. Instead we are looking three to five years ahead, asking: What can we invent that people actually need and will want to use? How can we learn, from what people are doing today, what products we should invest in for the future? What should those products enable? What is not a good idea? (see, e.g., Metcalf et al. 2008; Basapur et al. 2011).

You might think that the first three questions are the most interesting and fun, and you're probably right from the perspective of creating something cool, but the last question can actually be the most important from a business perspective. If you can tell a company what *not* to do, you have just saved them money, sometimes significant amounts of money that would have been invested in manufacturing and marketing a product that people will not use. That's why I say that it is the team's job to create design guidelines. These are as much about what not to do, and how not to do it, as they are about what to do and how to do it best. We call it *risk mitigation*. My team's job is to create a corpus of knowledge about interactive media behaviors that can be used to lessen the risk in creating new products.

But how do you get people in the rest of the company to listen to you? One of the greatest challenges, not only for design anthropologists, but for anyone in research, is to influence people in the rest of the company. Researchers in Kodak invented the first digital camera, but Kodak did not sell the first digital camera. Researchers at Xerox PARC developed the first graphical user interface (GUI) but Xerox never successfully commercialized it. These are just two well-known examples. And these were engineers trying to persuade other engineers. You, as a design anthropologist, are in a much worse situation. Trust me, I know.

The first time I told someone I was an anthropologist working in the high tech field, they asked, "What do you do, dig up old computers?" We both laughed, and I then explained what I did, but it highlights the difficulty we have when working with others outside our field. Not only do we have a hard time explaining what we are doing in an architectural office, a home appliance company, or a high tech communications company, but we have an even harder time influencing our colleagues.

The first hurdle is that we speak different languages. The good news is that this is relatively easy to overcome. It's like learning any new language. Listen, ask questions, and buy books. When I first joined Motorola I knew nothing about software development, yet it was usually the software functionality that I was trying to influence. So I bought a book on Java and even went to a couple of beginner tutorials. I still can't code, but I know enough of the language to understand what the developers are talking about and I can sometimes even figure out, just by looking at the code, what they are trying to get the software to do.

This speaks to the second hurdle I had to overcome, that anthropologists don't typically know very much about engineering and computer science. I sat in on meetings where the engineers were discussing system architecture, meetings where they were doing code reviews, meetings where they wondered why on earth I was there, essentially just to listen and ask questions. The best thing you can do, as a design anthropologist who hopes to influence the engineers and others around you, is to learn about what they do and the challenges they face. Learn enough to know whether something you are suggesting is easy or difficult and how long it might take to develop. If you suggest that the engineering team do X, you had better know if it's hard or easy because if it's hard you will have to be ready to argue the cost–benefit analysis. Imagine this:

> ANTHROPOLOGIST: I think we should have feature X added to the product.
> ENGINEER: That will take four months of work!
> ANTHROPOLOGIST: Oh, I didn't realize it would take that long.

I am sure you don't want to imagine the engineer's next comment. But consider this alternative:

> ANTHROPOLOGIST: There is a particular feature that I think should be added to this product. The problem is, I think it might require a significant amount of additional coding. It's X and I think we might need to add another service on the back end, and a new API . . . I'm not sure. The thing is, our research has shown that X is a highly desirable feature. How long do you think it would take, and is there some way you can think of to get this in? [Of course, because you have anticipated how long it might take and that you might receive pushback you are ready with the supporting facts about desirability should they ask.]
> ENGINEER: Well, let me think about it – at first glance this seems like about four months' worth of work . . .
> ANTHROPOLOGIST: I kind of thought so . . .

This conversation goes much better. You have demonstrated that you have an idea this might be difficult, you recognize their challenges, and you even know (kind of) what it might take to do it. You are also talking to them in their language. You are no longer the social scientist without a clue; you are the colleague with a different skill set who is working as part of a team. On the best teams there is joint accommodation, and the engineers, computer scientists, human–computer interaction (HCI) specialists, and others put in as much effort to understand the anthropologist as the anthropologist puts into understanding them.

So learning the language and learning about the discipline of those you work with takes care of influencing those you work with closely, but it's still a challenge to influence others in the company. Because people in the company who don't work with you closely will not make the effort to understand your discipline or methods, or anything else about you, it can be very difficult to influence them using just your research. No matter how rigorous you are, how good at communicating, or even (as I've found out later in my career) what position you hold, it is still a challenge to influence the creation of a new product if you and your team are not the ones building it.

I have found that my biggest problem, hands down, is getting people to listen to our research when they have their own experiences to guide them. This is extremely interesting, actually, but also quite frustrating. If you are a design anthropologist working on products for the country you are living in, and products that most of the people around you use or could see themselves using, this will probably be your biggest headache. In my experience, people in the high tech industry like to design for themselves. Even when they have evidence that not everyone has the same behavior pattern, they turn to their own behavior patterns to guide them in features, functionality, and design. If that engineer is Steve Jobs, this works out fine. Most of the time, however, the engineer who has decided they want the new product to do X is not Steve Jobs.

Luckily, over the years I have developed a reputation in our research organization for basing my reasoning solely on research and not my own behaviors or desires, so this is not an issue when the research organization is deciding what to build and how to build it. But as soon as we move to influence people outside of the research organization, in the product groups, it becomes a serious issue.

I have found that an excellent way to make your case is to develop a strong argument for the trustworthiness of your work. Peer review is, hands down, the strongest case you have for the rigor of your research. And you want to publish in journals that your colleagues believe are good, trustworthy sources. In my case the journals and proceedings that computer scientists and engineers pay attention to emerge from several important annual conferences, including those for CHI (Computer–Human Interaction), Mobile HCI, Pervasive Computing, UbiComp, EuroITV (interactive television), and DIS (Designing for Interactive Systems). Proceedings from these conferences are available online. We also publish through the IEEE (Institute of Electrical and Electronic Engineers). Many of these outlets have a 20 percent or lower acceptance rate, and all have a lower than 30 percent acceptance rate. If it's where your audience is looking for trustworthy research – go there and get published. I don't even think about publishing in the anthropological journals.

One of the main benefits of doing this kind of research inside a corporate research division is the ability to develop a body of knowledge in a particular domain area. Often design anthropologists are consultants, working on a project redesigning shopping carts one month, and coming up with new diaper concepts the next. And applied anthropologists of any stripe do not typically have years to focus on a particular type of activity. But a research team in a company that has a certain limited set of products that they create can define an area of research that has implications for all (or most) of the products the company produces. It is then your responsibility to develop a series of studies that impact multiple products in this domain area and build up your corpus of knowledge.

The long-term research agenda for my team is to answer these three questions:

1. How do people engage in media experiences across contexts, communities, and devices?
2. What media-based content creation, curation, and consumption experiences answer users' wants and needs?
3. What interaction paradigms are appropriate for different media contexts, communities, and devices?

But those are not the research questions we take into the field. Instead we do a three-month study on how people share photographs, a two-month study on how people share music, a five-month study on how people socialize during television viewing, and so on. Often we build something that we've thought of and give it to people to use in their homes. We then let them use it for four hours, or four weeks, learn how they use it, what features they use, and why.

We typically use ethnographic-style methods, the methods you find in H. Russell Bernard's books, and the LeCompte and Schensul books. We use multiple methods for data collection in every study. And we do rapid research. You have to. In industry you don't have the luxury of time. But this does not mean that you have to sacrifice rigor. Never sacrifice rigor. As far as I am concerned, if you cannot publish your research in a highly respected peer-reviewed journal you are not doing your job. It is ultimately your duty as a design anthropologist to make sure that any feature, functionality, or design guidance you give your organization is trustable and worth them listening to. This is how you build your reputation and your team's reputation. This is the one thing, in my mind, that is non-negotiable.

From my experience it is best to do this kind of ethnographic-style research with a team that consists of people from multiple disciplines. Why? Because, as we anthropologists know, there are multiple realities, and "truth" is best negotiated from multiple perspectives. I have much more confidence in research findings that have been analyzed and developed by several people who all come from different theoretical backgrounds than in research findings that were the work of a single person, or several people who all share the same background. As in traditional anthropological fieldwork, you are engaging in dialectic.

Frankly, it's also more fun to work on a multidisciplinary team. I can no longer imagine working on a team that consists of all anthropologists. I listen closely to my team and colleagues to hear and understand their perspectives on the data, and negotiate a shared understanding. The most interesting conclusions about what we are observing have always come from intense discussion about the interpretation and meaning of the data. Of course it's also more difficult, and time-consuming, and sometimes frustrating, to work on such teams, but it's worth it as long as all members of the team respect each other and what they are bringing to the table. As anthropologists, we have a special role to play in the team dynamics: we can influence the culture of our team. Transdisciplinary teamwork is achievable with the right attitude and through setting team-based goals (see Metcalf 2011).

Ultimately, the work of a design anthropologist is to make sure that companies are designing for people. It may sound strange, coming from an anthropologist who has spent almost 12 years in a for-profit industry, but I believe my purpose is to create things that make people's lives better. You can't do that from the outside: from the outside you can only critique (and there's certainly a role for that), but from the inside you can design. Design for people, design for good. It's my philosophy that if you do that, of course people will buy your product – it enriches their lives.

References

Baba, Marietta L. (1986) *Business and Industrial Anthropology: An Overview*. NAPA Bulletin 2. Washington, DC: National Association for the Practice of Anthropology, American Anthropological Association.

Basapur, Santosh, Gunnar Harboe, Hiren Mandalia, et al. (2011) "Field Trial of a Dual Device User Experience for iTV." In *EuroITV '11: Proceedings of the 9th International Interactive Conference on Interactive Television*. New York: ACM Press, pp. 127–136.

Briody, Elizabeth K. and Marietta L. Baba (1988) "Anthropology and International Business." *Practicing Anthropology* 10(1): 1, 7.

Burkhalter, S. Brian (1985) "If Only They would Listen: The Anthropology of Business and the Business of Anthropology." *Practicing Anthropology* 7(1): 18–20.

Metcalf, Crysta (2011) "Circulation of Transdisciplinary Knowledge and Culture in a High Tech Organization." *Anthropology News* 52(2): 28.

Metcalf, Crysta, Gunnar Harboe, Noel Massey, et al. (2008) "Examining Presence and Lightweight Messaging in a Social Television Experience." *ACM Transactions on Multimedia Computing, Communications and Applications (TOMCCAP)* 4(4): article 27.

Serrie, Hendrick (1983) "Anthropology and International Business." *Practicing Anthropology* 5(2): 12, 19.

Wasson, Christina (2000) "Ethnography in the Field of Design." *Human Organization* 59(4): 377–388.

Chapter 24

Environment and Resources

Robert Winthrop

Rob Winthrop provides us with a comprehensive look at the domain of professional environmental anthropology. He begins by defining the field – which includes both "environment" and "resources" – and charting its history as a practice arena, noting in particular how it has been put together in terms of areas of focus and action. Winthrop then proceeds to describe in detail the career arcs of seven environmental practitioners, beginning with himself and noting career highlights and major areas of focus. He concludes his chapter with a thoughtful discussion of lessons learned and some observations on the ethics of practice.

The views expressed here are the author's and do not represent the policies of the US Department of the Interior.

This chapter describes the work of professional environmental anthropology: its areas of practice and the skills that contribute to success. Environmental anthropology as a professional rather than an academic career deals with practical problems and their solutions: protecting subsistence economies challenged by energy development, designing biodiversity conservation programs that support rather than undermine local communities, and finding locally appropriate strategies for adapting to climate change. The range of this work is suggested by the seven careers profiled below.

The chapter title "Environment and Resources" acknowledges both the breadth of the field and its dual character. The *environment* stands apart from human agency, an intricate web of air, water, minerals, plants, and animals which must be con-

A Handbook of Practicing Anthropology. First Edition. Edited by Riall W. Nolan.
© 2013 John Wiley & Sons, Inc. Published 2013 by John Wiley & Sons, Inc.

served, for it forms the precondition and context for human social life. Humans also appropriate many elements of this environment. These become *resources*, valued for particular benefits, extracted, and used. Such resources include caribou for the Iñupiat of Alaska's North Slope and salmon for tribes of the Pacific Northwest, but also timber, oil, coal, and copper to feed a global industrial economy. In practice, environmental conservation and resource use are often in tension. Yet both are legitimate objectives for professional environmental anthropology.

Defining the Field

Emergence of environmental anthropology

Over the past century environmental anthropology emerged as a distinct field as it developed more detailed and theoretically sophisticated accounts of the influence of ecological factors on the organization and practices of small-scale societies. Yet from the human viewpoint nature is also culturally constituted, seen "through a screen of beliefs, knowledge, and purposes" (Rappaport 1979: 97). Thus the field must also be concerned with the culturally specific frames through which environments and resources are experienced and utilized. This dual perspective is exemplified by E. E. Evans-Pritchard's classic work *The Nuer* (1940: ch. 1), which demonstrates both the material constraints and the worldview associated with a pastoralist society.

Since the 1970s environmental and resource policy has changed from a specialized interest to a major focus of grassroots advocacy, and national as well as international policy. Anthropologists mirrored this transformation, often shifting their research to a regional, national, or international scale of analysis, recognizing the relevance of public policy, and considering external forces promoting environmental change – including migration, war, development, and tourism. This methodological shift included much greater attention to ethical and practical issues, including biodiversity conservation, environmental risk perception, human rights, and environmental justice (Kottak 1999: 25–30).

Varieties of practice

At least in the United States, an academic worldview has so pervaded the teaching of anthropology that it is very difficult to appreciate the opportunities and rewards of a professional career. In the academic world, a person is largely defined by a research topic, for example, Professor Jones *is* a specialist in Dravidian kinship systems. The professional world is far more fluid. A master's or a doctoral degree may provide an initial toolkit. But professional work is defined not by one's initial training but by the needs of employers and clients and by broader research and policy priorities, which change – often dramatically – over time.

An anthropological career centered on environment and resources can involve a number of roles, but four have particular importance: operations (including program development and implementation), policy development, applied research, and advocacy. Several types of organizations can serve as the foundation for a professional career, and it is common to move from one to another as opportunities change. The options include several private sector variants (self-employed to large corporations), nonprofit organizations, government agencies, international or multilateral institutions (e.g., the World Bank), and the applied or consulting arms of many universities.

Professional practice on environment and resources covers a wide and diverse territory. Here I can only suggest some important occupational niches and a few sources for further reading, organized around four broad topics: resource sectors, management systems, environmental rights, and change factors.

- Specific *resource sectors* are the focus for many anthropologists, such as water (Treitler and Midgett 2007), fisheries (Wingard 2000), and ranching (Brogden and Greenberg 2003).
- *Systems for managing environments and resources* provide a second set of topics, including co-management (Feit and Spaeder 2005) and other management structures, common-pool resources (Agrawal 2003), land tenure systems (Chapin et al. 2005), and local practices for managing subsistence resources (Smith and Wishnie 2000).
- *Environmental rights and ethics* form a third group: environmental justice (particularly effects on health) (Johnston 2011), cultural rights relative to proposed environmental change (Winthrop 2002), and intellectual property rights, typically involving traditional ecological knowledge (Posey and Dutfield 1996).
- *Responses to change* provide the focus for a fourth group, which may also involve issues of environmental rights. These include climate change (Crate and Nuttall 2009), natural disasters (Oliver-Smith 1996), species loss and biodiversity conservation (Orlove and Brush 1996), economic development (Godoy et al. 2005), and resource extraction and pollution (Paolisso and Maloney 2000).

Careers

Robert Winthrop

Cultural anthropology was my focus of study, both for my bachelor's degree from the University of California, Berkeley and for my doctorate from the University of Minnesota. The research theme for my PhD has remained relevant throughout my career. In the face of externally imposed change, how do communities preserve cultural autonomy and agency? How do established patterns of meaning and social organization (a "tradition" and "way of life") guide adaptation and innovation?

To date my working career has had two phases. Beginning in the early 1980s I lived the freedom and insecurity of small business, working in the western United

States primarily on conflicts between proposed development and American Indian cultural rights and values. In 2002 I shifted from the private to the public sector, from the west coast to the east, and from running Cultural Solutions (my small consulting practice) to leading the Socioeconomics Program at the Interior Department's Bureau of Land Management (BLM).

The decision to establish a small business reflected more fundamental choices: my wife (an archaeologist) and I weren't interested in academic careers, and we wanted to raise our family in southern Oregon. The business opportunity centered on abundant federal lands and resources in the Pacific Northwest, strong federal statutory protections for archaeological sites, and strong rights and interests of tribes over the use of public lands within their traditional territories. With another archaeologist partner we formed a small business, handling both archaeological and ethnographic studies.

My research was very field-focused, using ethnographic tools to decipher a problem involving specific communities, a specific terrain, and a specific proposal. My clients were companies proposing resource development involving federal lands or licensing, federal agencies managing those lands, and (occasionally) tribal governments. Regardless of who paid the bills, the ethical framework remained the same: to provide a professionally competent analysis of the issues in question, to work collaboratively and honestly with tribal communities, and – when consistent with the first two objectives – to help the client advance its goals.

Here is an example. State Power,[1] which operated a hydroelectric dam in Washington state, applied to the Federal Energy Regulatory Commission (FERC) to renew the facility's license. The dam lay within the pre-reservation territory of the River People, a federally recognized tribe, whose treaty provided significant rights over fishing, hunting, and gathering. After the River People intervened with FERC to oppose the facility's relicensing, FERC ordered the utility and the tribe to collaborate on a study of the effects of continued dam operations on traditional tribal uses of the area.

I was retained by State Power to conduct the study. Negotiating a research protocol with the River People took over a year. Among its provisions were that the utility would pay the salary and expenses of a tribal employee to work with me in a fully collaborative role, and any disagreements between the utility and the tribe regarding the interpretation of evidence, analysis of effects, or recommendations for mitigation would be fully documented in the report. My tribal colleague and I jointly conducted interviews and archival research and gave a joint presentation on our findings to a meeting of tribal council members and utility representatives. Our research broadly confirmed the adverse effects of continued hydroelectric operations: the decline of fishing-based communities above the dam, and the indirect effects on trade, travel, subsistence, and ceremonies across the region. Shortly after we presented our report, the utility board of directors and the tribal council began direct negotiations over the fate of the dam.

By 2000 I was ready for a change, but my anthropological training seemed rather narrow for a career switch. To get a broader grounding in the social sciences, I returned to graduate school for an interdisciplinary master's degree at George Washington University, which allowed me to study economics, political science, and business. In 2002, shortly after completing the degree, I was hired to lead the Socio-economics Program at the Interior Department's Bureau of Land Management in Washington, DC. The geographic canvas of the agency is very broad, ranging from the Arctic Ocean to the Mexican border. The organization's scale is also rather different from Cultural Solutions: some 10,000 agency employees, spread across some 150 offices and 12 regions, who manage an enormous range of land and resource uses.

My own work has two aspects. The first is programmatic: working with colleagues to provide capacity for effective socio-economic analysis across the agency through guidance, training, staffing, contracting, and quality assurance. The second involves responding to specific scientific and policy challenges. In some cases I do substantial work on a problem; in others my role is mainly to encourage and review the work of other colleagues. (Moral: If you need individual recognition, look for an academic job.) Many issues involve a combination of technical, policy, and organizational challenges. Examples of projects on which I've worked as part of a team include:

- revising BLM's planning regulations to give a stronger voice to local and state governments and tribes;
- identifying practical methods for modeling the human benefits of healthy ecosystems, to allow more realistic assessments of the costs and benefits of resource development;
- preparing a strategic plan for strengthening compliance with environmental justice principles across the agencies of the Interior Department; and
- advising the US Global Change Research Program on strategies for better integrating the social sciences into its predominantly natural science research program.

Diane Russell

Dr. Diane Russell's career has emphasized community-based conservation within the framework of international development. Her work has centered on the social and institutional dimensions of forestry and market-based approaches to conservation and natural resource management. She earned degrees in anthropology at Barnard College (BA) and Boston University (PhD), and subsequently completed a master's in environmental management at Yale University's School of Forestry and Environmental Studies. Diane Russell's field experience includes Central Africa and the insular Pacific.

From 2001 to 2005 Russell was based in Nairobi, Kenya as the program director for Trees and Markets at the World Agroforestry Centre. Since 2005 she has served as biodiversity and social science specialist with the US Agency for International Development (USAID) in Washington, DC. Russell's current work stands at the interface of livelihoods and conservation, advising USAID's efforts at headquarters and in overseas missions on the social and institutional aspects of biodiversity con-servation, climate change, and sustainable agriculture (Russell and Harshbarger 2004). Asked for an example of success, she noted:

> I've been working in Liberia since 2005 to help the USAID Mission develop a program in community forestry. This project helps put significant blocks of forest in the hands of local communities and has contributed to major changes in Liberia's Forestry Development Authority, which was once the tool of warlord Charles Taylor . . . It's been incredibly rewarding to . . . work with colleagues willing to take risks in trying a completely new approach to forestry in Liberia.[2]

Katy Moran

The anthropologist Katy Moran has had an accomplished career, serving as a legisla-tive aide in Congress, a program analyst for the Smithsonian, and director of the nonprofit Healing Forest Conservancy (HFC). Her work across these varied positions is linked by a common concern for the interrelation of environmental conservation and cultural integrity, and the search for policies and programs that promote both. Moran received an MA in applied anthropology from American University, writing a thesis on elephant management practices in Sri Lanka and their implications for wildlife conservation.

Based on her research on the social and economic dimensions of conservation, Representative John Porter hired her to coordinate a new policy effort, the debt-for-nature swap. *Debt for nature* is a policy that allows developing countries to be relieved of a portion of their debt burden in return for adopting environmental conservation measures: typically by preventing the degradation of forests or other designated habitat. Representative Porter's bill became law in 1989, establishing an important new tool in conservation policy.

Katy Moran established HFC in 1992 to foster the equitable provision of benefits for communities willing to share traditional ecological knowledge in the develop-ment of new pharmaceuticals, "biodiversity prospecting." As with the debt-for-nature swaps, with HFC Moran applied her anthropological and policy skills to formulate much needed solutions in another complex and controversial area of international policy, balancing conservation and the use of biodiversity (Moran et al. 2001).

Kevin Preister

Kevin Preister's career has focused on improving the quality of land use plan-ning and project design, both government and corporate, to achieve environmentally and socially sustainable outcomes. The central strategy of his work is understand-ing and engaging the local social systems that structure neighborhoods, communities, and regions in the search for innovative, locally acceptable solutions to complex environmental and resource decisions. Preister earned a PhD at the University of California at Davis with a dissertation on the economic transition of Oregon's south coast from natural resources to trade and services. As senior associate at James Kent Associates and subsequently director of the Center for Social Ecology and Public Policy, he has worked to build support for collaborative approaches to resource management, particularly among federal land management agencies.

Going beyond the often sterile procedures for public involvement, much of the work by Kevin Preister and his colleagues seeks to expand governments' capacity for effective engagement by stressing the value of two-way communication through informal social systems such as community networks (see www.jkagroup.com). Making this argument in the context of climate change policy, Kevin Preister and James Kent wrote:

> A central challenge for a new approach to global warming is the creation and integra-
> tion of scientifically-valid and culturally-appropriate policy strategies for addressing
> carbon emissions. If we as a global society are unable to link the formal institutions
> with the informal systems of communities concerned with survival and caretaking,
> the policy choices will by default become regulatory, draconian in their consequences,
> high in political and monetary costs, and limited in their effectiveness. (Kent and
> Preister 2012: 1–2)

Diane Austin

Diane Austin is associate research professor at the University of Arizona's Bureau of Applied Research in Anthropology (BARA), where she has worked since 1994. As an institutional base for anthropological practice, BARA represents an interesting hybrid, conducting applied studies that address a range of practical problems of the environment, development, and tribal cultural preservation while integrating these activities with scholarship and professional training (see http://bara.arizona.edu). Austin's training includes an MS in environmental engineering from the California Institute of Technology and an interdisciplinary PhD in natural resources and envi-ronment from the University of Michigan, which combined cultural anthropology, environmental policy, and environmental psychology.

Diane Austin has led applied research on a wide range of environmental topics, including social impacts of offshore oil and gas production on Gulf of Mexico communities, the impacts of natural resource development on Southern Paiute com-munities, and a range of projects addressing critical environmental health issues along the Arizona–Sonora border. Much of her work adopts a community-based participatory research approach, supported by long-term partnerships with govern-ment, nongovernmental organizations, universities, and businesses (Austin 2010). In a bi-national coalition that addresses water, waste, and air quality issues in the Arizona–Sonora border area, Austin has led group efforts to design and conduct initial assessments, develop pilot projects to convert waste products into resources, and promote the expansion of successful projects into larger initiatives.

Lucinda Power

Lucinda Power's work at the Environmental Protection Agency (EPA) focuses on watershed and ocean policy, and the local social systems needed for sustainable environmental management. She received a master's in applied anthropology from the University of Maryland in 2005, with concentrations in environmental anthropology and water resource management. Her master's research concerned environmental and heritage values in Maryland's Eastern Shore communities of Chesapeake Bay, as these shape the receptivity to state and federal watershed management programs (Power and Paolisso 2007). The Chesapeake Bay ecosystem, one of the world's largest and most productive estuaries, has been seriously compromised because of nitrogen and phosphorus pollution from wastewater treatment plants, agricultural runoff, and other activities. Restoring the ecological health of the bay is a major goal of current federal environmental policy.

While completing her graduate studies Power served on the staff of Coastal America, a partnership of federal, state, and local governments and nonprofit organizations to strengthen the management and health of America's coastal ecosystems. She began her career at EPA in 2007, working primarily on ocean policy and the development of environmental regulations. In 2011 Power became an environmental protection specialist at the Chesapeake Bay Program Office, coordinating state- and locally driven watershed restoration planning and project implementation. Her training and experience have been particularly valuable in two aspects of these efforts: understanding local social systems to enhance outreach and collaboration, and documenting local environmental knowledge to complement information on the Chesapeake Bay ecosystem provided by the environmental sciences.

Luisa Maffi

Luisa Maffi has combined linguistic and environmental anthropology to explore the relationship between sustaining the vitality of indigenous languages and cultures and conserving biological diversity. Maffi received her BA in linguistics from the University of Rome. After linguistic research in Somalia, she moved to the University of California, Berkeley for doctoral studies in anthropology, joining an ongoing research program in Chiapas on Tzeltal Maya ethnobiology. Moving from the conventional role of academic researcher to that of scholar-activist-NGO entrepreneur, Maffi provides an interesting case study in the changing nature of environmental anthropology.

The preservation of biodiversity is commonly thought to be incompatible with human activity, hence the frequent (but usually unsuccessful) conservation strategy of creating nature preserves walled off from human use. In 1996 Maffi and a number of colleagues founded Terralingua (www.terralingua.org), a nongovernmental organization which worked from a different premise, namely "that biological, cultural, and linguistic diversity are co-evolved, interdependent, and mutually reinforcing."

They termed this *biocultural* diversity: "Healthy environments, resilient cultures, and vibrant languages are a matter of social justice and basic human rights."[3] With Luisa Maffi as its director, Terralingua has pursued multiple strategies to support biocultural diversity. These include developing indicators of linguistic diversity and traditional environmental knowledge to quantify conditions and trends; supporting indigenous peoples' efforts to record their oral traditions; promoting international policy for biocultural diversity; guiding a community of practice, based on lessons from 45 biocultural diversity projects; and creating modules for teaching an integrated biocultural diversity curriculum in high schools (Maffi and Woodley 2010).

Summing Up

Professional effectiveness

Based on my own experience and the careers of the six colleagues described above, here are some recommendations for building a successful professional career.

- Pursue a professional career for the right reason. The professional practice of environmental anthropology is demanding, and failure to perform well has real life consequences. Those who see a professional career as a second-best to an academic one are advised to stay on campus or pursue another line of work.
- Do work that interests you. Given the many areas of professional practice involving environments and resources, there is opportunity for choice. If no job is available that fits your career goal, consider creating your own firm or nonprofit. Of the seven careers profiled here, four of us took that path. (Incidentally, it's not easy.)
- Maintain a scientific outlook, and communicate your findings clearly. Rigorous empirical research and clear conclusions are expected. Pseudo-philosophical reflections couched in postmodernist jargon are not. Diane Russell commented: "Get away from social science fads and jargon, as your work will be not be understood or used."
- Combine quantitative and qualitative methods whenever feasible. Traditionally, ethnography has involved both. Yet a 2010 study observes that recent publications in environmental anthropology "have substantially less quantitative and environmental data than in earlier decades" (Charnley and Durham 2010: 411). Ethnography is good at providing significant detail, but without quantification it is often impossible to discern patterns, to draw broader insights, or to contribute effectively to project teams usually dominated by natural scientists.
- The first lesson I learned as a consultant in Indian country was: collaborate or leave! The central role of collaboration is a common theme in many of the careers profiled here.

- Develop competence in more than one field. Most research, policy, and program development in the realm of environment and resources involves a mix of disciplines. Conversely, while ethnography has been anthropology's hallmark, many other disciplines now include training in qualitative methods. Additional skills translate to added effectiveness. As Diane Austin noted, "A solid background in the natural and physical sciences, along with an anthropological perspective, has been critical to my success."
- Understand the public policy relevant to your areas of practice. Treaties, laws, and regulations provide the institutional framework for managing environmental change. Working on environment and resource issues without understanding this framework is akin to navigating without map or compass.
- Develop good organizational skills. Employers will expect you to be competent at managing projects, preparing and tracking budgets, and organizing work teams.

Ethics

Conducting oneself with honesty, integrity, and fairness should be a cornerstone of any career in science, business, or government. Doing so successfully requires both attention to shared guidelines or principles, and one's own growing experience and judgment. To see how such principles can be translated into professional practice, consult the Society for Applied Anthropology's statement on "Ethical and Professional Responsibilities" and the National Association of Environmental Professionals' "Code of Ethics and Standards of Practice."[4]

Major resource management proposals often involve a powerful proponent with a large investment at stake (such as the Trans-Alaska Pipeline), a host of allies and opponents, and a government agency cast in the role of umpire. Yet in 20 years of consulting only once did I have a client try, unsuccessfully, to change my findings, and that was a government agency. Corporate clients understand the regulatory framework under which such decisions are made and, in my experience, generally abide by it. The lesson is: ethical professional engagement is enhanced by shared ground rules and a reasonably transparent decision process.[5]

Resources

Almost all effective anthropological practice in this area crosses disciplinary lines. Participating in the theoretical and practical discussion fostered by interdisciplinary organizations is an antidote to the self-reference and intellectual isolation that characterizes much contemporary cultural anthropology. Here are three groups appropriate to resource management and social impact assessment, each of which publishes an important journal:

- International Association for Society and Natural Resources (www.iasnr.org)
- National Association of Environmental Professionals (www.naep.org)
- International Association for Impact Assessment (www.iaia.org).

Finally, research-oriented environmental organizations can be excellent sources of information. I would recommend these two:

- Resources for the Future (www.rff.org)
- World Resources Institute (www.wri.org).

Notes

1　The names are pseudonyms.
2　Where not otherwise noted, quotations from the anthropologists profiled here are from email communications dated March and April 2012.
3　http://www.terralingua.org/about-2/, accessed Sept. 5, 2012.
4　http://www.sfaa.net/sfaaethic.html and http://www.naep.org/code-of-ethics, both accessed Sept. 5, 2012.
5　See Ch. 26 in this volume.

References

Agrawal, Arun (2003) "Sustainable Governance of Common-Pool Resources: Context, Methods, and Politics." *Annual Review of Anthropology* 32: 243–262.
Austin, Diane (2010) "Confronting Environmental Challenges on the U.S.–Mexico Border: Examining a Long-Term Community-Based Participatory Research Program." *Journal of Community Practice* 18: 361–395.
Brogden, Mette J. and James B. Greenberg (2003) "The Fight for the West: A Political Ecology of Land Use Conflicts in Arizona." *Human Organization* 62: 289–298.
Chapin, Mac, Zachary Lamb, and Bill Threlkeld (2005) "Mapping Indigenous Lands." *Annual Review of Anthropology* 34: 619–638.
Charnley, Susan and William H. Durham (2010) "Anthropology and Environmental Policy: What Counts?" *American Anthropologist* 112: 397–415.
Crate, Susan and Michael Nuttall (eds.) (2009) *Anthropology and Climate Change: From Encounters to Actions*. Walnut Creek, CA: Left Coast Press.
Evans-Pritchard, Edward E. (1940) *The Nuer: A Description of the Modes of Livelihood and Political Institutions of a Nilotic People*. Oxford: Clarendon Press.
Feit, Harvey A. and Joseph J. Spaeder (2005) "Co-management and Indigenous Communities: Barriers and Bridges to Decentralized Resource Management." *Anthropologica* 47, 147–154.
Godoy, Ricardo, Victoria Reyes-García, Elizabeth Byron, et al. (2005) "The Effect of Market Economies on the Well-Being of Indigenous Peoples and on their Use of Renewable Natural Resources." *Annual Review of Anthropology* 34: 121–138.
Johnston, Barbara R. (ed.) (2011) *Life and Death Matters: Human Rights, Environment, and Social Justice*, 2nd edn. Walnut Creek, CA: Left Coast Press.

Kent, James A. and Kevin Preister (2012) "Climate Change and the Language of Geographic Place." In H. Karl et al. (eds.), *Restoring Lands – Coordinating Science, Politics and Action.* Dordrecht: Springer.

Kottak, Conrad P. (1999) "The New Ecological Anthropology." *American Anthropologist* 101: 23–35.

Maffi, Luisa and Ellen Woodley (2010) *Biocultural Diversity Conservation: A Global Sourcebook.* London: Earthscan.

Moran, Katy, Steven R. King, and Thomas J. Carlson (2001) "Biodiversity Prospecting: Lessons and Prospects." *Annual Review of Anthropology* 30: 505–526.

Oliver-Smith, Anthony (1996) "Anthropological Research on Hazards and Disasters." *Annual Review of Anthropology* 25: 303–328.

Orlove, Benjamin S. and Stephen B. Brush (1996) "Anthropology and the Conservation of Biodiversity." *Annual Review of Anthropology* 25: 329–352.

Paolisso, Michael and R. Shawn Maloney (2000) "Recognizing Farmer Environmentalism: Nutrient Runoff and Toxic Dinoflagellate Blooms in the Chesapeake Bay Region." *Human Organization* 59: 209–221.

Posey, Darrell A. and Graham Dutfield (1996) *Beyond Intellectual Property: Toward Traditional Resource Rights for Indigenous Peoples and Local Communities.* Ottawa: International Development Research Centre.

Power, Lucinda P. and Michael Paolisso (2007) "Linking Estuarine Research to Local Community Heritage and Environmental Values: Lessons from the Chesapeake Bay." *Practicing Anthropology* 29(1): 29–34.

Rappaport, Roy A. (1979) "On Cognized Models." In *Ecology, Meaning, and Religion.* Richmond, CA: North Atlantic Books, pp. 97–144.

Russell, Diane and Camilla Harshbarger (2004) *Groundwork for Community-Based Conservation: Strategies for Social Research.* Walnut Creek, CA: AltaMira Press.

Smith, Eric A. and Mark Wishnie (2000) "Conservation and Subsistence in Small-Scale Societies." *Annual Review of Anthropology* 29: 493–524.

Treitler, Inga and Douglas Midgett (2007) "It's about Water: Anthropological Perspectives on Water and Policy." *Human Organization* 66: 140–149.

Wingard, John D. (2000) "Community Transferable Quotas: Internalizing Externalities and Minimizing Social Impacts of Fisheries Management." *Human Organization* 59: 48–57.

Winthrop, Robert H. (2002) "Defining a Right to Culture, and Some Alternatives." *Cultural Dynamics* 14: 161–183.

Chapter 25

Practitioners in Humanitarian Assistance

Adam Koons

Adam Koons directs a global relief and humanitarian assistance organization working across the world. He begins his chapter with a look at some of the challenges and issues faced by relief workers, and follows this with some frank talk about the constraints faced by anthropologists seeking to do this type of work. Teamwork, he emphasizes, is central to the success of this work. He describes in detail how to leverage anthropological skills, what practitioners need to learn in addition to their anthropology, and how to break into the field. Koons then describes what humanitarian work means for him personally, including both the challenges and rewards it offers.

Are you ready to spontaneously "mobilize" tomorrow, and arrive somewhere in the world within 48 hours?

Humanitarian assistance encompasses a broad range of activities and causes. These include disaster relief, which consists of an immediate spontaneous response to natural or man-made shocks, such as earthquake, hurricane, flood, or conflict. Some disasters or crises are long-term and not particularly spontaneous. Others, such as drought – which sometimes lead to famine – can often be predicted. Still other humanitarian crises are tragically protracted, such as multi-year droughts, or people forced from their homes and communities by conflict, called internally displaced persons (IDPS), or forced across national borders to become refugees.

In my current position as a global relief and humanitarian assistance director for a large international nongovernmental organization (NGO), I address all of these situations. We design and implement programs that provide food, water, shelter, and health support to natural disaster victims, and provide assistance to natural

A Handbook of Practicing Anthropology. First Edition. Edited by Riall W. Nolan.
© 2013 John Wiley & Sons, Inc. Published 2013 by John Wiley & Sons, Inc.

disaster- and conflict-derived IDPs and refugees. We go anywhere in the world where this type of assistance is required.

As relief and humanitarian director I have a number of roles. When an emergency occurs, the first priority is to get to the location and assess the situation and the needs. We often mobilize within 48 hours. I serve as team leader for a team of relief generalists or technical experts from our staff. I must ensure that we are effectively coordinating with every other stakeholder, for example, national and local governments, donors, UN agencies, and other international and local NGOs involved. I must swiftly ensure that our initial assessments and coordination result in funding proposals to donors so that we obtain the resources we need to implement our responses quickly. This also often involves negotiation with governments, donors, and sometimes armed groups. For protracted situations the needs may include finding and designing technical solutions and ensuring that programs are implemented smoothly.

A Few of the Key Issues and "Grand Challenges" Aid Workers Face

There are a number of both operational, and policy or paradigm, issues that we struggle with constantly in humanitarian assistance. The reality is that humanitarian response requires funding, and NGOs must obtain this externally, either through large national or international bodies, such as the US government's Office of Foreign Disaster Assistance (within the US Agency for International Development), or UN agencies such as High Commission for Refugees (which must in turn get its own funding from governments), or from individual, foundation, or corporate donors. But what criteria induce donors to provide resources?

For example, when does a crisis begin and how dramatic must it be? In those fortunate instances when we know an emergency is imminent, when do we act? Generally, when warning systems predict the arrival of a hurricane or cyclone, immediate steps are taken to reduce the impact. But when a drought in the Horn of Africa is building toward an inevitable famine, or when a political conflict is generating fatalities and refugees, why does it take so many extra months to react? What is the tipping point? Put very crudely, how many people have to die, or become refugees, for the gates to open? NGOs try desperately, through their advocacy efforts, to move that point closer and closer to the earliest warnings. It is not easy, since humanitarian responses can be extremely sensitive politically.

Another issue is reaction versus prevention. There is a growing, and very logical, movement toward undertaking disaster risk reduction (DRR), disaster mitigation, and disaster preparedness, to reduce the shocks, significantly reduce loss of live and property, and save tremendous amounts of money. But donors, the media, and the public react to dramatic images and crisis circumstances. Our challenge now is how to get at least some of the funds that are reserved for "emergencies" to be spent on reducing them. Or, at least, how to build into existing emergency responses longer-term reduction and mitigation mechanisms while still focusing on the crisis at hand and fulfilling the relief mandate. This is occurring, but far too slowly. How can we react and act quickly and in the short term while at the same time thinking and planning long-term?

An odd aspect of the work is the competition/collaboration dichotomy. In a very real, but often terribly uncomfortable way, all the agencies are competing for very scarce emergency funds. During a disaster, or protracted crises, there are only sufficient donor funds to support perhaps less than half of the agencies seeking to participate. We prepare "competitive" funding proposals, according to strict donor guidelines, and the "best" proposals – those that match donor objectives most clearly, are most technically sound, or present the most appealing technical solution and implementation plan – "win." During this process, relationships between agencies can sometimes be strained. Or else some agencies seek "strategic partnerships" with others to join forces on funding requests. At the same time, however, it is impossible to undertake programs without considerable collaboration. Agencies must complement each other geographically, or technically, or find synergies to increase efficiency and avoid duplication. And in fact, it is a rather small community of professional, full-time humanitarian specialists, and we often know each other well and see each other in response after response.

Another challenge, particularly sensitive for anthropologists and social scientists working in this domain, is the need to balance speed and efficacy against appropriateness. A feature of anthropology is that we take the time and effort to analyze sociocultural situations deeply and very carefully in order to derive a clear understanding of the many interconnected systems and networks that maintain a particular human setting.

In an emergency, we do not have that luxury. Everything is accelerated tremendously, and yet we must make decisions, in designing programs and activities, that will influence people's lives. Our job is to save lives, reduce suffering, preserve assets and livelihoods, and provide for the most basic needs – food, water, shelter, medical attention.

At the same time all aid workers are bound by the principle of "do no harm." We are required to interfere, but we must determine how to do so without further disrupting social, economic, cultural, and political systems which are already badly disrupted by the crisis. But this is where techniques such as (very) rapid unstructured assessment through observation, random sample consultation, and key informants is helpful. For example, as an anthropology undergraduate student I studied ethnographies of the Dinka and Nuer tribes of Sudan. I could hardly have every imagined that many years later I would be tasked with designing aid programs to promote and protect their well-being.

Another program challenge is merging the global and the local, the standardized and the tailored, to find the most appropriate response, at the time, for a particular place. Here there is also a distinction between the type of humanitarian response according to the situation. For a natural disaster and rapid response, the process can be clear and direct: in the fastest way possible, deliver food, water, shelter, and medical attention to save lives. But it is the next steps that are subject to careful design, including post-disaster, disaster "early recovery," and protracted humanitarian crises. Local perceptions and ideas about local solutions must be considered and integrated. While it would be unwise to entirely invent, or reinvent completely tailored programs – and far too time-consuming – it is also equally inappropriate to force a cookie cutter approach of structured and standardized solutions. That is why many of the widely endorsed key global standards for humanitarian response provide principles, guidelines, and criteria, and measures but are not prescriptive. For example, one of the largest and most successful humanitarian agriculture programs ever implemented, which I am proud to have designed, was conducted in Afghanistan but devised using key elements from a program in Lebanon.

An ironic challenge we are increasingly recognizing is how to leverage tragedy. As bad as things are, they also present an opportunity for real change and improvement; not just a post-disaster return to the horribly inadequate status quo. A phrase coined during the Indian Ocean tsunami serves as a guiding principle: *Build back better*. When the media, political, public, financial, and technical spotlight is on a disaster-hit country such as Haiti, it is a chance to put resources and policies and strategies into place that would not normally be so strongly promoted in regular times. And so in such cases, rather than the more traditional cultural anthropological tenet of preserving the status quo and allowing for organic cultural evolution, we are in fact actually the deliberate agents of change.

Some Constraints for Anthropologists Entering Humanitarian Work

The constraints for anthropologists in this type of work are that "anthropologists" are rarely, if ever, sought out for such positions. Anthropologists are perceived as academics. We are considered to be analysts who take too long to study narrow topics too deeply. Our overall set of very applicable skills are overshadowed by our image as thinkers rather than doers. And, of course, there are always those who ask (hopefully in jest) why we are not off somewhere digging up pots and bones. But we *are* hired because of our package of skills, capabilities, and experiences that are relevant to this kind of work. We are hired on the basis of delivering tangible and measurable results.

Another constraint is that "anthropology" per se is not part of the humanitarian skill set. It's also necessary to have, or to be knowledgeable in "real" technical skills, such as food aid logistics, water and sanitation, or shelter infrastructure. This is not a serious obstacle. Over the years I have managed to learn a significant amount about all of these and more – sufficient to design and manage programs – but we do not have these skills at the outset, unless we deliberately obtain them through additional training.

Who Is on the Team?

Because of the very broad range of humanitarian consequences and needs, from shelter repair to food aid, to medical attention, to mental health, there are a very wide variety of other professionals thrown together in this kind of work. For each new crisis there may be a slightly different tailored mixture, and it will also depend at the time on whether a particular response is "multi-sectorial," meaning we provide a mix of food, water, shelter, and health, or topic-driven, where we provide water delivery or food aid. Therefore, anthropologists interact on teams with engineers, sanitation experts, agronomists, health specialists, logisticians, accountants, finance analysts, communications and public relations experts, security specialists, and many others. But the domain is also composed of many generalists from international studies, development studies, political science, human rights, gender studies, who learn technical skills along the way, as I have had to do for almost all of the various activities. And in reality, response teams must be versatile, since so many of us must fill multiple technical roles at times.

Our mutual interaction is dictated more by common overall objectives and tasks than by specialty. Anthropologists and all the others work very well together because we recognize that we are mutually dependent and we all bring information, training, experience, and skills that complement the work of others. I have found that there is a general appreciation among my colleagues that I am an anthropologist, and a true interest in how I see things and what particular perspective I might bring. But mostly my "academic" background is far overshadowed by what experience, thoughts, and solutions I can bring to the particular challenge, no matter what my roots are.

Leveraging Our Anthropological Training and Perspective

In humanitarian assistance, in my experience, anthropologists can provide valuable sociocultural "reality checks" to program design. We are able, even in the compressed time allowable, to ask the right questions about how our programs will fit, leverage, integrate, or disrupt existing local systems. For example, every disaster-prone group has developed over time its own coping strategies which allow it to survive without needing assistance every single time there is stress. Anthropologists will ask what these are, and how to use such coping mechanisms to leverage, amplify, and complement external measures.

Anthropologists are particularly good at using a wide range of qualitative methods to rapidly assess crises. We are good at designing and using observation, engaging in local consultation, and working with key informants. In a particular setting we may even know of, or search for, existing past ethnographies and studies that will quickly inform our understanding of the local setting.

However, in full and honest disclosure, it is difficult to say realistically that anthropologists bring *unique* skills. We are certainly predisposed to immediately and automatically consider local social, economic, and cultural networks and systems, and to try to understand how not to disrupt them. But this frame of reference – largely due to social scientists' involvement over the years – is now a part of the skill set of many experienced and sensitive aid workers.

Either during field responses, or while quickly designing emergency activities, aid workers are thrown into a variety of new and unfamiliar cultures and settings. Our own previous personal experience and that of our team members can only go so far in helping us to cope with the variety of situations in which humanitarian aid occurs. But anthropologists are good at understanding different peoples and places. Our cross-cultural comfort level, our cultural versatility, and our capacity to adapt rapidly enable us to get going without culture shock or confusion.

Additionally, there are very often no initial hard statistics or relevant data with which to work, particularly in the early stages of a new crisis. Anthropological tools such as astute observation, key informant consultation, integration of qualitative analysis, and synthesis of diverse sources of existing information – all these make us good at deciphering complex situations so that culturally appropriate solutions and strategies can be developed. It is just that this process needs to occur significantly faster than most anthropologists are trained for or are accustomed to.

Of particular importance is something that generally comes naturally to those who are anthropologically trained: cultural sensitivity. Humanitarian assistance during its early years, and to some extent even now, is often externally conceived and implemented in a top-down manner, without a clear understanding of the short- or long-term implications or consequences. The idea is that quickly saving lives outweighs the time-consuming process of ensuring that activities are perfectly tailored to every local circumstance. But anthropologists are good at quickly identifying local perceptions, behaviors, and coping strategies that can inform, and even enhance and leverage external resources and assistance. We are trained to respect and recognize the knowledge and expertise of local people and the strength and logic of their own systems, and this allows us, as program designers and implementers, to integrate this understanding into how we work, so that we achieve the overall aid objectives in a "humanitarian" and locally appropriate manner.

What We Still Need to Learn

Humanitarian assistance operates on funding and so it is vitally important to be able to write these kinds of funding proposals, but such a skill is generally not part of an anthropologist's training or experience. This is a key issue. Depending on the tasks of the anthropologist in aid work, it may be necessary to assist in such proposals, to lead the process, or to write such proposals.

A number of skills are required to do this. In my current position I often have to draft entire funding proposals, or else supervise this process and ensure they are completed to a high standard. Each funding body has its own strict guidelines, formats, and templates. These must be followed precisely or a proposal will be rejected. Deadlines are very short – sometimes one to three weeks – and there is no flexibility. So work must be done extremely quickly and under considerable stress; this includes presenting a needs analysis, justification, goals and objectives, and a detailed description of implantation strategies and mechanisms, as well as a management plan, a monitoring and evaluation plan, and a detailed budget. Often there is a team working on such proposals, so on the one hand it is not a singular activity with all responsibility falling to one person, while on the other hand the coordination, collaboration, and teamwork must work perfectly. Whether the anthropologist is a team member or the actual team leader, they have to be prepared to pitch in and get the work done, up to and including preparing the budget.

Developing a professional writing style is another demand of the job. It is a real skill that is needed for situation updates, emergency assessments, field reports, funding proposals, progress reports, and sometimes public relations. Writing clearly and non-academically, and for a particular audience, is a key requirement. This means providing exactly the level of technical detail and context, using the appropriate jargon and key words, and responding precisely to guidelines while excluding irrelevant – but possibly very interesting or personally meaningful – text.

Staying calm under fire is critical. Humanitarian assistance, particularly in the early stages of a disaster response, can be chaotic, confusing, frustrating, and rapidly changing. Sights, sounds, living conditions (in the field), emotions (yours and those of others), all build up to extreme stress. Burnout is not unusual. It is necessary to find personal stress reduction and coping mechanisms, but that does not mean you have to deal with stress in isolation – others around you are in the same boat.

Depending on the level of responsibility, it may be necessary to make very rapid decisions that may well affect people's lives. Anthropologists are not accustomed to this, and we certainly do not learn this in our academic training. We need to take all of the information at hand, use our capacity for analysis, try to understand all of the choices and options, consult with others, and then trust our judgment and make our very best recommendation.

We often need to negotiate, to serve as humanitarian diplomats. We negotiate with other international or local aid agencies to collaborate or share programs, to operate in particular geographic locations, or to divide up respective activities. We negotiate with funding institutions for sufficient money, or to get them to pay for certain things, or to address their own policy or programmatic agendas. We negotiate with governments in affected countries, just to be allowed to provide aid, and on any number of issues, such as addressing their requests for money. Sometimes, we even negotiate with armed groups to reach disaster victims in locations they control.

We need to learn self-regulation. This is common to all aid workers, but anthropologists may have an even stronger sense of specific opinions, priorities, sensitivities, political views, and identification in certain settings. The humanitarian imperative dictates that aid comes first, regardless of intervening factors. For example, I have had to work in coordination with, and under the guidelines of, governments whose policies and practices and ethics I found to be repugnant, in order to be able to continue providing assistance to those who needed it most. It serves no one to get thrown out of a country and be unable to help anyone! Likewise, just as with stress, we must cope, and regulate our reactions, in the face of tragedy, trauma, and human suffering. We are not effective in our work if we empathize to the point of incapacity.

Anthropologists are trained to focus in on a particular situation and to understand it in depth. In humanitarian assistance this is an impossible luxury. Aside from fieldwork on a particular emergency response, the norm is cultural multitasking, or professional ADHD. In a single day, for example, I often address issues in Syria, Indonesia, Myanmar, Mozambique, and Ethiopia.

Getting Started and Breaking In

In all honesty my own path to humanitarian assistance was not planned. I fell into it or, more politely, I transitioned into it. I started in "traditional" development programs, working on agricultural and income generation projects, and as a monitoring and evaluation specialist with various NGOs. But then, because of my analytical and evaluation experience, I worked in Sudan for a USAID program called the Famine Early Warning System (now called FEWSNet), which began my involvement and deeper interest in human crisis. This was followed by what were intended to be development oriented assignments, but in countries – Haiti and Sudan – that were highly prone to disasters and humanitarian emergencies, and I found myself more and more thrown into the middle of relief responses. Then my role became doing it full-time.

There are a few potential approaches to entering this domain deliberately. The most likely route starts with short-term consulting field assignments, which will provide personal experience and help develop credibility, visibility, and contacts. There are specialized Internet job sites. Knowing who does what and matching your skills to their needs is the first step. For example, identify, from their websites, which UN agencies or NGOs focus on refugees, or child protection, or water, or shelter. Most of them do a range of things, but often are also particularly strong in certain areas. Then, according to your own skill set, undertake networking and find people with whom you can have "informational interviews." Stress both your technical skills, such as rapid assessment, language, a particular region or technical topic, and your personal traits that match emergency needs, such as versatility and durability.

Timing can be critical for entering this kind of work. Being able to go immediately to the right place at the right time is key. When a disaster strikes, and depending on the number of other new or ongoing global crises at the moment, agencies need "surge capacity." For this, they need additional external staff, fast.

Aid Paradigms Are Always Evolving

There are two current trends in humanitarian assistance that are well suited to the perspectives of anthropologists, and that many (but not all) other aid professionals struggle with. First, this is a movement by funding agencies to be more locally oriented in the countries in which they provide assistance; to insist on more local involvement and participation in planning and decision-making, more local leadership and locally linked solutions, and more capacity building to ensure handover and the future ability of local governments and local civil organizations to undertake their own assistance programs. Anthropologists fit right into this trend with our natural tendency to refer to, and to interact with, local systems and networks, even in emergencies.

Second, there is a movement toward longer-sightedness. These include ideas such as "early recovery," "disaster risk reduction," "emergency preparedness," and the enhancement of "resiliency." Practitioners are trying to look ahead, while still in the middle of immediate and severe present needs. For example, one can provide emergency water trucks during the height of a drought to save lives, but also be simultaneously building community-sized rainwater storage systems that will provide water during inevitable future droughts and eliminate the need for the tanker trucks. Again, anthropologists are good at this type of integrated, and consequence-oriented analysis and planning. We can assess and project current and recurrent behaviors, and use field methods to examine with communities appropriate long-term solutions. For instance, in the case of the water storage we can quickly examine water-sharing implications, management, maintenance, control, socially appropriate locations, and so on.

Aid Work for Me . . . So Far

I am not quite burned out yet. For me, working in humanitarian response has been, and continues to be, tremendously rewarding, as well as extremely stressful and exhausting. Typically, during the early stages of a disaster response, such as the earthquake in Haiti, or the Horn of Africa famine, the work is 16 hours a day seven days a week, while living in sometimes uncomfortable and makeshift accommodation. It sounds corny, but it's worth it. There is never the luxury of time; everything is urgent, everything must be done immediately. A tremendous amount of energy and stamina is needed. Stress levels can be enormous.

This is perhaps among the most perfectly suited jobs for (some sorts of) anthropologists and gets to the core of why many of us became anthropologists in the first place. I am frequently traveling to totally new locations, with cultures and social environments that are unique and very different. It's a variation on a classic travel or recruitment poster: travel the world and see many new places and people . . . and help them in crisis. Compared to other kinds of work I could imagine, the positive impacts are immediately visible and significant. We are literally helping keep people alive. For instance, in a particular year I have traveled to Ethiopia, Afghanistan, Sudan, and Tunisia.

Admittedly, even for mature veterans – and it may not be politically correct to say this among my colleagues – there is an energizing feeling: we are on the front lines; we are making things happen; we are taking part in what the rest of the world is only seeing in the media. While others may feel powerless to help, we are helping.

I have seen and felt that it is, at the same time, addictive. During a "deployment" the frenzy and pace may invoke dreams of retirement or career change. There is absolute exhaustion upon return home. But somehow, in a short time, my colleagues and I are ready and waiting for the next time – with both dread and excitement.

However, there are far too many crises and emergencies in the world. The number will not decline, and may well increase. Sadly, built into this is long-term job security. And it is all too easy to burn out. I have had to force myself to learn to at least try to balance work with life, with family, friends, and relaxation. For example, after being away from home for one or two months, I also have to remind myself not to stay in the office until 10 p.m.; to spend precious time with my family, since I do not have that option for many months during the year.

The spontaneity of the work is also exciting and appealing. In some cases – such as conflicts, droughts, and refugee crises – we see situations evolving and can prepare for them. But in others we cannot. Friends (my family knows better) often ask me when and where I will be traveling next. My "standard" reply is: "Watch CNN, then you and I will probably know at the same time." And my family and colleagues and friends always ask how long I'll be away. My standard answer (now a joke in my family) is three weeks. But it is almost never three weeks, and is often closer to six to eight weeks.

As careful human observers, we are privileged with a front row to many untold and powerful events. I have seen the best of people at their worst of times. It can be overwhelming and sometimes needs to be carefully kept in perspective. For example, I have seen again and again that we are not, as many of us like to believe – the "first responders" in disaster. Disasters can bring out the best in people, and that is tremendously inspiring.

For example, I had lived in Haiti for four years, working with an NGO, years before the earthquake of January 2010. During my poverty reduction work there at the time, I had noticed, as many of us had, that Haitians were not particularly interested in community or collective action or inter-household collaboration, like training each other (although this observation has been debated). However, when my team and I arrived in Haiti just days after the earthquake, we witnessed victims helping others in any way they could everywhere. In one case a team of young men who had lost their own homes were busy erecting emergency shelters from salvaged materials for whoever needed them. They would build one, give it away, and then begin another one. They told me they could not just sit by and watch the chaos while they had skills they could contribute.

In another example, a spontaneous community security patrol of young men self-organized to protect the neighborhood against looting and rape. And when we could not supply enough tarps to families, as is standard practice for emergency shelter, we found households voluntarily sharing theirs with neighbors until more tarps arrived. I believe that it is my past experience, combined with my anthropological predisposition to observe and examine social interaction, that led me to see beyond the immediate disaster response activities and to recognize the significance of these actions.

But sadly, we also see the worst of people. For example, during four years in Sudan I managed programs in Darfur, where I spent considerable time. Our programs helped save and preserve the lives of vulnerable and marginalized Sudanese against the deliberate and aggressive cruelty and inhumanity of other Sudanese of different tribes, ethnic groups, and political beliefs.

A Multitude of Ethical Issues and Challenges

The number, scope, importance, and urgency of ethical issues in humanitarian assistance are significant, and far exceed the scope of this chapter. I have presented entire seminars on this topic, and there are hundreds of meetings, conferences, papers, and articles that focus on any of the many challenges. Many of these are unresolved and debates continue.

But, importantly, we cannot wait for resolution. The often life-saving urgency of this work requires that we continue at full speed, regardless of the theoretical discussions in the background, and thus each organization, and each aid worker, myself included, has had to make their own choices about how to continue operating in spite of the ambiguity. For example, just a few of the issues that I face regularly include the following:

1. To what extent should aid agencies coordinate, collaborate, or cooperate with military actors when the two are in the same location?
2. In accepting funds from governments do we become party to political agendas? How do we avoid this? What happens when vitally needed funding is tied to certain approaches or strategies that have multiple objectives and agendas?
3. In the urgency of the moment, in order to help people quickly, is it acceptable to take actions that may influence cultural norms, standards, and practices, and ultimately induce social, economic, and cultural change?
4. When can we claim that we really do know best, and try to force our own strategies and approaches, in opposition to local authorities in whose country we are guests?

Parting Advice

Many of the realities and mechanics of working in this domain have been discussed in the previous section. So I will just reiterate a few key elements. Be flexible: a lot of the work is not distinctly anthropological. Package and present what anthropologists can *do*, not what we are: assessment, socio-economic analysis, applied data collection, interdisciplinary integration. Learn the humanitarian terminology, jargon, acronyms, and definitions. Have practical, applied, relevant field experience to bring to the table. And it is very helpful to have good solid knowledge in a key technical sector, such as nutrition, food security, water and sanitation, shelter, or livelihoods and income generation.

Part IV
Key Issues

Chapter 26

Ethics and Practicing Anthropology – Pragmatic, Practical, and Principled

Lenora Bohren and Linda Whiteford

"Ethics" in anthropology is all too often an abstract subject, but in this chapter, two anthropologists – one a university professor and the other a practitioner – engage in a professional dialogue about the ethical implications of a very specific environmental project. In this dialogue Whiteford and Bohren present us with a detailed case study of how the ethical issues and aspects of the project were approached, understood, and dealt with. They conclude their discussion with some thoughts about the particular ethical challenges and considerations of contracting and consulting work.

Introduction

We began this conversation about the role of ethics in practicing anthropology over coffee at the SfAA (Society for Applied Anthropology) meetings. Practicing and university-based anthropologists face distinct types of ethical dilemmas due to their different funding sources, different target audiences, different workplace expectations and products. While we all encounter ethical quandaries and must resolve them, this chapter focuses on the conversation we had about how one practicing anthropologist encountered and resolved a situation in her professional experience, and our shared analysis of that experience. We are two anthropologists: one is a research scientist (Bohren) directing the National Center for Vehicle Emissions Control and Safety (NCVECS) at Colorado State University (CSU), and the other an anthropologist (Whiteford) whose career has been primarily academically based at the University of South Florida (USF).

A Handbook of Practicing Anthropology. First Edition. Edited by Riall W. Nolan.

Part of that original conversation revolved around telling stories – something all anthropologists love to do – about the funny and sometimes awkward situations we found ourselves in professionally, and how we resolved them. What became clear in that conversation was that neither of us had any formal training in ethics while we were in graduate school and that, while some academic anthropology graduate programs now provide their students with training in ethics (at USF, for instance), we were both set loose as professionals without any formal training in ethics. Truth be told, while we did acquire some training and exposure to the professional ethics of our discipline along the way – with the codes and guidelines of professional organizations, for instance those of SfAA, American Anthropological Association (AAA), National Association for the Practice of Anthropology (NAPA), as well as those of institutional review boards (IRBs) – it became clear to us that this is still an area of relative opaqueness for many anthropologists. What follows in this chapter is a brief case study from Bohren's professional experience, and then a conversation between us about how to apply what we think is a simple and useful ethical problem-solving guide, the RICE Guide (Whiteford and Trotter 2008).

Ethical principles or guidelines exist to help resolve dilemmas caused by competing and equally justifiable courses of action. Where the courses of action are not in competition or where there is a clear and unambiguous course of action, there is no need to rely on a set of decision-making principles offered by ethical standards or codes of ethics. The classic ethical principles found in Western philosophy (and also significantly important in Eastern philosophy) are: (1) respect for others, (2) beneficence, and (3) justice. What these terms mean, and how to apply them, however, are more ambiguous questions, but they are clearly situated in personal and cultural values. For that reason, ethical decision-making processes include values clarification exercises as, for example, the RICE Guide, RICE being the acronym for "reflect, investigate, contemplate, and evaluate." It will be the basis for a conversation later in the chapter.

Anthropological practitioners are ideal consultants for many projects because of their holistic, culture-centered approach. A practicing anthropologist is an important part of a team consisting, as in the case we will present, of medical personnel, ergonomic and indoor air quality (IAQ) specialists, and engineers. Anthropologists' knowledge of the role of culture in decision-making could lead to the inclusion of questions resulting in a better understanding of the situation/context. In this conversation, we use the experience of one practitioner (Bohren) while she was employed by a large consulting company as an example of some of the ethical decisions, complications, and so on that come with the job of being a practitioner. As an environmental anthropologist, she was especially qualified (Bohren 2005) to be hired as a consultant on a project assessing the existence of sick building syndrome (SBS). Our conversation deals with her experience and reflections on the potential for ethical conflicts. The oil embargoes and worldwide energy crisis of the 1970s led to efforts to increase energy efficiency in buildings that had an unintended impact on the health of their occupants (Air Quality Sciences 2008). Engineers, building scientists, and architects began designing buildings that were as airtight as possible to reduce the energy burden from mechanical heating and cooling systems. While this practice resulted in reduced energy usage, it often resulted in inadequate circulation of fresh air.

The energy efficiency paradigm also led to many new products being designed to conserve precious energy. The use of formaldehyde was one more use of petro-chemicals that would eventually contribute to the hazardous mixture of chemicals that surround us in our homes. Engineered wood, which uses formaldehyde as a binder for wood pulp, gained in popularity in the 1960s, and was followed by urea-formaldehyde foam insulation (UFFI) in the 1970s. UFFI was marketed as one of the wonders of energy conservation in the wake of the oil embargo crisis, and over half a million consumers had this material pumped into the walls of their homes in the 1970s. By the end of the decade, complaints of adverse effects from urea-formaldehyde began to pour into health agencies. Investigations ensued and, given scientific evidence of a link between inhaled formaldehyde and cancer in laboratory animals, formaldehyde became the new topic of discussion in the health and build-ing industries (Ore 2007). In the early 1980s UFFI was banned in the United States and Canada, but formaldehyde continued to be used in many household products including engineered wood, fiberglass insulation, paint, carpeting, and upholstery.

The combination of tightened building enclosures, hazardous building products and materials, and occupant behaviors created unhealthy living and working condi-tions were created. What followed was the emergence of building-related illness (BRI) or sick building syndrome, a sharp increase in indoor mold growth, and the realization that formaldehyde and other volatile organic compounds (VOCs) in building materials expose occupants to unhealthy indoor environments (Kawamura 2011).

BOHREN: I was hired by Westat, a Washington, DC area survey research company, to help design and administer employee questionnaires at both the Library of Con-gress (LOC) and Environmental Protection Agency (EPA) headquarters buildings. As an anthropologist focusing on environmental issues, I was pleased to be involved in a study which had wide-ranging health and ethical implications. The health implications were evident; five employees of the EPA could no longer work in the Waterside Mall EPA headquarters building due to acute symptoms, and many others had serious complaints. These symptoms were thought to be caused by the building in which they worked. The ethical dilemma was that since ethics are a balance between the benefits and risks of choices and decisions and are embedded in cultural institutions (Whiteford and Trotter 2008), there was a conflict between choices that were in the interest of the individuals or occupants and those that were in the interest of the organization or businesses that owned or managed the buildings.

In the case of the buildings used to house the EPA offices, design, construction and remodeling decisions for the buildings were made in the interest of conserving energy and saving money. These decisions resulted in unforeseen consequences which did not take into consideration the health and well-being of individuals who were working in the buildings, especially the vulnerable populations such as those with asthma or those who were especially sensitive to environmental conditions. Indoor environmental hazards pose great risks to human health due to high levels of toxics associated with confined spaces and the significant amount of time people spend indoors. For example, the use of formaldehyde as a binder in wood products, fiberglass insulation, paint, carpeting, and upholstery and the use of or emissions from other volatile organic compounds exposed occupants to unnecessary health risks (Ore 2007). VOCs include emissions of chemicals such as ozone from copy machines. These unhealthy environmental conditions are often worsened by the lack of proper maintenance of air ventilation systems, including infrequent replacement of filters, which is often another cost-cutting decision.

Employees in both the Madison Building of the Library of Congress and the three EPA headquarters buildings in Washington, DC expressed concerns about the air quality and the work environment in their buildings. Employees in the LOC building had expressed complaints since the building opened in 1980. Employees of the headquarters buildings of the EPA in Washington, DC expressed similar complaints. In response, a study of both the LOC and EPA headquarters buildings used a similar study design to attempt to understand the nature of the employees' health symptoms and comfort concerns. The study investigated both the perceived (employee questionnaire) and actual (monitoring) quality of the indoor air and environment. Questions were asked at both locations in relation to health and comfort. Health questions addressed symptoms experienced while in the buildings and other risk factors such as contact lenses and eyeglasses wear, smoking, allergies, asthma, and ear, nose, and throat or respiratory irritations. Comfort questions addressed issues of temperature, humidity, air movement, noise, dust, light, odors, and furniture.

Results of the survey in the EPA building (81 percent response rate) showed that the most frequently reported health complaints were headaches, contact lens problems, stuffy nose, dry/itchy skin, dry/itchy/tearing eyes, strained eyes, and drowsiness (typical IAQ complaints). These complaints were reported as improving when employees left work. At the Waterside Mall location, the headquarters building with the most complaints, the employees reported that their symptoms reduced their ability to work and were perceived to be associated with the building. Comfort in the EPA headquarters buildings was generally satisfactory in terms of immediate workstations (chair, lighting) but employees were also dissatisfied with the air (too dry and too little movement) and the temperature, which was seasonally a problem. Symptoms such as headache, fatigue, and mucus membrane irritation are common complaints that have been reported in many published evaluations of IAQ (Westat 1989b).

WHITEFORD: Early on in the evolution of the SBS, complaints from people that their work places were making them sick, were often dismissed as having come from discontented employees. Did you ever feel any potential conflict between the legitimacy of the claims by the sick employees and power of an employer like the EPA? In some ways, one could see how a consultant might feel caught between two competing "good guys" – the sick employees and the Environmental Protection Agency. Did you feel any level of conflict from potential competing interests? If you did, how did you resolve the potential conflict of rights in this case?

BOHREN: I did not sense any potential conflict between the sick employees and the EPA. By the time the research team was brought in to study the situation, the employees were excited that the problem was being addressed. Perhaps there was a history of discontent, but I was unaware of its existence. A practitioner who is part of a larger research team is often at a distance and is not exposed to the underlying conflicts. Practitioners too often do not know the results of the study, that is, what is eventually done and whether the problem is resolved.

WHITEFORD: As a practitioner working as a consultant for a large company, did you have to go through something similar to the IRB process before you began your research? Academically based researchers must provide the IRB with information showing how they will protect the confidentiality of the people they interview. Did you do something like that?

BOHREN: As part of a larger team, the individual researchers did not have to go through a review board as I have to when I'm working on a project for NCVECS, which is university-based. The final report stated that both management and unions were given an opportunity to review the draft questionnaire, and their endorsements were communicated to all employees. The report also stated that stringent measures were taken to ensure the confidentiality of all responses; as a consultant, I never knew what these measures were.

WHITEFORD: How does working as a consultant for a large company shape the kind of research you can do? Can you design any type of methodology you think would be best in order to get the information needed? Who makes the decision about which kinds of methods will be use and who will be interviewed? In the case you are describing, did you get informed consent to participate from the people who were surveyed as part of the research?

BOHREN: Working for a large company is very different than working for NCVECS, where I make the decisions on research design. When you work for a large company, you can give input into the research design and specific questions, but the decisions are made by the company project managers who are ultimately responsible for the project. I did not find a reference to informed consent in the final report. The questionnaire was self-administered and was distributed to all employees. It was hoped that the endorsement from the management and unions would increase participation in the survey. The response rate at EPA was 81 percent; the employees I talked with were pleased that the study was being conducted – perhaps this showed an informal consent to participate.

Results of the survey in the LOC building (90 percent response rate) showed that the most frequent complaints were also associated with poor indoor air quality. These complaints were also reported as getting better when leaving work. The survey of comfort issues at the LOC showed that most respondents were satisfied with the physical environment (furniture, lighting) but were often dissatisfied with the air movement (too little) and humidity (too dry), and occasionally with temperature (seasonal) in their work space (Westat 1989b).

These complaints were described by the EPA (1991) as symptoms of sick building syndrome (SBS) and building related illness (BRI), terms used to describe a combination of ailments, symptoms, complaints, and discomforts associated with an individual's place of work or residence. It is a syndrome where you and/or your colleagues' symptoms are felt while in the building but tend to be alleviated when you leave the building. SBS came into being as a result of the oil embargoes of the mid-1970s which led to buildings with "tight" windows that didn't open and other efforts to conserve energy, as mentioned above. An unintended consequence was the entrapment of chemicals released or introduced into the building. A 1984 World Health Organization report suggested that up to 30 percent of new and remodeled buildings worldwide have experienced an increase in building-related complaints; roughly 21 million people might be at risk for developing SBS while at work (Brown 1996). Thus, most of the SBS complaints are related to poor indoor air quality.

The RICE Guide

One of the tools we found useful in "walking through" potential conflicts is the RICE Guide (Whiteford and Trotter 2008). The guide can be used before a consulting project begins to think through the situation and to clarify the values involved. A critical portion of any ethical decision-making process includes a value clarification exercise to identify what the underlying ethical principles may be that conflict with one another.

> WHITEFORD: As we try to understand the ethical dilemmas you encountered in the case study above, let's use the RICE Guide (Table 26.1) to identify the ethical dilemma, the values of the practitioner, and the resolution.

Table 26.1 The RICE Guide

Reflect: identify your own biases.
- What are your feelings about the case?
- What are the sources of your intuitions (i.e. your moral training, professional norms, personal history, social position, religious beliefs, relationship with the people involved?)
- What are the limitations to your objectivity?

Investigate: probe the facts as presented.
- What other information is relevant to the ethics of the case?
- Are other possibilities/resources available?
- Has any perspective been neglected?
- Are there unanswered questions?

Contemplate: prioritize information and identify ethical dimensions.
- What facts are particularly crucial?
- What ethical principles apply to the case?
- What values are in conflict?
- Are there underlying issues or hidden agendas?
- What social structures have contributed to this dilemma?
- What are the benefits and burdens of the available options?
- How does this case compare to others you have experiences or heard of?

Evaluate: analyze options and justify recommendations.
- What is the good act, and what makes it so?

Source: Whiteford and Trotter 2008: 113; used with kind permission.

BOHREN: Using the guide, I think about my responses this way:
Reflect: identify your own biases.

- I feel that it is crucial to revisit decisions that have been made with the good intentions of saving energy and/or money, but have had the unintended consequences of causing potentially serious health problems. Respect for others, with the intention of doing no harm, is essential.
- I come from a background that is grounded in a strong sense of justice – fairness for all. I find it difficult to justify actions that may harm others (especially those who are disadvantaged), even though it may save money.
- My limitations in this study were based on my role. I was only one of many researchers and was involved only in the development and administration of the questionnaire part of the study, not the decision-making.

Investigate: probe the facts as presented:

- I was pleased that action was being taken to investigate the scope and reality of the health concerns of the employees of both the LOC and EPA headquarters buildings and that an attempt was being made to identify the causes of their concerns.
- I continued to be concerned about what actions would be taken once the causes of the complaints were determined.
- I did not know to what extent solutions had been discussed, as I was a member of the research team, not the remediation team. This can often be a dilemma for a research team whose responsibility ends when the report has been made and the recommendations are turned in.
- I felt that the research team was inclusive: engineers, medical personnel, anthropologist, survey specialists, and indoor air and ergonomic specialists for designing the questionnaire and taking the needed measurements.

Contemplate: prioritize information and identify ethical dimensions.

- Make sure the questions are asked that get to the essence of the problem; in this case, I had to ensure that questions were asked that related to the disappearance or lessening of symptoms when employees were not in the buildings. That many of the symptoms continued to lessen over the weekend was important.
- All of the ethical principles are important: respect for persons, beneficence, and justice. I felt that justice was of primary importance, since many of the employees in the buildings had health issues which were magnified while in the building and in some cases were caused by being in the building. These health issues were often expensive to treat and caused financial problems for many of the employees.
- The issue underlying the conflict was what action would be taken to remedy the unhealthy situation.
- The underlying issue, or hidden agenda, was related to the idea of whether action would be taken, or if the activity of investigating the nature of the problem was meant to be part of the solution.
- The actions that had contributed to this dilemma included initial decisions in the interests of saving energy and cost taken by the building owners, which had negative/unhealthy effects on the employees; the positive aspect was that the decision-makers were taking actions to potentially remedy the unhealthy situation.

- The main benefit of the decision to research SBS was learning about the causes and effects of unhealthy buildings, which would enable action to be taken. However, the solutions for the problem were potentially costly.
- This was my first experience of studying SBS. I learned that it is important to review other SBS studies in order to understand what the potential problems were and what actions had been taken. Also, it was important to learn if the actions taken were appropriate, affordable, and effective.

Evaluate: analyze options and justify recommendations.

- There were two parts of the SBS study: development and administration of the questionnaire and actually monitoring and measuring the air quality. I participated in the questionnaire development and administration while the technical team measured the air quality. The results of our part of the study reported the data on numbers of employees with complaints, what the complaints were, and the locations of the employees with the complaints. We did not make recommendations for action; we reported data supporting the existence and extent of the complaints. The technical team confirmed the existence and location of the problems. The decision for action was left up to the LOC and EPA decision-makers. I do know that the EPA eventually moved to new headquarters buildings and that the LOC tried to correct as many problems as possible. The remediation of the problem at the LOC was difficult due to the nature of the library's role of preserving and storing books and documents over a long period of time; this process often gives rise to potentially toxic emissions. The good act was that the undertaking of the study showed respect for persons by trying to do no harm and to do them justice by protecting the right to fair and equitable treatment for all employees in terms of their health and well-being.

WHITEFORD: Did using the guide provide you with any insights into how to think through what could have been potentially troubling ethical dilemmas for you as a practitioner? Can you talk about what those insights were?

BOHREN: The guide was helpful in providing a context for understanding the ethical dilemma of a practitioner. A practitioner is hired to investigate a problem and to offer possible recommendations, but is not on the decision-making team. The guide provided a structure to assess the ethical questions that arose from a decision made earlier during the design or remodeling phase of building construction. It demonstrated the need for a design team that includes practitioners who are knowledgeable about the unintended consequences of construction or remodeling and of the people affected by the design.

In the case of the EPA Waterside Mall headquarters building, it was originally designed to be an open mall. The ventilation system was designed for an open space and did not have the capabilities to provide adequate ventilation for closed or divided spaces, especially ones that were utilizing furniture, carpeting, etc. made of composite materials that contained toxic chemicals. The unintended consequences of the remodel of the Waterside Mall were that many people developed IAQ complaints in relation to health and comfort and, as a result of these complaints, five people could no longer work in the building.

WHITEFORD: What happened to those people who could no longer work in the building? What happened to those who developed IAQ complaints? Did you feel any obligation to them? Did the agency who hired you act on any obligations to those now out of work? To whom are your primary obligations and responsibilities as a consultant? Is there any ethical conflict between those to whom the practitioner has primary responsibilities and those affected, whether intentionally or unintentionally, by the results of the research?

BOHREN: The five persons who could no longer work in the Waterside Mall building continued to work for EPA from home. Others who developed complaints from working in the building, planned to continue working for EPA as long as the problems were addressed. I was pleased to be working on a project that had the potential to solve serious health complaints in office buildings. I did not know which of the employees expressed concerns about their environment; the questionnaire was sent out to all employees. I do not think the agency who hired me felt any obligation toward those who were out of work; they were hired to do a research project.

As a consultant, my primary obligations were to Westat, the company that hired me as a researcher. I did not feel an ethical conflict between Westat and the employees of the LOC or EPA headquarters buildings. This project was one of many projects that Westat was hired to do. I believe Westat was selected to undertake the project because they do many health-related projects.

WHITEFORD: As a university-based anthropologist, the ethical quandaries that I most often see are those that involve a misuse of power and often are not a conscious action. However, since the 1960s and 1970s we have seen a codification of some of those power issues, such as relations between students and faculty when the faculty is in a position to evaluate or assess the student, the rights and responsibilities of faculty in relation to those who assess or evaluate them. This continued codification of what are essentially ethical decisions can be extended to the rights and responsibilities, and legal actions allowed, between faculty and the university administration.

WHITEFORD: In the role of a practitioner, are there similar codifications of rights and responsibilities between the practitioner and their employer? Can you identify some of those?

BOHREN: There are no codifications of rights and responsibilities between the practitioner and their employer, but the contract that is signed by both the contractor and the practitioner has well-defined rights and responsibilities for all the participants in the project. As a practitioner, I have found that it is essential to have the roles and responsibilities clearly outlined in order to know who is responsible for which task. Communication channels must also be established in order to discuss the project in an iterative fashion with the hopes of reducing the chances of unintended consequences.

An example of this in the case study was the design of the questionnaire by a diverse team whose specific task was to collect background data about the situation and the complaints, so that the data collected could be used as a basis for making the correct decisions about a solution. The questionnaire was designed by considering the situation from many viewpoints and conducting many pre-tests of it to be sure that the desired information was collected.

WHITEFORD: An impression students sometimes have is that university-based faculty are protected by bargaining agreements (if the university is unionized), and by organizations such as the American Association of University Professors (AAUP), and that faculty behavior should be guided by the codes and guidelines from our professional associations such as SfAA and AAA. But practitioners are not likewise protected. What protections are there for practitioners?

BOHREN: There are no real protections for the practitioners, since you are often regarded as independent contractors; however, you are guided by the ethics of your profession, as anthropologists are guided by the codes and guidelines of organizations such as SfAA, NAPA, and AAA. In my case, since NCVECS is housed in Colorado State University, we are bound by the contract agreements of the university which include approval from the offices of human subjects and contracts and grants. This approval process can be a deterrent to some contractors who prefer a less time-consuming and complicated process. Many consultants or practitioners have started their own consulting companies to avoid these complications.

WHITEFORD: Over the years, we have all heard or read about unethical conduct by university faculty, sometimes toward their students, sometimes involving the people they study, and sometimes involving the research results. We hear about those cases because they become public through articles, books, and in some cases legal challenges. However, in the case of practitioners, those problems may never become public because of the nature of the contract signed between the practitioner and the agency.

Can you talk about the kinds of ethical problems that might arise from the constraints (publications, secrecy, proprietary rights) included in a consulting contract?

BOHREN: One of the issues a practitioner is concerned with is intellectual property rights. If you are a practitioner representing the university, the output of your project becomes the intellectual property of the university. If you are a practitioner representing your own consulting company the final product belongs to you or the contractor (as specified in the original contract). You are free to publish or not publish as you wish; in fact, all that is often required is a final report to the contractor. An ethical dilemma that can arise is how the information will be used. The practitioner has to be careful to report the information learned in an unbiased manner and to include, if possible, a statement on how the information is to be used and/or not used. The practitioner has to be as true as possible to both informants and contractor.

WHITEFORD: The university-based anthropologist has a history of the academy to guide expectations of what their career might look like and on what success might be based. While there are certainly many unknowns in how are to achieve career advancement in a university setting, a tenure track assistant professor has some general expectations about how to achieve tenure and promotion and the ethical guidelines associated with that advancement. What can the practitioner expect about how to ethically to build a career and move toward advancement?

BOHREN: The practitioner at the university is "an employee at will" and is not on a tenure track; they can be let go at any time if they do not bring in funds to support their salary. The incentives for promotion, both inside and outside of the university, are that successfully managed projects and well-written reports can lead to project continuation and build a reputation that will result in more grants and contracts. Publications can be advantageous to both contactors and funding agencies, such as the National Science Foundation (NSF). Many other contractors are more inter-

ested in your track record of successfully completed projects both with them and
with other (often federal) agencies.

Conclusion

In condensing our rather long, amusing, and enlightening conversation, many interesting pieces of information about the competing and conflicting rights, for instance
of those advocating for the conservation of energy and those whose health is
affected by closed air systems, were lost. What became clear, however, is that while
both practitioners and university-based anthropologists share the core components
of their professional academic training, the conditions and constraints in which
these are applied are quite distinct.

In our discussion we applied the RICE Guide to facilitate value clarification so
critical to resolving potential or actual ethical dilemmas. That exercise raised a series
of questions we shared about the ethics of workplace activities (and the role of
institutional protection), the ethics of contracts and different kinds of proprietary
constraints, and finally the ethics of moving a career forward. In each of these situations, ethics play a central, if over overlooked, role. We hope that by sharing these
insights, experiences, and guidelines, the role of ethics will become clearer.

References

Air Quality Sciences (2008) *Energy Conservation and Indoor Air Quality: Benefits of Achieving Both in Homes.* At http://www.aerias.org/uploads/IAQ%20Energy%20Homes%20 FINAL.pdf, accessed Sept. 6, 2012.

Bohren, Lenora (2005) "Evaluation of Environmental Issues." In M. O. Butler and J. Copeland-Carson (eds.) (2005), *Creating Evaluation Anthropology: Introducing an Emerging Sub-field.* NAPA Bulletin 24. Berkeley: University of California Press, pp. 49–56.

Brown, Kathryn S. (1996) "Sick Days at Work." *Environmental Health Perspectives* 104: 976–982.

EPA (1991) *Indoor Air Facts No. 4: Sick Building Syndrome.* United States Environmental Protection Agency. Air and Radiation, Research and Development MD-56). At http://www.epa.gov/iaq/pdfs/sick_building_factsheet.pdf, accessed Sept. 6, 2012.

Kawamura, Shelley (2011) "An Evaluation of Green Home Weatherization and Remodeling Programs: What is Being Done to Promote Occupant Health and Recommendations for Best Practices." Paper presented at the HUD Healthy Homes Conference. At http://www.healthyhomesconference.org/presentations/Wednesday/4H-1_From%20 Isolation%20to%20Integration%20Strategies%20for%20Mixed%20Ability%20 Users.pdf, accessed Sept. 6, 2012.

Ore, Janet (2007) Poisonous Plywood: Environmental Hazards in Post-World War II Home Building." Paper presented at American Society for Environmental History conference on "Living on the Edge: Human Desires and Environmental Realities," Baton Rouge, LA, Feb. 28–Mar. 3.

Westat (1989a) *Indoor Air Quality and Work Environment Study: EPA Headquarters' Buildings*, vol. 1: *Employee Survey*. United States Environmental Protection Agency, National Institute for Occupational Safety and Health, Westat, Inc., John B. Pierce Foundation Laboratory at Yale University. Rockville, MD: Westat.

Westat (1989b) *Indoor Air Quality and Work Environment Study: Library of Congress Madison Building*, vol. 1: *Employee Survey*. National Institute for Occupational Safety and Health, United States Environmental Protection Agency, Westat, Inc., John B. Pierce Foundation Laboratory at Yale University, National Institute of Standards and Technology. Rockville, MD: Westat.

Whiteford, Linda M. and Robert T. Trotter II (2008) *Ethics for Anthropological Research and Practice*. Long Grove, IL: Waveland Press.

Chapter 27

The Academic–Practitioner Relationship

Linda A. Bennett and Shirley J. Fiske

Relationships between the world of practice and the world of the academy have been, at times, distant and somewhat strained, a fact of considerable concern to thoughtful people in both worlds. In this chapter, two experienced anthropologists – one academy-based and the other practice-based – engage in a dialogue about the relationship between practice and academia. In developing their conversation, Shirley Fiske and Linda Bennett draw extensively on their own backgrounds and experiences in order to illuminate key aspects of this relationship. In addition, however, they provide us with considerable detail about how five different anthropology departments have approached academic–practitioner relationships, what their experience has been, and what recommendations they would offer us. Fiske and Bennett then discuss these findings in terms of the mechanisms which promote and support strong academy–practice relationships, the value of these relationships for students, the barriers still standing in the way, and finally, some of the current positive trends.

Introduction

In writing this chapter, we acknowledge a basic working assumption that the discipline of anthropology benefits from constructive relationships between academically based and practicing anthropologists. Furthermore, we argue that although full-time careers in academia and careers in predominantly practitioner arenas represent two different types of work, with varying demands, talents, and rewards, important

A Handbook of Practicing Anthropology. First Edition. Edited by Riall W. Nolan.
© 2013 John Wiley & Sons, Inc. Published 2013 by John Wiley & Sons, Inc.

areas of commonality exist between them. In short, we observe that the boundaries between academia and practice are not as dichotomous as many anthropologists seem to believe. In this chapter we address four general questions dealing with academic–practitioner relationships: (1) What existing mechanisms encourage strong and positive relationships between practitioners and members of the academy? (2) Why are such relationships important for the education of anthropology students? (3) What barriers stand in the way of productive academic–practitioner connections? (4) And what positive trends promote building and sustaining constructive academic–practitioner affiliations?

As we approach this topic, we necessarily bring perspectives based on our own career experiences. Both our careers have benefitted from forging positive and strong academic–practitioner ties; and we believe that close ties are beneficial for everyone involved: students, faculty, practitioners, and the discipline of anthropology.

Reflections on Academy and Practice Perspectives

Both of us have a long history of attending to academy–practice relationships, and an account of our career trajectories may help clarify the roots of our perspectives. A glimpse into our career paths shows how the academic/practitioner dichotomy can be permeable rather than a rigid division and sheds light on how productive relationships between the two can be crafted.

In 1970 I (Linda) chose to begin doctoral studies at American University in Washington, DC, in large part because Washington was home to a substantial population of anthropologists who were working in a wide range of careers and organizations. The eclectic nature of anthropology in Washington, DC appealed to me as I anticipated possible career paths for myself. Furthermore, the Department of Anthropology at American University was committed to applied anthropology and several faculty members on full-time staff, or adjunct faculty members, had been or were employed in various federal agencies. For example, adjunct faculty member Bela Maday, the anthropologist at the National Institute of Mental Health, served as a member of my doctoral dissertation committee. Several other practicing anthropologists (e.g., Gordon Macgregor and Philleo Nash) taught in the department. Katherine Spencer Halpern, my main adviser, had conducted applied anthropological work with a number of Native American communities and had previously taught in social work programs in New York City and Boston.

An opportunity to take a job that did not fall within the traditional teaching arena came my way in 1974 as I was completing my dissertation. My job interview at the Center for Family Research in the Department of Psychiatry and Behavioral Sciences, George Washington University Medical Center, led to a 12-year history working with psychiatrist Steven J. Wolin on a series of three family and alcoholism projects, funded by the National Institute on Alcohol Abuse and Alcoholism. As a research faculty member, I was working collaboratively with colleagues from several disciplines on applied medical anthropology projects. A critical conversation took place when I completed my doctorate in 1976, when the director of the Center for Family Research, psychiatrist David Reiss, firmly advised me to retain my ties with my home discipline while working in the applied and interdisciplinary world.

I took his advice to heart. The timing was good since Washington, DC was home to both the Anthropological Society of Washington (ASW), which had been established in 1879, and the newly founded (1976) local practitioner organization (LPO), the Washington Association of Professional Anthropologists (WAPA). I had attended meetings of the ASW since arriving in Washington and from 1976 was active in both organizations, including serving in leadership positions. Between WAPA and ASW a very impressive and broad array of careers in anthropology were represented in the membership and in their lecture and publication programs. For example, the Smithsonian Institution anthropologists and many faculty members from throughout the DC area were regular participants in the ASW while many federal government employees and private consultants (among other work arenas) were active in WAPA. Academically based anthropologists – students and faculty – contributed to both, but WAPA was clearly an LPO organized to meet the interests and the needs of practitioner anthropologists whose main employment was not academic.

At the same time, many WAPA members taught as adjuncts at the numerous universities in the Washington, DC area. Members of the Consortium of Universities in the Washington Metropolitan Area include the Catholic University of America; George Washington University; the University of Maryland; American University; Georgetown University; Howard University; the University of the District of Columbia; George Mason University; Marymount University; National Intelligence University; National Defense University; Gallaudet University; and Trinity Washington University. Between the richness of anthropology as taught in these institutions of higher education and the complexity of the discipline as practiced in positions in a myriad of careers, including government agencies, private and voluntary associations (PVOs), and consulting, among many others, the Washington, DC area was an ideal landscape for witnessing the potential for intermingling between academic and practicing anthropology. Furthermore, this was a context with many resources for students studying anthropology in the area, such as me, who were interested in exploring a wide array of career trajectories in the discipline.

A major career shift for me occurred in 1986 when I took an academic tenure track position at the University of Memphis (then Memphis State University). This experience provided another rich, but different, opportunity for me to learn about and to contribute to an evolving relationship between academic and practitioner anthropology. Memphis's program was one of the few at the time that had explicitly developed as an applied anthropology MA degree (focusing on urban anthropology, medical anthropology, and public archaeology) with a pledge to help facilitate employment for the MA alumni as practitioners. During the job interview I was particularly impressed to meet Ron Register and Tim Bolding, who were recent alumni. Register (MA 1984) was working at Head Start and became its director, and Bolding (MA 1980) was working for Shelby County Government and later founded the nonprofit United Housing, Inc. in Memphis. I could sense immediately that the work of alumni from the MA program as practitioners within the wider Memphis–Mid-South community was going to be a major strength of the academic program and a promising model of academic–practitioner advancement of anthropology in the region and for the discipline.

Evidence of the long-term commitment by the faculty and alumni of the MA program can be seen in the fact that over 300 alumni have moved into primarily practitioner positions, many within the Mid-South region. In April 2012 the thirty-fifth-anniversary of the MA program was celebrated with an acknowledgment that anthropology alumni had "populated" the Memphis–Mid-South community. In this process, the alumni practitioners had become colleagues of the academically based faculty and mentors of the current generation of students. So, in this setting at least, anthropologists do not see a strict divide between academicians and practitioners. Faculty members acknowledge enthusiastically that educating students to enter the community as practitioner anthropologists depends on a close collaboration between academic faculty and alumni practitioners.

In summary, while I have mainly worked in academic settings (from 1966 on) over my professional career, I have always been committed to applied anthropology and to collaborative work between disciplines and between practice and the academy. This commitment has been strongly reinforced by the positive results for students, for faculty, and for practitioners when differences are muted and collaborations are developed and sustained.

I (Shirley) started in academia (University of Southern California's School of Public Administration) but my initial academic experience was quite different from my image of anthropology departments of the era. The school and faculty in public administration valued practice, and both practitioners and experience were continually integrated into the curricula, publications, and tenure and promotion process. I suppose I would say that my initial academic experiences predisposed me to seeing practice and academia as lifelong partners.

I actively sought a government job in DC – it was not a "last choice" on my list of desirable employment opportunities. I was in Washington, DC in 1980. WAPA had just been formed, and through personal networks in California and anthropology I was recruited to join WAPA, which became a lifeline for me to other anthropologists working across government, consulting firms, and academia. WAPA brought together anthropologists in diverse careers, and was an incredibly valuable network for those of us working beyond academia, but at the same time it had academic members, and connected us to multiple universities across the metropolitan area (as Linda describes above). I recall that one of the first activities WAPA undertook was a set of workshops for anthropology graduate students, provided on campuses of regional universities on skills for job seeking outside academia – again, providing and promoting connections between practitioners and academia and students.

Through my career in both the executive and legislative branches I constantly connected to universities, bringing my experience and thoughts to classrooms, other colleagues – who also happened to be faculty – and to leadership in practice-oriented organizations like WAPA and NAPA – as well as the Anthropological Association of America (AAA) and Society for Applied Anthropology (SfAA). All these organizations play important and integrative roles in my life.

In 1984 the Anthropology Department at the University of Maryland was establishing its master's in applied anthropology. The department chair, Erve Chambers, asked two practitioners – Bob Wulff and me – to develop and teach a new core course for the MAA program called "Strategies for Cultural Understanding." It was sheer genius on the department's part to prepare students for job skills for the "real" world and for productive employment outside of academia. Here is what we included, in a quote from the original syllabus:

> The course provides the student with a framework for understanding the utilization of sociocultural information in government and industry. It explores the criteria for useful information, the organizational and environmental constraints surrounding useful information, and the problem-solving or policymaking process in which information plays a part. We will explore these topics through case studies, exercises, group discussion, and presentations, and lectures. As in organizational life in general, much of the learning will come from the experience and participation of the class participants.

The "Cultural Strategies" course was one of the conceptual foundations for the MAA and the department, I would like to believe – perhaps a little grandly. The department went on to develop the applied master's program and to incorporate internship requirements as part of the MAA degree preparation; they invited practitioners to be members of graduate committees, developed courses that include literature by practitioners, practitioners as lecturers and mentors, and practitioners as adjuncts teaching courses. This is true across the University of Maryland's cultural anthropology track as well as also its archaeology track, especially because historic and public archaeology are very strong at Maryland, with Mark Leone and Paul Shackel as leaders in the field. Naturally, the intensity of my personal relationship with the department waxed and waned over the years after the 1980s, depending on my employment requirements, the department's needs, and my colleagues' classes and research needs; but it has been an extremely positive institutional and intellectual relationship from my perspective as a practitioner.

I (Shirley) would like to offer a few observations on why the relationships with practitioners have been generally positive over the years. The department faculty have a positive cultural mindset toward practice and have adopted a positive and welcoming attitude to it; in addition they have consciously created a number of opportunities to involve and highlight practitioners' work during the year, such as inviting them to give the keynote talk at the annual colloquium, a rite of passage for graduating MAA students, where the graduates present their internship experiences and research projects. As another example, the department has incorporated a career-building class into their undergraduate and graduate programs, and invited practitioners to advise and to lecture on the course, thus providing students with the opportunity to learn critical career strategies from practitioners. And finally, as many departments have discovered, whether or not they are applied, it is important to keep the links with graduates alive and active, because they can be enormously helpful to current students – as lecturers in classes, as "ports of entry" into internships and career paths for graduates. The department has a robust mailing list of alumni, invites them to a number of events during the year, and works with them to develop internships.

Is the gap between practice and academia closing? While it is hard for me to generalize beyond universities that have applied anthropologists programs, I would say that, among those programs at least, the gap with practice is narrowing in certain ways. There are a lot of external variables that affect the narrowing gap as well, such as the growing trend in anthropology for faculty to undertake applied consulting or research projects with corporations, nonprofits, or local, state, or federal agencies, which in turn leads to greater appreciation of the work of practitioners and greater contact with the world of practice. The applied anthropology field is probably changing because of its increased focus on contemporary issues, alongside the public anthropology movement. In any case it takes long-term effort by departments with a pro-practice attitude. From my perspective as a practitioner with a long and generally positive association with academia in general, there seems to be growing acknowledgment and respect for anthropologists who have careers outside academia. At Maryland, in particular, there is a very close association with cultural and archaeological practice (public archaeology, historic archaeology, and historic preservation) and practitioners which has been well integrated into the graduate program's process and departmental curricula. Adjuncts who are practitioners routinely teach courses and lecture. The model that Linda describes above at the University of Memphis, where practitioner alumni become colleagues of department faculty, is excellent goal and outcome of a 35-year program which has welcomed and nurtured practitioner participation over time; this commentary should be an incentive to other programs to do the same.

Five Departments Report on the Academic–Practitioner Relationship

Recognizing that we have our own particular views on the relationship between academic and practitioner worlds – as shown in the previous section – we thought it would be useful to draw on the observations and opinions of colleagues from five specific anthropology departments which have a long-standing track record of educating and training students for applied and practicing work. We have particularly close working ties with two of them.

Colleagues in these five departments of anthropology were questioned about four issues with regard to academic–practitioner relationships: (1) efforts that have worked well; (2) challenges they faced in developing productive relationships and initiatives with anthropological practitioners; (3) recommendations based on their positive and challenging experiences in integrating anthropological practice with departmental educational and research goals; and (4) the role of local practitioner organizations (LPOs) in the departments' educational and research programs. The five departments were:

- University of North Texas (BA, MA, MS in applied anthropology, dual degrees in applied anthropology and public health);
- Wayne State University (BA, MA, PhD in anthropology);
- University of Memphis (BA, MA in anthropology);
- University of Maryland (BA, MAA in applied anthropology, PhD in anthropology);
- University of South Florida (BA in anthropology, MA in applied anthropology, PhD in anthropology).

Efforts that have worked well

The types of successful activities mentioned most frequently include class projects that get students out into the community to work in agencies and organizations. In turn, such community-based experiences can provide organizational bases for practicums and internships, and the possibility of bringing practitioners into academically based roles such as advisers on thesis projects. Departments also report that practitioners can do class presentations work on jointly funded research projects. In short, there is a myriad of roles practitioners are taking within departments.

Location is pertinent to the kinds of practitioner resources available. In Washington, DC area, for example, the University of Maryland has many highly qualified practitioners involved with the department due to the proximity of WAPA and a high density of anthropological practitioners in the federal government, consulting firms, and nonprofits. Quite a lot of these colleagues have been adjunct faculty members on both undergraduate and more specialized graduate courses. Depending on the location, each department is likely to draw on the expertise of practitioners from a wide variety of occupational arenas. For one department, the most important strategy for developing and maintaining relations with practitioners has been the internship program. The main goal is to make sure that students use their knowledge of anthropological theory and methods and their research skills to provide a service that an organization or agency needs. A second objective is for students to be able to collect data for their thesis or dissertation.

Another valuable strategy is to facilitate research activities through classes. Students usually make contact with more than one community agency and involve them as much as possible in the research project. The results are always presented back to the agencies, and ideally they should be useful for collaborations between the researchers and the local community.

Developing alumni networks and groups with the graduates of the programs is a very important way to develop relationships with practitioners. The alumni network can be expansive enough to encompass practitioners who are working locally, but who graduated from other academic programs.

Faculty members' local networks for developing projects, writing grants, doing community outreach, and placing students in internships and practica are also critical. Support by the university for integrating local and regional research and practice can be very helpful. The University of Memphis encourages collaborative research on urban issues. The degree to which universities emphasize community service and serving local needs is important, especially at the local and regional levels. Programs that involve reciprocity between faculty, students, and practicing anthropologists are very important. Perhaps the most fundamental program has been the practicum project, which often leads to joint research projects and permanent jobs.

Faculty serving on joint university–community task forces and committees and on community-based boards can facilitate and sustain the relationships necessary for a healthy academic–practitioner relationship. Advisory boards are an especially important means for involving alumni, community partners, and faculty in joint initiatives beneficial to both the academic and practical arenas.

Challenges to academic–practitioner relationships

The traditional demands for tenure and promotion for anthropology faculty can pose obstacles for personal and program success. Despite all the merits of collaborative work between academically based and practicing anthropologists, when it comes to tenure and promotion decisions most credit is given to faculty for focusing on research partnerships, grant writing, and "traditional" academic activities.

> Joint research efforts between practitioners and faculty can be difficult to get started and maintain due to obstacles posed by campus. Once the campus–community relationships are established a particular challenge is just trying to maintain and support the relationships and networks that are available to us, especially among our own practitioner graduates. I feel that we faculty, and especially our students, benefit more from some of the relationships than do practitioners. Finding ways for them to benefit more is always a challenge.[1]

Offering compensation to practitioners to make the time they need to invest in the course they are teaching worthwhile for their livelihood is a difficulty. Online courses have the potential to expose students to some amazing practitioners, but finding the appropriate compensation is a challenge.

Development and management of internship programs is a challenge. Departments noted the difficulty in securing paid internships. They also noted that staff and the management of internships require a dedicated leader, and in many cases this is not possible given limited departmental finances.

A major challenge of working with practitioners is understanding the mission and realities of the agency or organization; in turn, practicing anthropologists face challenges in providing students with sufficient mentoring.

Recommendations from departments

Get as many practitioners to campus as possible so that students have an opportunity to talk with them.

> Most academics have limited experience of working as practitioners and, frankly, we need the practitioners to help us guide the students on careers. Additionally, we need to compensate the practitioners fairly or have some other incentive that will make it worth their time away from their job. The COPAA Visiting Fellows Program is a good place to apply for funding.

> After more than a quarter of a century, I feel we are at a point where the distinction between practitioner and academic is quickly fading. Our faculty are fully applied, each in their own way, and connected in their research and interests with many of the same agencies and issues that engaged local practitioners. So my recommendation is that [good practitioner–academic relationships] work best if a department has made a full and unambiguous commitment to applied research and recognition that many of their graduates will not pursue careers in academia.

Maintain a constant presence in the local communities through participation in local events. This allows the department to have visibility and recognition and fosters good will.

If the budget permits, have a position dedicated to overseeing and coordinating activities that involve local communities and the universities. Establish and maintain strong local relations with alumni groups, local practitioner organizations, interest groups, and so on. Carrying out specific activities such as workshops, brown bag talks, small conferences, and so on is especially valuable.

> My primary recommendation is that both the academic and practicing anthropologists keep the vision that we are jointly creating a knowledge base that can make a huge difference in how programs and policies are created and implemented. Both are learning together so that programs and policies are shaped in a manner that improves the quality of life for the communities we are working in, local, regional, or international. To accomplish this end the commitment to understanding and using participatory action research is critical.

The role of local practitioner organizations (LPOs)

> Over the years, our local practitioner organization has risen and fallen several times. In a mid-size city such as ours, relationships are key and not organizations, per se. Both academic and practicing anthropologists work at relationship building through a variety of activities including parties, dinners, conferences, committees. Creating an environment and events that foster interaction and relationship building has been key in the experience here. After all, people get together mainly because they want to see and talk with each other.

LPOs can help by

> providing a network for students to meet practitioners. LPOs can play an important role in allowing students to network with practitioners, which in turn provides a wonderful opportunity not only for internships, but also for future research and employment opportunities.

> To date, such an involvement has been relatively limited. We are more likely to draw on our own (deep) networks of program alumni who live in the region to help out with departmental initiatives. It would be good to strengthen our relationship with the LPO, but most of our focus is on strengthening the alumni network and ties in the area.

> One of our faculty members and a couple students started an LPO several years ago, but it only lasted a year. We haven't had any problems getting practitioners to speak to our classes, but we had less success with the LPO.

> Our relationship with our LPO here has been an important one, especially, although certainly not solely, for our students. The relationship varies from year to year, depending in part on how much energy comes out of the LPO at any given time, and in part on the extent to which faculty make a point of encouraging student involvement. Last year we hosted an LPO meeting on campus, for the first time ever. I think that worked well.

Discussion and Conclusions

Drawing on our own experiences, the reports of the five departments, and a myriad of conversations with colleagues from across the country over our careers, we return to the initial issues raised in this chapter: What existing mechanisms encourage strong and positive relationships between practitioners and the academy? Why are such liaisons important for the education of anthropology students? What barriers are there to productive and smooth academic–practitioner relationships? What positive trends promote the building and sustaining of academic–practitioner bonds?

Mechanisms for advancing academic–practitioner relationships

To be successful in establishing these relationships, faculty members in anthropology programs within the academy and their practicing anthropology partners need to be firmly committed to developing them at local, regional, national, and/or international levels. Without firm commitment, collaborations are apt to founder and fail. Depending on the scholarly and teaching interests of anthropologists in a particular university or college, different collaborative projects should be developed which involve students. It is important to recognize from the start that such collaborations typically take considerable time to establish and to sustain, and it is important that all parties see the benefit of investing in such projects. Being intentional and transparent are helpful qualities. It is important to recognize that in order to develop such collaborative programs, *relationships* must be created and nourished. That is critical to success.

Benefits to students

We take the position that it is essential, not optional, to facilitate and encourage student connections with anthropological practitioners and others outside of the academic realm. Anthropological organizations, departments, and individual anthropologists have recognized for decades that increasing numbers of anthropologists with doctoral degrees and virtually all with master's find jobs outside of academic settings. Aside from all the qualitative benefits that can accrue to students who are educated in programs which prepare them for a range of occupational niches (in short, giving them options), anthropology programs have a responsibility for (1) opening students' minds to occupational choices and (2) providing the necessary education, training, and experience for students to be able to enter a range of job sectors. Both of these objectives are much more likely to be realized if anthropology faculty and practicing anthropologists work together for the benefit of students. We argue that anthropology programs which do not address this reality in helping to prepare their students for a range of occupational sectors are behaving irresponsibly. At the same time, practicing alumni can play a very important role in departments by coming on campus to teach classes or by offering distance learning classes. In fact, practicing alumni can be a tremendous resource for departments through serving in collaborative adjunct, advisory, and research positions.

Barriers

To be perfectly honest, these kinds of goals are not easy to attain. For a department to be successful with plans for robust academic–practitioner collaborations, a consensus among faculty is important. Ideally all faculty members buy into such a mission; at the very least, a majority of the faculty should make such a commitment. That does not mean that all faculty need to be working in a particular subfield of anthropology; a mixture is often preferable. Practitioner anthropologists are active in all subfields of anthropology. When the department has made a commitment to offer applied and practicing anthropology, developing such collaborations tends to be easier since it fits the "mission." Additionally, within the university setting, the more the university envisions itself as an engaged institution, the greater the chances that such initiatives from anthropologists will be applauded, supported, and rewarded. When that kind of agreement does not exist, it can be a formidable barrier.

Another type of barrier has to do with the employment demands of many working practitioners. They are typically rewarded for different activities and products than academically based anthropologists. Rather than peer-reviewed, refereed articles or monographs, they tend to produce reports to agencies or to consultant firms, and so on. In short, the day-to-day lives of practitioners and academic anthropologists differ in terms of reward structures and time frames. If such differences are acknowledged and allowance made for them in collaborative work, they can be transformed from barriers to benefits for students, especially as they learn from both worlds.

Positive trends toward integration

Over the past decade a number of developments within anthropology demonstrate movement in the direction of more and closer ties between academic and practicing anthropologists. There has been a notable increase in master's and doctoral programs focused on applied anthropology which, in turn, tend to be more open to establishing productive working relationships with practitioners. This growth in applied degree programs is reflected in the creation (self-organization) of the Consortium of Practicing and Applied Anthropology Programs (COPAA) in 2000, currently with 28 member departments (www.copaa.info). COPAA is an independent consortium dedicated to encouraging greater collaboration across departments to advance the place of practicing and applied anthropology within the discipline.

Second, attention to practice has increased in our national anthropology organizations in significant ways. The Society for Applied Anthropology and the National Association for the Practice of Anthropology both have ongoing efforts to link graduate students to employment opportunities (such as the NAPA-sponsored Employer Expo) and to increase the role and importance of practicing and applied anthropology in annual meetings.

In addition to these opportunities, in 2007, on the recommendation of the Practicing Advisory Work Group (PAWG), the AAA agreed to establish a new standing committee that cuts across all sections and sub-disciplines in anthropology, providing a voice for common interests of practice, applied, and public interest anthropologists and greater visibility within the organization. The Committee on Practicing, Applied, and Public Interest Anthropology (CoPAPIA) was created to undertake initiatives that deal directly with the issues of the academy–practice relationship. One of the first initiatives was to develop baseline survey data on the growth and status of master's-level graduates in anthropology and their careers and employment (Fiske et al. 2010). In addition, CoPAPIA has established a continuing line of communication with section leaders on topics of concern to them each year, such as creating "Places and Spaces for Practitioners" in sections (Colwell-Chanthaphonh et al. 2009: 20; 2010: 13). In 2010, CoPAPIA, in collaboration with COPAA, acknowledged the need to address tenure and promotion standards which undervalue the kinds of products (reports, videos, community service work) of academically based anthropologists who are practicing, applied, public interest, or engaged anthropologists as they apply for tenure and promotion. The "Guidelines for Evaluating Scholarship in the Realm of Practicing, Applied, and Public Interest Anthropology for Academic Promotion and Tenure" (AAA 2011) were approved by the AAA Executive Board in 2011 and are posted on the AAA website for departments' use.

Another reflection of increasingly positive connection with practice is the increase in the number of publications that deal directly with preparing for careers and employment outside of academia, that is as practicing anthropologists. Examples of recently published books include Stephens (2002); Gwynne (2003a, 2003b); Nolan (2003); Briller and Goldmacher (2009); and Ellick and Watkins (2011).

At the department level, the growth in the number of departments that have developed interactive alumni networks is an impressive marker of growing integration of practice and applied academic interests. Alumni networks provide a sense of continued belonging to alumni who are in practicing positions. Newsletters are very helpful in communicating occupational possibilities for students and advance a sense of belonging to one's home department. Some departments hold alumni reunions. In April 2012 the University of Memphis' Department of Anthropology celebrated the thirty-fifth anniversary of its master's program in applied anthropology with a reunion that drew alumni from all over the country as well as the Mid-South. The engagement with practitioners in Memphis has been a positive success story, culminating in graduates who have pursued successful careers and return to campus as colleagues and peers of faculty who had encouraged them 35 years earlier.

We would like to conclude with the observation that anthropology alumni – whether they enter academic employment or become practicing anthropologists (or some of both) – offer an invaluable resource as our academic programs at undergraduate, master's, and doctoral levels aim to provide and facilitate movement toward positive academic–practitioner relationships.

Note

1   This and subsequent quotations in this section are from email communications with our colleagues, whose input to this chapter we acknowledge: Sherylyn Briller (Wayne State University); Erve Chambers (University of Maryland); Lisa Henry (University of North Texas); Stanley Hyland (University of Memphis); and Nancy Romero-Daza (University of South Florida).

References

AAA (2011) "Guidelines for Evaluating Scholarship in the Realm of Practicing, Applied, and Public Interest Anthropology for Academic Promotion and Tenure." At http://www.aaanet.org/resources/departments/upload/Final-T-P-Document-2011.pdf, accessed Sept. 6, 2012.

Briller, Sherylyn and Amy Goldmacher (2008) *Designing an Anthropology Career*. Lanham, MD: AltaMira Press.

Colwell-Chanthaphonh, Chip, Linda A. Bennett, and Nathaniel Tashima (2009) "Places for Practitioners in AAA Sections." *Anthropology Newsletter* 50(5): 20.

Colwell-Chanthaphonh, Chip, Linda A. Bennett, and Nathaniel Tashima (2010) "Places for Practitioners in AAA Sections II." *Anthropology Newsletter* 51(2): 13.

Ellick, Carol J. and Joe E. Watkins (2011) *The Anthropology Graduate's Guide: From Student to a Career*. Walnut Creek, CA: Left Coast Press.

Fiske, Shirley J., Linda A. Bennett, Patricia Ensworth, et al. (2010) *The Changing Face of Anthropology: Anthropology Masters Reflect on Education, Careers, and Professional Organizations. The AAA/CoPAPIA 2009 Anthropology MA Career Survey*. Arlington, VA: American Anthropological Association.

Gwynne, Margaret A. (2003a) *Anthropology Career Resources Handbook*. Boston: Pearson Education.

Gwynne, Margaret A. (2003b) *Applied Anthropology: A Career-Oriented Approach*. Boston: Pearson Education.

Nolan, Riall W. (2003) *Anthropology in Practice: Building a Career outside the Academy*. Boulder, CO: Lynne Rienner.

Stephens, W. Richard (2002) *Careers in Anthropology: What an Anthropology Degree Can Do for You*. Boston: Allyn & Bacon.

Chapter 28

Professional Communication

Nathaniel Tashima and Cathleen Crain

The ability to communicate clearly and persuasively to diverse audiences is a key professional prerequisite. Niel Tashima and Cathleen Crain draw on their extensive experience in doing just this, to provide us with a clear and practical chapter which looks in detail at some of the most important forms of professional communication, and how to approach them effectively. They first cover oral presentations, including the use of visuals, offering a variety of tips on avoiding the common pitfalls. They then discuss interviews (and being interviewed) and different types of written presentations.

Introduction

Learning to communicate effectively is an important part of becoming a successful professional anthropologist. Our communications are the means by which we can make a difference in people's lives through our professional work. As professionals we are called on to present information to other professionals, to community audiences, and to students. We must be equally effective in sharing our information in accessible and appropriate ways, regardless of who the audience is.

In this chapter we will discuss some of the key elements in professional communication. We will deal with ways to ensure that it is effective and also highlight some of the difficulties anthropologists encounter and the ways to overcome them. We will address both written and verbal communications.

A Handbook of Practicing Anthropology. First Edition. Edited by Riall W. Nolan.
© 2013 John Wiley & Sons, Inc. Published 2013 by John Wiley & Sons, Inc.

Oral Presentations

We have all endured oral presentations where the presenter could have emailed the presentation to each of us and we would have learned as much and been more entertained. Typical problems include:

- reading a paper without any audience contact;
- failing to stay within the time allotted;
- discarding sections of your presentation on the fly, leaving the audience puzzled at the key points and logical connections;
- reading PowerPoint slides verbatim while facing the screen;
- speaking too softly; and
- using language that the audience does not understand.

There are a number of other offenses committed by presenters that result in the audience not being engaged and the important information to be communicated being obscured. Knowing how to present well is a critical skill that will help you to succeed as a professional. We will discuss some ways of ensuring that you and your ideas are well received.

Assess your audience

As students, we are trained to present to professors and other students and to demonstrate our grasp of our discipline; we know this audience and how to impress it. The challenges are different for professionals, as there will be many audiences with diverse information needs, to which we should tailor our response to ensure their maximum learning. Therefore, it is essential that before you start to develop a presentation you do your best to understand who your audience will be and what their level of topic engagement is, that is, are they a lay or a professional audience for your area of presentation? Assess the level of language that will be appropriate to use in making your presentation. Presenting in a way that is inaccessible to your audience will not advance your interests or theirs. Try to think about what will be of special interest to your audience in your presentation; if they are advocates, for example, then you can shape your message to be most appropriate to them. In some instances, you will be invited to present because the sponsor believes that you have ideas or information to share that meets their needs.

Determine key points to communicate

Create a presentation that will allow you to make your key points and to have time (within the construction of the presentation) for questions and answers. Too often speakers fail to prioritize what is most important for the audience to learn. The tendency to pack it with too much information can make for a rushed presentation in which there is more than an audience can reasonably take in and appreciate. This is a critical point that we will come back to when we discuss other kinds of presentations. You must carefully gauge the time you have with each audience and their capacity to take in and understand what you are trying to say. If you try to communicate too much, the danger is that you will lose the audience and fail to communicate anything.

Practice, practice, practice

As you become more confident in making successful presentations, you will be able to draw up your presentation in a form that will allow you to speak on key points without having to read each sentence. While highly technical presentations may necessitate a verbatim rendering of information, anthropologically based presentations will rarely require such exactitude. Again, as noted earlier, avoid the use of highly technical language or jargon unless you are presenting to a technically or disciplinarily congruent audience. It may convey the exact meaning of your idea, but too often an audience will either be intimidated or tune you out if they are not similarly trained. Neither case will help you to communicate effectively.

You should know your topic and your materials well enough to be able to discuss them with an audience rather than reading a script. Here are some ideas on how to become comfortable with your presentation content:

- Your presentation should be about content that forms a linked group of ideas; if it does, you will be able to follow your own logic more easily.
- Begin by telling the audience briefly the purpose of your presentation, what you will present, and where you will end; this reinforces the logic and the construction of the presentation.
- Present each point in order, so that both you and your audience will understand where you are going and how you will get there.
- As anthropologists, one of our key skills is to capture and share the stories that illustrate important points about our subject. Using brief stories will help to illuminate data and to translate it into illustrations that the audience will retain long after the data have faded.
- Finally, sum up by briefly reviewing what you have presented and the conclusions.

Practice your presentation first for the amount of time it takes to make the full presentation with time for questions and answers if those are included in your allotted time. Most speakers find that when they are in front of an audience they are a bit nervous and tend to talk faster. You will need to practice speaking at a pace that will allow others to understand your points. Don't unnaturally slow your speech, but pace yourself so that you are not rushing through points.

Once you are clear on what you are going to say and the time you have, practice your presentation with a friend or speak in front of a mirror. See how your words sound and listen to what you say. If you practice with a friend, let them ask questions at the end to get comfortable with audience engagement.

Sharing your ideas

Determine whether it is usual for the venue of your presentation to provide handouts. These may be PowerPoint notes or a one-page synopsis of your presentation. If you are providing PowerPoint notes you should ensure that they are available to the audience before you begin. Enlisting someone to hand out the notes is better than trying to do it yourself, especially if you are nervous about the presentation. One-page summaries may be handed out before or after the presentation but are likely to be less disruptive to the overall flow of a panel if distributed before; again, it is best to ask someone else to hand them out. If you do give out PowerPoint notes or summaries, use this time to make eye contact with members of the audience, to walk through the space, and to be in comfortable charge of what is happening.

Take down the walls

One of the challenges for a good presenter is to reduce the distance between them and the audience. The distance, as indicated earlier, may be topic- and content-related, it may be presentation style, or it may be physical. We are going to continue to focus on some of the ways to reduce the psychic distance between you and your audience and then to address physical barriers.

Visual aids

Visual aids can be a wonderful way of illustrating what you are trying to communicate to your audience. We believe that may people are graphic learners, that is, they learn best through illustrations. So consider using graphics in addition to your words to convey meanings. And in using graphics and other illustrations, think about some of the following points.

PowerPoint is one of the most commonly used (and sometimes overused) visual aids at meetings. PowerPoint is ubiquitous at meetings in which oral presentations are made. Few people who use PowerPoint appear to have been trained to present information in a format that is helpful to the audience in understanding the points that the presenter is making. Having a well-crafted presentation that illustrates your presentation rather than duplicates it can make your points easier for the reader to grasp. Edward Tufte, who trained as a statistician, is an expert on visual presentations and has published a number of books on the subject (1990, 1997, 2001 [1983],

2003a, 2006). As an aspiring or new professional, you may find it helpful to read some of his work before using PowerPoint at professional meetings. He has particular criticisms of the use of PowerPoint, the ways in which it forces information to be presented and in which presenters utilize it as a tool. In an article entitled "PowerPoint is Evil" (2003b) Tufte writes:

> Presentations largely stand or fall on the quality, relevance, and integrity of the content. If your numbers are boring, then you've got the wrong numbers. If your words or images are not on point, making them dance in color won't make them relevant. Audience boredom is usually a content failure, not a decoration failure.
>
> At a minimum, a presentation format should do no harm. Yet the PowerPoint style routinely disrupts, dominates, and trivializes content. Thus PowerPoint presentations too often resemble a school play – very loud, very slow, and very simple.
>
> The practical conclusions are clear. PowerPoint is a competent slide manager and projector. But rather than supplementing a presentation, it has become a substitute for it. Such misuse ignores the most important rule of speaking: Respect your audience.

Whether or not you become an expert, here are some simple guidelines that will help you to make your presentation accessible and useful to your audience:

- Do not crowd the slide with narrative; use key points to which you provide the narrative.
- When showing charts and graphs, be sure that they are large enough to be read easily when projected, including any legends.
- Do not use highly colored or complicated PowerPoint templates as they will likely distract from the important points you want to make.
- When using a colored background, be sure that the font color provides sufficient contrast that it can be easily read.
- Do not use complicated bulleting or numbering systems as they will likely not enlighten the audience and may confuse them.
- Do not use fancy fonts as they are often difficult to read.
- Do not use more slides than you need to illustrate your key points; again, the slide should be ancillary to what you are saying.

And, in respect to your audience, do not read PowerPoint slides to them. There is nothing as dull as watching the back of the presenter's head as they read the slides. Maintaining eye contact with the audience is an important part of engaging people, as we will discuss further along.

Setting the stage

Before any presentation, try to go to the room in which the presentation will be made. The following are some things to look for in the venue.

- Sit in various places in the room to see what sight lines are like; if there are obstructed places you may want to ask people to move before you begin.
- Look at the size of the room and think about it in relationship to how many people are expected to attend the presentation. If the room is very large and the audience is expected to be small, then be prepared to ask the audience to move forward.
- For formal presentations at meetings, rooms are often set up classroom-style. In such a setting, the audience will likely respond as students. If you want them to be active as part of your presentation, you will need to think about either changing the set-up, or finding another way to overcome it.
- If the room is set up for the presentation, try speaking to see what you will sound like; if you will be using a microphone, try to practice with it so that you become more comfortable. Enlist a friend to work with you to help you to modulate your voice; being either too loud or too soft makes it difficult for the audience to listen to you comfortably.
- If you are making a presentation and are given the option to determine how the room is to be set up, take the opportunity to make it as appropriate for your presentation as possible. Here are some ways to consider your presentation space:
  - If you are doing a formal presentation at a meeting, then the formal classroom style is probably fine. If however, you are presenting material that is conducive to engaging the audience, then consider other set-up styles.
  - If you are training and want to be able to engage with individuals in a room, consider an open U-shape; this configuration allows you to stand at the end and see everyone's face. It also allows you to move into the U to engage with participants. This configuration also allows all participants to see one another easily which can encourage discussion within the group.
  - If you are conducting an informal discussion-type of presentation you may want simply to have chairs in a circle or a semi-circle.

As you gain experience in presenting, think about each presentation and how you will manage it for the best outcome.

Owning the room

Learning to act confidently will help you to feel confident in making presentations. Many presenters act out their lack of confidence and this is transmitted clearly to the audience. In this section, we will talk about some of the ways to engender confidence in you both in yourself and in the audience.

The physical aspects of presenting

Most presentations will be set up with a podium and a computer. This set-up creates a box into which most people feel they are expected to work. In some cases, you may decide that it is best to work within the box. However, stepping outside of the box changes both you and your relationship with the audience.

Take command of the space Move out from behind the podium if the venue and the kind of presentation allows for it. This immediately places you in a better relationship with the audience. If you know your material, the podium will not be necessary; PowerPoint can be run by someone else or with the remote. You can have notes to which you refer even as you move away from the podium. Eventually this kind of movement will become very natural and a normal part of your presentation style. When you first use it, you may want to assume a position near the podium or even to to place your notes on the podium. Moving to different positions at the front of the audience may also allow you to address different parts of the audience and to signal changes of subject.

Use your voice It is important to remember that part of being a good presenter is to use your voice to illustrate your thoughts. You can be serious without speaking in a monotone; you can be funny without shouting or laughing. Varying your tone also helps to signal to the audience the content they are hearing, reinforcing and deepening what you are saying.

While a presentation is not strictly theater, it is a form of art to engage, educate, and entertain. You may be asking why we should care about the entertainment aspect of presentations. The answer is simple: It is our experience that when people are being entertained, they pay better attention than when they are listening to a lecture. When people smile or laugh, they open up to new learning. We often present on very serious topics and use entertaining illustrations or even cartoons to make a point; people remember the points. We are not suggesting that you should try to do stand-up comedy but rather that you think about keeping people engaged and learning from your presentation.

Make eye contact One of the very distracting things some speakers do is look at anything except the audience. This is particularly easy if they are reading their paper or the PowerPoint slides. An easy way to make eye contact is to pick several people in the room as points to focus on: near, far, left, right, center. Then speak to them. It will shift your focus, makes the audience feel as though you are really talking to them personally. This technique will also help you to remember not to focus on any one point in the room.

Enjoy your presentation This may be particularly difficult for those who find presenting to be one of the levels of hell. You are a professional who has been afforded an opportunity to share knowledge with others. You have an audience that is interested in hearing what you have to say. You have the opportunity to educate people by engaging them on a topic that has been important and interesting to you. And remember to smile – everything you say is not deadly serious.

In this section we have discussed how to make an in-person presentation; if your presentation is to be conducted electronically, by webcast, or over another electronic medium, the same principles apply.

Interviews

Being the subject of an interview can be particularly challenging for anthropologists as well as for other social scientists. In this section we will present some of the challenges and the ways to address them. Most of the information in this section will work well for interviews that are broadcast or presented in print.

Setting the context and rules

Most interviews are set up to be unscripted, even if topic-centered. That opens the door for the interviewer to ask any question that occurs to them, whether or not it is germane to your work. No matter how clever and educated someone is, it is easy to be dragged into talking about things about which you know nothing. "So, Dr. X, you were looking at housing patterns for USAID in Z country. How do religious and sexual customs affect the migration of people to the cities?" Well, you can either try to answer the question and perhaps find yourself wandering in the wilderness and saying unusual things; or try to reframe the question so that it bears some relation to what you were actually doing in country Z without alienating the interviewer or embarrassing your sponsor.

To reduce the likelihood of such an awkward situation, the first issue in agreeing to an interview is to discuss how the interview will be conducted and what topics will be covered. Ask the interviewer to send you the questions that they want to discuss several days in advance of the interview. Read the questions carefully and send back corrections to the assumptions that are unclear or incorrect. Then ask for agreement about the final list of questions. Also, be clear about who will be conducting the interview; if Howard Stern is the interviewer it may present particular challenges to a serious discussion of your research. You also need to know who the audience will be, how long the interview will last, and in what specific fora the final product will be used (newspapers, magazine, e-zine, etc.). You need to be sure that the information will not be used to embarrass your sponsor, employer, or you. It is important to remember that you are sharing your intellectual capital with others and that the way in which is it represented is important to you.

Conducting the interview

Whether the interview is live or is being recorded for transcription, it is important to take your time in answering a question. It is easy to be nervous, rush into an answer, and say something less than profound. There are lots of ways to think while considering your response. Some of those ways include repeating the question in an affirmative way, taking a drink of water, asking for clarification, verbally analyzing the question and then choosing the parts you want to take on and the order in which you answer them (or don't). And, if the question is outside of your area of expertise or comfort, you can deflect the question by saying so, and at the same time reframe it to focus on your area of expertise and/or comfort.

If in setting the context and rules for the interview, you have specified that there are areas that are out of bounds, you should deflect any question that violates the rules. This can be done diplomatically by saying something like, "Sorry Howard, as we discussed, that's not an area on which I can comment." You need to be confident and in control of where the interview goes and that it does not violate your boundaries. If an interviewer repeatedly tries to go past your boundaries, you may want to stop the interview.

After the interview

If the interview is for an article, you can ask to see the article before it is published; this should be a part of the context and rules. Many journalists will be uncomfortable with that kind of request, but writers for magazines or websites may be more accommodating. It is important to emphasize that your interest is in fact checking, not in trying to challenge their journalism. If you see errors in fact, you should correct them. If you find that they have misconstrued something, you should present them with information that corrects it. Most journalists want their interviews to result in something that will inform a particular public.

Written Presentations

Written presentations are likely to be the kind of presentation that you have the most experience in developing. Term papers are probably most familiar for new and aspiring professional anthropologists, followed by theses and dissertations. Some people will have been encouraged to develop journal articles either as a function of solo research or as part of team research. The development of these kinds of documents is important in learning how to create the structure of a document, present information clearly, and be held to rigorous standards regarding the quality of your science. There will be a variety of new types of documents that you, as a professional anthropologist, will need to learn to develop for a variety of non-academic audiences.

No matter what the presentation, there are some general guidelines that will support the effectiveness of the document.

- Set out the document in an outline that includes topic sentences before beginning to write.
- Use language that is accessible and meaningful to the audience.
- Use both narrative and illustrations (graphics, charts, tables) to make your key points.

- Don't overcrowd pages; use white space to let the reader rest.
- Use simple fonts and avoid excessively large or small fonts.
- Use a standard structure for your outline; avoid using too many levels that may confuse the reader.

Possibly the greatest challenge for anthropologists is to determine the level and amount of information that is needed. Leveling the presentation so that the audience can understand and appreciate what is being presented is critical, as discussed earlier. This is about the topical depth of knowledge needed to understand your point, as well as the sophistication of the language you use. If, for either reason, your reader cannot understand what you are saying, then the document cannot succeed.

The amount of information that is presented to the reader is a second challenge. For many anthropologists, there appears to be a biological imperative to present everything known about the topic. For most professional writing, you will need to determine how much a reader needs to know to understand your point, and then craft your presentation to meet that need. For some presentations, such as a briefing document or even an executive summary, you will need to distill your information to the most important few points. This is a challenge to accomplish when you believe that the reader needs to understand the whole history or the whole body of evidence. As a professional, your purpose is to move a policy or program agenda forward, to provide information from which people can made decisions or advocate. Your ability to present credible, succinct information will be an important part of becoming a professional anthropologist.

In this section, we will discuss some ways of planning and developing two kinds of effective documents.

Proposals

Developing proposals is a part of daily life for many professional anthropologists. A proposal challenges us to set out a project idea clearly and persuasively, how it will be conducted, what will come from the project, the time line in which it will be conducted, who will work on the project, and, finally, what it will cost. A proposal is a persuasive document and should be crafted to lead the reader to the understanding that you and your group are skilled, competent, and ready to conduct the project. In this section, we will briefly review some of the ways to make a proposal competitive.

Know the rules For most proposals, there is a request for application (RFA) or a request for proposal (RFP). In these or similar documents, the potential donor, sponsor, or funder sets out what they want to fund and what they need to know about you in order to consider your proposal. They will generally tell you how they want the document to be formatted, how long it should be, and what should go into any appendices or annexes. It is a bonus if you are given guidance on how each topic within a section is to be addressed.

If, when you review an RFP, there are items that are unclear or are in conflict with other instructions in the RFP, prepare and submit questions. Most sponsors are more than willing to respond to questions, as they want the proposals they receive to be responsive to their needs.

The very first activity in preparing a proposal is to develop an outline that includes all the required elements. As with any other document outline, this one should be specific and should include topic sentences. And if the RFP calls for the same or closely related information to be presented three times, present it three times or however often it is requested. It is important to remember that the proposal is for the sponsor and they set out the requirements; your job is to follow the requirements carefully.

For proposals, it is useful to add the evaluation points or weight to each section in the outline; that will help you to remember how the sponsor views the importance of the section. Give yourself an estimate of how many pages it will take to cover the topic fully, making sure that the number of pages overall doesn't exceed the allowed number.

Once you have answers to your questions, a clear outline, and a firm grasp of what the sponsor wants, you are ready to write. The rules for this kind of writing are not significantly different from those cited in the section on written presentations. The one significant difference, however, is that this is a document that aims to persuade the sponsor both that you know how to do the work that is being contemplated and that you will be the best person to do it. This is particularly challenging for anthropologists who tend not to be forward about being great at their jobs. This is the time to advance that case without being arrogant or less than factual. Saying that you have five years of professional evaluation experience in sub-Saharan Africa is factual; saying that you have five years of successful evaluation practice with international donors and nongovernmental organizations working across sub-Saharan Africa adds important but still factual elements to the statement.

When you have finished the proposal, ensure that you have covered the following points before submitting:

- The page and font limits, and other construction requirements, have been carefully followed.
- The proposal structure reflects what was requested in the RFP and corresponds to the evaluation criteria.
- You have made a clear and persuasive argument for the soundness of your approach, your capabilities, and the skills of the team.

Reports

A report is a formal vehicle for presenting information regarding a project or research. You should view a report as an opportunity to showcase the work that has been conducted and to share salient findings and recommendations. All the guidelines that have been provided earlier in this chapter are relevant to the development of reports. Reports are special in that they can be enduring documents that represent a body of work. They are also a product that you and your sponsor need to work together to design.

The purpose and audience for the report should be determined with the sponsor before any writing is undertaken. There may be several possible purposes for a report, which may include accounting for the funding spent on a program; sharing interesting findings with a larger audience; publicizing the utility of an initiative with internal organizational sponsors; and reporting findings back to partners or a community. Clearly, the purposes and audiences are going to drive how the report is designed, including the level of language used. And the report may have multiple purposes and multiple audiences, requiring a high degree of finesse to speak clearly to each.

Generally, reports will have the following features:

- An executive summary: This is a document that summarizes the whole report in a few pages; this is where the topline findings are particularly important. This is a very important section, as it may be the only one policy-makers and funders actually read. Generally the executive summary is written last.
- An introduction and background section: This section allows you to set out the context for the work that was conducted and to introduce the report to the reader. Remember the good writing adage: tell them what you will tell them, tell them, and then tell them what you told them. This is particularly important for reports that may be long and complex documents, as it frames the report and guides the reader.
- A section on the methods used to develop the information that you are reporting (if applicable) is standard. This does not have to be a long section but should provide the reader with an overview of how you designed the study, evaluation, or research; how you collected and managed the information (including appropriate participant protection measures); and how you analyzed the information.
- The body of the report should focus on the reporting of the information that you are presenting.
- A section on conclusions and recommendations should be the last section of the report.
- Appendices and annexes may be provided as appropriate.

As a good anthropologist, you will have observations and stories from your work, some of which should be included to illustrate your key points.

The length of the report should be in keeping with its purpose and audience, which you and your sponsor will have discussed. A big report does not necessarily accrue extra points in professional life.

Final Thoughts

You will have interesting opportunities as a professional to share your insights with others both through presentations and through written documents. Taking those opportunities and maximizing the potential for the best communication will be a challenge. If you communicate well, your potential for influencing and affecting the field in which you work will increase.

References

Tufte, Edward R. (2001 [1983]) *The Visual Display of Quantitative Information*, 2nd edn. Cheshire, CT: Graphics Press.

Tufte, Edward R. (1990) *Envisioning Information*. Cheshire, CT: Graphics Press.

Tufte, Edward R. (1997) *Visual Explanations: Images and Quantities, Evidence and Narrative*. Cheshire, CT: Graphics Press.

Tufte, Edward R. (2003a) *The Cognitive Style of PowerPoint*. Cheshire, CT: Graphics Press.

Tufte, Edward R. (2003b) "PowerPoint is Evil." *Wired* 11(9). At http://www.wired.com/wired/archive/11.09/ppt2.html, accessed Sept. 6, 2012.

Tufte, Edward R. (2006) *Beautiful Evidence*. Cheshire, CT: Graphics Press.

Chapter 29

Working on Cross-Disciplinary Teams

Mari H. Clarke

Teamwork is stressed by almost all practicing anthropologists as a key element in today's workplace, and yet most of us are still trained as individual researchers. Mari Clarke discusses teamwork in this chapter, and in particular, teamwork with people from diverse disciplines. Drawing on her own professional experience in a variety of settings, Clarke shows how communication and an appreciation for how people from other disciplines think can enhance professional effectiveness. She provides details of how she worked as an anthropologist practitioner in a variety of contexts, and offers an extensive list of tips and suggestions for teamwork, team building, and training.

Some say that anthropological training does not prepare students for cross-disciplinary teamwork, but that was not my experience. I sought out cross-disciplinary opportunities for the same reason that I switched from psychology to anthropology for my undergraduate major – I was intrigued by the relationships between the various domains carved out by different disciplines. Anthropology's holistic perspective, with the four-field approach encompassing cultural anthropology, physical anthropology, archaeology, and linguistics, as well as its human or social focus, was much more intellectually challenging to me than other, more narrowly focused, disciplines. I also found collaborative work much more appealing than working as a solitary scholar. So my own inclinations and a great deal of luck set me on a path that provided me with valuable skills and some excellent opportunities for practicing anthropology on cross-disciplinary teams. Viewing each new challenging combination

A Handbook of Practicing Anthropology. First Edition. Edited by Riall W. Nolan.
© 2013 John Wiley & Sons, Inc. Published 2013 by John Wiley & Sons, Inc.

of people and disciplines as a learning experience was very important in helping me keep my eyes and ears open to new perspectives, approaches, and opportunities.

Anthropological Building Blocks for Cross-Disciplinary Teamwork

Cultural ecology and regional research

Practical, hands-on "learning by doing" is an effective approach to fieldwork and to understanding the perspectives and approaches of other disciplines. My graduate study at the University of Pennsylvania focused on cultural ecology, mentored by Robert Netting (1977, 1980). Our readings reached out beyond anthropological literature to ecology and systems theory. My interest lay at the interface between social organization, economy, and environment as they changed over time. Netting facilitated my opportunity to work on the regional Argolid Exploration Project, led by classical archaeologists, which examined structures and artifacts from prehistoric to modern times. The cross-disciplinary team included classical archaeologists, medieval and modern historians, geographers, geologists, and specialists in soil science, carbon dating, plants, shells, aerial photography (using a hot air balloon), and pottery restoration as well as anthropologists. My role, along with that of three other fellow anthropologists, was to explain how contemporary villagers used the material culture excavated by the archaeologists. My experience in undergraduate archaeology summer field schools and conservation work during the year enabled me to participate at the prehistoric site. This provided a better understanding of the regional project and an opportunity to explore potential field sites. Unlike my previous excavation experience, there was a gendered division of labor. Women washed and cataloged finds (fragments of pottery, shells, bones, stone tools) while men oversaw the male Greek workers who excavated the site, in the tradition of classical archaeology. Participating on the archaeological team enhanced my credibility. We also had a strong champion in the project director, Michael Jameson, who persuaded others that our work was important. Recognition of our value to the project continued to grow as our knowledge of the cultural ecology of the region deepened beyond mere background reading knowledge to a grounded understanding of how people used the environment and the material culture. We worked with villagers in their fields and households, growing, processing, and celebrating the crops and livestock (New York Academy of Sciences 1976; Sutton 2000).

Public policy and families

Finding a useful role that complements the team and builds on your strength, but does not infringe on the roles of other team members, has been valuable throughout my career. During my graduate studies I worked as a program coordinator for anthropologist Carol Stack, at Duke University Institute of Policy Sciences and Public Affairs. This raised my awareness of public policy and advocacy as well as the contributions an anthropological perspective can make to changing stereotypes and policies (see Stack 1973 for an example of this). With a grant from the National Institute of Health, Stack established a postdoctoral program guiding social scientists' research on the impacts of public policies on American families. The fellows included three anthropologists, a historian, and an attorney. One way I was able to make myself useful to Stack and the fellows was by editing drafts of advocacy papers on their policy studies and assisting in organizing a large conference on the family and the state – thus enriching my toolkit of skills to bring to other interdisciplinary settings where the differences in perspective were much greater.

Adding Cross-Disciplinary Communication Skills

Good communication skills are essential in cross-disciplinary work and teamwork across and within disciplines. Excellent writing skills are necessary but not sufficient; a multimedia approach is required, with the use of sound and image as well. Even more important are active listening skills – granting your colleagues the same undivided attention you give to informants in fieldwork. At the University of Pennsylvania, I took courses on kinesics (the study of human body motion and communication) from Ray Birdwhistle (1970), who also discussed the work of Edward T. Hall and Erving Goffman, and which broadened my understanding of non-verbal communications. I was fortunate to have additional opportunities to broaden my communication horizons early in my career.

AAAS Mass Media Fellows program

Aiming to enhance the quality of science journalism, the American Association for the Advancement of Science initiated a Mass Media Fellows program to encourage a wide array of scientists, including social scientists, to contribute to science news coverage. After a crash course in news writing, we fanned out across the country to newspapers, magazines, and television and radio studios. I worked at the *Raleigh News and Observer*, covering medical research in the Research Triangle.[1] Multiple red marks on my initial copy persuaded me to use plain English and emulate Ernest Hemingway, not Claude Lévi-Strauss. Work in the newsroom also introduced me to real deadlines. The need to get words on paper, ready for publishing, shortly after doing interviews, was in sharp contrast to the lengthy pondering, reviewing, discussion, and rewriting that accompanied my academic writing. The ability to write clearly and rapidly is a valued asset on any team.

Instructional design and educational media

Adding another field to one's professional repertoire enhances opportunities and gives a deeper basis for cross-disciplinary collaboration. As a visual thinker, I was drawn to the instructional design program in the School of Education at the University of North Carolina in Chapel Hill because the director of the program, Ralph Wileman (1980), emphasized the transformation of complex information into simple, bold, visual communications. The program also had links to international development work opportunities through instructional design graduates and Wileman's own international work. I learned a systems approach to instructional design (Gagné and Briggs 1979) which provided solid grounding in evaluation methodology, adult learning theory, and active learning. Also valuable was the requirement to do internships to apply classroom learning in work settings. I worked for the Environmental Protection Agency, developing training modules on pollutants and their sources, and helping to transform very technical material into concrete practical words and pictures that non-technical readers could understand. My internships provided valuable additions to my résumé which, at that time, was very thin on employment experience.

Practicing Anthropology on Cross-Disciplinary Teams

As I moved on to employment, my learning continued on the job in my work on various aspects of international development, with colleagues from different disciplines. I highlight a few examples that illustrate the challenges faced and the approaches that have worked for me in cross-disciplinary teamwork.

Program for International Training in Health

My degree in instructional design opened the door at the Program for International Training in Health (INTRAH), which focused on maternal and child health and family planning in Africa and the Middle East. Doctors and public health professionals, as well as nurse midwives, led INTRAH. I was the only anthropologist. Our team of four instructional designers developed training materials for nurse midwives and health educators, including a manual on *Teaching and Learning with Visual Aids* (Fetter et al. 1987). We worked with health professionals as subject matter experts who ensured that the materials we produced were technically correct. I incorporated an anthropological perspective in this work by providing suggestions for the adaptation of training materials to take into account the cultural and social practices are well as the specific health needs in different countries. This fitted well with health behavioral change communication research findings showing the influence of sociocultural factors on health-related behavior. It was important to find a niche for anthropological inputs that was compatible with the health professionals' goals and models.

INTRAH also had a small evaluation unit staffed by health evaluation professionals. Recognizing a good opportunity, I participated in the evaluation coordinating group that included members from different units. Thus I enhanced my experience with evaluation methodologies, a very important area of expertise in a practicing anthropologist's toolkit.

There was also a training unit focused on training health professionals from Africa and the Middle East. I was also involved in training nurse midwives in Egypt, Turkey, Kenya, and Sierra Leone in how to use visual aids effectively to teach people about maternal and child health. In preparation for this work, INTRAH sent me to an intensive trainers' course on participatory training for adults. As I have continued to hone these skills through other training opportunities and practice, active listening, facilitation, group dynamics, and experiential learning have served me very well, enabling me to design and deliver culturally informed participatory training (see Table 29.1).

Table 29.1   Training skills

Active listening focuses on the verbal and non-verbal messages of the person speaking in order to understand what they are saying and then repeats what you have understood in the form of a question. It is not necessary to agree with the speaker, just to understand their message.

Facilitation makes it easy for others to talk and learn together. An effective facilitator does the following:
- reminds the group of their experience and expertise;
- listens more than talks;
- keeps the group focused on task and process;
- remains neutral;
- asks frequently if there are questions;
- recognizes signs of confusion (puzzled looks, asking neighbors questions, resistance);
- encourages everyone to participate;
- recognizes that individuals participate in different ways – some may talk only in small groups, others constantly but contribute little;
- helps keep the group within time constraints;
- protects participants from attacks by others;
- energizes the group or slows it down as needed;
- recaps, occasionally, what happened in the training event and helps the group make connections between sessions.

Group dynamics includes the communication patterns, decision-making methods, member behaviors and relationships within groups. This includes the *content* of the group discussions, tasks, debates, and the *process* by which the group functions – interpersonal relations, and the handling of disagreements.

Experiential learning provides learners with opportunities to apply what they are learning through role play, group problem solving, and on-site activities followed by analysis and discussion of the experience. This active learning approach sharply contrasts with the pedagogical approach based on lectures and exams where learners are passive recipients of knowledge.

USAID Office of Women in Development

Working in the United States Agency for International Development (USAID) Office of Women in Development (WID) plunged me deeply into the bureaucratic realities of bilateral development agency operations, as well as engagement in internal advocacy on gender issues at a time when this was viewed as a marginal special interest. I rapidly learned the USAID language of acronyms and commonly used phrases drawn from military and sports, such as bringing someone "on board" or "going on TDY."[2]

I joined the team as one of two anthropologists. The other anthropologist covered monitoring and evaluation while I focused on labor-market issues. There was also a trainer, an economist, a media specialist, and three civil service employees. Most of us worked as contractors for a technical support project. Our team conducted participatory gender and development training for USAID staff in Washington and on country missions, did policy analysis, provided inputs on project designs and evaluations, conducted gender analyses of country project portfolios, prepared briefing books for agency leaders, and engaged with the Development Assistance Committee Gender Working Group and the United Nations Commission for the Advancement of Women for UN Preparatory Conferences.

Kay Davies, the office director, and former congressional staffer of many years, mentored us on how to work the system. This included cultivating individual male champions for gender in development, building alliances with departments within USAID, cultivating support at the highest possible levels of leadership for attention to gender in agency policy, and building evidence for the economic case for addressing gender issues in development programs and policies – that investing in women and girls as well as men and boys promotes economic growth. Within USAID, we interfaced with economists, agronomists, labor analysts, evaluation experts, and career bureaucrats – both civil service and foreign service – as well as political appointees. Under Davies's guidance, we learned the hierarchies, roles, and power relationships of these players.

This was my first collaboration with economists. Anthropologist Gloria Davis's comparison of economists and anthropologists is a good reflection of the disciplinary differences that I faced. Where anthropologists and sociologists analyze people in their social context, looking at value and norms, economists usually examine individual economic responses to economic incentives and information, and characterize social factors as "extraneous variables." The anthropological analysis is holistic, contextual, qualitative, and often participatory with an emphasis on process, whereas the economic analysis is technically rigorous and quantitative, focusing on inputs and outputs. Both approaches have limitations. The economic approach is too reductionist to adapt to diverse situations; the anthropological approach is often too complex and context-specific to be policy-relevant (see Davis 2004 and Clarke 2012).

To bridge this disciplinary gap, I identified myself as an economic anthropologist with research experience on household economics.[3] I used economic terminology such as "distributional issues," "value-added," and "supply side" and "demand side." Also helpful was the growing interest in the "new institutional economics"[4] at high levels in USAID, which examine the social and legal norms, and the rules, that underlie economic activity. I rapidly added terms such as "transaction costs," "rent seekers," and "freeloaders" to my vocabulary. However, it was most effective to find areas of common ground on which I could support the most gender-resistant economists in meetings and through technical assistance. The head of the Economic Affairs Office was particularly resistant. I began to win him over by supporting his position on an issue in a large meeting of different offices, much to his surprise. He later turned to me when there was a concern about the keynote speaker for the annual USAID Economists Conference. A scholar from the University of Chicago was a rising star in the field but his paper consisted almost entirely of equations that the Economic Affairs Office staff could not understand. I called my academic mentor, Robert Netting, for advice. With is usual pragmatism, he said, "You are an anthropologist. This guy can talk. Ask him what the paper is about." I called the economist, explained the situation, asked for the core message of the paper, and recommended minimizing equations. The result was that his presentation was clearly understood and a great success, and this greatly enhanced my credibility and ability to work with the Economic Affairs Office.

Working in the WID Office raised my awareness of the importance of organizational culture and the differences between the organizational cultures in which we worked – United Nations agencies; other US government agencies such as the Department of Labor and the Census Bureau; other bilateral donors such as England, Norway, and Japan; as well as multilaterals such as the World Bank, and nongovernmental organizations such as CARE and Catholic Relief Services. Working with these different players in development required more than crossing disciplinary boundaries. It also entailed negotiating differences in organizational goals, policies, procedures, and acronyms, interlaced with cultural differences.

The Office of Private and Voluntary Cooperation

I directed a technical support contract for the USAID Office of Private and Voluntary Cooperation (PVC). I took over from a person who had moved to a position with USAID. Staff were already in place to arrange meetings of the Advisory Committee for Voluntary Foreign Aid,[5] provide technical support to PVC office operations, conduct special studies, work on evaluations, and manage the grant program, which included identifying technical reviewers for NGO grant proposals. The background of my young staff included two Peace Corps volunteers, an events manager, and an administrative assistant. Our team was dispirited by difficult personalities in the PVC office and uncertainties due to turnover in the management of the firm employing us. I organized an off-site participatory team-building retreat. Teams of two each organized team-building sessions so that everyone had a leading role. We looked at our working styles after taking a modified version of the Myers Briggs test for personality type, and assessed each other's strengths and weaknesses. In another team-building exercise, three people were blindfolded while others directed them to untangle a rope, but one was tasked to give them the wrong information. The team-building retreat helped me connect with my young staff members, boosted our morale in a difficult working situation, and developed better working relationships on our team. The stages of team development and tasks for team leaders at each stage summarized in Table 29.2 provide a useful guide for team maintenance.

Table 29.2   Stages of team development and tasks of team leaders

1. *Orientation:* exposure to different needs and styles creates ambiguity and anxiety.
   - Establish safe open environment for teamwork.
   - Facilitate learning about each other.
   - Clarify team purpose and tasks.
   - Provide structure through task and role clarification.
   - Set norms for interaction.
   - Encourage participation by everyone.
   - Promote open communication.
2. *Conflict:* direct or indirect challenges to leadership as individuals attempt to gain influence.
   - Clarify what the conflict is about through dialogue until all points of view are understood.
   - Identify common goals, find common ground, and establish members' preferred outcomes.
   - Discuss options to meet goals.
   - Define what can and cannot be done to change the situation.
   - Settle on a solution that everyone can accept.
   - Help all members understand what the solution means for them and to view it as a win–win situation.
3. *Collaborating:* members pull together as a cohesive unit, begin to negotiate roles; trust deepens.
   - Talk openly about issues and team members' concerns.
   - Encourage team members to provide feedback.
   - Delegate as much as possible to team members.
   - Use consensus decision-making.
4. *Productivity:* members are working together as a fully functioning team.
   - Collaboratively set goats to challenge all team members.
   - Look for ways to enhance team excellence.
   - Acknowledge individual contributions.
   - Use coaching and feedback to develop members' potential.
5. *Transformation:* team has reached intended goal and needs to redefine purpose or disband.
   - Facilitate decision-making on whether to redefine purpose or disband.
   - If disbanding, celebrate the accomplishments of the team.
   - If redefining purpose, review process of team development.

Based on Dearden et al. (2002).

These stages of team development are drawn from organizational theory on the common phases that most new teams go through as they evolve. For each stage of team development, the key tasks of team leaders are noted.

Centre for Development and Population Activities

After working with USAID on various contracts in Women in Development, Education, and Private and Voluntary Cooperation for nearly 15 years, I ventured into a new arena, assisting international NGOs in writing proposals for USAID funding. CEDPA (Centre for Development and Population Activities) soon hired me full-time to expand their US government funding. Other staff focused on corporate funding, foundations, and individual gifts. CEDPA's technical specialists came from public health, youth, leadership, advocacy, and evaluation, in addition to financial and human resources staff. CEDPA was known for its flagship women's leadership training and its capacity building for local organizations working on women's reproductive health issues. What was unique to CEDPA, and in contrast to my previous experience, was the predominance of women at all levels of the organization. Even the Board of Directors was primarily female. The organizational culture was very participatory and woman-friendly. Pregnancies were celebrated and maternity leave and other benefits were generous. However, the business model was not working.

USAID grants to NGOs such as CEDPA had been dramatically cut, replaced by large cooperative agreements and contracts awarded competitively to large consortia of private sector and NGO bidders. So CEDPA had to adapt and develop additional funding streams to survive. I was charged with making this happen in government funding, which necessitated teaming up with other organizations in large bids because CEDPA was too small to take the lead.

In addition to the cross-disciplinary perspectives that had to be taken into consideration when cultivating these bidding partnerships, there were also the competing business interests of the private sector firms and of other groups also vying for a place on a bid with the lead organization that appeared to have the best chance of winning. I rapidly researched existing contracts and the organizations working in CEDPA's areas of expertise, reviewed announcements on forthcoming requests for proposals (RFPs), and networked with former colleagues to identify potential funding opportunities, promising partnerships, and strengths and weaknesses of competitors. I arranged meetings to cultivate potential partners and persuade them that CEDPA brought a wealth of grassroots experience and expertise that could help them win the bid. Before these meetings I briefed CEDPA leaders about the organization's interests, capabilities, and competitive advantages, as well as those of competitors.

Watching the increasing amounts of funding that were going into HIV/AIDS prevention and treatment, I persuaded CEDPA leaders that this was an important direction for us to pursue and encouraged them to recruit HIV/AIDS experts. I also helped develop a PowerPoint presentation showing how CEDPA's grassroots women's reproductive health experience was important for HIV/AIDS prevention. This required research on HIV/AIDS prevention to ensure that we presented the right messages. Our pitch was successful. Once a piece of the project activity was negotiated for CEDPA, an agreement was signed; CEDPA focused on the prevention of mother-to-child transmission through women's reproductive health care and grassroots capacity building for HIV/AIDS support organizations.

Then the hard work of proposal writing began. Because the health professionals were also working on other projects, the time they had available for technical input or writing sections of proposals was limited. Coordinating with the schedules of the specialists of bidding partners made completing and harmonizing the pieces of the proposals all the more challenging. As initial screening of the proposals would be done using a checklist based on the RFP, we knew it was absolutely essential that our proposal responded to what USAID was looking for, particularly the criteria by which the proposals would be assessed, and that it included all the required documentation such as overhead rate, audits, board members, and staff bios. Although I concluded that the orchestration of multi-organizational proposals was not the way I wanted to spend the rest of my career, the time was well spent. I soon learned that proposal development skills enhance an anthropologist's "value added" on cross-disciplinary teams. Most of my recent work at the World Bank has been funded by trust funds for which I wrote or co-authored the proposal.

World Bank gender and infrastructure

In my most recent cross-disciplinary teamwork I have engaged with transport and mining engineers, water and energy experts, information technology specialists, and housing and municipal planning experts. Unlike USAID where the staff are American citizens with security clearance, the World Bank staff are very international at all levels except for the president. Michael Bamberger, a former World Bank evaluation expert, hired me as a graduate student to do a literature review on survival strategies of the poor in Kenya. When a colleague asked him to work on a gender and transport guide that they had initiated before he retired, Bamberger proposed me instead and briefed me on the initiative. I worked with team leader George Banjo, a transport specialist in the Africa region, and Wendy Walker, a fellow anthropologist who had already done work on the social dimensions of transport. The guide expanded from an Africa-specific list of points to a globally focused overview with an extensive virtual library on gender and transport.[6] Working on this guide provided me with a crash course on transport issues and technical constraints, and an entry point for additional work on gender and transport and other infrastructure sectors.

Fellow anthropologist Reidar Kvam, who currently leads the Quality and Policy Assurance Unit of the International Finance Corporation (IFC), uses an aerial photo of a road passing through a densely populated squatter settlement to contrast the mindset of road engineers, who want nuts-and-bolts solutions to transportation-related problems, with that of social scientists who analyze the complex dynamics in the "messy" margins where the road and human activities meet (Kvam 2010). Road engineers look for simple, technically sound solutions to problems. For example, maps showing increasing HIV/AIDS transmission along new roads convinced road engineers the solution to the problem was to require contractors to provide HIV/AIDs prevention education to construction workers and neighboring communities. Social scientists approach HIV/AIDS by looking at cultural concepts of masculinity, gender roles, and other factors affecting risky sexual behavior that leads to HIV/AIDS infection, the increasing care burden of HIV/AIDS-affected families, and the stigma attached to persons living with HIV/AIDS.

With the image of the messy margins of the road in mind, I present gender issues in transport in very concrete, operational, terms and engage supportive transport specialists to make the case to their counterparts.[7] I also conduct an extensive literature review on gender and other sociocultural dynamics in every country where I provide technical support so that I can share relevant data with transport task teams.

Supporting rural transport project task teams in in Papua New Guinea (PNG) and Vietnam, I focus on identifying women's as well as men's transport needs, involving women as well as men in routine road maintenance, incorporating erosion prevention measures in maintenance where possible, providing roadside market areas where needed, and, in PNG, developing women-owned transport for women to reduce the gender-based violence and theft experienced by women traveling to market. I am drafting a proposal for funding for a pilot on business development support for women road maintenance teams, market entrepreneurs, and transport entrepreneurs in PNG.

In summary I offer a few tips for anthropologists working on cross-disciplinary teams.

1. Learn the language of the disciplines represented on the team. Familiarize yourself with key assumptions, terminology, acronyms, and the aims of the practitioners for each discipline by reading recent reports, web pages, and other sources.
2. Learn the organizational culture and dynamics. Find out who the key stakeholders are, what the power relations are, who makes the decisions, and who allocates resources.
3. Provide clear, simple communication of necessary information:
   • avoid anthropological jargon;
   • avoid unnecessary complexity in presenting findings and recommendations;
   • provide only the necessary information, taking into account the role/task of the recipient (the higher the level, the more succinct and targeted the message needs to be).
4. Use a client-focused approach: be responsive to the client's priorities, rather than acting as an expert who arrives with all the answers. It is often necessary to help the client clarify objectives and prioritize what needs to be done so

they have a sense of ownership and commitment to the actions. It is also important to demonstrate practical knowledge of their sectors.

5. Focus on solutions. Critiques and problem analysis are not enough. Relevant, practical recommendations and strategies and approaches to solve problems are essential, phrased in terms that make sense to all disciplines involved.

6. Cultivate "champions" in other disciplines who recognize and promote the value of your skills and expertise.

7. Find points of common agreement rather than debating differences. Teamwork is about building trust and common understanding. An excellent way to do this is to support the perspectives and priorities of those from other disciplines when you agree with them.

8. Demonstrate your usefulness by finding opportunities to assist other team members or colleagues in achieving their goals rather than promoting yours. This not only enhances the trust and respect of your colleagues; it also can provide an entry point for your own agenda.

9. Pay attention to team dynamics. Talk about "us" not "me." Respond to different needs and styles. Facilitate participation by all and open communication. Clarify goals and mediate conflict. Celebrate accomplishments.

10. Acknowledge that reports, training events, and so on are authored and "owned" by the team. The products will be different from what you would produce on your own. It is essential to compromise unless there is a factual or policy error. Recognize members' contributions in meetings, report acknowledgments, and so on.

11. Use participatory facilitation techniques – create learning experiences rather than simply lecturing team members. Education research has demonstrated that learning is more effective and long-lasting when learners, particularly adults, have opportunities to apply new skills and knowledge and discuss the experience with others.

Notes

1. The Research Triangle area of North Carolina includes Raleigh (North Carolina State University), Durham (Duke University); Chapel Hill (University of North Carolina at Chapel Hill), and Research Triangle Park, the home of a range of pharmaceutical and other for-profit research institutions.

2. Bringing someone "on board" refers to hiring them or adding them to the team. "Going on TDY" (literally, "temporary duty assignment") refers to an overseas assignment of any length.

3. My dissertation research (Clark 1988) looked at household transformation in Greece, focusing on the changing interface between economic and social aspects of households as nearby Athens expanded. In addition to Netting and colleagues' *Households: Comparative and Historical Studies of the Domestic Group* (1984), and my own experience of working in international development at INTRAH, I was influenced by Smith (1976) and Wallerstein (1974).

4 People at high levels in USAID were reading North (1990), who defined institutions as humanly devised constraints that structure political, economic, and social interaction. Formal constraints include laws and property rights; informal constraints include customs and taboos.

5 The Advisory Committee for Voluntary Foreign Aid was established after World War II to provide a link between the US government and nongovernmental organizations active in humanitarian assistance.

6 The *Gender and Transport Resource Guide* is available online at http://www4.worldbank. org/afr/ssatp/Resources/HTML/Gender-RG/index.html, accessed Sept. 11, 2012.

7 Interviews that I conducted in preparation for a workshop on gender and transport revealed that transport professionals look to their peers to solve problems and find innovative approaches rather than to handbooks or other types of experts.

References

Birdwhistle, Ray (1970) *Kinesics and Context: Essays on Body Motion Communication.* Philadelphia: University of Pennsylvania Press.

Clark [Clarke], Mari H. (1988) *The Transformation of Households on Methana, Greece 1931–1987.* Ann Arbor, MI: UMI Dissertation Information Service.

Clarke, Mari (2012) "Engendering Transport: Mapping Men and Women on the Move." In Christina Wasson, Mary O. Butler, and Jacqueline Copeland-Carson (eds.), *Applying Anthropology in the Global Village.* Walnut Creek, CA. Left Coast Press, pp. 57–92.

Davis, Gloria (2004) *A History of the Social Development Network at the World Bank, 1973–2002.* Social Development Paper 56. Washington, DC: World Bank. At http://siteresources. worldbank.org/INTRANETSOCIALDEVELOPMENT/214578-1111735201184 /20502396/History+of+SD+in+WB.pdf, accessed Sept. 10, 2012.

Dearden Philip, Steve Jones, and Rolf Sartorius (2002) *Tools for Development: A Handbook for Those Engaged in Development Activity.* London: Performance and Effectiveness Department, United Kingdom Department for International Development (DfID).

Fetter, Katherine A., Catherine Murphy, Jo Ella Walters, and Mari Clark (1987)*Teaching and Learning with Visual Aids: A Resource Manual for Family Planning Trainers and Health Workers in Africa and the Middle East.* New York: Macmillan.

Gagné, Robert and Leslie Briggs (1979) *Principles of Instructional Design.* New York: Holt, Rinehart and Winston.

Kvam, Reidar (2010) "Gender Responsive Social Analysis in Transport Projects." Presentation at workshop on "Designing Inclusive Transport Operations," Jan. 28, Washington, DC. World Bank.

Netting, Robert (1977) *Cultural Ecology.* Menlo Park, CA: Cummings Publishing Co.

Netting, Robert (1980) "The Ecological Perspective: Holism and Scholasticism in Anthropology." In E. Adamson Hoebel, Richard Currier, and Susan Kaiser (eds.), *Crisis in Anthropology: View from Spring Hill.* New York: Garland Publishing, pp. 271–319.

Netting, Robert, Rick Wilk and Eric Arnould (1984) *Households: Comparative and Historical Studies of the Domestic Group.* Berkeley: University of California Press.

New York Academy of Sciences (1976) *Regional Variation in Modern Greece and Cyprus.* New York: New York Academy of Sciences.

North, Douglass (1990) *Institutions, Institutional Change and Economic Performance*. Cambridge: Cambridge University Press.

Smith, Carol (ed.) (1976) *Regional Analysis*, vol. 1: *Economic Systems*. New York: Academic Press.

Stack, Carol (1973) *All Our Kin: Strategies for Survival in a Black Community*. New York: Basic Books.

Sutton, Susan (ed.) (2000) *Contingent Countryside: Settlement, Economy, and Land Use in the Southern Argolid since 1700*. Stanford: Stanford University Press.

Wallerstein, Immanuel (1974) *The Modern World System: Capitalist Agriculture and the Origins of the European World Economy in the Sixteenth Century*. New York: Academic Press.

Wileman, Ralph E. (1980) *Exercises in Visual Thinking*. New York: Hastings House.

Chapter 30

Professional Networking for Practitioners

Paula Chambers

Paula Chambers freely admits that she is not an anthropologist. What she is, however, is the founder of one of the most successful professional networking and development sites for non-academic PhDs. She gives us a detailed look at how her own career developed after graduate school, how and why she decided to start her website, and what she has learned along the way. Anthropologist practitioners are not alone, and it is through networking with other professionals that practitioners come to see that there are not only common challenges, but common strategies for overcoming those challenges and building one's personal and professional capacities. Networking is essential for professional effectiveness, and Chambers provides both advice and encouragement for people at all stages of their careers.

Confession: I am not an anthropologist. I am a rhetoric and composition person who went through that PhD program in the English Department at Ohio State in the late 1990s. But my journey has a lot in common with yours. Like some of you, I was in the middle of my PhD program when I realized I would probably be happier in a non-academic career. I did leave the academy after finishing, then groped around for a satisfying career, slowly re-fashioning myself from academic, to ex-academic, to the new, completely different "applied" creature that I am today.

If you read no further than this paragraph, let me at least get across that there are many exciting futures out there for you – many possible versions of "you." Your identity is not fixed or stable. You are evolving now and will evolve further as a result of new experiences. You do not have to choose the "correct" post-academic career

A Handbook of Practicing Anthropology. First Edition. Edited by Riall W. Nolan.
© 2013 John Wiley & Sons, Inc. Published 2013 by John Wiley & Sons, Inc.

immediately on leaving the academy. You can start with just a *job*. From that job, whatever it is, you will visit new worlds, learn new things, meet new people, and relate with them. Through those experiences and relationships, you will evolve into your own "applied" self, with new skills, new knowledge, and many friends around you. No matter which direction(s) you take, other people, your friends and allies, will play important roles in your self-reinvention.

Here's how it happened for me. Though I enjoyed graduate school and had great advisers, I realized mid-program that I was temperamentally ill-suited to academic life. I loved teaching and research, but my proactive, impatient temperament made me feel a little out of step with the academy. I am highly social, curious about different cultures (as anthropologists, you probably share that curiosity), and preoccupied with the question "What impact am I having on society?" I want to solve problems and I want to solve them now.

Teaching initially seemed like a very impactful, problem-solving activity: in my mind, I was preparing the activists of the future to change the world with their fantastically persuasive writing. Several years and classes later, however, I came to feel one step removed: even if my students did go out and change the world as I hoped they would (which I had started to doubt), it would be them taking all the risks and having all the fun, not me. Also, I noticed that the further I advanced in my program, the smaller my reading audience became. My dissertation would be read by my committee, a dozen scholars, a couple of close friends, and my parents – at most.

Finally, I noticed how slowly things change in the academy. Problems in academic institutions seem to take forever to solve, particularly systemic problems. Like, for example, the problem that nobody had much information about what else a humanities PhD might do besides teach and do research. My institution didn't have information for me and neither did the Internet (this was 1999, when there was hardly anything out there on this topic). I thought to myself, "Somebody ought to create a mailing list server about non-academic careers for humanities PhDs, so we can support each other and exchange information without losing our academic reputations." Being a self-starter who likes to take initiative – knowing there were others out there who needed this information as much as I did, and craving a dissertation procrastination project! – I went ahead and created this mailing list server in June of 1999, calling it WRK4US (Work for Us) – "work" meaning non-academic careers, "us" meaning humanities PhDs. Since I hadn't a clue myself as to what humanities PhDs did outside the academy, I started hunting them down using simple web research and bringing them onto the list as guest speakers to share their experience. Word got around and the list grew.

This early little episode of my story illustrates several things, which were not clear to me at the time but are crystal clear now:

• People are driven by their temperaments. Looking back, I see that being an impatient self-starter has been a major factor again and again in my life. Your temperament has no doubt already driven many of your choices. And it has

absolutely nothing to do with your choice of academic discipline. All temperaments are probably present in all disciplines.

- Procrastination is not only tempting; it is actually good because it reveals what
you care about and enjoy. Ask yourself: when you are supposed to be doing one
thing, but really doing something else, *what is the something else*? Look there for
insight into yourself and what you may have to offer the world.

So back to my story. I graduated in December 2000, got married, moved back
home to Los Angeles with my Ohio-born husband, and embarked on my own rather
awkward post-academic career. At that point, I had pretty much the same skill set
that anthropology PhDs and, in fact, all humanities and social science PhDs have
at graduation: research, writing, persuasion, teaching, organizing, critical thinking,
qualitative research, project management, problem identification and analysis. I also
had a certain image of who I was and what I could do. Through my experiences as
an academic, I had come to see myself as a "teacher of writing." I later discovered
that was way too specific – there was much more to me than that – but that's what
I thought at the time, just like you think you are X right now. That belief is heavily
conditioned – in fact created – by your experiences to date; more aspects of "you"
will emerge with new experiences.

Believing that I was a writing teacher, I attempted, quite logically, to export that
identity into the non-academic world as a communications consultant, pitching
myself as a freelance trainer who teaches corporate employees how to write better.
It seemed like a good plan at the time. However, I failed. Though I was certainly an
excellent writing teacher, I had no contacts in the corporate world, no track record
of success as a corporate trainer, no understanding of any of the industries I was
targeting, and a profound "values disconnect" with the very people I had imagined
would hire me (corporate HR professionals). They expected me to show them how
my training services would increase their bottom line. I was never able to address
that question in any but the vaguest terms, and I privately thought they were a little
stupid for thinking that way. Didn't they know how important good writing is, just
because? I did not share their values at all.

With hindsight, my mistake at that juncture was twofold: (1) I saw myself and
my options too narrowly. I thought I had one skill (teaching writing) when really I
had many more. (2) I did not know that it is more than just skill that gets you work.
It is also familiarity with the "world" you are trying to inhabit, including its values.
Therefore, anything you can do to get familiar with different worlds will be tremendously beneficial to you.

In 2002, while still trying to be a consultant, I had a series of positive experiences
volunteering for local nonprofits that I cared about. I felt comfortable with the
nonprofit people; for them, it wasn't about the bottom line, but it was about making
an impact on the world. I grasped that instantly, and by the fall of 2002 had decided
to change course: I would enter the nonprofit sector, leveraging my writing, research,
persuasion, organization, and project management skills (the very same skills you
probably also have) to become a grant writer. Much better: now I was using more

of my skills, in a non-academic world, where I had at least a tiny bit of experience and whose basic values I shared.

Still, it was hard for a PhD with little experience to break in. I applied for dozens of positions and did not get a single interview. The turning point came in January 2003, when I finally persuaded an environmental nonprofit to use me two days a week as a volunteer grants associate. It was a huge breakthrough. That one volunteer assignment, which I held for six months, gave me contacts, references, a little track record, plus exposure to daily life and operations inside a nonprofit. After six months of that, I updated my résumé and, wow, what a difference! I applied for six jobs, was interviewed for three, and was offered two. Hallelujah! I accepted a position as foundation grant writer at a national Latino civil rights nonprofit.

Note: from the day I was hooded in December 2000 to the day I started that first "real" job as a grant writer, it took two and a half years and one major self-reinvention. I have since learned from observing thousands of PhDs and ABDs leaving the academy that a two- to three-year time frame is common. It takes many of us that long to find our footing and reinvent ourselves. Sometimes there is a false start, as there was with me. There may be periods of unemployment, volunteering, or a "survival job" or two before the first real job is found. Even the best, smartest people go through this. It is very common. And there is no shame in it. Every experience you have is shaping you and developing your identity as a professional. No single choice defines you for life.

So, anyway, in June 2003 I started my first real job! Took the subway, carried a briefcase, reported to an office, and everything. Adapting to this new office-based lifestyle was a challenge, but there I was, on my way, learning new tasks, meeting new people, and experiencing a world unlike any I had previously known. There were moments when my cluelessness showed. I was still very naive about workplace politics, plus I was in the surprisingly precarious position of being a white person in a movement of color. I made mistakes and looked like an idiot many times. But I did my actual job well (hooray for those research, writing, persuasion, organization, and project management skills!) and developed a little fan base. Kind people took me under their wing. By being friendly to me and modeling successful workplace behaviors, they taught me stuff like how to be a team player, how to navigate tricky situations, how to help and protect your friends as well as yourself. My co-workers were a critically important resource, as yours will be for you. I am still in touch with some of them today, eight years later.

Meanwhile, all this time, I continued managing WRK4US. I started doing panel discussions with multiple guest speakers, got support from the Woodrow Wilson National Fellowship Foundation and later Duke University, expanded the list to include social sciences, and kept making time for the list in my increasingly busy post-academic life. Sometimes, under stress, I would fantasize about making my living through managing the list, but always concluded it was impossible, thinking, "Yeah, right. If only!"

After a year in the grant writing job, I wanted more variety and responsibility; I wanted more different things to do and more authority to do them my way. So

I applied for and got a director of development position at a much smaller organization. Be careful what you ask for. As a one-person development department, I was responsible for all revenue streams, but had no teammates, no support staff, and little experience of other aspects of fund-raising besides grant writing. Still, it was a huge step up in both variety and responsibility, just like I wanted.

Thank goodness someone told me about AFP, the Association of Fundraising Professionals. Those monthly meetings were a godsend. It was great to be with other development professionals who had faced similar challenges themselves and were full of wise advice. And I noticed new positions opening up all the time in other organizations; these AFP meetings were where the news would spread (nice to know there are options, and also nice to help friends by letting them know of positions that might interest them). Also helpful were short training classes in various aspects of fundraising, where again I made new friends while learning the profession and about mailing list servers for fund-raising professionals.

As my career bumped along, I consistently turned to others for help, got it, and offered them help when I could. You should do the same. The "others" can be within your organization or outside it. They can be geographically close or distant, peers or superiors, similar to or different from you. Whatever you are doing, attend meetings. Take classes. Join associations. Say yes to invitations. These all represent new networks for you to join. A network is really nothing more than a collection of people. The more people you are connected to, the more resources you will have at your disposal: information, moral support, job announcements.

In my two and a half years in that director of development position, my biggest successes, overall, were doubling the size of the grants program, quintupling major gifts revenue and instilling in the board a deeper sense of leadership and personal responsibility for fund-raising than they had felt before. My biggest failure was also related to the board: I failed to grasp certain key things about the board–development director relationship, so, even while instilling those things, I had been irritating some of them all along without knowing it. After a staff change immediately above me, my protector was gone and within months I was on thin ice politically with several members of the board. That faction gained power, my life became increasingly unpleasant, and I saw no light at the end of the tunnel.

The day I updated my résumé in November of 2006 was the day I discovered, to my own surprise, that I had accomplished so much in the position that I really was free to leave. Thanks to my rather obsessive habit of writing down everything I had done and sending it to myself as an email every Friday (highly recommended, by the way), I knew exactly what I had achieved and it was all true, no exaggeration. Bullets on the new résumé included: "Built grants program from 12 active grants in 2004 to 20 in 2006"; "Worked with program staff to increase outreach program from a 20K annual loss to a 20K annual gain"; "Established major gifts program, increasing major gifts revenue from $45,000 to $242,984 and the number of major donors from 22 to 78." (This is the kind of thing you can say only when you have kept accurate records.)

So I resigned with confidence, knowing that after a little much needed rest, it would be pretty straightforward for me to get a job. And I knew exactly what kind of position to aim for: grants manager at a larger organization, which would highlight my strongest skill set, grant writing and grants program management, while insulating me a little bit from my weak point, board politics. Perfect!

Note: In just a few short years since getting that first real job, I had morphed from "awkward ex-academic trying to break into Field X" to "highly employable professional with a documented track record of success and a clear idea of the next step." Despite the challenges I faced in both organizations, I forged partnerships, joined communities, accomplished many meaningful tasks, and learned the ropes of an interesting profession that could easily absorb all of my skills. In those general terms, my journey was completely typical of what many PhDs and ABDs experience on leaving the academy: a tough time getting the first job, but once that first job is secured, rapid learning, prompt advancement, and, within a few years, a solid career in a stimulating field. This is more or less what you can expect if you leave the academy.

Had it not been for WRK4US, this would be the happy ending of my story of transformation. Today I would probably be grants manager or director of corporate and foundation relations at a large nonprofit with a support staff of two or three working under me, whom I would happily see as students or mentees. But thanks to the online community I had created and nurtured, my dissertation procrastination project, there were big surprises in store.

A few months before I resigned the director of development position, I was invited to speak at a conference of university career counselors, who had long felt that WRK4US was one of the best career resources out there for humanities PhDs. Meeting this group for the first time was a life-changing experience. The passion these people felt for graduate students and their careers was electric and awakened in me a new sense of my own identity. I was one of these people. This was my tribe. I can hardly describe the sense of joy and belonging I felt at that conference, and the sense of having made an impact. They told me how much WRK4US had helped them and their students, and I saw what a difference my work had made, what a problem-solver my list was for these people. As a result of that conference, I resolved that if there were ever an opportunity for me somehow to build on the success of WRK4US and dedicate myself completely to that work, I would do it.

Fast forward about nine months. Shortly after I left the director of development job, the opportunity came. I was incredibly fortunate to receive a financial windfall which expanded my options. I could continue my development career as planned, *or* I could act on my resolution and build on the success of WRK4US. After much agonizing (looking back, I can't believe I agonized so much!), I chose the latter. That choice put me on a beautiful new path. I dedicated myself completely to solving that one problem that had bugged me so much when I was in the academy: the lack of information and cultural support for graduate students interested in non-academic careers.

Figuring out how to transform a free mailing list server into a revenue-generating operation was the big challenge, but with the help of my community, I did it. Over a period of several weeks, I had long phone conversations with 50 stakeholders, mostly prominent list subscribers and university career counselors. Each conversation yielded at least one good idea, and I synthesized all the good ideas together to create a workable business model. The name would change to "The Versatile PhD"; it would be a website not a mailing list server; and it would be supported by institutional subscriptions to a premium content area, which would contain fabulous new materials that I would have to create. Again, community support was crucial. I established genres (the career autobiography, the hiring success story), recruited community members to write them, and used my composition teaching experience to work with the authors to make each piece as useful and pleasing as possible. Without the enthusiastic support of my community, I would never have come up with the model, much less actually pulled it off.

Today I am the proud founder and full-time manager of The Versatile PhD. Same mission, same wonderful community, only now there's a business to support it. I find PhDs outside the academy and invite them to write about their post-academic career journeys and share the résumés and cover letters that got them their first post-academic jobs. Universities pay an annual subscription fee so their graduate students can access these materials. As of this writing in April 2012, I have 40 fine universities as subscribers, 16,000 individual members, and am on track to recoup my start-up expenses by the end of this, my third year in business. Next year, Versatile PhD will expand to include STEM, at which point its impact on the academy will about double.

The "applied creature" that I am today is a thrilling thing to be. I play a shifting kaleidoscope of roles: editor, writer, educator, community organizer, marketer, administrator, analyst, and strategist. Every day I use all of my skills and then some because, to be honest with you, as a business owner with zero business experience or training, I am on a steep learning curve. Sometimes it's a little too steep, but it always seems to flattens out just in time (right before I lose my mind), and the lifelong learner in me is secretly delighted by the demand that I constantly learn new things, meet new people, join new communities.

Most importantly, every day I fulfill my personal mission to help graduate students and new PhDs identify, prepare for, and excel in non-academic careers. I help people by maintaining the community and delivering great content. I help universities by providing an easy, inexpensive solution to the problem of how to help grad students in this area. I educate people about the Versatile PhD resource. And I am part of a national community of practice: people who, from within and outside the academy, share my passion for graduate student professional development and for the great capabilities of PhDs and ABDs. My work is absolutely fascinating and suits my temperament perfectly. And none of it would have happened without the help and support of other people, coupled with my own willingness to seek it out.

Okay, enough about me. Let's talk about you. As advanced PhD students and recent PhDs in anthropology, you have pretty much the same skill set as all humanities and social science PhDs: research, writing, persuasion, teaching, organizing, critical thinking, qualitative research, project management, problem identification and analysis. And you are a fast learner, interested in many things. These skills are all valued outside the academy. And you are not alone: you are part of a nationwide "network," if you will, of humanities and social science PhDs – others like yourself who have similar skills and face similar challenges in their careers. That network can be a tremendous resource for you.

More specifically, as anthropologists you have a special ability to understand cultures and sub-cultures. You also have a bit of a public perception problem because very few members of the general public understand what anthropology is. They think "bones and stones," Jane Goodall, gorillas, and the like. So you will always be faced with the need to explain your version of anthropology. Fortunately, it makes sense when explained. Many people will readily grasp the importance of cultural insight. All organizations, be they for-profit, nonprofit, or government, have their target audiences and need to understand those audiences.

Becoming a practitioner is a big trade-off that is different for each person. For example, you may have to give up on a cherished dream in order to gain something else of value, such as the ability to live near your family, earn more income, or any number of things. That, my friends, is life. Life is a series of trade-offs and you seldom get 100 percent of what you want. The academic lifestyle gives you, at the very least, a high degree of control over your schedule, access to the many resources of a college or university, and the opportunity to have teaching and research be your main activities. Perhaps you take pleasure in your identity as an academic; you identify with your institution, and others are impressed when you say, "I teach anthropology at X University." If you have tenure, you have job security, which is a very rare thing in this world.

On the other hand, non-academic careers present significant advantages too. Just the geographical freedom alone is huge: you can live wherever you choose. The upside of less job security is more diverse opportunities. Tired of your current job? No problem, get another one. Salaries tend to be higher outside the academy, promotions more frequent, and the sheer variety of experiences available to you is, for me anyway, a tremendous plus. There are so many ways you can go: different job, different organization, different career trajectory, a different version of *you* – and you are in the driver's seat.

Neither world is perfect or will make your life nirvana. You will face major life challenges at some point no matter where you work. And both worlds have their pleasures, perks, and irritations. The academy is not blissfully free from commercial and economic influences. Nor is the business world devoid of moral goodness, intellectual challenge, and socially positive impact. These are myths, oversimplifications that blind us to surprisingly interesting realities and reduce the number of options we believe are open to us. Both the academic and non-academic worlds are populated with a mixture of nice people and nasty people, smart people and not so smart, all driven by a rainbow of human motivations. Reputation, relationships and communities are important in both worlds. And politics are everywhere. So try to get over any belief you may have that the academy is safe and wonderful whereas the applied world is harsh and scary. It's not true. You can lead a happy (or miserable) life in either world.

Whatever your path, whether you are inside the academy, outside, or somewhere in between, there are people around you who can and will become your friends and allies. You don't necessarily have to create an online community like I did. In fact, because I did create it, you can now simply join it (at http://versatilephd.com) and link up with thousands of peers who understand exactly what you are going through and are someplace on that same road themselves: graduate students, new PhDs, ABDs, all either contemplating applied careers or already in them. Some of them are even anthropologists. Other online communities exist that are more narrowly focused on anthropologists; search for applied anthropology groups on LinkedIn and through the AAA.

Equally important are your own networks, the people you have access to in your neighborhood, at the gym, at work, on campus, on mailing list servers and websites, in that club you belong to or that place you sometimes go. You are surrounded by people who, like you, are a mixture of strengths and vulnerabilities. They know stuff you don't, yet may at some point need information that you have. Cultivate an interest in others. Learn about their work and their lives and listen for opportunities to help, such as by sharing information or introducing them to someone. Ask for help when you need it, offer help when you can. That's what "networking" is all about: mutual aid. If you can't meet the need yourself, refer them to a resource or introduce them to someone else better suited. Expose yourself to new communities by attending new events, saying yes to invitations, seeking out local chapter meetings of non-academic professional associations related to your interests. Be friendly, honest, and real.

The word "networking" may seem weird to you, like some sort of strange, unpleasant ritual that vaguely resembles selling, pushing, intruding, or arm-twisting. But it is really just interacting with people and building positive relationships. Any set of people can be seen as a network. Your peers, your family, the people you see at conferences, even your students – these are all networks that graduate students typically have. Then you get your first job and new networks open up to you. Anytime you venture into any unfamiliar group, such as when you take a class, attend a meeting of a professional association, join a mailing list server or online group, even when you say yes to an invitation to an event you would not normally attend, you are exposing yourself to a new network. First you're a newbie, with everything to learn; then, over many instances of asking for help and eventually giving it, you become part of the group and, voila, you are changed by the experience. Your professional identity has evolved.

The "asking for help" part can be challenging for academics. We don't want to impose; we think our needs are already obvious to everyone, or that asking for help is somehow bad because smart people are supposedly self-sufficient. Let me tell you: self-sufficiency is severely overrated. Helping others is pleasurable. It makes you feel good, right? Therefore it feels good to others to help you. People helping people is what makes the world go round.

And it is *not* obvious to everyone what you want and need. People are generally so wrapped up in themselves that the only person who spends more than a nano-second thinking about you and your career is you. Tell people what you are looking for! "I am looking for a job or internship where I can use my communication skills." "I want to meet someone in industry X and do an informational interview with them." "I would like to join your team and work for your organization someday." All these are perfectly good things to say, which help others understand what you want and need. Not everyone will be able to help you, but some definitely will. Thank everyone for their help, encourage them to ask you for help in the future, and you are on your way to developing your own network of friends and allies.

These best practices hold true in the academy as well. Cultivating people-positive habits in yourself will make you a better colleague and provide a gentle assist to your academic career at every stage. Wherever we are, inside the academy, outside, in some world we haven't even imagined yet, we all get by with a little help from our friends.

Chapter 31

Drug Resistance and Biosocial Analysis in Practice

Amy S. Porter and Paul E. Farmer

*Helping people to understand the complex relationships which connect medical prob-
lems with large-scale social forces, and in ways which illuminate workable solutions, is
a formidable task. In this chapter Amy Porter and Paul Farmer present two examples
of how to frame medical issues within a larger context. Drawing on their work with
tuberculosis in Russia and HIV/AIDS in South Africa, the authors demonstrate how
and why the challenges and opportunities presented by chronic infections today cannot
be effectively understood without a biosocial analysis.*

Introduction

Five years ago, Harvard Medical School added a mandatory course called "Introduction to Social Medicine" to its curriculum. Both of us were involved in this process,
one as professor and the other as student, and so experienced at first hand reactions
both positive and negative. Happily, the former dominated. Students who reported
dissatisfaction with the course focused on a single complaint: Course materials were
deemed "extraneous." In other words, a substantial proportion of Harvard medical
students regarded history, medical anthropology, medical sociology, and even epidemiology as peripheral to their medical training.

Surely this called for improvement in course design. But it also signaled short-
sightedness, widespread in clinical medicine, of the mechanisms by which large-scale
social forces come to influence both the distribution and the outcome of disease.
This is true of cancer, heart disease, and other non-communicable diseases; it is
especially true of the pathologies we study, including chronic infections like AIDS

A Handbook of Practicing Anthropology. First Edition. Edited by Riall W. Nolan.
© 2013 John Wiley & Sons, Inc. Published 2013 by John Wiley & Sons, Inc.

and tuberculosis (TB). In the last few decades, both of the causative pathogens – HIV and *Mycobacterium tuberculosis* – have been fully characterized on a molecular level. But they've also been altered on the molecular level, in part from selective pressures stemming from the therapies introduced in the post-antibiotic era. In some of the settings in which we work, there has been a startling collision of epidemics and therapeutic regimes. In South Africa, the wealthiest and most inegalitarian nation in southern Africa, for example, AIDS and tuberculosis are bound in noxious synergy; these diseases are also being treated, however ineffectively, at a level hitherto unknown. These challenges and achievements of modern medicine cannot be understood, we argue here, without fully *biosocial* analysis.

We hope this chapter, which explores some of the complexities, challenges, and advantages associated with being an anthropologist and a practitioner of clinical medicine (as both of us are), will offer one response to the critiques presented by these students at Harvard Medical School. In two short ethnographic vignettes drawn from our work in South Africa and Siberia, we seek to highlight the need for full biosocial analysis linked to engagement in service delivery – the vitality of praxis – when tackling the most difficult global health problems today, such as drug-resistant tuberculosis and AIDS.

The Challenge of Biosocial Research

Every practitioner of what has been termed "global health" yearns for specific and quick-fix – in public health jargon, "vertical" – interventions capable of saving millions of lives and preventing needless suffering among the world's poor and otherwise vulnerable. The allure of such interventions is hardly difficult to understand. The greatest threats to human health – cardiac disease, diarrheal disease, AIDS, tuberculosis, diabetes, malaria, cancer, to name just a few – cause severe disability and death around the world every day. They each demand an urgent response. One recent study found that 52 out of 53 patients with extensively drug-resistant tuberculosis and AIDS in Tugela Ferry, a town in KwaZulu Natal, South Africa died within an average of 16 days after diagnosis (Gandhi et al. 2012). In Haiti, a cholera epidemic erupted in October 2010 which in 18 months claimed more than 7,000 lives and infected well over half a million people, or 5 percent of Haiti's population (MSPP 2012). All of our patients and colleagues in countries rich and poor dream of magic bullets that are able to eliminate these pathologies.

Acting rapidly – immediately – is perhaps the only option when confronted with needless suffering and death. But we don't have to be trained in history or anthropology to understand that there are inevitably unintended consequences of purposive social action (Merton 1936). The challenge is acting in a way that minimizes unintended consequences and confers greatest gain to the intended beneficiaries. Anyone familiar with the history of "international health" and "colonial medicine," the antecedents of global health, knows the potential for good intentions to sour amid the profound biosocial complexity endemic to the field. Sterilization, quarantine, imprisonment, unethical experimentation, cost-saving instead of life-saving approaches – the list of abuses is long and beyond the scope of this chapter.[1]

One way to minimize such unintended consequences is, we contend, to *resocialize* the emerging field of global health. Policy-makers in any field must reduce some the level of complexity to some extent in order to formulate actionable strategy. Policy is, by definition, an exercise in simplification. Why take on urban crime, the scarcity of healthy foods in low-income neighborhoods, the soda industry's promotion of sugar consumption, or funding shortfalls for health education when blood pressure can be lowered with an ACE inhibitor – a drug used to treat hypertension – and coronary disease can be managed with a cardiac catheterization? Why try to change the entrenched labor migration system in southern Africa, when condom use and abstinence promotion might convince migrant workers not to engage in concurrent sexual relations and thus slow the spread of HIV? Why try to promote the right to safe drinking water when people can be exhorted to wash their hands and put chlorine tablets into the water they haul from streams and lakes? Our challenge as physician-anthropologists is to resocialize global health problems: to conceptualize and design interventions that address the social determinants of health just as they do the biological ones. This work demands, in other words, a fully biosocial approach.

Some scholars and practitioners have argued that the term "biosocial" is itself jargon that does not advance practical efforts to better understand and respond to global health challenges (Howe 2011). But our motivation for considering the biological and social roots is as much practical as epistemological: ignoring social factors, at least in the resource-poor settings in which we work, is a sure way to limit the effectiveness of interventions – and to fundamentally misunderstand the pathologies of poverty that determine the distribution and outcomes of the diseases we diagnose and treat. Even diseases attributed to single genetic mutations, such as sickle cell anemia, are entangled in a complex web of political and economic decision-making, social networks, differential access to diagnostics and therapeutics, and determinations of scientific truth and validity, as Duana Fullwiley's (2011) recent ethnography of sickle cell disease in Senegal reveals.

We both work on diseases – drug-resistant forms of both tuberculosis and HIV – that more plainly require such biosocial understandings, since it is social intervention (the introduction of antibiotics) that has altered these pathogens at the molecular level. Drug resistance highlights different tiers of biosocial analysis. On one level, resistance-conferring mutations in viruses, bacteria, and other pathogens must be identified; risk factors for treatment interruptions that can lead to drug resistance must be modeled. Equally, we must ask what forms of social, political, and economic inequality undermine access to primary health care (including prompt and accurate diagnosis and daily care for chronic disease), generate migration-dependent livelihoods, and perpetuate shoddy housing conditions – all of which often shape drug resistance in the settings in which we work (Farmer 1999; Vearey et al. 2010). We must also ask what counts as a risk factor and what does not, and whose job it is to do this defining. The ethnographic vignettes that follow explore the need for biosocial analysis in the context of drug-resistant tuberculosis in Siberian prisons and drug-resistant HIV in South Africa.

Cruel and Unusual: Resurgent Tuberculosis in Russia's Prisons

Russia, 1998

Sergei was tall and thin, with black horn-rim glasses that gave him more the look of an owlish accountant than a felon.[2] His fellow prisoners and their guards were silent as he told me (Farmer) his story. The only other sound aside from his soft voice was that of coughing: like him, all the other young convicts who crowded the cell were sick with pulmonary tuberculosis. At times Sergei seemed bored with the tale, at times intimidated by the hush. He punctuated his sentences with a rattling cough of his own, raising, as an afterthought, a long pale hand to his mouth.

Shortly after the breakup of the Soviet Union in 1991, Sergei explained, he became involved in a complicated scam – something to do with fake checks. Arrested in the Siberian city of Kemerovo, he was held in pre-trial detention for more than a year. Although Russian law prohibits such prolonged pre-trial detention, and the Ministry of Justice has issued statements deploring the delays, the courts have been, by all accounts, overwhelmed by ever growing caseloads: rates of imprisonment in Russia have doubled since the collapse of the Soviet Union.[3] And so the jail in Kemerovo was dank and crammed with other young men awaiting trial, most accused of non-violent crimes like the one Sergei readily admits to having committed. Food and sanitary conditions were wretched, and Sergei began to cough and lose weight well before his case came to trial. "I knew I had tuberculosis," he said simply, "because that's what everybody else had." After his trial, the diagnosis was confirmed by prison health authorities, and Sergei was transferred to a "TB colony" – a prison facility dedicated to the detention and care of convicts ill with tuberculosis. Since Colony 33, in the nearby town of Mariinsk – once notorious for its especially grim conditions – was already overflowing, Sergei was sent instead to a colony at Vladimir, about 60 miles east of Moscow. He began his therapy at precisely the time that Russia's massive tuberculosis infrastructure began to crumble. The political and economic upheavals associated with the dissolution of the Soviet Union meant drug stockouts, failure to pay prison officials, and a dramatic weakening of the civilian tuberculosis services.[4] Sergei completed a year of erratic treatment about seven years ago.

For about two years after his initial treatment Sergei felt, he said, "just fine." Rather than being moved back to a regular prison, however, he was offered the chance to stay on at Vladimir and complete his sentence as a medical orderly assisting the nursing staff of the Vladimir colony. Three years later, he recalled in a low voice, his symptoms returned.

At this point in his narrative, Sergei paused, looking at the prison doctor. "He's due to be released soon," interjected the young doctor grimly, "but he's not responding to therapy." She had already informed me that the prison hospital under her direction had in recent months continued to face drug stockouts, a lack of X-ray film, and even food shortages. She did not add, as had the warden earlier, that her own pay was in arrears for months; her worries were solely about her patients.

The doctor handed me Sergei's chest films and I placed them in a view box affixed to the examining room wall. I tried not to wince. In recent months, there had been a marked enlargement of the cavities in Sergei's right upper lobe. Spreading inexorably, the recrudescent tubercle bacilli had already reduced the top half of that lung to Swiss cheese. It was also clear that the disease had spread to his left lung, which only a few months previously had been unaffected.

Long and erratic treatment had done Sergei little good. Such haphazard therapy is one of the best ways of inducing the tubercle bacillus to acquire drug-resistance. But Sergei – along with about 30 other Vladimir inmates – was to be sent home, in all likelihood carrying infectious, drug-resistant tuberculosis with him. He was to spend the harsh Siberian winter cooped up in a tiny wooden house with his wife and children. The one thing that might protect his family was that they might already be infected with latent tuberculosis. Quiescent infection with *Mycobacterium tuberculosis* likely confers some immunity to the drug-resistant strains pouring out of Russia's vast prison network. In Siberia, incidence of tuberculosis trebled in the decade after Sergei was arrested.[5]

Handing the X-rays back to the doctor, I smiled encouragingly at Sergei and wished him luck. He made a small, polite bow, and said nothing, as he was once again coughing. But he managed a smile as he tried to suppress his paroxysm; the other prisoners also murmured their farewells. After the doctor and I left the crowded cell, and we were more or less alone, my questions began in earnest. Although she had heard them all before, she listened patiently. With what drugs were Sergei and the other prisoner patients being treated, I asked? Are you having trouble with drug supply? Do the prisoners take their medications? Is each dose directly observed? Is there adequate food? She nodded politely. Food was scarce, she allowed, but they were managing to scrape by. Some of the guards, although themselves grossly underpaid, shared their own food with the prisoners. Sergei was receiving isoniazid, rifampin, and ethambutol – three of the strongest (or so-called first-line) drugs; his previous regimen had included streptomycin. The dosages were correct, and the staff observed him taking the pills. Yet each month, his doctor explained, microscopic examination of Sergei's sputum continued to reveal signs of persistent tuberculosis.

My final question, and perhaps the first one my colleague found pertinent, concerned microbial resistance to drugs. Most tuberculosis patients who fail to respond to treatment do so because they're not taking their medications regularly. In the Russian Federation this may have been due to the commonplace drug stockouts, or to patients' failure to take their drugs. But with directly observed therapy, failure to respond to powerful drugs is usually a sign that the tubercle bacillus has acquired resistance to them. An infecting strain that is resistant to at least isoniazid and rifampin – the two most powerful first-line drugs – is termed multidrug-resistant tuberculosis (MDRTB). When patients have MDRTB, they require longer periods of treatment – about two years of a multidrug regimen. This compares with six to nine months of treatment for disease due to drug-susceptible strains. Five first-line drugs are available for treating tuberculosis; at most eight second-line drugs also have proved effective, if less so than isoniazid and rifampin, against *M. tuberculosis*. But, in Russia in 1998, strains of MDRTB exist that are resistant to all the first-line and most of the second-line drugs. (We had already treated patients in Peru who were sick with strains resistant to 10 and 12 twelve drugs – which would later be termed after the Tugela Ferry outbreak – "XDRTB," extensively drug-resistant tuberculosis, as if it were a new strain (Gandhi et al. 2006). It was not.)

Sergei's doctor was well aware of this problem: "There are, as you might say, superbugs loose in our jails and prisons. We know how to manage the cases, even the drug-resistant ones. But we don't have the resources." The annual medication budget for the entire Vladimir colony was the equivalent of about US$2,000, less than a fifth of what it had been a decade previously, when drugs were virtually free and plentiful – and there were, by all accounts, fewer cases and far less drug resistance. Thus, the colony could now afford only an irregular supply of certain first-line drugs and no second-line drugs. The facility was also chronically short of syringes, masks, X-ray film, and other supplies.[6]

Conditions in Russia's TB colonies were nothing short of dismal. The prison personnel, at least the medical corps, struck me as professional and conscientious. They were well liked, by and large, by the prisoners.[7] Indeed, they compared favorably to many of their international interlocutors. But the overall effect of a modern Russian TB colony was one of gloom, shabbiness, and desuetude, and a stark lack of necessary supplies. The prisons were either too hot or too cold, airless in winter, and always short of light. Morale was poor, but it was not as poor as I had expected. Throughout the Russian Federation, prison medical staff continued to show up for work, whether or not they are paid.

If left untreated, each smear-positive pulmonary tuberculosis patient can, in turn, infect a dozen or more new contacts every year.[8] The transmission rate was surely higher within an overcrowded penitentiary system in 1998. One in every 10 (or approximately 110,000) Russian prisoners were estimated to have active tuberculosis. Bad as that is, prisoners have two further strikes against them. First, even those sick with drug-susceptible strains are having them transformed into superbugs through inadequate treatment regimens. Second, prisoners who have acquired MDRTB will then infect others with drug-resistant strains.

In 1998 about a quarter of the prisoners with active tuberculosis probably had MDRTB. If Sergei has MDRTB and is receiving a regimen based on first-line drugs, he will not be cured – but his germs may acquire greater drug resistance even as he follows his well-intentioned and well-trained doctor's orders. The same point should have been made a decade later in South Africa. The patients who died in Tugela Ferry died in part because they followed their doctors' orders to show up to clinic. With no access to second- and third-line treatment, nor to the laboratory tests that can identify drug resistance, the patients received both the wrong medications (first-line medications are the wrong treatment for drug-resistant infections, whether HIV, tuberculosis, or both) and the wrong counsel (come to clinic, the place where they were likely infected with XDR strains).

What of prisons elsewhere in the former Soviet Union? In the past decades we've visited detainees in Latvia, Azerbaijan, and Kazakhstan. In each of these places, our fears were confirmed: tuberculosis is out of control throughout the region's jails and prisons. Just as in the time of Dostoyevsky and Chekhov, tuberculosis is again the leading cause of death of young prisoners. According to the International Committee of the Red Cross, it accounts for up to 80 percent of deaths in many prisons (Coninx et al. 1995; see also Baussano et al. 2010). Worse, highly and extensively resistant strains are already entrenched. An epidemiological catastrophe has come to pass inside these prisons: Drug-resistant disease has resulted from ineffective treatment regimens, and since only the susceptible strains are being treated effectively, the proportion of superbug cases continues to grow.

International expert opinion has tended to blame poor treatment outcomes on the hapless tuberculosis services, both prison and civilian, or on a lingering "Soviet culture," rather than on the social and economic conditions that are at the heart of both the epidemic of imprisonment and the epidemic of tuberculosis.[9] Worse still, many international experts continue to insist that the prescription for Russia's runaway tuberculosis epidemic should include only the wise use of first-line drugs – this at a time when fully half of all patients with active disease are sick with strains resistant to isoniazid or streptomycin.[10]

No epidemic of drug-resistant disease on this scale had ever before been documented. It is unquestionably true that prisons were an important factor in New York's MDRTB epidemic of the early 1990s. The New York State Department of Health reported that this outbreak consisted of 1,279 cases from 1991 to 1994, with no figures available for 1990.[11] According to a report issued by city health authorities, 80 percent of all MDRTB cases could be traced back to prisons and homeless shelters (Garrett 1994: 524). According to some estimates, the epidemic cost more than US$1 billion to bring under control. In fact, the logic of cost-effectiveness was invoked to justify extraordinary expenditures in New York:

> The costs of the resurgence of tuberculosis have been phenomenal. From 1979 through 1994, there were more than 20,000 excess cases of the disease in New York City . . . Each case cost more than $20,000 in 1990 dollars, for a total exceeding $400 million. In addition, as many as one third of patients with tuberculosis were rehospitalized because of inadequate follow-up . . . There were additional expenditures for renovation of Rikers Island . . . the renovation of hospitals . . . Care will be required for those who become ill in the years and decades to come. These costs easily exceed $1 billion and many reach several times that amount. Thus, despite their cost, efforts to control tuberculosis in the United States are likely to be highly cost effective. (Frieden et al. 1995: 232)

Compare that with what is unfolding in Russia (or South Africa). Precisely the opposite argument – that tuberculosis control is too costly, especially if it involves treating prisoners with MDRTB – continues to hamper efforts to check the most serious epidemic of tuberculosis ever to hit an industrialized country.

As elsewhere, the Tomsk prisons and jails – in western Siberia – have served as breeding grounds for difficult-to-treat strains of drug-resistant tuberculosis. In a 1998 survey of 212 prisoners with active, pulmonary tuberculosis, three-quarters had drug-resistant tuberculosis. Among prisoners with a history of previous antituberculous therapy – and this was the majority – most had resistance to more than one first-line drug (Farmer et al. 1999: 56–57). The mean age of the Tomsk patients was 27. Here as elsewhere, the disease was again the leading cause of death of prisoners.

The mutant microbes were not long deterred by prison bars. Inside the nearby Tomsk civilian sanatorium, one-third of all patients suffered from MDRTB. According to the director, no fewer than half of all the past year's deaths in the hospital were due to MDRTB. Many of these patients had been in prison; some were prison staff. But some patients appeared to have become infected in hospitals and other institutions. Still others were homeless coughers or alcoholics.

There were probably more MDRTB patients in Tomsk Oblast alone, with its million or so souls, than there were at the height of the outbreak in New York. But the tuberculosis services there, in 1998, had a budget that amounted to less than 5 percent of that of New York's tuberculosis bureau.

What was to be done? Most international health experts argued that Russia needed to pare back its large, unwieldy tuberculosis-control system, which relied on in-patient services and individualized treatment regimens. Patients should be treated at home, said the international experts; all Russian patients should be treated with standardized doses of the same drugs – what is termed in the jargon "short-course chemotherapy." But the Russians countered that many of their patients had complex social problems (it's hard to treat someone at home if they have no home; alcoholics cannot always adhere to out-patient therapy). Their "case mix" was too complex, they said, for a one-size-fits-all approach to tuberculosis treatment and control.

MDRTB certainly proved their point. If someone is sick with MDRTB, giving that patient short-course chemotherapy is tantamount to doing nothing – worse than nothing, given the toxicity of the drugs. As for cutting back expenditures in the middle of a burgeoning epidemic, one can only liken it to conserving water when your house is on fire.

That these complexities were acknowledged only in the late 1990s, a decade into the epidemic, was a shame, and, for some patients, an irreparable one. But some groups have been trying to repair the damage. In Tomsk, a novel effort brought together all parties – the Russians and their international interlocutors; doctors and nurses and patients; prison and civilian authorities; public and private donors – in order to make sure that every patient received high-quality care. For years, the

British nongovernmental agency Merlin and the Public Health Research Institute worked with Tomsk's civilian and prison authorities to respond effectively and in a coordinated manner to resurgent tuberculosis. What was missing was the ability to treat patients with MDRTB. That meant second-line drugs, specialized laboratory capacity, and some technical assistance.

At the close of the twentieth century, after careful evaluation of local capacity to use the drugs correctly, Partners in Health purchased some of the second-line medications required by the prisoner patients. By 1999, prisoners with MDRTB finally had access to the drugs that might save their lives, and hundreds were treated. Adequate resources to rebuild the tuberculosis infrastructure, including increased laboratory capacity, were finally brought to bear on this problem.

What happened once the biosocial complexity of this epidemic was embraced and adequate resources were marshaled to try to stop it? In 1999 Partners in Health (with funding from the Russian government and the Gates Foundation, among others) joined forces with Tomsk prison officials to identify patients with drug-resistant tuberculosis and to design treatment regimens based on these laboratory findings. This was not an attempt to build an MDRTB program so much as an acknowledgment of drug resistance as an important driver, if not *the* most important driver, of runaway tuberculosis epidemics and high mortality in the prison system. We found that many patients had MDRTB, by the definition noted above, and others had XDRTB, as it would later be termed. That year, case-fatality rates of tuberculosis in the prison system were 26 percent. In other words, a quarter of all patients, most of them young men receiving *treatment* for tuberculosis died while on therapy. There were, as noted, many discrepant explanations for this staggering failure (Farmer 1999: 228–261). But the team in Tomsk soon had reason to believe that our hypothesis was correct: within a year of introducing proper care for drug-resistant tuberculosis to all prisoner patients with that diagnosis, the case-fatality rate dropped to zero (Shin et al. 2006). This was a great victory for medicine and public health, and was celebrated as such by the Tomsk prison authorities and their partners.

However, the question remained: since tuberculosis is never reined in by bars but instead reaches out to civil society, what would be the impact of this intervention beyond the prison system? And to return to a perennial question: what is the impact of treatment programs on the burden of disease? Would plunging case-fatality rates decrease prevalence in Tomsk Oblast, and if so when? Although claims of causality are fraught, as any medical anthropologist knows, the trends are surely positive: Russian tuberculosis authorities now report that, for the first time in decades (if ever), Tomsk-wide tuberculosis prevalence has dropped not only below all other Siberian oblasts but also below nationwide levels (Sarayeva 2012). It might be argued in retrospect that only an acknowledgment of the enormous biosocial complexity of this epidemic, rooted in social disruption, might permit such results within a decade. That would be our conclusion, as well as that of our Russian colleagues.

Livelihoods and Drug Resistance in South Africa

South Africa, 2012

"There was no job security in Joburg," explained Nothando, a 28-year-old mother of three whom I (Porter) met in a clinic in Cape Town, the capital of the Western Cape province. Nothando and I sat in a small consulting room at the end of the clinic's long hallway. A TB and HIV patient at the clinic, Nothando had agreed to tell me why she had left her family home in the rural Eastern Cape province and come to urban Cape Town. She perched herself on the edge of an office chair, pushed up against the wall, catty-corner to an old desk, and I sat to her right, facing the desk. As we began talking, she took off the straw hat that had been shielding her face, and I saw the protruding clavicles of her emaciation. It was one of the first cloudy days of fall; not much light snuck into the room through its three small windows. Intent on sharing her story, Nothando looked straight at me, but just behind her left shoulder I could see the township and its rows of corrugated metal shacks, spread vertically up the mountainside above the clinic.

Born in a rural area in the Eastern Cape (the former Transkei region), Nothando first left her home in 1997, at the age of 14, shortly after her mother died. After her father remarried, his new wife forced her out of the house. She moved to Johannesburg, where she completed three more years of school, married, and had her first child before relocating to Cape Town in search of work. Her father, who also now lives in Cape Town, has developed dementia; she is his principal caregiver. On the hill above the clinic, in a one-room metal structure that can only be called a shack, she lives with her youngest child, her husband, her father, and her brother, who is also looking for work. She does not consider this house, in which she has spent much of the last several years, a home – but rather a place to live while she searches for a livelihood. Working a few hours per week cleaning in a local restaurant, she is the family's sole provider.

Nothando began losing weight and developed a chronic cough around the time she arrived in Cape Town. She did not go to a doctor because she attributed her symptoms to the stress of not being able to find work. She feared learning what she assumed was inevitable: that she was infected with HIV. In 2005, when she was 22, her husband was diagnosed with HIV and started on antiretroviral therapy (which the South African government began providing free of charge that year). She also tested positive for HIV, but was not judged to require antiretroviral medications after a high CD4 count suggested her immune system was fairly intact.

In 2010 Nothando became pregnant again, and was started on treatment as part of the government antenatal prevention of mother-to-child transmission program. By then her cell-mediated immunity, which helps protect against certain infections (including tuberculosis), had weakened significantly. Her cough and weight loss worsened, and she was finally diagnosed with tuberculosis – the most common opportunistic infection in South Africa. These diagnoses made her eligible for a government disability grant, which Nothando used to build a one-room house with a corrugated metal roof in her ancestral home in the Eastern Cape. She spent four months building the house – she could only access the money piecemeal every few weeks – and then returned to Cape Town to continue searching for a job. Though no one currently lives in the Eastern Cape house, she explained that it was critical for her to build so she and her other family members can one day be buried near their ancestors. The empty house waits for her to return home to die.

Nothando lives within walking distance of the clinic in which we met. She knows the doctors, nurses, and counselors well, and she refills her antiretroviral medications regularly. When she returns to her home region, however, she has trouble finding decent medical care. The nearest government clinic is several hours' walk (or an expensive minibus ride) away. It is run by a single nurse and poorly stocked – yet is responsible for serving everyone within more than a 100 km radius. This clinic requires a referral letter for an appointment, and during her most recent trip home, Nothando had left hers in Cape Town. During the four months she spent building her family a house in their ancestral home, she was unable to refill her antiretroviral medications.

This scenario was hardly new to Nothando. She is herself a *sangoma* (a traditional Xhosa healer), and her family had long made do with traditional practices in the absence of modern biomedical care. But this time, on antiretroviral treatment, her continuity of treatment is essential. She reported "no problems" during the time off treatment, and most of the time, she said, she felt pretty well. But when she returned to Cape Town, the clinic found that her CD4 count had dropped from 480 cells to 282 cells per microliter. Though she had been counseled that an interruption in her antiretroviral treatment would weaken her immune system, she understood the drop in her CD4 count to be a result of financial stress. She has no money to buy meat for her family; she feels like she is failing to support them, which is something she cannot hope to do except in Cape Town, through wage labor.

There is also a great uncertainty facing Nothando and her providers in the formal biomedical sector. It is an uncertainty facing many in settings in which two epidemics have collided and in which some medical care, including treatment for AIDS and tuberculosis, is available. Is she sick with drug-resistant pathogens? It is impossible to know, to date, as Nothando's lab work has not yet been reported, and in South Africa's public sector health system, there is little access to drug-resistance testing. Based on her history of sporadic treatment, however, resistance is deemed likely. Extended interruptions in antiretroviral therapy are among the best ways to fan drug resistance (Graham et al. 2012; Luebbert et al. 2012). If the infecting HIV strain does demonstrate resistance to the first-line medications, she (and her family) will be in no small trouble. Second-line HIV drugs are expensive and almost entirely unavailable to the poor in South Africa. (Wealthy populations in Cape Town a few miles from the hill where Nothando lives, on the other hand, have little trouble finding such medications, though drug-resistant disease is, for them, uncommon.)

Her rationale behind building the house in the Eastern Cape might well be a self-fulfilling prophecy.

South Africa is, as noted, the epicenter of a new and complex epidemic due to the collision of HIV and *M. tuberculosis* and the antibiotics needed to treat or cure them. The toll of these pathogens is just now being acknowledged; the toll of drug resistance is still poorly understood. While working in the tuberculosis ward of a government hospital in the Eastern Cape, I watched helpless as Lucky, a young migrant worker, lay dying of AIDS and tuberculosis. When his mother noted that he had just returned from Cape Town, I tried to imagine why, after developing symptoms, Lucky had left the relative medical abundance of Cape Town for the scarcity of the rural Transkei region.[12] But this story, like Nothando's, was sadly typical of those South Africans who live between two disparate places that together constitute "home." A number of demographic studies have shown that labor migrants (or more appropriately, people who move in pursuit of livelihoods) often return home to die when they get sick with AIDS, tuberculosis, or both (Clark et al. 2007; Collinson et al. 2007; Collinson 2009; Vearey et al. 2010; Vearey 2012).

In the absence of systems to coordinate care across South Africa's provinces, drug resistance has already begun to crop up among mobile populations (MacPherson et al. 2009). The conditions facing South Africa's labor migrants are particularly severe. Epidemiologists have estimated that 17 percent of the world's HIV-positive people – some 5.6 million – live in South Africa (JUNP and WHO 2010). As the relatively new AIDS epidemic converges with a long-standing tuberculosis epidemic, co-infection rates have soared. Meanwhile, high unemployment (Ngonini 2010), geographic inequalities (Collinson 2009), and the history of apartheid (Burawoy 1976; Posel 2006) drive circular, seasonal labor migration (Packard 1989; Wilson 2001; White and Lindstrom 2005). Indeed, the South African economy has depended on labor migration since colonial times. Moreover, the links between labor migration and infectious disease are well known: All of the sub-Saharan African countries most heavily hit by AIDS have substantial populations of migrant laborers (Zimmerman et al. 2011). Xhosa-speaking South Africans, in particular, bear disproportionate burdens of AIDS, tuberculosis, and labor migration (Statistics South Africa 2005).

More labor migrants originate in the Eastern Cape – South Africa's poorest province – than in any other province (Statistics South Africa 2005), and most of them look for work in or around Cape Town, the largest city in the wealthier Western Cape province. HIV prevalence in the Eastern Cape is estimated at 30 percent (South African Department of Health 2010), compared to 16–18 percent in the Western Cape (JUNP and WHO 2010; South African Department of Health 2010). The Western Cape also has more public and private resources dedicated to fighting AIDS than the Eastern Cape. Since the end of the apartheid regime in 1994, the former African labor reserves ("homelands"), including the Transkei, have remained politically and economically disadvantaged (Collinson 2009). Health care (or lack of it) tracks with such disparities. Recent funding mechanisms like the

Global Fund to Fight AIDS, Tuberculosis and Malaria, and the US President's Plan for AIDS Relief (PEPFAR) – which together increased global health funding tenfold – have also flowed primarily into South Africa's cities. The landscape labor migrants traverse between the Western Cape (workplaces) and the Transkei (home communities) spans highly unequal biomedical resources.

It is easy to feel helpless observing interactions between patients, family members, and providers, having casual conversations with the relatives and neighbors of patients with end-stage HIV disease, or talking to taxi drivers about their fees for transporting sick patients or even deceased patients' bodies back "home" to the Transkei. Just last week, while sitting on a narrow bench next to a small clinic that serves a community of mostly internal migrants who have settled, at least partially, outside of Cape Town, I spent hours talking with patients and community care workers. They told stories of how they or family members have negotiated access to care as they traverse the fragmented worlds between the Western and Eastern Cape. These migrants have pragmatic suggestions for reform. Transregional systems of care could enable migrant workers to continue taking drugs for tuberculosis and for AIDS despite the unpredictable and mobile nature of their livelihoods. Disruptions in care are common for all migrant workers (the only livelihood available to them, in most cases). For example, an elderly family member living in the rural Eastern Cape suddenly requires care after the sister-in-law who had been running the household got a job in Cape Town; money runs out for a return taxi fare after traveling home to the Eastern Cape for the Easter long weekend; the financial burden of a family member's funeral increases the number of work hours necessary to keep the household solvent, and thereby prevents a planned trip home to the Eastern Cape or a planned return to Cape Town.

Of course, attending to the needs of such migrants would mean, on some level, tackling inequities that are deeply entrenched in the political economy and history of the region. This would take time and broad coalitions. Nurses are needed to assess their signs and symptoms, as are doctors to help with diagnosis and to decide on treatment regimens. Community health workers are needed to provide directly observed care (to improve adherence) and psychosocial support to patients in their homes. Policy-makers are needed to build platforms of coordinated care and transregional communication. Demographers are needed to track migration flows – and epidemiologists to track pathogen flows. Anthropologists are needed – I contend – to map out how complex political, economic, and social inequalities find their way into the bodies of migrants as disease and disability. But there is more progress to be made on all of these accounts. Even as the South African government has succeeded in rolling out the largest antiretroviral treatment program in the world, policy-makers have paid scant attention to the links between labor migration and the AIDS and tuberculosis epidemics. Over the last decade, as the South African government and the country's healthcare workforce have worked hard to get treatment to all HIV-infected citizens, coordination across regions has rarely entered policy planning conversations. As a result, the systems in place today still make it difficult – sometimes impossible – for migrants to access life-saving care consistently.

Conclusion

There is, in anthropology, a literature on resistance: the resistance of the poor and otherwise oppressed to social and economic structures that shape the global burden of disease and disability. These structures are plainly visible in the lives of Sergei and Nothando. But this chapter seeks to move beyond such broad-brush generalizations to the biosocial causes and consequences of their illnesses. Both are sick, it is true, with chronic infections (in the case of Nothando, at least two of them). It is also likely that both are sick with drug-resistant infections, even though advanced laboratory work to definitively determine drug resistance is often unavailable in the worlds Nothando traverses.

The term "antibiotic" does not refer to antibacterials alone, but to anti-infectives, including antibacterials, antiparasitics, and antivirals. The first antibiotics developed include the antibacterial sulfadrugs, and also streptomycin, discovered by Selman Waxman in 1943, which was, and is still today, used as an anti-tuberculosis agent. During the first large-scale clinical trial of streptomycin, five years after Waxman isolated the drug, many patients were cured; but many others had recurrent disease (Medical Research Council 1948). Mycobacterial isolates cultured from these patients were found to be resistant to streptomycin (Pyle 1947). Resistance has thus been a constant companion to the therapeutic advances of the post-antibiotic era. Multidrug regimens were, in fact, originally developed to prevent the emergence of drug-resistant mutants, the natural response to challenges from a single anti-infective.

The rate at which drug resistance emerges varies according to the pathogen in question. According to one theory that has, in large part, stood the test of time, when multidrug regimens are used to suppress or cure an infection, adherence (usually daily) to the regimen determines the rate of resistance. The mechanism is straightforward: both naturally occurring mutants and those stimulated into being by antibiotic challenges will be "covered" by multidrug regimens. Although this theory has never been disproven, in the post-antibiotic age, many primary infections – whether of HIV, *M. tuberculosis*, or other pathogens – occur with drug-resistant strains. This was certainly not the case in 1943. In a setting of poor adherence and acquired drug resistance, and its transmission as primary drug-resistant infection, there is a wide range of adverse possibilities – one of which has been termed *cryptic monotherapy*, in which both patient and provider believe that an infection is being treated with multiple drugs, when in fact only one or two of these drugs is effective against the infecting strain (Farmer 2005: 170–171).

These biological explanations of drug resistance do not even consider the impact of the large-scale social forces that have rendered both Sergei and Nothando unable to adhere to complex multidrug regimens. Such forces delay – or postpone indefinitely – diagnosis, interrupt supply chains, and erect barriers to care such as long commutes to clinic and prohibitively expensive user fees. The examples considered in our ethnographic vignettes build on work by Margaret Lock and Vinh-Kim

Nguyen (2010) exploring the social and economic structures that shape the emergence of drug resistance.[13] The modern drama of drug-resistant disease therefore begs questions of structure and agency that vexed the great nineteenth-century thinkers who laid the foundations of modern social science.

No single discipline can hope to explain the range of forces, from the biological to the social, that led Sergei and Nothando to become sick; no single branch of medicine can fully explain, or alleviate, their suffering and that of their families. It is our hope, nonetheless, that biosocial analysis, drawing on fields from molecular epidemiology to anthropology, linked to the delivery of services, has the potential to advance efforts against tuberculosis and HIV – in their drug-resistant and drug-susceptible forms – and the other modern pathologies afflicting Sergei and Nothando and so many others around the globe.

Notes

1 For more on the mixed history of colonial medicine and international health, see, e.g., Randall Packard (1989); Vaughan (1991); Warwick Anderson (2006).
2 This section has been adapted with permission from the University of California Press from Farmer (2005: ch. 4). Sections of the text have been reproduced verbatim. For a more extended discussion of the social origins and implications of drug-resistant tuberculosis in Russian prisons, please refer to the original essay.
3 As Juviler (2000: 119) notes: "The Ministry of Justice took control of prison facilities from the Interior Ministry (in charge of police and special forces) in September 1998. The head of the Ministry of Justice may openly deplore conditions, a Duma committee may investigate them, and a president's commission may propose reforms, but they all lack the means to carry them out."
4 For more on the complex impact of Russia's recent social and economic transformations on the quality of tuberculosis care, see Farmer et al. (1999).
5 In much of Siberia, case notifications increased from 30 per 100,000 population to over 100 per 100,000. Rates were, in the mid-1990s, 40 to 50 times higher within prisons. For a review of tuberculosis epidemiology in Russia, see Farmer et al. (1999).
6 For more on the collapse of the Russian healthcare system and the deteriorating health of its citizens over the past decade, see Laurie Garrett's informative series, "Crumbled Empire, Shattered Health," that appeared in *Newsday* in the fall of 1997. Murray Feshbach (1995) and Martin McKee (Walberg et al. 1998) are among those who have written about the Russian "mortality crisis."
7 This seemed to be the case even in the nineteenth century, if Dostoyevsky's *House of the Dead* – based on his four years in a convict prison in Omsk, Siberia – is to be believed: "The way the common people see it is that they are to be given treatment by their masters, for the doctors belong to a higher social class than they. However, when they get to know the doctors better (though there are exceptions, this is mostly true) all these terrors disappear, a fact which to my mind redounds to the honour of our medical men, most of whom are quite young. The majority of them know how to win the respect and even the love of the common people" (1985: 224).
8 Karel Styblo (1984) and others estimated that a smear-positive patient infects 10–14 susceptible contacts with *M. tuberculosis* each year (see also Sutherland and Fayers 1975).

9   In the words of one high-ranking World Health Organization official, the Soviet victory over tuberculosis bred "a tremendous pride on the Russian side" (quoted in Zuger 2000). This and similar attitudes, rather than the gutting of health budgets, were held to be in part responsible for ineffective responses to the later resurgence of tuberculosis.

10 Most surveys of drug-susceptibility profiles within prison populations show that a majority have drug-resistant disease; as many as two-thirds are resistant to streptomycin. These data are reviewed in Farmer et al. (1999: ch. 2). This suggests, of course, that novel strategies, and more than first-line drugs, will be required to arrest tuberculosis in the former Soviet Union. It is disturbing in this context to note that many experts have called for the universal use of short-course chemotherapy; some have even suggested fixed-dose combinations of these drugs. Either of these two prescriptions will fail to cure patients with MDRTB. For a review of this debate, see Coker (2000) and Farmer and Kim (2000).

11 For more on the recrudescence of drug-resistant tuberculosis in New York, see the review by Frieden et al. (1995).

12 The former Transkei region of the Eastern Cape province was a dispossessed homeland under the apartheid regime and one of the poorest regions in South Africa today.

13 Nguyen (2010), for example, considers how the public health imperative to treat more people led providers in Côte d'Ivoire during the mid-1990s to offer dual antiretroviral therapy instead of triple therapy, even though the latter does a better job preventing drug resistance. His ethnography limns political and economic forces – the availability of international funding hinged on the dual, not triple, therapy approach – that manifest themselves as drug-resistant HIV in the bodies of poor people in Côte d'Ivoire.

References

Anderson, Warwick (2006) *Colonial Pathologies: American Tropical Medicine, Race and Hygiene in the Philippines.* Durham, NC: Duke University Press.

Baussano, Iacopo, Brian G. Williams, Paul Nunn, et al. (2010) "Tuberculosis Incidence in Prisons: A Systematic Review." *PLoS Medicine* 7: e1000381.

Burawoy, Michael (1976) "The Functions and Reproduction of Migrant Labor: Comparative Material from Southern Africa and the United States." *American Journal of Sociology* 81: 1050–1087.

Clark, Samuel J., Mark A. Collinson, Kathleen Kahn, et al. (2007) "Returning Home to Die: Circular Labour Migration and Mortality in South Africa." *Scandinavian Journal of Public Health Supplement* 69: 35–44.

Coker, Richard (2000) "'Extrapolitis': A Disease More Threatening than TB in Russia?" *European Journal of Public Health* 10(2): 148–150.

Collinson, Mark A. (2009) *Striving against Adversity: The Dynamics of Migration, Health, and Poverty in Rural South Africa.* Umeå: Umeå University.

Collinson, Mark A., Stephen Tollman, and Kathleen Kahn (2007) "Migration, Settlement Change and Health in Post-Apartheid South Africa." *Scandinavian Journal of Public Health Supplement* 69: 77–84.

Coninx, Rudi, Bruce Eshaya-Chauvin, and Hernán Reyes (1995) "Tuberculosis in Prisons." *Lancet* 346: 1238–1239.

Dostoyevsky, Fyodor (1985) *The House of the Dead.* London: Penguin.

370   *Amy S. Porter and Paul E. Farmer*

Farmer, Paul E. (1999) *Infections and Inequalities: The Modern Plagues.* Berkeley: University of California Press.

Farmer, Paul E. (2005) *Pathologies of Power: Health, Human Rights, and the New War on the Poor.* Berkeley: University of California Press.

Farmer, Paul E. and Jim Yong Kim (2000) "Resurgent TB in Russia: Do We Know Enough to Act?" *European Journal of Public Health* 10: 150–152.

Farmer, Paul E., Alexander S. Kononets, Sergei E. Borisov, et al. (1999) "Recrudescent Tuberculosis in the Russian Federation." In Program in Infectious Disease and Social Change (ed.), *The Global Impact of Drug-Resistant Tuberculosis.* Boston: Program in Infectious Disease and Social Change.

Feshbach, Murray (1995) *Environmental and Health Atlas of Russia.* Moscow: PAIMS; Bethesda, MD: Foundation for International Arts and Education.

Frieden, Thomas R., Paula I. Fujiwara, Rita M. Washko, and Margaret A. Hamburg (1995) "Tuberculosis in New York City." *New England Journal of Medicine* 333: 229–233.

Fullwiley, Duana (2011) *The Encultured Gene: Sickle Cell Health Politics and Biological Difference in West Africa.* Princeton: Princeton University Press.

Gandhi, Neel R., Anthony Moll, A. Willem Sturm, et al. (2006) "Extensively Drug-Resistant Tuberculosis as a Cause of Death among Patient Co-infected with Tuberculosis and HIV in a Rural Area in South Africa." *Lancet* 368: 1575–1580.

Gandhi, Neel R., Jason R. Andrews, James C. Brust, et al. (2012) "Risk Factors for Mortality among MDR- and XDR-TB Patients in a High HIV-Prevalence Setting." *International Journal of Tuberculosis and Lung Disease* 16: 90–97.

Garrett, Laurie (1994) *The Coming Plague: Newly Emerging Diseases in a World Out of Balance.* New York: Penguin.

Graham, Susan M., Zahra Jalalian-Lechak, Juma Shafi, et al. (2012) "Antiretroviral Treatment Interruptions Predict Female Genital Shedding of Genotypically Resistant HIV-1 RNA." *Journal of Acquired Immune Deficiency Syndromes* 60: 511–518.

Howe, Jeff (2011) "Crossing Over: A Review of *Anthropology Now.*" *American Anthropologist* 113(1): 145–146.

JUNP and WHO (2010) *Global Report: UNAIDS Report on the Global AIDS Epidemic.* Geneva: Joint United Nations Program on HIV/AIDS and World Health Organization. At http://www.unaids.org/en/media/unaids/contentassets/documents/unaidspublication/2010/20101123_globalreport_en.pdf, accessed Sept. 7, 2012.

Juviler, Peter (2000) "Political Community and Human Rights in Postcommunist Russia." In Adamantia Pollis and Peter Schwab (eds.), *Human Rights: New Perspectives, New Realities.* Boulder, CO: Lynne Rienner, pp. 115–137.

Luebbert, Julia, Hannock Tweya, Sam Phiri, et al. (2012) "Virological Failure and Drug Resistance in Patients on Antiretroviral Therapy after Treatment Interruption in Lilongwe, Malawi." *Clinical Infectious Diseases* 55: 441–448.

Lock, Margaret and Vinh-Kim Nguyen (2010) *An Anthropology of Biomedicine.* Oxford: Wiley-Blackwell.

MacPherson, Douglas W., Brian D. Gushulak, William B. Baine, et al. (2009) "Population Mobility, Globalization, and Antimicrobial Drug Resistance." *Emerging Infectious Diseases* 15: 1727–1731.

Medical Research Council (1948) "Streptomycin Treatment of Pulmonary Tuberculosis." *British Medical Journal* 2: 769–782.

Merton, Robert K. (1936) "The Unanticipated Consequences of Purposive Social Action." *American Sociological Review* 1: 894–896.

MSPP (2012) "Rapport du 23 Avril 2012." *Ministère de la Santé et de la Population*. Downloadable at http://www.mspp.gouv.ht/site/index.php?option=com_content&view=artic le&id=120&Itemid=1, accessed Sept. 7, 2012.

Ngonini, Xola (2010) "Anxious Communities: The Decline of Mine Migration in the Eastern Cape." In J. Crush and B. Frayne (eds.), *Surviving on the Move: Migration, Poverty and Development in Southern Africa*. Cape Town: Idasa Publishing.

Nguyen, Vinh-Kim (2010) *The Republic of Therapy: Triage and Sovereignty in West Africa's Time of AIDS*. Durham, NC: Duke University Press.

Packard, Randall M. (1989) *White Plague, Black Labor: Tuberculosis and the Political Economy of Health and Disease in South Africa*. Berkeley: University of California Press.

Posel, Dori (2006) "Moving On: Patterns of Labour Migration in Post-Apartheid South Africa." In M. Tienda et al. (eds.), *Africa on the Move: African Migration and Urbanization in Comparative Perspective*. Johannesburg: Wits University Press.

Pyle, Marjorie (1947) "Relative Number of Resistant Tubercle Bacilli in Sputa of Patients before and during Treatment with Streptomycin." *Proceedings of the Mayo Clinic* 22: 465–473.

Sarayeva, Darya (2012) "Disease of the Century." *Tomsk News* (Mar. 28). Available in Russian at http://tomsk-novosti.ru/bolezn-veka/, accessed Sept. 7, 2012.

Shin, Sonya S., Alexander D. Pasechnikov, Irina Y. Gelmanova, et al. (2006) "Treatment Outcomes in an Integrated Civilian and Prison MDR-TB Treatment Program in Russia." *International Journal of Tuberculosis and Lung Disease* 10: 402–408.

South African Department of Health (2010) "The South African Department of Health Study, 2010." At http://www.avert.org/south-africa-hiv-aids-stastistics.htm

Statistics South Africa (2005) *Documented Migration Report, 2003*. At http://www.info.gov.za/view/DownloadFileAction?id=112066, accessed Sept. 11, 2012.

Styblo, Karel (1984) *Epidemiology of Tuberculosis*. The Hague: Royal Netherlands Tuberculosis Association.

Sutherland, Ian and Peter M. Fayers (1975) "The Association of the Risk of Tuberculosis Infection with Age." *Bulletin of the International Union against Tuberculosis* 50: 70–81.

Vaughan, Megan (1991) *Curing Their Ills: Colonial Power and African Illness*. Stanford: Stanford University Press.

Vearey, Joanna (2012) "Learning from HIV: Exploring Migration and Health in South Africa." *Global Public Health* 7(1): 58–70.

Vearey, Joanna, Ingrid Palmary, Liz Thomas, et al. (2010) "Urban Health in Johannesburg: The Importance of Place in Understanding Intra-urban Inequalities in a Context of Migration and HIV." *Health and Place* 16: 694–702.

Walberg, Peder, Martin McKee, Vladimir Shkolnikov, et al. (1998) "Economic Change, Crime, and Mortality Crisis in Russia: Regional Analysis." *British Medical Journal* 317: 312.

White, Michael J. and David P. Lindstrom (2005) "Internal Migration." In Dudley L. Poston and Michael Micklin (eds.), *Handbook of Population*. New York: Springer, pp. 307–342.

Wilson, Francis (2001) "Minerals and Migrants: How the Mining Industry has Shaped South Africa." *Daedalus* 130(1): 99–122.

Zimmerman, Cathy, Ligia Kiss, and Mazeda Hossain (2011) "Migration and Health: A Framework for 21st Century Policy-Making." *PLoS Med* 8(5): e1001034. doi:10.1371/journal.pmed.1001034

Zuger, Abigail (2000) "Russia has Few Weapons as Infectious Diseases Surge." *New York Times* (Dec. 5). At http://www.nytimes.com/2000/12/05/science/russia-has-few-weapons-as-infectious-diseases-surge.html?pagewanted=all&src=pm, accessed Sept. 13, 2012.

Chapter 32

High-Performing Applied Programs

Elizabeth K. Briody and Riall W. Nolan

Elizabeth Briody and Riall Nolan were curious about how anthropology departments approached the issue of training future practitioners, and in 2010 they conducted a Delphi survey of 15 institutions. They have combined the results of this survey with data from several other recent surveys of students, faculty, and departments to present a picture of how training is being done today, how this differs from the past, and what experience so far may mean for students, faculty, and departments as they seek to improve training and to respond to new opportunities. The authors discuss how training has changed, how applied programs have evolved, and what their main commonalities and differences are. They look in detail at four flagship programs – Memphis, Maryland, Northern Arizona, and North Texas – and how they grew. Finally, the authors offer advice to students on choosing a program.

A gradual but steady transformation has been occurring within US-based anthropology departments. Since the late 1970s, increasing numbers of these departments have been offering coursework, community and organizational learning experiences, and career skills to their students to prepare them for the job market. This trend is a response, in part, to the dearth of academic job opportunities, and to the demand by master's level students for training that will give them a competitive edge over peers in other disciplines. In this chapter, we look at several of these programs in terms of their origins, similarities, and differences.

In general, applied anthropology programs are characterized by an emphasis on problem-solving and collaboration. *Problem-solving* refers specifically to the

A Handbook of Practicing Anthropology. First Edition. Edited by Riall W. Nolan.
© 2013 John Wiley & Sons, Inc. Published 2013 by John Wiley & Sons, Inc.

identification of, and engagement with, organizational, community, and societal issues. *Collaboration* can be understood as a joint cooperative activity, not just between students and professors, but between students and professors *and* clients, community members, and others who contribute to the discovery and solution of problems by working together. In the programs we looked at, both the focus of the problem-solving and the form and extent of collaboration are influenced by such factors as the university and college mission, the setting (e.g., local, global) in which the joint activity occurs, and the economic climate.

We wrote this chapter to speak to the concerns of both students and faculty. Students should find this chapter useful for the contrasts we draw between academically oriented and applied programs, commonalities and differences between applied programs, and ideas for selecting an applied program. Faculty should benefit from our discussion of the applied program life cycle, the ability to craft an applied program with a high degree of fit between faculty and student interests and local conditions, and the hopes and expectations expressed by students for future applied program offerings.

The Emergence of Applied Programs

If there were ever an American theme that captured the essence of Elizabeth Briody's graduate training in anthropology, we believe it was self-reliance. The requirements of her program – core classes, thesis, language proficiency, qualifying exams, fieldwork, and final defense – provided a structure for her MA and PhD training (1978–85). However, she quickly perceived her graduate experience as isolating from both a peer-relationship and a learning standpoint. Her classmates tended to keep to themselves, working independently as they absorbed classroom lectures, prepared for exams, and planned and conducted field projects. Briody found few opportunities for interactions or joint activities. Those professors who served as mentors and provided guidance on her academic work were training her to become what they were – academicians who worked on their own anthropological studies and contributed to scholarship mainly through sole-authored publications. Briody figured out that if she were to succeed, she would have to rely largely on herself in making her own way.

Contrast Briody's graduate experience with that of Marisa Deline a generation later. Deline was enrolled in an applied anthropology program from 2007 to 2009, and graduated with a master of Applied Anthropology degree.[1] The theme of collaboration is exemplified in two particular experiences that were part of Deline's training. First, one requirement for her pre-internship class was to conduct 10 informational interviews with organizational and community members. That exercise turned out to be an initial step in building her network of professional contacts. In addition, she and another classmate conducted the interviews together, which enabled them to cooperate on the assignment, learn from each other, and reduce their initial nervousness associated with interviewing. At another point in her program, Deline accessed her professor's contacts and approached a practitioner (also a departmental adjunct) to work with her on an independent study. The readings, discussions, and final product – a realistic work plan that Deline developed – occurred within the context of a strong mentoring relationship. Career questions and advice flowed freely. Both of these experiences illustrate how much some anthropology programs have evolved from the academically oriented programs, and the benefits to learning and networking from the wider community that can result.

We have tried to capture key dimensions of this change by comparing academically oriented programs of the 1980s with programs today (see Table 32.1). Three broad themes run through changes in anthropological training. First, training is no longer solely grounded in the academy. While the basic research paradigm continues to predominate in many academically oriented programs (particularly those granting PhD degrees), there has been a growth of interest and activity in application. Today, there are 28 anthropology departments that are members of the Consortium of Practicing and Applied Anthropology Programs (COPAA 2012). In many of these

Table 32.1 A comparison of academically oriented and applied anthropology programs

	Academically oriented programs (early 1980s)	*Applied programs (late 2000s)*
Culture	Autonomous, self-reliant, independent, somewhat isolated; characterized by the "lone anthropologist"	Group-based, collective, integrated; characterized by people working together
Course content	Theory, method, and substantive area	Theory, method, and applied courses and experiences
Goal	Academic position	Non-academic positions, and sometimes options for additional academic training
Career-related preparation	Own field project, teaching and research assistant positions	Internships, class projects, own field projects
Skills	Developing theoretical abilities, designing and conducting field research, scholarly writing, teaching	Integrating theory with problem-solving, working with others to diagnose issues and implement solutions
Mentoring	Done by individual professors	Done by professors, adjuncts, alumni, practitioners, students
Networks	Dependent on self or on own professors	Dependent on self, but typically aided by others
Professional anthropology associations	Little direct outreach to students	Some outreach to students, with benefits to students specified

departments, coursework, class projects, and internship preparation and follow-up have been designed to connect students with community and organizational issues, hone their problem-solving skills, and ready them for the job market.

Second, anthropological training is now more likely to be collaborative in programs with an applied focus. Students may work with other students on a class project that is guided by both a professor and a client, linking together theory and practice. Master's-level applied programs are the most likely to offer internships, where the student, faculty adviser, and client identify and complete an agreed set of goals. When it is done well, such cooperation brings multiple perspectives and experiences to bear on real world issues. The student benefits from hands-on work experience, the faculty adviser from community connections, and the client from the student and faculty efforts and insights. Recommendations are typically posed and discussed by the applied project team and client. Applied programs today are also more likely to be linked to applied and practice-oriented professional associations including the Society for Applied Anthropology (SfAA), the National Association for the Practice of Anthropology (NAPA), or the aforementioned COPAA.

Third, the internal, disciplinary focus within many anthropology programs is shifting outward (Bartlo 2012). This change is noticeable in several ways: in application-oriented coursework, readings, and internships; in the integration of practitioners as lecturers and mentors into academic programs; and in the growth of program linkages with outside constituencies. As this shift occurs, programs benefit from increasingly wider networks, providing visibility and the potential for support.

We believe that comparing the Briody and Deline cases is instructive in another way. Although self-reliance has always been fundamental to any job search, today's recent applied graduates have "practiced" the craft of job market engagement as part of their formal training. While they rely primarily on themselves, they have also learned that it is useful – and professionally expected – that they will connect with others for advice and support, and develop this network of contacts in a variety of ways. These entrepreneurial skills, together with their anthropological toolkit, give them a high probability of finding interesting and challenging work throughout their career.

Continuity with the Past

A "must read" for those thinking about applied anthropology programs is *Anthropology for Tomorrow* (Trotter 1988). Its framing and messages continue to be useful for anthropologists who are either developing applied programs or expanding existing ones. The book's orientation can be likened to a two-way flow in which academia can play a significant role in human problem solving, and anthropological practice can have an important presence in the broader context of student training. The future is viewed as encompassing both worlds, even as they are in a continual state of flux, through a willingness to connect and collaborate as an integrated whole.

Elizabeth K. Briody and Riall W. Nolan

This orientation to the connection of theory and application is part of a broader movement within the discipline to draw attention to the value of applied anthropological training and anthropological practice. For example, Rylko-Bauer (2006) and her colleagues point out that applied anthropology has contributed significantly to the "shaping of professional organization, evolution of disciplinary subfields, and establishment of ethical standards . . . [along with being] a productive source of anthropological concepts, perspectives, and theory." Other researchers highlight the rise in anthropology graduates who find work outside academia (Price 2001; Fiske et al. 2010), and the obligation to broaden student training beyond presumed academic positions. Indeed, early arguments for the professionalization of the discipline (Chambers and Fiske 1988; Nolan 1998) are part of the ongoing characterization of anthropological practice and the "professional" anthropologists associated with it.

Growth and Development

Applied anthropology programs exist within a particular historical, institutional, socio-economic, and political context. Such programs are shaped by features internal to the departments as well as external to both the university and the wider community. Faculty contemplating the development of applied programs should look to the ways in which the faculty composition, university mission and constraints, and the local setting can be leveraged as assets in developing and structuring the curriculum and hands-on work experiences.

The applied anthropology program life cycle

We recently carried out a CoPAPIA-sponsored study to examine how and why programs of applied anthropology become established and sustained (Briody and Nolan 2011). We used the Delphi method to gather perspectives from 23 faculty members at 15 institutions. Respondents indicated that internal factors such as faculty expertise and faculty consensus in relation to program goals and structure had a considerable effect on the character of their program as it developed. They pointed to external factors such as the availability of job opportunities, local interests and expectations, and university pressure and constraints as major influences.

Our study also revealed some of the obstacles that applied programs face as they develop. First, there was typically a lack of consensus within anthropology departments about the role of application – often because a number of faculty members had little experience or interest in applied work. Second, tension often emerged between anthropology departments and university administrators. For example, there may be opposition to applied programs in a basic research university, or concerns expressed about adding more graduate programs. Third, applied programs typically ran into resource shortages relating to personnel and funding.

Fortunately, according to our Delphi respondents, applied programs generally learn to deal with the obstacles they face. Consensus within the departments improved through such means as faculty willingness to build relationships (e.g., with practitioners, community members), commitment to the program, and hiring. Tension with the university administration tended to dissipate as the program incorporated the university mission into its planning and as its value to the university became evident. And, while resource shortages might continue to exist, creative solutions were often devised to cope with them. Thus, by the time an applied program has "gone to scale" and engaged the wider university and local community, it was likely to offer greater stability and fewer unexpected challenges to entering students. Of course, even applied programs that have been active for many years may experience disruption if departing faculty leaders are not replaced, if funding is curtailed, or if program interest and energy dissipate.

Collaboration and problem-solving at the core of applied programs

Effective applied programs require collaboration and partnership, as well as significant long-term effort. At a minimum, applied programs require faculty to reach consensus on the curriculum, and community partners to serve as supervisors and mentors to students. Applied programs, collaborative by design and execution, create interdependencies between the faculty, students, and outside partners. Applied programs also extend and reinforce the decades-long growth in action anthropology and community-based participatory research spearheaded by applied anthropologists such as Tax (1960, 1964), Dobyns et al. (1971), and DeWalt (1979), and adapted for use with today's challenges through such means as rapid assessment techniques and new technologies (Kedia 2008; Briody et al. 2010).

The applied program orientation to collaboration and partnering fits well with some broader societal trends. Social networking sites, for example, are booming. Organizations enter into joint ventures, strategic alliances, and non-equity collaborations. Mentoring programs have become a common way for young, less experienced people to benefit from the knowledge and competencies of seasoned professionals. Collaboration enables individuals, groups, and organizations to engage in greater outreach and to benefit from a broader range of learning opportunities.

Problem-solving is the other prominent element associated with applied anthropology programs. It is most often evident in class projects for clients, internships, and job searches. For example, projects are undertaken not solely because of their theoretical merit, but because there is a problem or issue that warrants a solution. The investigation of a particular issue might be proposed by faculty or students, or by a client. The goal is typically to describe and explain what's going on and then offer potential solutions to address the problem. Students frequently gain experience in problem-solving through internships and other kinds of volunteer and work opportunities. Recognizing, understanding, and solving problems are an ongoing part of the world of work, and students use their internships as a way to improve their skills in problem identification and resolution.

Problem-solving is also linked with the search for employment. Since relatively few jobs for master's-level graduates have the title "anthropologist," an array of strategies, including networking, may be necessary to find a desirable position. Applied programs help to develop and hone that problem-solving orientation – a critical skill in the anthropological toolkit, and highly useful in the job hunt.

Applied Program Commonalities

Perhaps the most common feature distinguishing applied from academically oriented anthropology programs is the internship or practicum option. CoPAPIA also sponsored a recent interview-based study of 20 applied faculty members and students/recent graduates (Bartlo et al. 2011). Nine of the 10 applied programs represented in the study offered internships as a key part of their program requirements. This experience, including its preparatory and post-internship/practicum phases, became a mechanism for connecting theory with practice, books and lectures with experiential learning, and the university with the broader community. The internship was also an effective way to link students with the job market since the majority of students in applied programs used these experiences and the networks associated with them to identify post-graduation employment.

Applied programs shared other elements as well. CoPAPIA interviewees reported that seven of the 10 applied programs integrated job skills into the core curriculum through such means as methods courses, applied courses, and grant and résumé writing. Six of the 10 programs encouraged networking opportunities with alumni. Five of the 10 programs brought or encouraged students to attend anthropology conferences. Four of the 10 programs held workshops or other kinds of exercises to help students translate anthropological skills to the job market. In addition, four of the 10 programs recommended that students network with practitioners, including adjunct members of the anthropology department, as a strategy for understanding the job market, getting advice, setting up some informational interviews, and following up on job placement leads.

Applied Program Differences

Applied programs are not monolithic in their history, development, or current approach to student training. Indeed, we discovered no single model that explains how they are structured or operate. The applied programs we looked at were at different stages of their life cycle and/or were subject to different kinds of constraints (e.g., related to size, faculty interests). Some programs were quite new and had only one or two faculty members engaged in applied program and curriculum development. Other programs had been around for years – even decades. In general, newer programs and those in which few faculty members consult for organizations and communities tended to have relatively fewer offerings compared with larger, more mature applied programs.

The CoPAPIA interview-based study also explored some of the specific features of four mature and long-standing applied programs (Bartlo et al. 2011) which we summarize here.

The University of Memphis

The University of Memphis Anthropology Department, which grants both a bachelor of arts and a master of arts degree, was established in 1972 and celebrated its thirty-fifth anniversary of the master's applied program in 2012 with special events for those connected with the department past and present (University of Memphis 2012). Memphis, located on the banks of the Mississippi river, initiated its applied master's program in 1977. The program offers dual concentrations in (1) medical anthropology, and (2) globalization, development, and culture.

Faculty members in the Memphis program actively cultivate and integrate community members – especially alumni – into all aspects of program functioning. Alumni are viewed as the lifeblood of the program because they are so much a part of its "everyday activities" (see Figure 32.1). They serve as part-time instructors. They help students network. They also hire interns and graduates of the program, as indicated in this statement:

> Our graduates are in the (local) job market. A lot are called back (to campus). We've had opportunities to meet with them. We can network with them. We can volunteer our time with them to get our foot in the door.

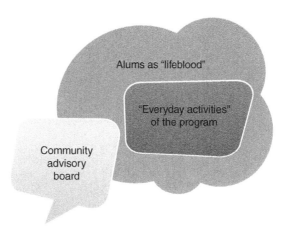

Figure 32.1 Visual representation of the applied anthropology program at the University of Memphis

Faculty members appreciate the "critique and evaluation of the program" that they receive from alumni. Such feedback, along with input from the program's Community Advisory Board, helps to guide the program and keep it fresh. Alumni connections to the program are robust and long-lasting. For example, when the SfAA held its annual meeting in Memphis in 2008, we were told that about "150 alums came . . . This number of alums represented about half of our alums." It is the strength and durability of the alumni network, in particular, that gives this applied program its strong practice foundation. That network is fueled in part by job market connections in the surrounding area.

The University of Maryland, College Park

The Maryland Anthropology Department was established in 1974. In 1984 it became the first program in the United States to offer an MAA. degree – a master of applied anthropology – which is the only master's degree offered by the department. The department also grants a bachelor of arts degree and began granting a PhD degree in 2007. The department has three specialization areas including (1) anthropology of environment, (2) anthropology of health, and (3) anthropology of heritage with a focus on historical archaeology and applied cultural anthropology.

Adjunct faculty members are one of the key ways in which Maryland's applied program is distinctive (see Figure 32.2). Many anthropologists work for the federal government and various other organizations and institutions in and around Washington, DC – just 11 miles from College Park. Twenty-two anthropologists are listed as adjuncts on the website (University of Maryland 2012). They perform the same kinds of functions as alumni at the University of Memphis: giving lectures, supervising independent studies, offering career advice, and assisting with the job search. For example, we were told that:

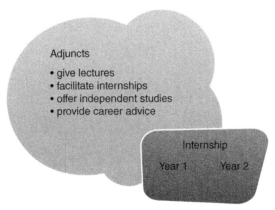

Figure 32.2 Visual representation of the anthropology program at the University of Maryland, College Park

Our department uses the adjunct members well. Yesterday, an M.A.A. student defended his proposal. The student will work at the Bureau of Land Management. An adjunct faculty found that opportunity.

The timing of the internship, between the first and second years of the M.A.A. program, emphasizes its centrality to learning. Adjuncts help to facilitate internships – both through their networks and their ability to find placements for students. As one interviewee reported:

> The value of the adjunct is enormous. It is important to reach out to them. They can help you understand how your interest in anthropology can translate to a career.

In the last few years, adjuncts have begun working with faculty and students on research grants as well.

Northern Arizona University

The Anthropology Department at Northern Arizona University was created in 1985. At that time, faculty members undertook an intensive effort to design and implement an applied master's program which would operate alongside the more academically oriented thesis program. Located in Flagstaff (elevation nearly 7,000 feet) and surrounded by a large pine forest, the department grants a bachelor of arts and a master of arts degree (Northern Arizona University 2012). The master of arts offers three emphasis areas: (1) archaeology, (2) sociocultural anthropology, and (3) linguistic anthropology.

The culture of this applied program is built around neither alumni nor adjuncts, though both are important to how the program functions. Instead, the centerpiece of the program is the "cohort philosophy" (see Figure 32.3). Program faculty developed

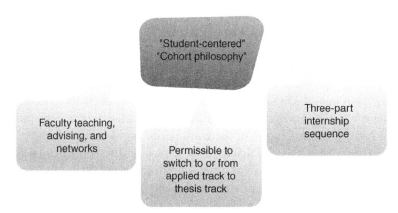

Figure 32.3 Visual representation of the applied anthropology program at Northern Arizona University

consensus around using the structure of the cohort progression to build and extend student networks. Entering cohorts are encouraged to build their own networks, taking advantage of those of their student peers, faculty, and others connected with the program. These networks are a contributing element to an individually tailored curriculum, and ultimately individual career paths. A three-part internship sequence, including the periods prior to and following their internship experience, is a core part of student learning and job preparation. Later, students discover that "the cohort effect is a deliberate part of the job search process. Even after the end of the program, they [applied students] are helping each other." Locally, the archaeology graduates have found that their "cohort networks maintain [the] level of staffing" in the national parks and national forests. The cohort philosophy engenders strong, tight-knit connections among the students, so much so that we were told, "The thesis students asked if the department could create a cohort progression for them" – which subsequently occurred.

The University of North Texas

The Anthropology Department at the University of North Texas uses its website to teach prospective students about anthropology, applied anthropology, and the range of anthropological careers. The program, which is part of a college of applied social sciences, grants a bachelor of arts, a master of arts/science (both on-campus and online options), and a dual master's in applied anthropology and public health. Located in Denton, Texas, the department was established in 1990 and formalized its applied focus by 1997. Today, the program offers several specializations including (1) business, technology, and design anthropology, (2) migration and border studies, (3) medical anthropology, (4) anthropology of education, and (5) environmental and ecological anthropology.

The University of North Texas program stresses "the practical use of anthropology to solve problems and improve people's lives" (University of North Texas 2012). Students engage in multiple client interactions over the course of the program through various project experiences (see Figure 32.4). We were told, for example, that some of the required core classes "had a client attached to them and almost all of the electives had them." Class projects are a key mechanism for exposing students to issues facing organizations and communities, sharpening their research skills, and engaging them in problem solving and decision making. One student indicated that the professor "set up a project before the class even started. So they (the professors) sort of used their connections in the community or wherever." Another type of project experience is the practicum (now known as the applied thesis), a type of internship in which the student designs and carries out a major client project. As in the other three applied programs, students are expected to find their own clients. A formal agreement is created with the client such that "There is a three-way between the student, the professor, and the [client]." The combination of the class projects and the practicum/internship experience prepares students well for the job

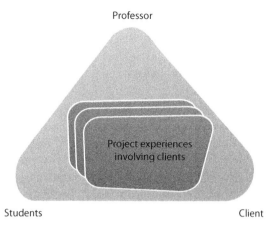

Figure 32.4 Visual representation of the applied anthropology program at the University of North Texas

market, enables them to make an impact on both local and global community issues, and helps fulfill the mission of the College of Public Affairs and Community Service.

These four applied programs build on their individual strengths to create interesting and challenging learning experiences. Each operates using a collaborative orientation with the potential to benefit all parties involved (e.g., students, faculty, community members). Each figures out its own ways to connect with and beyond the locale in which it is situated and offers mechanisms for integrating alumni, adjuncts, and other groups into the university setting. Finally, each trains students to be problem-solvers who seek solutions to thorny organizational and community challenges. The diversity of these four models suggests that prospective applied anthropology programs have many options open to them. Faculty members can take stock of their own competencies and interests, and the local conditions, and then develop and execute a plan that is consistent with them, making periodic adjustments as necessary.

Student Reactions to Applied Training

At least three recent studies have sought student feedback on master's-level training. NAPA sponsored a survey in 2000 of 113 graduates from six applied master's programs in the United States. One question asked for recommendations for improving applied program curricula. Dozens of suggestions emphasized "specific work management and workplace interaction skills" along with particular work-related skills (e.g., data collection and analysis, report and grant writing, evaluation, networking) (Harman et al. 2004: 5–6). The study also found that more recent graduates reported greater continuity between the training they received and its applicability to their jobs. The authors speculated that applied programs may be keeping pace with updating their curricula to be responsive to workplace environments generally.

In 2009 CoPAPIA conducted a large survey of 758 anthropology master's graduates – both applied and academically oriented – from 128 US, 12 Canadian, and two Mexican universities (Fiske et al. 2010). Respondents expressed an overall satisfaction with their master's education. Consistent with the earlier NAPA study, respondents confirmed the importance of workplace preparation and application skills within the master's-level curricula. Their top recommendations included technical writing (e.g., proposals, grants), project design, development, and management, presentation skills, budget preparation, analysis and execution, and networking.

The 2010 CoPAPIA interview-based study solicited suggestions for improving preparation for the job market within applied anthropology programs (Bartlo et al. 2011). Recommendations were associated with six domains. First, students desired more "professionalization" preparation, including better training on how to sell anthropological skills as well as develop proposals. Second, they sought more real world experiences such as internships and "smaller projects on tighter deadlines." Third, mentoring and guidance were seen as important – "someone pointing out my strengths and skills," or an opportunity for "long-term relationship building." Fourth, they stressed the value of face-to-face access with anthropological practitioners. For example, "In school . . . you could also bring in guests who could speak, or who could give an inspirational talk." Fifth, they emphasized virtual access to practitioners: "Having a more active on-line community . . . to learn about professional opportunities . . . students who are looking for internships right now for the coming summer could really benefit from that." Finally, students wanted more coverage of survey and focus group methods as well as quantitative analysis. All of these suggestions reflect a desire for improved alignment between applied program training and current employment options. There is no evidence in the study that students want to undercut the educational content of their program. What is required is an appropriate balance between orienting students to the job market while ensuring that the substantive course material is robust and useful.

Choosing an Applied Program

To conclude, we'd like to offer some thoughts on how students might choose an applied anthropology program. In choosing a program, it is helpful to have a general understanding of the kinds of work in which anthropologists are engaged. There are many resources available to assist with that search.

A good place to start is with the career DVDs offered through the American Anthropological Association (Briody and Bodo 1993; Smiley 2006; Altimare 2008). There are publications describing jobs held by anthropologists (Wasson 2006; Guerrón-Montero 2008; Strang 2009), or planning an anthropological career (Nolan 2002; Briller and Goldmacher 2009; Ellick and Watkins 2011). Workshops offered through anthropological organizations (e.g., SfAA, NAPA) can assist in a non-academic career search (Nolan 2010). Some websites are worth exploring (including

AAA 2012), as well as various online groups such as LinkedIn Groups (e.g., Ethnographic Praxis in Industry Conference, Consumer Anthropology, NAPA).

Websites are also informative. Anthropology department websites provide considerable insight into the people, scope, and requirements of applied programs. The philosophy, areas of concentration, research interests, and courses are listed. The work of departmental members, including students or recent graduates, may be featured and often enhanced with photos or video clips. Departmental newsletters and current events may be posted.

Informational interviews with faculty and students can be used to confirm what was learned via websites and to gather additional information. Questions can be posed about such matters as program structure, expectations, workload, graduation rates, and post-graduation job placement. These conversations can reveal how much energy and enthusiasm permeate the program, the likelihood that solid working relationships can be formed, and the extent to which departmental members share common interests. Finding a good "fit" between the program and the prospective student is the goal. Documenting the entire investigative activity – what is absorbed from websites, conversations, campus visits, and other means – enables informed decision-making. Some additional networking and/or some guidance from a mentor are likely to be helpful in sorting out priorities.

There is an important long-term benefit to this process: the knowledge acquisition, coordination, and relationship building skills used in an applied program search are essential in the training, employment pursuits, and career development of practitioners. Establishing a base of support, working cooperatively with others, and partnering on projects when appropriate make a valuable connection between anthropology's traditional value of self-reliance and that of collaboration. While the graduating anthropologist still approaches the job market and career prospects as an individual, they do so within the context of a networked community that they have created.

Note

1   We thank Marisa Deline for her helpful comments on an early draft.

References

Altimare, Emily L. (2008) "Beyond Ethnography: Corporate and Design Anthropology" (DVD). Careers in Anthropology 2. Arlington, VA: American Anthropological Association.

AAA (2012) "Career Paths and Education." *American Anthropological Association*. At http://www.aaanet.org/profdev/careers/Careers.cfm, accessed Sept. 11, 2012.

Bartlo, Wendy D. (2012) "Crossing Boundaries." *Anthropology News* 53(2): 24.

Bartlo, Wendy D., Keri Brondo, Elizabeth K. Briody, and Shirley J. Fiske (2011) "Linking Anthropology Graduates to the Job Market." Report to CoPAPIA (Feb. 26).

Briller, Sherylyn H. and Amy Goldmacher (2009) *Designing an Anthropology Career: Professional Development Exercises.* Lanham, MD: AltaMira Press.

Briody, Elizabeth K. and Dawn Bodo (1993) "Anthropologists at Work: Careers Making a Difference" (DVD). Arlington, VA: American Anthropological Association.

Briody, Elizabeth K. and Riall W. Nolan (2011) "Bringing Practice into Your Department: Results of a Delphi Survey." Paper presented at Society for Applied Anthropology meetings, Seattle, WA, Mar. 29–Apr. 2.

Briody, Elizabeth K., Robert T. Trotter, II, and Tracy L. Meerwarth (2010) *Transforming Culture: Creating and Sustaining a Better Manufacturing Organization.* Basingstoke: Palgrave Macmillan.

Chambers, Erve and Shirley Fiske (1988) "Involving Practitioners in Applied Anthropology Programs." In Robert T. Trotter, II (ed.), *Anthropology for Tomorrow: Creating Practitioner-Oriented Applied Anthropology Programs.* Washington, DC: American Anthropological Association: 47–56.

COPAA (2012) "Programs in Applied Anthropology (COPAA Members)." Consortium of Applied and Practicing Anthropology Programs At http://www.copaa.info/programs_in_aa/list.htm, accessed Sept. 11, 2012.

DeWalt, Billie J. (1979) *Modernization in a Mexican Ejido: A Study in Economic Adaptation.* Cambridge: Cambridge University Press.

Dobyns, Henry F., Paul L. Doughty, and Harold D. Lasswell (1971) *Peasants, Power, and Applied Social Change: Vicos as a Model.* Beverly Hills, CA: Sage.

Ellick, Carol J. and Joe E. Watkins (2011) *The Anthropology Graduate's Guide: From Student to a Career.* Walnut Creek, CA: Left Coast Press.

Fiske, Shirley J., Linda A. Bennett, Patricia Ensworth, et al. (2010) *The Changing Face of Anthropology: Anthropology Masters Reflect on Education, Careers, and Professional Organizations. The AAA/CoPAPIA 2009 Anthropology MA Career Survey.* Arlington, VA: American Anthropological Association.

Guerrón-Montero, Carla (ed.) (2008) *Careers in Applied Anthropology in the 21st Century: Perspectives from Academics and Practitioners.* NAPA` Bulletin 29. Oxford: Blackwell.

Harman, Robert C., Jim Hess, and Amir Shafe (2004) "Report on Survey of Alumni of Master's Level Applied Anthropology Training Programs." Report sponsored by the National Association for the Practice of Anthropology, Long Beach, CA: California State University Long Beach. At http://www.copaa.info/documents/Alumni_Survey.pdf, accessed Sept. 11, 2012.

Kedia, Satish (2008) "Recent Changes and Trends in the Practice of Applied Anthropology." *National Association for the Practice of Anthropology Bulletin* 29(1): 14-28.

Nolan, Riall W. (1998) "Teaching Anthropology as if it Mattered: A Curriculum for 21st Century Practitioners." *Practicing Anthropology* 20(4): 39–44.

Nolan, Riall W. (2002) *Anthropology in Practice: Building a Career Outside the Academy.* Boulder, CO: Lynne Rienner.

Nolan, Riall W. (2010) "Becoming a Practicing Anthropologist: A Workshop for Students Seeking Non-Academic Careers." Society for Applied Anthropology workshop, Merida, Yucatan, Mexico, Mar. 24–27.

Northern Arizona University (2012) "Anthropology." At http://nau.edu/sbs/anthropology/, accessed Sept. 11, 2012.

Price, Laurie J. (2001) "The Mismatch between Anthropology Graduate Training and the Work Lives of Graduates." *Practicing Anthropology* 23(1): 55–57.

Rylko-Bauer, Barbara, Merrill Singer, and John van Willigen (2006) "Reclaiming Applied Anthropology: Its Past, Present, and Future." *American Anthropologist* 108(1): 178–190.

Smiley, Francis E. (2006) "Anthropology: Real People, Real Careers" (DVD). Careers in Anthropology 1. Arlington, VA: American Anthropological Association.

Strang, Veronica (2009) *What Anthropologists Do*. Oxford: Berg.

Tax, Sol (1960) *Documentary History of the Fox Project, 1948–1959: A Program in Action Anthropology*. Chicago: University of Chicago Press.

Tax, Sol (1964) "The Uses of Anthropology." In Sol Tax (ed.), *Horizons of Anthropology*. Chicago: Aldine, pp. 248–258.

Trotter, Robert T., II, (ed.) (1988) *Anthropology for Tomorrow: Creating Practitioner-Oriented Applied Anthropology Programs*. Washington, DC: American Anthropological Association.

University of Maryland (2012) "Department of Anthropology." At http://www.bsos.umd.edu/ anth/, accessed Sept. 11, 2012.

University of Memphis (2012) "The Department of Anthropology." At http://www.memphis. edu/anthropology/, accessed Sept. 11, 2012.

University of North Texas (2012) "Anthropology." At http://anthropology.unt.edu/index.php, accessed Sept. 11, 2012.

Wasson, Christina (ed.), *Making History at the Frontier: Women Creating Careers as Practicing Anthropologists*. NAPA Bulletin 26. Berkeley, CA: University of California Press for National Association for the Practice of Anthropology.

Part V
Conclusion

Chapter 33

The Future of Practice
Anthropology and the Grand Challenges

Riall W. Nolan

In this concluding chapter, Riall Nolan looks at the grand challenges of our age, and how anthropology has responded to these. At a time when other disciplines are reorienting themselves to address the grand challenges, anthropology's response has remained largely individual and piecemeal. Ironically, practitioners are deeply involved in many of today's grand challenges, and have been for some time. Recent calls within the academy for more public engagement on the part of the discipline is highly encouraging, but Nolan argues that anthropology's potential contribution to some of our most pressing problems will be realized only if we can overcome the split which we have created between academia and practice, if we develop a true profession, and work with others to promote the needed changes in our institutions. If we can do this, the future for anthropology, and for practice, is very bright.

To conclude this book, I want to look briefly at several linked issues: what we as a society need to pay attention to these days, what anthropology has done to help us with this, and how anthropology might become more useful to us in the future.

Today's World

Our world, it hardly need be said, is becoming more diverse and complex with every passing day. Communication and transport have moved difference in next door to each of us, both literally and metaphorically. We value this diversity; we celebrate

A Handbook of Practicing Anthropology. First Edition. Edited by Riall W. Nolan.
© 2013 John Wiley & Sons, Inc. Published 2013 by John Wiley & Sons, Inc.

and extol it. And yet, to a large extent, we remain profoundly ignorant of the cultural worlds of others, even as we try to connect with them. Pico Iyer cautioned us:

> Insofar as we try to love our neighbors as ourselves, we have to admit that our neighbors are people with whom we share no common language, or past, or value. (1994: 13)

What we *do* share, however, are predicaments, the ones we've come to call "grand challenges." These include such problems as climate change, sustainable energy, global health, and poverty. These problems are not merely "grand," they are *wicked*. "Wicked" problems share a number of characteristics: they are hard to formulate and resolve; every solution brings consequences of its own; stakeholders disagree about almost every aspect of the problem, from its shape to its solution; and wicked problems are intertwined and connected in dynamic ways. Perhaps the worst – and most important – characteristic of wicked problems is that we can't afford not to address them.

Our current attempts to deal with these wicked problems are spearheaded by disciplines such as science, engineering, and agriculture, which in turn are driven by a mindset that is highly empirical, focused on efficiency, profit, and speed, in which cultural factors, if they appear at all, tend to be considered as obstacles.[1]

We've seen this mindset at work, for example, with two of our biggest problems – war and poverty – issues which in many parts of the world are linked, in both straightforward and highly complex ways. Our attempts to confront these problems have tended, on the whole, to be highly technical in nature, and, for the most part, these approaches have failed. Ambrose Bierce once remarked that war was the way God taught Americans about geography. I believe that war and poverty are also teaching us, in rather painful ways at times, about culture.

Human culture – its nature and its consequences – are a huge missing piece of our attempts to create better and more sustainable futures for ourselves and for others. Whatever their accomplishments thus far, science and technology alone are unlikely to be sufficient for resolving the problems and challenges which now confront us.

This presents clear and enormous opportunities for anthropology, which works to situate objects, events, and ideas within a broader context. Failure to do this almost inevitably leads to problems. As George Dyson (2011) reminds us, "information is cheap, but meaning is expensive."

Anthropology's Response So Far

Many universities – and some entire disciplines – now speak of repositioning themselves to confront these "grand challenges" in a strategic manner, developing new programs and curricula, and organizing the work of faculty differently. Anthropology would seem to have much to contribute here, but in many institutions its voice so far seems muted. Although anthropology takes as its brief all human issues, the people actually writing about these issues – and whose books reach the general public – are rarely anthropologists. We have no disciplinary project, so to speak, for addressing any of our global problems in coherent, coordinated, intentional ways.

Our discipline does not talk collectively about "grand challenges" or "wicked problems." Indeed, with respect to war and poverty in particular, the discipline has sometimes seemed intent on marginalizing the anthropologists actually working in those areas, thus ensuring that anthropology's contribution to – and learning from – these difficult problems will remain minimal.

There is still far more rhetoric than there is action from the anthropological mainstream. Thirty years ago, Paul Bohannan's (1980) statement, "You can't do nothing," was a plea for the application of anthropology to world problems. Five years later, Sue Estroff reminded us of this again, in words that I have quoted many times over the years:

> The next decades will present us with choices that we have avoided making explicitly and with intention for a very long time . . . None of these agonizing choices can be made humanely without the kind of understanding of these "different others" and their worlds that anthropologists can provide. (1984: 369)

But, truth be told, anthropology isn't actually providing much in the way of understanding. We can't simply assert, as we often do, that anthropology is essential to solving our global problems. It's not that we haven't been involved in global issues (see Checker 2009, for example). It's just that we haven't been very effective in that arena. We need to actively figure out how to bring anthropology into the global conversation.

Instead, we've chosen to focus on other things. Controversy continues among academics concerning the proper role of practice, and the appropriate status to be accorded practitioners. In the conference halls there is still intense debate over how far anthropology should go in pursuit of public goals, what means and methods should be used, and what roles anthropologists should adopt. But there's very little in the way of a coherent plan.

This isn't new. It was noticed many years ago. In 1981 Rynkiewich and Spradley commented:

> We are doing all this [work] in anthropology is a planless sort of way . . . with no under-standing or knowledge of how we are distributing manpower in anthropology, and therefore, necessarily no understanding of how we should distribute our efforts except through rarely voiced but deep prejudices that the best schools should concern them-selves with the most esoteric work in the most ivory tower manner. (1981: 179–180)

Today, more graduates are choosing practice, rather than being pushed into it. In the fields in which they work, they are increasingly skilled and influential. These practitioners, for the most part, have made their peace with issues of engage-ment. Practitioners now look outside the academy for inspiration, validation, and professional satisfaction. Practitioners are slowly transforming the public face of anthropology into something that looks much more like a profession. To do this, however, they will need to connect more effectively with each other, by creating communities of practice. And this they are beginning to do.

The disconnect between the academy and the world of practice is neither as dire nor as pronounced as many might think, but it is still significant, and particularly so when we consider the present stagnation in academic employment and the fact that most of our graduate students are still being prepared for academic careers. There is an obvious synergy here between the strengths of practitioners and the strengths of the core discipline, but this synergy is not, for the most part, being captured.

Where We Go from Here

The main task in the future for anthropology, it seems to me, is to succeed in bringing sociocultural data and perspectives into our efforts to address global problems. To do this, anthropology needs to be much more involved with public life. Erve Chambers reminded us years ago that anthropology is more than a science: "it must also be a form of participation in human affairs" (1985: 189). If we want to be more influential in the wider society, we will need to enter into that society more fully. We will be listened to because of our skill and experience, not as anthropologists per se, but as problem-solvers. Action does not challenge anthropology's traditional role – it extends it.

We will also need to repair the split we have created between academia and practice. We're not the only discipline which needs to do this, of course. Ernest Boyer (1997), who wrote extensively on the role and mission of the university in today's society, believed in what he called the "scholarship of application." He felt strongly that it should have equal place in the academy beside research.

But sadly, many of us continue to feel that practice is what anthropologists do if they're not good enough to be academics. And many of us also feel that it is unethical to work for change, at whatever level. We seem preoccupied with disciplinary purity, focused on controversies which seem irrelevant to many, and increasingly isolated in significant ways from what's actually going on out on the street, so to speak.

As long as we continue to believe these things, anthropology will have little or no effective voice in world affairs. As Pat Fleuret, a development practitioner, said years ago:

> The notion of a value-free, non-directed applied science that is uninterested in achievement is absurd. Most anthropologists ... are cripples as applied scientists because they are unwilling – or simply unable – to accept service in the search of improvement as a measure of professional performance. (1987: 271)

More recently, Kamari Clarke framed the issue this way:

> Such compartmentalization [between theory and praxis] is false and has no place in the context of an unfurling new world order in whose presence anthropology has a far from public face and risks becoming divided between those in "ivory towers" and those who are exiled from academia because of the work they do. (2010: S311)

Whereas a discipline generates knowledge, a profession puts it to use, within specific domains, for clients (Greenwood 1957). Bringing the academy and the world of practice together will involve conscious recognition of the professional, as opposed to purely disciplinary, face of anthropology.

The longer we delay advancing the profession of anthropology, the higher the risks to the discipline. As the recognition of the need for social knowledge grows, so do the opportunities for anthropologists. But if we don't promote our discipline professionally, then others will eventually own what we do, and how we do it. And at that point, there will be no further need, so to speak, for our services. Choosing to remain on the sidelines will all but ensure that others will seize these opportunities, imposing their preferred solutions. "The dogs bark," as they say, "but the caravan moves on."

Becoming more involved with public life will also have the effect of allowing us to develop a true theory of practice – a set of propositions and principles for bringing anthropology to bear on real life situations, which is intellectually sound, practically relevant, and effective. Essential to the development of theory is of course a supporting literature of practice – "thick description" accounts of how practitioners actually work. Practice is an unfolding field test of anthropological method and theory, and understanding how practitioners do what they do will greatly enrich our discipline.

Thanks to practitioners, anthropology is today increasingly present and influential in our public life. Practitioners are involved at every level with the issues of our time. As a result, our students now have more options available to them regarding what to do with what they have learned. Years ago, Laura Nader (1972) exhorted us to "study up," and it's still good advice. But for many practitioners, it's now also a case of "studying in" – of looking at these organizations from the inside out. And while I'd freely admit that not everyone has to "go inside," I'd also maintain that without that authentically insider's viewpoint, we're missing much of the picture. So – to be direct about it – not all of us have to work for the World Bank, or for the military, or for a corporation. But we need to listen to our colleagues who do, learn from them, and put that knowledge to good use.

Much of life today, across the globe, is influenced by large, powerful, and relatively impersonal organizations which seem to have great difficulty understanding and acknowledging the importance of culture. Changing the way these institutions think is a very difficult task, but it is not impossible. And however difficult it may appear, it needs to be done. Years ago, I said this, with reference to the international development industry:

> We have no other way, ultimately, to effect change on a global scale than through our institutions. They are human creations, built by us, products of our minds. As we created them, so can we reshape them. (Nolan 2002: 281)

Anthropology today is very different from anthropology of 20 or 30 years ago. We now have a majority of practitioners, and they work at every conceivable job. It's time we made use of their collective skill and experience to find more effective ways to speak truth to power. Because if we don't take up this challenge, we're going to get what we've gotten so far – institutions that find it very difficult to think across cultural boundaries.

No one would call that a desirable state of affairs. The ability to work productively and sustainably with culture and cultural difference is very clearly central to America's story in the twenty-first century – to our democracy, to our values, and to our continued economic prosperity. It is also central to our attempts to join with others across the globe to address our common problems. Helping our institutions transform themselves into global learning organizations will not be done easily or quickly, but it can be done if we – academics and practitioners alike – work together, and with others, carefully and confidently.

It has always seemed to me that anthropology unites two very basic human impulses: a curiosity about the people living over the next hill, and a desire to make a lasting contribution. Anthropological practice is in many ways a fulfillment of these impulses, and I believe that it has a very bright future.

Note

1   I've characterized this mindset as "technicist thinking," and have elsewhere explored its manifestations and implications in development work (Nolan 2002: 45–50, 233–234).

References

Bohannan, Paul (1980) "You Can't Do Nothing." *American Anthropologist* 82: 508–524.

Boyer, Ernest (1997) *Scholarship Reconsidered: Priorities of the Professoriate.* San Francisco: Jossey-Bass.

Chambers, Erve (1985) *Applied Anthropology: A Practical Guide.* Prospect Heights, IL: Waveland Press.

Checker, Melissa (2009) "Anthropology in the Public Sphere, 2008: Emerging Trends and Significant Impacts." *American Anthropologist* 11: 162–169.

Clarke, Kamari M. (2010) "Toward a Critically Engaged Ethnographic Practice." *Current Anthropology* 51(S2): S301–S312.

Dyson, George (2011) "Information is Cheap, Meaning is Expensive." European (Oct. 17). At http://theeuropean-magazine.com/352-dyson-george/353-evolution-and-innovation, accessed Sept. 12, 2012.

Estroff, Sue (1984) "Who Are You? Why Are You Here? Anthropology and Human Suffering." *Human Organization* 433: 68–70.

Fleuret, Patrick (1987) "Comment on Natural Resource Anthropology." *Human Organization* 46: 271–272.

Greenwood, Ernest (1957) "Attributes of a Profession." *Social Work* 2: 44–55.

Iyer, Pico (1994) "Strangers in a Small World." *Harper's Magazine* (Sept.), 13–16.

Laura Nader (1972) "Up the Anthropologist – Perspectives Gained from Studying Up." In Dell H. Hymes (ed.), *Reinventing Anthropology.* New York: Pantheon Books, pp. 284–311.

Nolan, Riall (2002) *Development Anthropology.* Boulder, CO: Westview Press.

Rynkiewich, Michael A. and James P. Spradley (1981) *Ethics and Anthropology: Dilemmas in Fieldwork.* Malabar, FL: Robert E. Krieger.

Further Readings

We asked our contributors to suggest additional readings which they had found particularly helpful in their work. Some of their suggestions, of course, duplicated references already provided in other chapters, and in most cases we have included these here.

Anthropological practice is a huge field, and evolving very rapidly. No list is definitive, and it was not our intention to provide such a one. Our contributors' suggestions, grouped loosely below, are not intended to be either authoritative or exhaustive. Rather, they are signposts and suggestions for further reading which we thought would be both interesting and helpful to readers of this volume.

General: Textbooks, Edited Collections, and Key Articles

Baba, Marietta L. (1994) "The Fifth Subdiscipline: Anthropological Practice and the Future of Anthropology." *Human Organization* 53(2): 174–186.

Baba, Marietta L. and Carole E. Hill (eds.) (1997) *The Global Practice of Anthropology*. Williamsburg, VA: Studies in Third World Societies.

Basch, Linda G., Lucie Wood Saunders, Jagna Wojcicka Sharff, and James Peacock (eds.) (1999) *Transforming Academia: Challenges and Opportunities for an Engaged Anthropology*. American Ethnological Society Monograph Series 8. Washington, DC: American Anthropological Association.

Chambers, Erve (1985) *Applied Anthropology: A Practical Guide*. Prospect Heights, IL: Waveland Press.

A Handbook of Practicing Anthropology. First Edition. Edited by Riall W. Nolan.
© 2013 John Wiley & Sons, Inc. Published 2013 by John Wiley & Sons, Inc.

Chambers, Erve (1987) "Applied Anthropology in the Post-Vietnam Era: Anticipations and Ironies." *Annual Review of Anthropology* 16: 309–337.

Eddy, Elizabeth M. and William L. Partridge (eds.) (1987) *Applied Anthropology in America*. New York: Columbia University Press.

Ervin, Alexander M. (2004) *Applied Anthropology: Tools and Perspectives for Contemporary Practice*, 2nd edn. Boston: Allyn & Bacon.

Fiske, Shirley and Erve Chambers (1996) "The Inventions of Practice." *Human Organization* 55(1): 1–12.

Foster, George M. (1969) *Applied Anthropology*. Boston: Little, Brown and Company.

Gwynne, Margaret A. (2002) *Applied Anthropology: A Career-Oriented Approach*. Boston: Allyn & Bacon.

Hill, Carole E. and Marietta L. Baba (eds.) (2000) *The Unity of Theory and Practice in Anthropology: Rebuilding a Fractured Synthesis*. NAPA Bulletin 18. Washington, DC: American Anthropological Association.

Hill, Carole E. and Marietta L. Baba (eds.) (2006) *The Globalization of Anthropology*. NAPA Bulletin 25. Arlington, VA: American Anthropological Association.

Kedia, Satish and John van Willigen (2005) *Applied Anthropology: Domains of Application*. Westport, CT: Praeger.

Painter, Michael (2000) "Nonacademic Experience and Changing Views of the Discipline." In Paula Sabloff (ed.), *Careers in Anthropology: Profiles of Practitioner Anthropologists*. NAPA Bulletin 20. Washington, DC: American Anthropological Association.

Partridge, William L. (1985) "Toward a Theory of Practice." *American Behavioral Scientist* 29(2): 139–163.

Redfield, Alden (ed.) (1973) *Anthropology beyond the University*. Southern Anthropological Society Proceedings 7. Athens: University of Georgia Press.

Spicer, Edward H. (ed.) (1952) *Human Problems in Technological Change*. New York: Sage.

Trotter, Robert (ed.) (1988) *Anthropology for Tomorrow*. Washington, DC: American Anthropological Association.

van Willigen, John (1980) *Anthropology in Use: A Bibliographic Chronology of the Development of Applied Anthropology*. Pleasantville, NY: Redgrave Publishing.

van Willigen, John (1991) *Anthropology in Use: A Source Book on Anthropological Practice*. Boulder, CO: Westview Press.

van Willigen, John (1993) *Applied Anthropology*, rev. edn. South Hadley, MA: Bergin & Garvey.

van Willigen, John, Barbara Rylko-Bauer, and Ann McElroy (eds.) (1989) *Making Our Research Useful: Case Studies in the Utilization of Anthropological Knowledge*. Boulder, CO: Westview Press.

Wasson, Christina, Mary O. Butler, and Jacqueline Copeland-Carson (eds.) (2011) *Applying Anthropology in the Global Village*. Walnut Creek, CA: Left Coast Press.

Wulff, Robert M. and Shirley J. Fiske (eds.) (1987) *Anthropological Praxis: Translating Knowledge into Action*. Boulder, CO: Westview Press.

Training for Practice

Angrosino, Michael V. (1981) "Practicum Training in Applied Anthropology." *Human Organization* 40(1): 81–84.

Bennett, Linda A. (1988) *Bridges for Changing Times: Local Practitioner Organizations in American Anthropology.* NAPA Bulletin 6. Washington, DC: American Anthropological Association.

Bennett, Linda, T. J. Ferguson, J. Anthony Paredes, et al. (2006) *Final Report: Practicing Advisory Work Group (PAWG).* Arlington, VA: American Anthropological Association. At www.aaanet.org/cmtes/copapia/PAWG.cfm, accessed Sept. 18, 2012.

Briller, Sherylyn H. and Amy Goldmacher. (2009) *Designing an Anthropology Career: Professional Development Exercises.* Lanham, MD: AltaMira Press.

Ellick, Carol J. and Joe E. Watkins (2011) *The Anthropology Graduate's Guide: From Student to a Career.* Walnut Creek, CA: Left Coast Press.

Fiske, Shirley J., Linda A. Bennett, Patricia Ensworth, et al. (2010) *The Changing Face of Anthropology. Anthropology Masters Reflect on Education, Careers, and Professional Organizations.* Arlington, VA: American Anthropological Association.

Harman, Robert C., Jim Hess, and Amir Shafe (2004) "Report on Survey of Alumni of Master's Level Applied Anthropology Training Programs." Report sponsored by the National Association for the Practice of Anthropology. Long Beach, CA: California State University Long Beach.

Hyland, Stanley and Sean Kirkpatrick (1989) *Guide to Training Programs in Applied Anthropology.* Memphis, TN: Society for Applied Anthropology.

Mitchell, Lesli (1996) *The Ultimate Grad School Survival Guide.* Paterson, NJ: Peterson's.

Price, Laurie J. (2001) "How Good is Graduate Training in Anthropology?" *Anthropology News* (May), 5–6.

Price, Laurie J. (2001) "The Mismatch between Anthropology Graduate Training and the Work Lives of Graduates." *Practicing Anthropology* 23: 55–57.

Schön, Donald (1983) *The Reflective Practitioner: How Professionals Think in Action.* New York: Basic Books.

Schön, Donald (1987) *Educating the Reflective Practitioner: Toward a New Design for Teaching and Learning in the Professions.* San Francisco: Jossey-Bass.

Smiley, Francis E. (2006) "Anthropology: Real People, Real Careers" (DVD). Careers in Anthropology 1. Arlington, VA: American Anthropological Association.

van Willigen, John (1987) *Becoming a Practicing Anthropologist : A Guide to Careers and Training Programs in Applied Anthropology.* NAPA Bulletin 3. Washington, DC: American Anthropological Association.

Wasson, Christina, Keri Brondo, Barbara LeMaster, et al. (2008) "We've Come a Long Way, Maybe: Academic Climate Report of the Committee on the Status of Women in Anthropology." American Anthropological Association. At http://www.aaanet.org/resources/departments/upload/coswa-academic-climate-report-2008.pdf, accessed Sept. 18, 2012.

Jobs and Careers

American Anthropological Association (1982) *Getting a Job Outside the Academy.* Washington, DC: American Anthropological Association.

Basalla, Susan and Maggie Debelius (2001) *"So What are You Going To Do With That?"* A Guide to Career-Changing for M.A.'s and Ph.D.'s. New York: Farrar, Straus and Giroux.

Bolles, Richard (1978) *The Three Boxes of Life.* Berkeley, CA: Ten Speed Press.

Bolles, Richard (2001) *What Color is Your Parachute?* Berkeley, CA: Ten Speed Press.

Briody, Elizabeth K. and Dawn Bodo (1993) "Anthropologists at Work: Careers Making a Difference" (DVD). Arlington, VA: American Anthropological Association.

Brondo, Keri Linda Bennett, Harmony Farner, et al. (2009) "Work Climate, Gender, and the Status of Practicing Anthropologists: Report commissioned by the Committee on the Status of Women in Anthropology." Washington, DC: American Anthropological Association. At http://www.aaanet.org/resources/departments/upload/ES_COSWA-2009REPORT-2.pdf, accessed Sept. 18, 2012.

Camenson, Blythe (2000) *Great Jobs for Anthropology Majors.* Lincolnwood, IL: VGM Career Horizons.

Ellick, Carol and Joe E. Watkins (2010) *The Anthropology Graduate's Guide: From Student to Career.* Walnut Creek, CA: Left Coast Press.

Everett, Melissa (1995) *Making a Living While Making a Difference: A Guide to Creating Careers with a Conscience.* New York: Bantam Books.

Green, Marianne E. (1997) *Internship Success.* Lincolnwood, IL: VGM Career Horizons.

Guerrón-Montero, Carla (ed.) (2008) *Careers in Applied Anthropology in the 21st Century: Perspectives from Academics and Practitioners.* NAPA Bulletin 29. Oxford: Blackwell.

Gwynne, Margaret A. (2002) *Anthropology Career Resources Handbook.* Boston: Allyn & Bacon.

Hanson, Karen J. (ed.) (1988) *Mainstreaming Anthropology: Experiences in Government Employment.* NAPA Bulletin 5. Washington, DC: National Association for the Practice of Anthropology, American Anthropological Association.

Hefland, David P. (1999) *Career Change: Everything You Need to Know to Meet New Challenges and Take Control of Your Career*, 2nd edn. Lincolnwood, IL: VGM Career Horizons.

Kedia, Satish (2008) "Recent Changes and Trends in the Practice of Applied Anthropology." In Carla Guerrón-Montero (ed.), *Careers in Applied Anthropology in the 21st Century: Perspectives from Academics and Practitioners.* NAPA Bulletin 29. Washington, DC: American Anthropological Association, pp. 14–28.

Koons, Adam, Beatrice Hackett, and John P. Mason (eds.) (1989) *Stalking Employment in the Nation's Capital: A Guide for Anthropologists.* Washington, DC: Washington Association of Professional Anthropologists.

Newhouse, Margaret (1993) *Outside the Ivory Tower: A Guide for Academics Considering Alternative Careers.* Cambridge, MA: Office of Career Services, Harvard University.

Nolan, Riall (2003) *Anthropology in Practice.* Boulder, CO: Lynne Rienner.

Omohundro, John T. (1998) *Careers in Anthropology.* Mountain View, CA: Mayfield Publishing.

Peters, Robert L. (1992) *Getting What You Came For.* New York: Farrar, Straus and Giroux.

Pillsbury, Barbara (2008) "Applied Anthropology and Executive Leadership." In Carla Guerrón-Montero (ed.), *Careers in Applied Anthropology in the 21st Century: Perspectives from Academics and Practitioners.* NAPA Bulletin 29. Washington, DC: American Anthropological Association, pp. 131–151.

Sabloff, Paula L. W. (ed.) (2000) *Careers in Anthropology: Profiles of Practitioner Anthropologists.* NAPA Bulletin 20. Washington, DC: American Anthropological Association.

Secrist, Jan and Jacqueline Fitzpatrick (2001) *What Else Can You Do with a PhD: A Career Guide for Scholars.* Thousand Oaks, CA: Sage.

Stephens, W. Richard (2001) *Careers in Anthropology: What an Anthropology Degree Can Do for You.* Boston: Allyn & Bacon.

Strang, Veronica (2009) *What Anthropologists Do.* Oxford: Berg.

Sweitzer, H. Frederick and Mary A. King (1999) *The Successful Internship*. Pacific Grove, CA: Brooks/Cole Publishing.

Troutman, Kathryn K. (2011) *Federal Resume Guidebook: Strategies for Writing a Winning Federal Resume*, 5th edn. Indianapolis: JIST Publishing.

Wasson, Christina (ed.)(2006) *Making History at the Frontier: Women Creating Careers as Practicing Anthropologists*. NAPA Bulletin 26. Berkeley, CA: University of California Press for National Association for the Practice of Anthropology.

Methods and Workplace Operations

Bamberger, Michael, Jim Rugh, and Linda Mabry (2006) *Real World Evaluation: Working under Budget, Time, and Political Constraints*. Thousand Oaks, CA: Sage.

Beebe, James (2001) *Rapid Assessment Process*. Lanham, MD: AltaMira Press.

Berkun, Scott (2008) *Making Things Happen: Mastering Project Management*. Sebastopol, CA: O'Reilly Media.

Bernard, H. Russell (2011) *Research Methods in Anthropology: Qualitative and Quantitative Approaches*. Lanham, MD: AltaMira Press.

Block, Peter (2001) *Consulting Fieldbook and Companion: A Guide to Understanding Your Expertise*. San Francisco: Jossey-Bass/Pfeiffer.

Block, Peter (2011) *Flawless Consulting: A Guide to Getting Your Expertise Used*. San Francisco: Pfeiffer.

Fetterman, David (1983) "Guilty Knowledge, Dirty Hands, and Other Ethical Dilemmas: The Hazards of Contract Research." *Human Organization* 42: 214–224.

Fetterman, David M. and Abraham Wandersman (eds.) (2005) *Empowerment Evaluation Principles in Practice*. New York: Guilford Press.

Fisher, Roger and Alan Sharp (1998) *Getting It Done*. New York: Harper Business.

Fisher, Roger and William Ury (1981) *Getting to Yes: Negotiating Agreement without Giving In*. Boston: Houghton Mifflin.

Fowler, Alan and Chiku Malunga (eds.) (2010) *NGO Management: The Earthscan Companion*. London: Earthscan.

Gluesing, Julia et al. (2003) "The Development of Global Virtual Teams." In Cristina B. Gibson and Susan Cohen (eds.), *Virtual Teams that Work: Creating Conditions for Virtual Team Effectiveness*. San Francisco: Jossey-Bass, pp. 353–380.

Hamada, Tomoko and Willis E. Sibley (eds.) (1994) *Anthropological Perspectives on Organizational Culture*. Lanham, MD: University Press of America.

Hyatt, Carole and Linda Gottlieb (1993) *When Smart People Fail*, rev. edn. New York: Penguin.

Project Management Institute (2008) *A Guide to the Project Management Body of Knowledge*. Newtown Square, PA: Project Management Institute.

Puntenney, Pamela (ed.) (1991) "Commentary: Communicating Anthropological Insights." *Practicing Anthropology* 13(3): 23–28.

Schensul, Jean J. and Margaret D. LeCompte (1999) *Ethnographer's Toolkit*. Lanham, MD: AltaMira Press.

Schwartzman, Helen B. (1993) *Ethnography in Organizations*. Newbury Park, CA: Sage.

Singer, Merrill (1994) "Community-Centered Praxis: Toward an Alternative Non-dominative Applied Anthropology." *Human Organization* 53: 336–344.

van Willigen, John, Barbara Rylko-Bauer, and Ann McElroy (eds.) (1989) *Making Our Research Useful: Case Studies in the Utilization of Anthropological Knowledge*. Boulder, CO: Westview Press.

Vella, Jane (2002). *Learning to Listen, Learning to Teach: the Power of Dialogue in Educating Adults*. New York: Wiley.

Wasson, Christina (2006) "Being in Two Spaces at Once: Virtual Meetings and Their Representation." *Journal of Linguistic Anthropology* 16(1): 103–130.

Wilson, Valerie and Anne Pirrie (2000) *Multidisciplinary Team Working: Indicators of Good Practice*. Edinburgh: Scottish Council for Research in Education. At http://modern-timesworkplace.com/good_reading/GRWhole/Multi-Disciplinary.Teamwork.pdf, accessed Sept. 18, 2012.

The Military

Albro, Robert, George Marcus, Laura A. McNamara et al. (eds.) (2011) *Anthropologists in the SecurityScape: Ethics, Practice and Professional Identity*. Walnut Creek, CA: Left Coast Press.

Fosher, Kerry (2010) "Yes, Both, Absolutely: A Personal and Professional Commentary on Anthropological Engagement with Military and Intelligence Organizations." In John D. Kelly et al. (eds.), *Anthropology and Global Counterinsurgency*. Chicago: University of Chicago Press, pp. 261–271.

Frese, Pamela R. and Margaret C. Harrell (2003) *Anthropology and the United States Military: Coming of Age in the Twenty-First Century*. New York: Palgrave Macmillan.

Gusterson, Hugh (2007) "Anthropology and Militarism." *Annual Review of Anthropology* 36: 155–175.

Lucas, George R., Jr. (2009) *Anthropologists in Arms: The Ethics of Military Anthropology*. Lanham, MD: AltaMira Press.

McNamara, Laura A. and Robert A. Rubinstein (eds.) (2011) *Dangerous Liaisons: Anthropologists and the National Security State*. Santa Fe, NM: School for Advanced Research Press.

Rubinstein, Robert A., Kerry Fosher, and Clementine Fujimura (eds.) (2012) *Practicing Military Anthropology: Beyond Expectations and Traditional Boundaries*. West Hartford, CT: Kumarian Press.

Tortorello, Frank, Jr. (2005) "The Movement of American Infantry in Anthropological Perspective." *Journal for the Anthropological Study of Human Movement* 13(2): 87–106.

Tortorello, Frank, Jr. (2010) "An Ethnography of 'Courage' among U.S. Marines." Ph.D. dissertation, University of Illinois at Urbana-Champaign. Downloadable at http://hdl.handle.net/2142/16110, accessed Sept. 18, 2012.

Tortorello, Frank, Jr. (2010) "Women Can't Do It and Men Can't Change: Some Thoughts on Agency and Gender in U.S. Marine Corps Training." *Journal for the Anthropological Study of Human Movement* 17(1): 1–54.

Health and Medicine

Biehl, João (2009) *Will to Live: AIDS Therapies and the Politics of Survival*. Princeton: Princeton University Press.

Bock, Naomi, Paul Jensen, Bess Miller, et al. (2007) "Tuberculosis Infection Control in Resource-Limited Settings in the Era of Expanding HIV Care and Treatment." *Journal of Infectious Diseases* 196(Suppl 1): S108–S113.

Carrasco, Lorena Núñez, Jo Vearey, and Scott Drimie (2011) "Who Cares? HIV-Related Sickness, Urban–Rural Linkages, and the Gendered Role of Care in Return Migration in South Africa." *Gender and Development* 19: 105–114.

Chesluk, Benjamin and Eric Holmboe (2010) "How Teams Work – or Don't – in Primary Care: A Field Study on Internal Medicine Practices." *Health Affairs* 29: 874–879.

Farmer, Paul (1999) *Infections and Inequalities: The Modern Plagues*. Berkeley: University of California Press.

Farmer, Paul (2003) *Pathologies of Power: Health, Human Rights, and the New War on the Poor*. Berkeley: University of California Press.

Han, Clara (2012) *Life in Debt: Times of Care and Violence in Neoliberal Chile*. Berkeley: University of California Press.

Hunter, Mark (2010) *Love in the Time of AIDS: Inequality, Gender, and Rights in South Africa*. Bloomington: Indiana University Press.

Israel, Barbara A., Eugenia Eng, Amy J. Schulz, et al. (2005) "Introduction to Methods in Community-Based Participatory Research for Health." In Barbara Israel et al. (eds.), *Methods in Community-Based Participatory Research*. San Francisco: Jossey-Bass, pp. 3–26.

Joseph, Galen, Nancy Burke, Noe Tuason, et al. (2009) "Perceived Susceptibility to Illness and Perceived Benefits of Preventive Care: An Exploration of Behavioral Theory Constructs in a Transcultural Context." *Health Education and Behavior* 36(S1): 71S–90S.

Keshavjee, Salmaan and Paul Farmer (2010) "Picking Up the Pace – Scale-Up of MDR Tuberculosis Treatment Programs." *New England Journal of Medicine* 363: 1781–1784.

Keshavjee, Salmaan and Paul Farmer (in press) "Tuberculosis, Drug Resistance and the History of Modern Medicine." *New England Journal of Medicine*.

Kim, Jim Yong et al. (2003) "From Multidrug-Resistant Tuberculosis to DOTS Expansion and Beyond: Making the Most of a Paradigm Shift." *Tuberculosis* 83(1–3): 59–65.

Kleinman, Arthur (2006) *What Really Matters: Living a Moral Life amidst Uncertainty and Danger*. New York: Oxford University Press.

Livingston, Julie (2005) *Debility and the Moral Imagination in Botswana*. Bloomington: Indiana University Press.

Lock, Margaret (1994) *Encounters with Aging: Mythologies of Menopause in Japan and North America*. Berkeley: University of California Press.

Lock, Margaret and Vin-Kim Nguyen (2010) *An Anthropology of Biomedicine*. Oxford: Wiley-Blackwell.

Mitnick, Carole et al. (2003) "Community-Based Therapy for Multi-Drug Resistant Tuberculosis in Lima, Peru." *New England Journal of Medicine* 348: 1219–1228.

Nguyen, Vin-Kim (2010) *The Republic of Therapy: Triage and Sovereignty in West Africa's Time of AIDS*. Durham, NC: Duke University Press.

Packard, Randall (1989) *White Plague, Black Labor: Tuberculosis and the Political Economy of Health and Disease in South Africa*. Berkeley: University of California Press.

Robbins, Steven (2010) *From Revolution to Rights in South Africa: Social Movements, NGOs, and Popular Politics after Apartheid*. Oxford: James Currey.

Vearey, Joanna (2008) "Migration, Access to ART, and Survivalist Livelihood Strategies in Johannesburg." *African Journal of AIDS Research* 7: 361–374.

Wendland, Claire (2010) *A Heart for the Work: Journeys through an African Medical School.*
    Chicago: University of Chicago Press.
World Health Organization (2010) *Multidrug and Extensively Drug-Resistant TB (M/XDR-
    TB): 2010 Global Report on Surveillance and Response.* Geneva: World Health Organiza-
    tion. At http://whqlibdoc.who.int/publications/2010/9789241599191_eng.pdf, accessed
    on Sept. 18, 2012.

Advertising, Marketing, and Consumer Research

Malefyt, Timothy de Waal (2011) "Using Anthropology to Understand the American 'Dinner
    Dilemma'." In *CourseReader eBooks*. Belmont, CA: Wadsworth Cengage Learning.
Malefyt, Timothy de Waal and Brian Moeran (eds.) (2003) *Advertising Cultures.* Oxford:
    Berg.
Malefyt, Timothy de Waal and Robert Morais (2012) *Advertising and Anthropology.* Oxford:
    Berg.
McCracken, Grant (1990) *Culture and Consumption.* Bloomington: Indiana University Press.
Miller, Daniel (1998) *A Theory of Shopping.* Ithaca, NY: Cornell University Press.
Moeran, Brian (1996) *A Japanese Advertising Agency.* Honolulu: University of Hawai'i Press.
Sunderland, Patricia and Rita Denny (2007) *Doing Anthropology in Consumer Research.*
    Walnut Creek, CA: Left Coast Press.

Business and Corporate Anthropology

Baba, Marietta (1998) "Anthropologists in Corporate America: Knowledge Management and
    Ethical Angst." *Chronicle of Higher Education* (May 8), B4–B5.
Briody, Elizabeth (2011) "Handling Decision Paralysis on Organizational Partnerships." In
    CourseReader eBooks. Belmont: Wadsworth Cengage Learning.
Briody, Elizabeth, S. Tamer Cavusgil, and Stewart Miller (2004) "Turning Three Sides into a
    Delta at General Motors: Enhancing Partnership Integration on Corporate Ventures."
    Long Range Planning 37: 421–434.
Briody, Elizabeth, Robert Trotter, and Tracy Meerwarth (2010) *Transforming Culture:
    Creating and Sustaining a Better Manufacturing Organization.* Basingstoke: Palgrave
    Macmillan.
Cefkin, Melissa (ed.) (2009) *Ethnography and the Corporate Encounter: Reflections on Research
    in and of Corporations.* New York: Berghahn Books.
Ferraro, Gary and Elizabeth Briody (2013) *The Cultural Dimension of Global Business*, 7th
    edn. Upper Saddle River, NJ: Prentice Hall.
Jordan, Ann (2003) *Business Anthropology.* Prospect Heights, IL: Waveland Press.
Morais, Robert and Timothy de Waal Malefyt (2010) "How Anthropologists Can Succeed in
    Business: Mediating Multiple Worlds of Inquiry." *International Journal of Business
    Anthropology* 1(1): 45–56.
Wasson, Christina (2000) "Caution and Consensus in American Business Meetings." *Prag-
    matics* 10: 457–481.

Design

Altimare, Emily L. (2008) "Beyond Ethnography: Corporate and Design Anthropology" (DVD). Careers in Anthropology 2. Arlington, VA: American Anthropological Association.

Beyer, Hugh and Karen Holtzblatt (1997) *Contextual Design*. San Francisco: Morgan Kaufmann.

Isaacs, Ellen and Alan Walendowski (2001) *Designing from Both Sides of the Screen*. Indianapolis: Sams Publishing.

Metcalf, Crysta (2011) "The Circulation of Transdisciplinary Knowledge and Culture in a High-Tech Organization." *Anthropology News* 52(2): 28.

Squires, Susan, and Bryan Byrne (eds.) (2002) *Creating Breakthrough Ideas: The Collaboration of Anthropologists and Designers in the Product Development Industry*. Westport, CT: Bergin & Garvey.

Development

Cernea, Michael (ed.) (1991) *Putting People First: Sociological Variables in Rural Development*. Oxford: Oxford University Press.

Cernea, Michael (1994) *Sociology, Anthropology, and Development: Annotated Bibliography of World Bank Publications*. Washington, DC: World Bank.

Davis, Gloria (2004) "A History of the Social Development Network at the World Bank 1973–2002." Social Development Paper 56. Washington, DC: World Bank. At http://siteresources.worldbank.org/INTRANETSOCIALDEVELOPMENT/214578–1111735201184/20502396, accessed Sept. 18, 2012.

de Haan, Arjan (2009) *How the Aid Industry Works: An Introduction to International Development*. West Hartford, CT: Kumarian Press.

Dearden Philip, Steve Jones, Rolf Sartorius, et al. (2002) *Tools for Development: A Handbook for Those Engaged in Development Activity*. London: Performance and Effectiveness Department, Department for International Development.

Durr, Kenneth (2010) *The First 40: A History of DAI*. Bethesda, MD: Development Alternatives, Inc. At http://dai.com/sites/default/files/DAI-HISTORY-BOOK.pdf, accessed Sept. 18, 2012.

Fechter, Anne-Meike and Heather Hindman (eds.) (2011) *Inside the Everyday Lives of Development Workers: The Challenges and Futures of Aidland*. West Hartford, CT: Kumarian Press.

Gow, David (2002) "Anthropology and Development: Evil Twin or Moral Narrative." *Human Organization* 61: 299–227.

Grammig, Thomas (2002) *Technical Knowledge and Development: Observing Aid Projects and Process*. London: Routledge.

Guggenheim, Scott (2004) "Crises and Contradictions: Understanding the Origins of a Community Development Project in Indonesia." Jakarta: World Bank. At http://siteresources.worldbank.org/INTINDONESIA/Resources/Social/KDP-Crises.pdf, accessed Sept. 18, 2012.

Marshall, Katherine (2008) *The World Bank: From Reconstruction to Development Equity*. London: Routledge.

Nolan, Riall (2002) *Development Anthropology: Encounters in the Real World.* Boulder, CO: Westview Press.
Scudder, Thayer (2005) "The Lesotho Highlands Water Project (2003) and Laos' Nam Theun 2 Dam" (2003 with 2005 updating). Unpublished manuscript. At http://www.hss. caltech.edu/~tzs/Lesotho%20&%20Laos%20Cases.pdf, accesssed on Sept. 18, 2012.

Disaster and Humanitarian Aid

Bankoff, Greg, George Frerks, and Dorothea Hilhorst (2004) *Mapping Vulnerability: Disaster, Development and People.* London: Routledge.
Blaikie, Piers, Terry Cannon, Ian Davis, et al. (1994) *At Risk: Natural Hazards, People's Vulnerability and Disasters.* London: Routledge.
Button, Gregory (2010) *Disaster Culture, Knowledge and Uncertainty in the Wake of Human and Environmental Catastrophe.* Walnut Creek, CA: Left Coast Press.
Cuny, Frederick (1983) *Disasters and Development.* New York: Oxford University Press.
Erikson, Kai (1994) *A New Species of Trouble.* New York: W. W. Norton.
Ferris, Elizabeth and Daniel Petz (2012) *The Year that Shook the Rich: A Review of Natural Disasters in 2011.* Washington: Brookings Institution. At http://www.brookings.edu/ research/reports/2012/03/natural-disaster-review-ferris, accessed Sept. 18, 2012.
Hewitt, Kenneth (1983) *Interpretations of Calamity from the Viewpoint of Human Ecology.* Boston: Allen & Unwin.
Hewitt, Kenneth (1997) *Regions of Risk: A Geographical Introduction to Disasters.* Boston: Addison Wesley Longman.
Hoffman, Susanna and Anthony Oliver-Smith (eds.) (2002) *Catastrophe and Culture: The Anthropology of Disaster.* Santa Fe, NM: SAR Press.
Lewis, James (1999) *Development in Disaster-Prone Places: Studies of Vulnerability.* London: Intermediate Technology.
Mitchell, James (1999) *Crucibles of Hazard: Mega-Cities and Disaster in Transition.* New York: United Nations Press.
Oliver-Smith, Anthony (1986) *The Martyred City: Death and Rebirth in the Peruvian Andes.* Albuquerque: University of New Mexico Press.
Oliver-Smith, Anthony and Susanna Hoffman (eds.) (1999) *The Angry Earth: Disaster in Anthropological Perspective.* New York: Routledge.
Tobin, Graham and Burrell Montz (1997) *Natural Hazards: Explanation and Integration.* New York: Guilford Press.
Van Arsdale, Peter and Derrin Smith (2009) *Humanitarians in Hostile Territory: Expeditionary Diplomacy and Aid Outside the Green Zone.* Walnut Creek, CA: Left Coast Press.
Walker, Peter and Daniel Maxwell (2009) *Shaping the Humanitarian World (Global Institutions).* New York: Routledge.
Women's Refugee Commission (2009) *Building Livelihoods: A Field Manual for Practitioners in Humanitarian Settings.* New York: Women's Refugee Commission. Downloadable at http://womensrefugeecommission.org/component/docman/doc_download/281-building-livelihoods-a-field-manual-for-practitioners-in-humanitarian-settings-building-livelihoods-a-field-manual-for-practitioners-in-humanitarian-settings?q=building+liveliho ods, accessed Sept. 18, 2012.

Higher Education

Altbach, Philip, Patricia J. Gumport, and Robert Berdahl (eds.) (2011) *American Higher Education in the Twenty-First Century: Social, Political, and Economic Challenges*, 3rd edn. Baltimore: Johns Hopkins Press.

Bergquist, William (1992) *The Four Cultures of the Academy: Insights and Strategies for Improving Leadership in Collegiate Organizations*. San Francisco: Jossey-Bass.

Bergquist, William H. and Kenneth Pawlak (2008) *Engaging the Six Cultures of the Academy*. San Francisco: Jossey-Bass.

Birnbaum, Robert (1988) *How Colleges Work: The Cybernetics of Academic Organization and Leadership*. San Francisco: Jossey-Bass.

García, Mildred, and Yolanda T. Moses (eds.) (2000) *Succeeding in an Academic Career: A Guide for Faculty of Color*. Westport, CT: Greenwood.

Gunsalus, C. Kristina (2006) *The College Administrator's Survival Guide*. Cambridge, MA: Harvard University Press.

Schein, Edgar (2010) *Organizational Culture and Leadership*, 4th edn. San Francisco: Jossey-Bass.

Environment and Resources

Crumley, Carole L. (ed.) (2001) *New Directions in Environmental Anthropology: Intersections*. Walnut Creek, CA: AltaMira Press.

Dove, Michael R. and Carol Carpenter (eds.) (2008) *Environmental Anthropology: A Historical Reader*. Oxford: Blackwell.

Haenn, Nora and Richard R. Wilk (eds.) (2006) *The Environment in Anthropology: A Reader in Ecology, Culture, and Sustainable Living*. New York: New York University Press.

Index

A Handbook of Practicing Anthropology. First Edition. Edited by Riall W. Nolan.
© 2013 John Wiley & Sons, Inc. Published 2013 by John Wiley & Sons, Inc.

Waitzkin, Howard, 216
Walberg, Peder, 368n
Walker, Wendy, 339
Wallerstein, Nina, 218–19, 220n, 341n
Walloo, Keith, 202
Warry, Wayne, 212
Washington Association of Professional
    Anthropologists (WAPA), 20, 135–6,
    182, 305, 306
Wasson, Christina, 62, 235n, 260
Watkins, Joe E., 315
Wayne State University, 309
Weber, Max, 216
websites, 100, 192, 219, 276, 350, 384–5
Westat, 292–301
Wexley, Kenneth N., 73
What Color is Your Parachute (Bolles), 37
Wheeler, John, 110
White, Michael J., 365
Whiteford, Linda, 291, 296–301
Wiedman, Dennis, 186, 189–92
Wileman, Ralph, 333
Williams, Holly Ann, 62
Williams, Jody, 119

Wilson, Francis, 365
Wingard, John D., 268
Winthrop, Robert H., 268–70
Wishnie, Mark, 268
Wolfe, Alan, 108
Wolfe, Tom, 108
Wolin, Steven J., 304
Womack, Mari, 62, 213, 217
Wooley, Sabra, 219n
working relationships *see* teamwork
working style, 4–5, 31, 64–5, 251–3,
    286–7
work–life balance, 142, 193
World Bank, 150–8, 159n, 224, 235n,
    339–40
Wray, Jacilee, 181
writing skills, 100–1, 216, 325–8, 332
WRK4US (mailing list), 345, 347, 349
Wulff, Bob, 307

Yin, Robert K., 206, 217

Zimmerman, Cathy, 365
Zuger, Abigail, 369n

CPSIA information can be obtained
at www.ICGtesting.com
Printed in the USA
BVOW08s0259180817

492411BV00007B/22/P